Ilex Foundation Series 6

The *History* of Beyhaqi

Also in the Ilex Foundation Series

Poet and Hero in the Persian Book of Kings
by Olga M. Davidson
third edition

Comparative Literature and Classical Persian Poetics
by Olga M. Davidson
second edition

Ferdowsi's Shāhnāma: *Millennial Perspectives*
edited by Olga M. Davidson and Marianna Shreve Simpson

Global Medieval: Mirrors for Princes Reconsidered
edited by Regula Forster and Neguin Yavari

Erin and Iran: Cultural Encounters between the Irish and the Iranians
edited by H. E. Chehabi and Grace Neville

Dreaming across Boundaries:
The Interpretation of Dreams in Islamic Lands
edited by Louise Marlow

The Rhetoric of Biography: Narrating Lives in Persianate Societies
edited by L. Marlow

Ruse and Wit: The Humorous in Arabic, Turkish, and Persian Narrative
edited by Dominic Parvis Brookshaw

Persian Literature and Judeo-Persian Culture:
Collected Writings of Sorour S. Soroudi
edited by H. E. Chehabi

On the Wonders of Land and Sea: Persianate Travel Writing
edited by Roberta Micallef and Sunil Sharma

Methodists and Muslims: My Life as an Orientalist
by Richard W. Bulliet

Naqqali Trilogy
by Bahram Beyzaie
translated by Richard Saul Chason and Nikta Sabouri

Cyrus the Great: Life and Lore
edited by Rahim Shayegan

more at *www.ilexfoundation.org*

The *History* of Beyhaqi

(The History of Sultan Masʿud
of Ghazna, 1030–1041)

by

Abu'l-Fażl Beyhaqi

Translated with a historical, geographical,
linguistic and cultural commentary and notes by

C. E. Bosworth

Fully revised and with further commentary by

Mohsen Ashtiany

VOLUME II

Translation of
Years 424–432 A.H. = 1032–1041 A.D.
and the History of Khwarazm

Ilex Foundation
Boston, Massachusetts

Distributed by Harvard University Press
Cambridge, Massachusetts and London, England

The *History* of Beyhaqi (The History of Sultan Masʿud of Ghazna, 1030–1041) by Abu'l-Fażl Beyhaqi

Translated with a historical, geographical, linguistic and cultural commentary and notes by C. E. Bosworth; and fully revised and with further commentary by Mohsen Ashtiany

The *History* of Beyhaqi project was sponsored by the Center for Iranian Studies, Columbia University.

Published by the Ilex Foundation, Boston, MA
Third printing, April 2023

Distributed by Harvard University Press, Cambridge, MA and London, England

Cover design: Joni Godlove
Printed in the United States of America

Library of Congress Cataloging-in-Publication Data

Bayhaqi, Abu al-Fazl Muhammad ibn Husayn, ca. 996-1077.
[Tarikh-i Bayhaqi. English]
The history of Beyhaqi : (the history of Sultan Mas'ud of Ghazna, 1030-1041) / by Abu'l-Fazl Beyhaqi ; translated with a historical, geographical, linguistic and cultural commentary and notes by C.E. Bosworth ; fully revised and with further commentary by Mohsen Ashtiany.
v. <1-3> ; cm.
Translated from Persian.
Includes bibliographical references and index.
ISBN 978-0-674-06233-7 (alk. paper) -- ISBN 978-0-674-06234-4 (alk. paper) -- ISBN 978-0-674-06235-1 (alk. paper) -- ISBN 978-0-674-06236-8 (alk. paper) -- ISBN 978-0-674-06238-2 (alk. paper) -- ISBN 978-0-674-06239-9 (alk. paper)
1. Ghaznevids. 2. Iran--History--640-1256. 3. Afghanistan--History. I. Bosworth, Clifford Edmund. II. Ashtiany, Mohsen, 1943- III. Title.
DS288.7.B313 2011
955'.022--dc23

2011028511

Contents

[The Year 424
(/7 December 1032–25 November 1033)]

[Gh 361, F 460] The year 424 began. The beginning of the month and of the year fell on a Thursday. En route, a letter from the postal and intelligence officer of Ray arrived, with the news that "Tāsh Farrāsh has had an awe-inspiring impact here, and the Son of Kāku and all the others in the surrounding regions have had to knuckle under and bow down to him. Ṭāher the secretary is pursuing his job as counsellor and administrator in a laudable manner, and all is well and under control. [F 461] The son of Gowhar-āgin Shahrnush[1] had risen up and seized Qazvin, which belonged to his father. Ṭāher despatched Tāsh and the Keeper of the Royal Wardrobe Yāruq-tughmush, together with several tough commanders, and the Treasurer Gowhar-āyin,[2] Khumārtāsh and a contingent of Turkmen cavalry, and they put an end to this God-forsaken fellow's delusions.[3] Tāsh now intends making a progress round the territory in order to parade the power of the royal rule further, and a great feeling of fear and perturbation has arisen in Western Persia."[4]

Reply letters went out expressing approbation, to the effect that "We have left Bost and have headed for Herat. When we arrive there, we shall appoint a trusty person and will send, through his agency, robes of honour for Tāsh, Ṭāher the secretary and those commanders who had gone to fight Gowhar-āgin Shahrnush, together with orders for proceeding to Ray, Jebāl and Hamadan." When the Sultan reached Herat, these robes of honour were entrusted to and sent with Masʿud b. Moḥammad b. Leyth. He was a person of high resolution, wisdom and shrewdness, who had been in the Amir's service at Herat and who had had a fine upbringing amongst the outstanding men of his age.[5] With him went the message that [Gh 362] "The exalted banner will very shortly set out for Nishapur in order to spend this winter and spring there." Masʿud set off with the robes of honour.

On 10 Moḥarram [/16 December 1032] Khᵛāja Aḥmad b. Ḥasan became seriously ill, for his end was near. He was unable to come to his Divān and directed affairs from his own palace. Meanwhile, he was having people arrested, and he himself was being maligned by the public at large. [F 462] He began to persecute Abu'l-Qāsem b. Kathir, who had been head of the Divān of Khorasan,[6] and instituted an auditing of his accounts. He meant to inflict serious harm on him, to the extent that he ordered a flogging-frame,[7] whips and a flogging master to be brought in, and wanted to have him beaten. Abu'l-Qāsem appealed to my master for redress. My master wrote a note to the Sultan, and through ʿAbdus sent him a verbal message with the words, "I do not say that what belongs to the royal coffers (*divān-e mamlakat*) should not be recovered, and what is due from Abu'l-Qāsem should be extracted down to the last drop;[8] but the lord's retainers and servants, those raised up to prominence by the Sultan your father, should not be deliberately destroyed. This Vizier is grievously ill and has despaired of his own life, and is bent on settling old scores before he dies. Bu'l-Qāsem b. Kathir has a right of consideration for his long service and is a person of some standing. If the exalted judgement sees fit, he should be delivered from this plight."

When the Amir learnt of this situation, he gave orders, saying, "You, Bu Naṣr, must go to the Grand Vizier on the pretext of making a bedside visit, and ʿAbdus will go immediately after you to make a visit on our behalf, and whatever needs to be done regarding this matter, he will do." Bu Naṣr went away. When he arrived at the Vizier's palace, he saw Abu'l-Qāsem b. Kathir on the dais while an inquisition into his financial dealings was in progress. A man skilled in exacting money,[9] a flogging-frame, whips and instruments of torture had been brought in and a flogging master had come, and they were plying him with threatening words from the Grand Vizier. Bu Naṣr said to the man skilled in exacting money and the other there, "Suspend your proceedings for an hour while I see the Grand Vizier," and he went into the Vizier's presence. He saw him propped up in his place, a solitary figure, deeply sunken in reflection and in pain. Bu

Naṣr said, "How is the lord?" The Vizier replied, "I feel better today, but I am troubled all the time because of this offspring of Kathir. This wretched fellow has stolen a substantial sum of money and he thinks he can get away with it, not realizing that before I die I am going to squeeze every penny of it out of him. I am giving orders for him to be stretched out on the flogging-frame and they are going to keep on beating him until he disgorges what he has appropriated." Bu Naṣr said, "Why is the lord upsetting himself so much? [F 463] Abu'l-Qāsem will never have the audacity to get away with money from the state treasury. If you just say the word, I will go to him and [Gh 363] knock some sense into him."[10] He replied, "It's not worth it, he's going to get what he deserves."

While they were talking, ʿAbdus came in. He offered up formal greetings and said, "The lord Sultan is enquiring after you and is asking, 'How does the Vizier fare today?'" He kissed his pillow[11] and said, "Through the lord's beneficent power, things are better now. At some point in these next two or three days I should be able to come to the court and render service." ʿAbdus said, "The lord says, 'We hear that the Grand Vizier is under unbearable pain and anxiety through his concern for the activities of Bu'l-Qāsem b. Kathir regarding the taxation money. No-one has the temerity to get away with money appropriated from the state treasury; he should not burden himself with this. Let him write down the sum of money which should be extracted from Bu'l-Qāsem, and give it to ʿAbdus so that Bu'l-Qāsem can be brought to the court, and before the sun goes down, he will be made to disgorge the money." The Vizier ordered the accounting officials to write out a list of what was owed[12] and they gave it to ʿAbdus, and he also ordered that Bu'l-Qāsem should be sent to the court with ʿAbdus. Bu Naṣr and ʿAbdus said, "If the lord's judgement sees fit, let him come into the lord's presence and take his leave with us." He replied, "No, not on any account!"[13] They answered, "He's an old man, and rights of service are owed to him." They spoke at length in this vein until the Vizier gave his permission. They then brought in Bu'l-Qāsem. He performed the acts of obeisance in an impeccable fashion, and the Vizier bade him sit down.

The Vizier said, "Why don't you hand over the Sultan's money?" He replied, "May the lord's life be prolonged! I am ready to hand over everything which is justly due and which will alleviate the lord's ill humour with me." The Vizier said, "Give back what you have embezzled, and get the idea of becoming a vizier out of your head, and no-one will bother you." He answered, "I am obedient to the command, and I will give back everything which is rightfully due. But I do not, and never have harboured, any notions of attaining the vizierate. If I had harboured such an idea, the Grand Vizier would not now be enjoying his present high office, considering those dangerous plots which they hatched against him." He said, "Did they emanate from you or from someone else?" [F 464] Bu'l-Qāsem reached his hand into the leg of his boot, brought out a letter and gave it to an attendant, and the latter placed it before the Vizier. He picked it up and read it, folding the scroll from the top as he perused the contents. When he reached the end, he rolled it up again, keeping the superscription hidden, and placed it in front of himself. For a while he appeared very preoccupied and somewhat embarrassed. Then [Gh 364] he said to 'Abdus, "Go back, and tonight I will give an order for the total sum due, and what remains to be paid by him, to be set down clearly and brought to the court with him tomorrow so that the lord may ordain whatsoever he sees fit."

'Abdus took his formal leave and went back, and he waited outside the palace until Bu Naṣr came out. When they met up with each other, 'Abdus said to Bu Naṣr, "I've just seen a most incredible occurrence. A man was brought in all tied up, with a flogging frame ready, and on the brink of execution. A message arrives from the Sultan concerning this, a paper is put into the Vizier's hand, he reads it and the grilling[14] stops!" Bu Naṣr laughed and said, "O noble sir, you're too young to understand! He is now, moreover, going to release him. Bu'l-Qāsem is coming to my house; you should likewise come!" At the time of the evening worship, Bu'l-Qāsem came to Bu Naṣr's house, and gave thanks to him and to 'Abdus for their concern in the affair, and he offered up profuse prayers on behalf of the Sultan for that great act of solicitude which he had vouchsafed. He asked them to speak well of him to the Amir and to explain that "Nothing owing the state treasury was due from me, but a small number of additional sums have been collected together, and the accounting officials, fearful of the Grand Vizier Aḥmad, added up the monies which I and my personnel had expended on our own subsistence during the period when I was head of the Divān [of Khorasan] and the monthly stipends (*moshāhara*) which were due, and they built them up into a great sum. Whatever I possess is at the lord's command, since he did not allow them to bring about my ruin."

Bu Naṣr said, "All this will be expressly stated, and even more; but explain the episode of the letter, what exactly was it that made Khᵛāja Aḥmad so compliant when he read it, so that ʿAbdus can relate it all to the Amir tomorrow?" Bu'l-Qāsem explained, "It was a command from Amir Maḥmud, with his official emblem and signature, ordering the execution of Khᵛāja Aḥmad (i.e. the Grand Vizier) on the grounds that it had been made necessary as an act of retaliation for the blood shed on his orders. [F 465] I went against the orders of a monarch like Maḥmud and gave the reply that 'It's not my business,' so that the man might live.[15] If I had so wished, he would have been killed instantly. When the Grand Vizier read the letter, he was overcome with shame, and after your departure, he offered profuse apologies".

ʿAbdus went off and retailed what had happened. The Amir said, "How is the Vizier?" He replied, "He is in an enfeebled state. I asked the physician, and he responded, 'He is at the end of his allotted span, and is afflicted by two or three discordant maladies,[16] and this makes any treatment difficult; it will be remarkable if he comes out of this affliction alive.'" The Amir said, "Bu'l-Qāsem b. Kathir must submit himself to the Vizier's wishes and not behave in an obdurate and intransigent way towards him, for he will not be unjustly treated. We intend during this week to go to Nishapur. Bu'l-Qāsem should remain here with the Vizier until one can see what the outcome of his illness will be." This gave Bu'l-Qāsem a new lease of life. [Gh 365]

On 18 Moḥarram [/24 December 1032], the Sultan set out from Herat heading for Nishapur, while the Vizier remained in Herat with all the local financial officials and tax collectors.[17] On 1 Ṣafar [/6 January 1033] the Amir took up residence at Shādyākh. It was bitterly cold that day with a heavy snowfall. He had given orders for the gholāms' quarters and the smaller residences[18] to be erected in Nishapur near to himself and for the rest of the troops and retainers to be stationed further away.

On Saturday, a courier of the postal and intelligence service arrived from Herat with the news that Khᵛāja Aḥmad b. Ḥasan had passed away a week after the royal departure and after he had ill-treated a substantial number of local financial officials.[19] When my master read the letter, he went into the Amir's presence and showed him the letter, saying, "May the lord of the world endure for ever! The Grand Vizier Aḥmad has entrusted his soul to the Court of Heaven." The Amir replied, "Alas for Aḥmad, the unique figure of the age! Men like him are hard to find!" He was plunged into sadness and expressed his grief, saying, "Were it possible to bring him back to life, we would spare no costs." Bu Naṣr said, "It is sufficient happiness for this servant that he passed away in the lord's full approbation [of him]." [F 466] He came to the Divān, and for an hour or two remained pensive, and then composed a piece of poetry (*qeṭʿa*) elegizing him. It was lost amongst other documents, and I could only recall this one verse: (Poetry)

1. *O you sad harbinger of the eclipsing of the sun and the moon, tidings of loss, disgrace and trouble have been announced to you.*[20]

With the death of this outstanding figure, courage, piety, prowess and greatness also passed away. But there is no permanence in this transitory world; all of us are in a caravanserai, we pass along one after the other, with no permanent halting-place for anyone. One must live in such a manner that, after death, one is remembered favourably in prayers. Khᵛāja Bu Naṣr Moshkān, who composed the elegy for this outstanding person, likewise died at Herat; I shall set this forth in its appropriate place. Ebn al-Rumi has written well on this theme: (Poetry)

1. *The days are robbing me of everything which was entrusted to my care, and there is no good in anything which is snatched back and of which one is stripped.*
2. *They garbed me in a cloak of youth and a girdle, but that in which they previously clothed me they will strip away.*[21]

[Gh 366] I remain astonished at people's greed and feuding with each other, and at so much vice and corruption, and reckoning and punishment. For when death arrives at the door, there is nothing to distinguish a starving beggar and his miserable existence from a rich person with all his wealth. The truly noble man is that person whose good name lives on after his death. Rudaki says: (Occasional verse, *qeṭʿa*) [F 467]

1. Whether life be brief or long, is not death the end of it all?
2. No matter how long be the rope [of life], the noose awaits at the end.
3. Whether you live in hardship and deprivation or whether in security of life and in the lap of luxury,
4. Whether you receive very little from the world or as much as from Ray to Ṭarāz,
5. All of this is nothing but demonic whisperings into the human soul,[22] like a dream, with no power except that of illusion.
6. All appear the same on the day of death; you can no longer recognize one from another.

After the court session ended, Amir Masʿud had a private meeting with the eminent men and pillars of state, and the Commander-in-Chief ʿAli Dāya, the Great Chamberlain Bilgetegin, Bu'l-Fatḥ Rāzi, the Head of the Army Department Bu Sahl Ḥamdavi, and Bu Naṣr Moshkān. Then he said, "The Grand Vizier Aḥmad has passed away. He was an old man of great learning and knowledge and with a long-established lofty reputation, and we used to have no worries during his lifetime. We cannot manage without a vizier, for without such an intermediary, things will not run smoothly. Whom do you know who can measure up to such a crucial task as this?" They replied, "The lord knows his servants, including both his own protégés and those whom the late sultan raised up in his service. Whoever the lord chooses will be obeyed by everyone and the dignity of his office will be respected, and no-one will have the insolence to criticize the lord's exalted will." He said, "Go along to the Divān and sit down together in a private conclave in the place where the secretaries work." They sat down in the open loggia which is in the midst of the garden and which was the place where the Chancery functioned.[23]

He recalled Bu Naṣr, and said, "At that time when my father had Aḥmad detained, he had mentioned several possible names before the decision fell on Ḥasanak. Tell me the names of those persons." Bu Naṣr replied, "The Sultan said, regarding Bu'l-Ḥasan Sayyāri, 'He's a capable man, but I don't like his demeanour and his bearing. He is cut out for the office of head of the Divān (i.e. as Chief Secretary), for he is both efficient and trustworthy.' Regarding Ṭāher the accounting official, he said, 'He is [Gh 367] the best of the lot,[24] [F 468] but he is slow-moving and circumspect and I am impetuous by nature; I shall lose my temper, and he will lose his grip on affairs. As for Bu'l-Ḥasan ʿAqili, he enjoys a good reputation and status, but he is something of a lumbering yokel[25] and does not act decisively upon my commands; whereas I am used to straightforward talk and a firm response. Now for Bu Sahl Ḥamdavi, he is our own protégé and has spent much of his time as assistant to Aḥmad b. Ḥasan; but he is still young and should continue with his apprenticeship until he becomes more mature and polished, and then he will be fit for an important office.[26] Moreover, the job of looking after Ghaznin and its adjoining regions is a very onerous one, and must be held by someone who causes us no headaches. Regarding Ḥasanak, he has acquired much prestige, but he does not know accounting and secretarial practice, although his deputies are carrying on the governing of Nishapur very competently and are able to do this through his power and eminence. Regarding Aḥmad b. ʿAbd al-Ṣamad, he is the most suitable of them all. But Altuntāsh has no-one of his calibre to replace him, and Khwarazm is an important frontier province.' "

"In this manner—may the lord's life be prolonged—the respective traits and merits of these men were discussed. In the end, the Sultan conferred the vizierate on Ḥasanak, and came to regret it. At the present time, all of these persons, with the exception of Ḥasanak, are alive. The lord likewise has suitably qualified servants and retainers." The Amir said, "The names of these people should be written down and shown to the leading men in the state." Bu Naṣr wrote them down and presented them to those notables. They said, "They are all equally worthy of the task; the lord will know in whom he should put his trust."

The Amir said to Bu Naṣr, "Bu'l-Ḥasan Sayyāri is head of the Divān of Ray and Jebāl, and thanks to his direction, it is well regulated. Bu Sahl Ḥamdavi will go to Ray, since nothing can be expected from Ṭāher the secretary except wine-drinking and frivolous behaviour. Ṭāher the accounting official is of value in the Accounting Office, and we need Bu'l-Ḥasan ʿAqili at court. Just as the late Sultan had made up his mind at the end, my mind is fixed on Aḥmad b. ʿAbd al-Ṣamad, for he managed to bring such an enormous army, together with the corpse of the Khwarazm Shah, to Āmuy. [F 469] Moreover, he is well versed in the arts of secretaryship, financial accounting and administrative transactions, and is nimble-witted and far-sighted." Bu Naṣr replied, "That's an excellent idea. In the days of the 'Abbasid caliphs, and in those of the Samanids, the vizierate was often given to the counsellors and administrators (*kadkhodāyān*) of local rulers and army commanders. Kathir was the counsellor and administrator of Bu'l-Ḥasan b. Simjur, and Bu'l-Qāsem is his grandson. On several occasions the Samanids tried [Gh 368] to take Kathir away from Bu'l-Ḥasan in order to appoint him as their own vizier, and Bu'l-Ḥasan had to dissuade them by resorting to intercessors and pleading that he had no-one else to put in his place. At the present time, the affairs of Khwarazm are in an orderly state and well regulated, and Khᵛāja Aḥmad [b. 'Abd al-Ṣamad]'s son 'Abd al-Jabbār should be able to cope there after his father's appointment as Grand Vizier." The Amir ordered the inkstand to be brought and wrote out, in his own hand, a confidential letter to Aḥmad with this offer, "We have an important task for the Khᵛāja involving the governance of the whole realm, and this swift courier has been despatched post-haste. As soon as you have perused this missive written in our own hand, you must come to the court via the Nasā route[27] and not stay a moment longer in Khwarazm."

He gave the confidential letter to Bu Naṣr and said, "Write something further in your own hand, addressing him by the official form of address 'My Master and My Trusted One' (*Sheykhi va-Moʿtamadi*),[28] and mention that[29] he should have a trustworthy person in Khwarazm as his own replacement as counsellor and administrator, in case there is trouble in his absence. He is to bring his son 'Abd al-Jabbār with him so that, when the latter has seen for himself the sanctity of the exalted court, he can return to Khwarazm with a robe of honour and tokens of favour in a stately and ceremonious manner. Also, indite a letter from yourself, and spell out clearly for him that he has been summoned in order to receive the vizierate, and that the Sultan has told you this in confidence, so that he may be reassured."

Bu Naṣr wrote out the Sultan's letter in his inimitable way, since he was the master of the age in such epistolary skills, and on his own behalf he composed this private missive, "May the life of the noble Khᵛāja be prolonged, and may he live for many years in exalted office and good fortune! Let him be aware that, hidden in the bosom of

Fate there have been many fixed decrees and that the Almighty God is fully aware of those secrets, since He is the author of the decree. Moreover, he should also know that the lord, the great Sultan, the dispenser of bounties, [F 470] has deliberately chosen this friend of Aḥmad b. ʿAbd al-Ṣamad, that is, Bu Naṣr Moshkān, as the repository of that secret, and I myself have written out the Sultan's letter at the exalted command, *may God increase him in lofty status*, in my own hand, and it has been strengthened with the royal emblem and motto. A confidential letter in the royal hand is enclosed within that. I have written this letter of mine likewise at the exalted command. To be brief, let him come very quickly, since the exalted position of the vizierate awaits its rightful occupant, and that person is our master the Khᵛāja himself. So let him reach here speedily, and by his very appearance add lustre to the lives of us lesser mortals." [Gh 369] *May God Most High grant him long life and make him perpetually mighty and powerful*,[30] *and may He bring him to the farthest extent of his intentions and bring me, in the course of this, to what I have wished for him of God's favour!*" The Amir affixed his emblem and signature. One of the swift-riding dare-devil cavalrymen (*az kheyltāshān-e div-sovārān*)[31] was chosen and charged with going to Khwarazm and then returning to Nishapur within ten days. He left at once.[32]

On 7 Ṣafar [/12 January 1033] a letter arrived from Bost by courier of the postal and intelligence service with the news that the jurist Bu Bakr Ḥaṣiri, who had been ill there for some time, had passed away. How remarkable are the ways of Fortune that the passing of the late Vizier Aḥmad b. Ḥasan and that jurist—who had always been at daggers drawn—should fall so close together!

Meanwhile, news arrived that Bu Bakr Soleymāni, the envoy of the caliph al-Qāʾem be-amr Allāh, had reached Ray, and that he was accompanied by a eunuch attendant from the closest circle of the caliph's household attendants[33] bearing gifts and other noble manifestations of favour, while the envoy himself was in charge of other matters of high import. The Sultan ordered lavish preparations to be made for their arrival. They halted for a week and were looked after most hospitably. They came to Nishapur with a full escort and with staff charged with attending to their daily needs. [F 471] The Amir ordered that persons should go out speedily, and food and fodder[34] and supplies were got ready in the rural district of Beyhaq. On 8 Rabiʿ II [/11 April 1033], the jurists, judges and leading dignitaries of Nishapur went forth to welcome the incoming party. On the Wednesday,[35] the holders of court offices and those charged with the entertainment and accommodation of visiting envoys went forth. From the Gate of the Ray Road to the entrance of the Friday mosque, the way as well as the markets had been decorated. Large quantities of dirhams and dinars, pieces of sugar loaf and sweets were scattered and thrown down as alms, and the newly-arrived envoys were lodged in the Garden of Abu'l-Qāsem Khᵛāfi.[36] At the time of the midday worship great piles of tasty delicacies, prepared with care, were brought forward, together with 10,000 dirhams for petty and other expenses;[37] and every day there was some new manifestation of beneficence.

When a week had elapsed and they had sufficiently rested, a cavalcade was formed to go from the gate of the Shādyākh Garden to the gate of the envoy's residence. The whole of the troops, the great men of state and the senior officers were on their steeds with banners in their hands, and the infantrymen, with a great panoply of weapons, were stationed in front of the cavalrymen, while the holders of court offices formed up in two lines. The Amir was seated upon his throne on the dais, and there were the commanders and chamberlains with their two-pointed hats. It was a day of great splendour. The official charged with the envoys' reception and hospitality had gone at dawn to the envoy's residence with a chamberlain, several black-uniformed attendants and door-keepers, shield bearers, led horses and twenty mules for carrying the robes of honour and had conveyed those presents. They set the envoy and the caliph's household attendant on mounts, and they loaded up the robes of honour sent by the caliph in chests on the backs of mules, with the assistants of the treasury taking guard over them, and with eight horses [Gh 370] led by their halters and with gold-adorned saddles and accoutrements. One cavalryman with a furled standard in his hand and another one with the investiture patent and letter of appointment folded up in black satin brocade in his hand, went before the envoy, keeping carefully to their stations. Preceding them came the chamberlains and holders of court offices.

The blast of trumpets and the clamour of the barrel-shaped drums arose, and the thunderous jubilation of the troops went up as if it were the Day of Resurrection itself.[38] [F 472] Several elephants were stationed there. They led the envoy and the caliph's household attendant forward and brought them into the Amir's presence. The envoy kissed the Amir's hand and the attendant kissed the ground before him and they both stood in attendance. The Amir said, "How is the lord, the dispenser of favours, the Commander of the Faithful?" The envoy answered, "He is in a most happy and serene state, with all the affairs of the realm going according to his wishes, and he is pleased with the Exalted Sultan (*solṭān-e moʿaẓẓam*)—may he endure perpetually—who is his main pillar of support." The chamberlain Bu Naṣr took the envoy's arm and led him from the middle of the dais to close proximity of the throne and seated him there. On this dais there were seated the Commander-in-Chief ʿAli Dāya and the Head of the Army Department, but there was no vizier in post at that time, as I have recounted.

The envoy said, "May the lord's life be prolonged! When I returned to the caliphal court, I described for it the meticulous manner in which the Sultan had manifested his obedience and allegiance, and how he had fulfilled what he had deemed his duty in observing the mourning ceremonies for the death of al-Qāder be'llāh, and, after that, how he had proceeded to celebrate the Commander of the Faithful's glorious accession to the caliphal throne, how he had ordered the *khoṭba* to be proclaimed and enunciated, how he had performed the requirements of affirming his allegiance (*beyʿat*) and how he had despatched me homewards in a fitting manner. [When I had conveyed all these things,] the Commander of the Faithful, in a manner befitting his august state, sat on the caliphal throne and during that week held a general, open court audience so that he saw everyone who came before him. He found it an apt occasion to speak highly of the Sultan and to lavish praise upon him to the extent that he proclaimed that 'The greatest of our pillars of support and the most powerful today is the Upholder of the Religion of God and Protector of God's Servants, the One who Wreaks Vengeance on God's Enemies (*Nāṣer Din Allāh va-Ḥāfeẓ ʿEbād*[39] *Allāh, al-Montaqem men Aʿdāʾ Allāh*), Abu Saʿid Masʿud.' Also in that same court session, he had decreed that an investiture patent should be written out in the Sultan's name regarding his lands and possessions, both those inherited and those gained by his own efforts or about to be acquired in the near future, and he had it read out to the assembled audience. An inkstand was brought, and he adorned the investiture patent with the exalted signature and official emblem while invoking a blessing on the deed. Then he gave orders for it to be sealed, and after that, it was entrusted, together with the letter, to the household attendant while the caliph offered up invocations. He gave order for a standard and it was brought, and he fastened it with his own hand [F 473]. The collar, belt, neckband and crown were brought forward. One by one he handed them to the attendant and offered up prayers to the Almighty God [Gh 371] that He might bless them. Sewn garments were brought in, and he expressed adulatory words at each of these occasions, and likewise in respect of the special mounts which had been held at the rear of the hall.[40] Likewise, when the turban cloth and the sword were brought in, the caliph pronounced, 'This turban cloth, which has been wrapped round with our own hands, must reach the Upholder of Religion (*Nāṣer-e Din*) just like this, and he must place it on his head after the crown.' He drew the sword and said, 'The Zanādeqa and Qarāmeṭa[41] should be uprooted, and the established custom of his father Yamin al-Dowla va 'l-Din must be maintained in this regard. Moreover, by the might of this sword other lands which are in the hands of our enemies must be seized.' All this was delivered to me in that court session; now it has been conveyed to the Sultan so that he may ordain whatever he deems fit in this regard."

The Amir made a sign to Bu Naṣr b. Moshkān to receive the investiture patent and the letter. Bu Naṣr came forward out of the line and spoke to the envoy in Arabic. The latter then rose to his feet, bore that investiture patent wrapped in its black satin brocade cover before the Amir, and laid it on the throne. Bu Naṣr took it, and retired some distance away and stood there. The envoy, still standing there, asked the Sultan that, if he so considered it fitting, he should come down from the throne so that he might don, as an auspicious and blessed act, the Commander of the Faithful's robe of honour. The Amir ordered a prayer rug to be laid down. The Keeper of the Royal Weapons[42] had one with him and laid it down. The Amir faced towards the direction of Mecca.[43] The golden trumpets, which had been positioned in the midst of the Garden, were sounded, and their noise [F 474] was joined to the blast of other trumpets to form a tumultuous crescendo. At the court itself, large kettledrums were beaten, trumpets sounded and the glittering metal accoutrements of the elephants[44] jangled; one would have said that it was Resurrection Day. Bilgetegin and the other high-ranking commanders hastened forward and took the Amir's arms so that he descended from the throne and sat on the prayer rug. The envoy asked for the chests containing the robes of honour, and they were brought forth. They took out seven ceremonial, loose-fitting and cordless *faraji* robes,[45] one of them of black silk brocade and the rest of sundry material, and precious garments of Baghdadi cloth. The Amir kissed them, performed two prostrations of the worship and came to the throne. The crown set with jewels, and the collar and the neckband likewise set, were all brought forward, were kissed and were laid on the throne at his right hand. The household attendant brought forward the already folded and made up turban, the Amir kissed it, took off his hat and placed the turban on his head. He grasped the standard with his right hand and he girded on the sword and its belt. He kissed them and then laid them at one side. [Gh 372] Bu Naṣr Moshkān read out the caliph's letter and gave a Persian translation of it, and he read out the investiture patent. They set about showering largesse to such an extent that the scattered coins turned the floor of the dais golden and the emptying out of the purses made the garden glitter like silver. The envoy was conducted back, and rare and precious objects were scattered in unlimited quantities. With such pomp and ceremony on this scale did the envoy reach his house at the time of the afternoon worship. For several days successively, all was merry-making and joyfulness, and people were engaged in feasting and merriment night and day; no-one could recall such celebrations on that scale ever before.

In the midst of all this, news had arrived that the son of Yaghmur the Turkmen, and the sons of other Turkmen chiefs whom Tāsh Farrāsh, the Commander-in-Chief of Western Persia, had ordered to be put to death while he was on the way to Ray, had poured in from Balkhān Kuh with large numbers of other Turkmens. They were harrying the fringes of the realm wreaking vengeance on Muslims in order to avenge their fathers.[46] The Amir ordered the Commander-in-Chief ʿAli Dāya [F 475] to go to Ṭus and the Great Chamberlain Bilgetegin to go to Sarakhs, and they were to send out scouts and secure intelligence on what the Turkmens were doing. The Great Chamberlain Bilgetegin set out from Nishapur with his gholāms and cavalrymen, and the Commander-in-Chief ʿAli Dāya rode out the next day, Wednesday. Letters were despatched to Bā Kālijār by swift camels enjoining him to be alert and vigilant and to send a strong force to Dehestān to take up its position at the frontier post of Dehestān and guard the roads.[47] Letters were likewise despatched to Nasā and Bāvard ensuring that the military governor[48] and the people of those regions would obey the instructions of the Commander-in-Chief ʿAli and the Great Chamberlain Bilgetegin.

The swift-running envoy who had gone to Khwarazm to Khᵛāja Aḥmad b. ʿAbd al-Ṣamad, brought back his response to the letter. He said that the Khᵛāja had kept him there for two days, had presented him with a valuable horse, twenty sets of clothing and 20,000 dirhams, and had said that he would follow him in three days' time. The reply read as follows: "The exalted command arrived, written in the hand of Khᵛāja Bu Naṣr Moshkān, and adorned with the royal emblem and motto, and enclosed within its folds was the confidential letter written in the exalted hand of the Sultan which I reverently placed on my head and eyes. Bu Naṣr Moshkān had likewise written a confidential letter at the exalted behest, and has implanted certain words in my ear that have filled me with apprehension, for I heard something of which I am not worthy, something which had never passed through my mind and which I know I am not capable of fulfilling. I have sent back the envoy and I shall entrust my present duties to Bu Naṣr Barghashi, who is competent and well-thought of.[49] Hārun is most [Gh 373] sensible and self-disciplined, and, God willing, will remain thus in my absence. I am bringing along with me ʿAbd al-Jabbār, in accordance with the exalted command, so that, having had the good fortune to serve at the royal court, he will gain experience before returning home to Khwarazm. I shall follow the envoy and leave here in three days' time so that I can arrive soon at the exalted court."

The reply to my master was also written with the customary form of address: "To the Exalted, Noble Sheykh (*al-Sheykh al-Jalil al-Sayyid*) Abu Naṣr b. Moshkān from Aḥmad, son of ʿAbd al-Ṣamad, *his insignificant and humble servant*," and he had written to him at length and in a deferential manner so that Bu Naṣr was astounded at that, [F 476] and he commented, "This great master is indeed a perfect man; I knew him well but had not realized his true stature," and he took the letters to the Amir.

When news arrived that the Khᵛāja had approached Nishapur, the Amir ordered that everyone should go out to meet and escort him back. But by the time people had been told and were ready to set off, he and his son had already reached the court, this being on Wednesday, 1 Jomādā I [/4 April 1033]. People began to arrive and offer him their greetings. The Amir held court, and he was informed that Khᵛāja Aḥmad had arrived. He gave orders that he was to come into his presence. He kissed the ground at two or three places and stood by the corner of the dais. The Amir made a sign in the direction of Bilgetegin, and Bilgetegin made a sign to a chamberlain and gave orders for him to be conducted to the dais and to be set down some distance from the throne. A thousand dinars were scattered on behalf of Khᵛāja Aḥmad.[50] He brought out from his sleeve a bejewelled collar, said to be valued at 1,000 dinars; the Great Chamberlain Bilgetegin took it from him and gave it to the General Bu'l-Nażr[51] and he placed it before the Amir. The Amir said to Aḥmad, "How did you leave the affairs of Khwarazm, and Hārun, and the army?" He replied, "Through the resplendent power[52] of the exalted rule, everything is going in accord with the royal wishes and there are no setbacks." The Amir said, "You must be weary after your journey and should now rest." He took his formal leave and went back. A horse specially designated for him was summoned and speedily got ready,[53] and he went back to the mansion of Bu'l-Fażl of the Āl-e Mikāl, which had been refurbished and prepared for him, and installed himself there, with his son in another residence near his father's house. The Amir had ordered the intendant of the household to have them supplied with a complete array of comestibles and delicacies. Each day, Aḥmad would come to the court, offer up his respects and then go back.

When three days had gone by, the Amir gave orders for him to be given a seat in the loggia near the dais. The Amir further made his court session a private one. Bu Naṣr Moshkān, Bu'l-Ḥasan ʿAqili and ʿAbdus acted as intermediaries, conveying messages (i.e. between the Amir and Aḥmad). The private session went on till the time of the midday worship, [F 477] and there was much discussion concerning the vizierate. Aḥmad appeared reluctant to accept it and said, "I am but an outsider [Gh 374] in this present company (i.e. those of the court circle and the central administration), and I don't know the ways of service here. It would be better for me to remain the apprentice and aide that I am"—but to cut a long story short, he finally consented and accepted the post of vizier. He was brought before the Amir, and found himself much heartened by the royal presence and verbal encouragement, and then he went back in order to write out the customary contractual agreement in which he made request for the conditions of his employment.[54] The horse specially designated for him by personal name (i.e. not yet in the name of him as vizier) was now summoned. When people ascertained that he was to become vizier, they came to present themselves to him and to render service.

He wrote out the contractual agreement and sent it to my master. The Amir wrote out his own response in his own hand, and graciously accepted all those conditions that the Kh^{v}āja had sought and requested. An especially fine robe of honour was prepared, and on Monday, 6 Jomādā I [/9 April 1033] he was enrobed with it. The outfit included a belt set with a thousand pearls. The Great Chamberlain Bilgetegin took his arm and sat him down near the throne. The Amir said, "May the robe of honour be auspicious for us, for the Kh^{v}āja, for the army and for the subjects!" The Kh^{v}āja stood up, offered up obeisance, and set before the Amir a bejewelled collar valued at 5,000 dinars. The Amir placed in the Kh^{v}āja's hand a turquoise ring with the Amir's name engraved on it, and said, "This is the ring of state (*angoshtari-e mamlakat*), which we have given to the Kh^{v}āja, and he is now our deputy. He must set about the job with a stout heart and the utmost vigour, for his command comes immediately after our own command in regard to every sphere of activity which appertains to the welfare of the empire and the realm." The Kh^{v}āja said, "I am obedient to the command, and as your faithful servant will do my utmost, in acknowledgement of what is due to the lord for his favours," and he kissed the ground and went back. A gholām of his was given a robe of honour [F 478] as if he were a chamberlain, and departed with him.[55] When he was installed at his house, all the retainers, notables and leading personalities of the court went to convey their congratulations, and offered large amounts of money and presents. A list was made of all the gold, silver and whatever had been brought to him, a very substantial sum, and he sent it to the Amir. He also sent along, as a separate account, what he had brought from Khwarazm,[56] together with the son of

Tāsh Māhruy.[57] (Both he and his father were strikingly handsome; Tāsh had been killed in the forefront of the Khwarazm Shah's army fighting against 'Alitegin.)[58]

The Amir was pleased with all this and placed this son of Tāsh amongst his closest retainers, since there were not three or four individuals like him in the three or four thousand gholāms. Many became envious of him or fell in love with him, including some from amongst the palace gholāms. It so happened that, one night, a companion from the same barracks came to him with the intention of seducing him—for he was enamoured of him [Gh 375]—and Tāsh's son stabbed him with his dagger and the gholām was killed. *We seek refuge in God from the onslaught of evil!* The Amir decreed that legal retaliation of a life for a life (*qeṣāṣ*) should be taken. The major-domo of the palace (*mehtar-e sarāy*) said, "May the lord's life be prolonged! It would be a shame to consign such a handsome face below the earth!" The Amir replied, "He must be beaten with a thousand strokes and then castrated; if he dies, retaliation will have been exacted, and if he lives, we will look and see what job he is suitable for." He did live, and regained his former lustre; now as a eunuch attendant, he appeared a thousand times more attractive and beautiful than before, and became the Amir's Inkstand Bearer. His ultimate fate was as follows. During the reign of 'Abd al-Rashid, allegations were made that he had colluded with the Amir Mardān Shāh who was incarcerated in a fortress, and that he had pledged his allegiance to him. Mardān Shāh and a group of other persons, including the hapless son of Tāsh, were put to death. They were impaled on the tusks of elephants, with several of the leading commanders, prominent men and senior officers, brought out of the square and then thrown down. God's mercy be upon them all![59] [F 479]

Khᵛāja Aḥmad sat down in his place in the Divān and embarked on his task as a vizier in a most accomplished manner. He established order and regularity, for he was highly competent, well-qualified, deliberate, learned and cultured, and was thoroughly acquainted with administrative procedures and transactions; and in addition to all these admirable qualities, he was also a perfectly fine man. This noble person performed such good works that it became evident what a genuinely great man he was. It is as if these two verses were composed about him: (Poetry)

1. *The vizierate came to him, showing its obeisance all the way* (lit. "dragging along its skirts").
2. *It fitted no-one else but him, and he fitted naught else but it.*[60]

As well as being so capable, he displayed much bravery and courage, for during the blessed reign of this monarch he led many an army and performed several memorable feats. During his entire tenure of office, he was only faulted on one or two issues (the man exempt from all faults does not exist!). One was that, in the early days of his vizierate, one day, in full public audience, he spoke some harsh words to the Khᵛājas ʿAli and ʿAbd al-Razzāq, the sons of Khᵛāja Aḥmad b. Ḥasan [Meymandi], and in the course of them mentioned their father, a man of such commanding stature, in slighting terms. People, from the noble and humble classes alike, took umbrage at this. The other was that, at the end of his tenure as Amir Mowdud's vizier, [Gh 376] he uttered some words in regard to Ertegin,[61] whose sister was one of the Amir's wives,[62] such as to make this Turk weary and resentful against him, and this led to the Vizier's downfall. I shall recount this story in its appropriate place, for it is a notable one. *But where are really refined and presentable men to be found?*[63]

On Friday, 10 Jomādā I [/13 April 1033], the Amir gave orders that the Vizier's son, ʿAbd al-Jabbār, [F 480] should be garbed in a robe of honour. At the same time he ordered that the stipulated tribute from Bā Kālijār, the governor of Gorgān, should be demanded and that his daughter, who had already been contracted in marriage to the Amir, should be sent to the court before its departure from Nishapur. It was decided that ʿAbd al-Jabbār, the Vizier's son, should be sent there on an embassy, together with a religious scholar and several servants and attendants, according to the customary practice. The Amir pointed out to Aḥmad, "This is the first mission which has been entrusted to your son." My master Bu Naṣr prepared the drafts of the letters and the sets of instructions which were to be communicated verbally,[64] and they were written out. The religious scholar Bu'l-Ḥasan Qaṭṭān,[65] who was one of the outstanding students of the Judge, the Imam Ṣāʿed, was attached to ʿAbd al-Jabbār, as also the trusted attendant of Sultan Maḥmud, Kāfur Maʿmari.[66] The (bridal) litter was got ready, as also the various servants and the presents, according to the practice and custom. On 12 Jomādā I [/15 April 1033] ʿAbd al-Jabbār set out from Nishapur for Gorgān with his party.

Section concerning the present world[67]

I shall recount a section about the artful ways of this present world, which doles out pieces of sugar with one hand and deadly poison with the other.[68] Some people it has tested through adversity, while others have been attired in blissful felicity, so that the wise can discern the futility of pining for the riches of this world. Motanabbi says: (Poetry)

1. *He who keeps company with the present world for any length of time finds all its aspects, exterior and interior, turned upside down, until he sees that its truthfulness is all lies.*[69]

I had brought this volume of the History thus far when the monarch Farrokh-zād gave up and entrusted his sweet and precious soul to the One Who Seizes Souls. They performed for him the funerary ablutions and laid him on a wooden bier,[70] and from all those numerous pleasure gardens and the buildings and palaces [F 481] inherited from his grandfather, father and brother, he had to make do with a plot of ground four or five *gazs*'[71] long, and they heaped up the earth over him. Daqiqi has a poem in this vein: (Poetry)[72] [Gh 377]

1. Alas for Amir Bu Naṣr, and alas! For your youth brought you precious little happiness![73]
2. But the all-conquering heroes of this world are like roses: They have but a brief season.

Poetry

1. *Where is Kesrā, Kesrā of the kings, Anushervān, or where, from the days before him, is Sābur?*
2. *And where are the noble, pale-faced ones* (banu 'l-aṣfar), *kings of the earth* [moluk al-Rum rather than al-arż in the original Arabic]? *Not a memory of them has endured.*
3. *And where is the ruler of al-Ḥażr (Hatra), who once built it and for whom the taxation of the Tigris and Khābur used to be collected?*
4. *The blows of ill fortune did not fear him, and thus royal power departed from him, and his portals are now forsaken.*

5. *Then they passed on, as if they were leaves which became dry and shrivelled, and the east and the west winds snatched them away.*[74]

By Abu'l-Ṭayyeb al-Moṣʿabi[75]

1. O World, you are all teasing and playful diversion; not staying long with anyone and chiming with none!
2. Moon-like in your display but a thorn to touch; snatching away your victim like a falcon or a hawk.
3. You taste like poison but are mellifluous as a harp; you bite like the wind and cut through like a diamond. [F 482]
4. You are like the aloes wood from Qemār[76] and the musk of Tibet; or like the amber of the Yemen and the Ḥejāz.
5. Outwardly, a mansion of Āzar,[77] the idol-maker, resplendent with figurines; Within, a filthy pig and a wild boar.
6. You appear as paradise to one, and as hell to another; the pits of an abyss for some, the very summit for another.
7. You are like an orchard, drooping with bounties: strictly barred to one, but most welcoming to another.[78]
8. All is trial and tribulation, all is appearance and spectacle, all is humbug and highfalutin' talk,[79] as you strut like a well-plumed fowl.[80]
9. It is you that enables chess players to inflict checkmate (i.e. death); it is you who hands out the pieces when playing the game.[81]
10. Why do bright and talented people exist in such dire straits, and why do the foolish and ignorant bask in opulence?
11. Why is the life of the peacock and the francolin short? Why do the snake and the vulture live for years?[82] [Gh 378]
12. A country yokel (*mard-e gharcha*) lives for a hundred odd years; why did that man of the Arabs (*mard-e tāzi*, i.e. the Prophet Moḥammad) live for only sixty-three?[83] [F 483]
13. Perversity is your hallmark, or else, why do you favour the least noble the most?

14. But verily, O world, all this is of no import to you! It is we who are the sinners, while you are a mere prop for our greed and passions.

The One who decrees the span of lives, the Creator of night and day, the Mighty, the Overpowering One, the One who wields authority over kings, His eminence is exalted and His names sanctified, had allotted such a small span of life in this world and period of kingly power for the Amir Farrokh-zād, God's mercy be upon him. There was great sadness among all ranks of people at his passing away while still in his youth, with so many praiseworthy deeds and memorials left behind, and such a clear sense of justice that his fame had reached the four corners of the world. (Poetry)

1. *Man is nothing but a good tale, so be a good tale for the person who understands!*[84]

When he passed away, the Almighty God brought to the seat of government the memorial of the emperors and the choicest of the monarchs, the exalted Sultan, the dispenser of favours, Abu'l-Moẓaffar Ebrāhim b. Nāṣer Din Allāh, in felicity, happiness and good fortune, and by taking up his seat there he added lustre to the throne of his forefathers. The elders of the state saw visible manifestations of those noble qualities and achievements of the bygone era of Maḥmud and Masʿud which had since fallen into abeyance.[85] May this monarch be always granted enjoyment of life, and may he long enjoy royal power, youth and prosperity! On Monday, 19 Ṣafar of the year 451 [/6 April 1059], the day when I had brought this History up to this point and when the exalted Sultan Abu'l-Moẓaffar Ebrāhim b. Nāṣer Din Allāh gave lustre to this great domain, the occasion itself reflected these words in a most eloquent manner: (Poetry) [F 484]

1. A monarch of pure, noble character has passed away, but in his place there sits a ruler of angelic descent.[86]

2. All the world grieves for the departed king, and all the world rejoices for the newly-enthroned one.

3. If God took away from us a lamp, He put a fresh torch in its place.[87]

4. We, who have lost the Shāh Farrokh-zād, have gained a sovereign like Ebrāhim.[88]

One of the manifestations of the majesty of this monarch was that, out of the darkness of a fortress,[89] a sun with such brilliance which reached its zenith of nineteen degrees[90] illuminated the world. Furthermore, when he came to rule, he treated the retainers and courtiers and his subjects in general [Gh 379] according to their status and degree, brought them close and distributed favour amongst them in accordance with what reasons of state and the considerations of the realm required. He displayed and made manifest to people his imperial aura by his instructions and his words, and the first thing he ordained was a period of mourning for his brother. Rest assured that a shepherd has come to this flock, and the subjects will no longer suffer harm from wolves and savage beasts. A scattered and demoralised army was given new life and united through his royal bounty; he listened to the complaints of those who had undergone tyranny or who had endured affliction, and redressed their grievances. May he be shielded for ever from malevolent fortune, for he is a second Nushirvān![91]

Some might say, "Great and exalted is the exercise of rulership! If it comes into the hands of a mighty monarch, one blessed with good fortune and knowledgeable about affairs, he will succeed by some means or other and will discharge his responsibilities in such a way that he will achieve both spiritual salvation and worldly success. But if it comes into the hands of a weak and helpless being, he will fall into a quagmire himself and drag down his people with him."

God forbid that [F 485] a person who is heavily indebted in gratitude to their royal bounty should utter untoward and ungracious words about the way this house have conducted themselves as monarchs! Nevertheless, from the time of Adam up to our own day, it has been customary for those old and experienced enough to have been through the ups and downs of this world to say, out of pure compassion and genuine concern, that so-and-so person acted well whereas another person acted wrongfully.[92] It is written in the historical traditions (*khabar*): *"A man came to the Prophet, may God grant him and his family blessings and peace, and said, 'What a reprehensible thing it is to exercise rulership over people.' He replied, peace be upon him, '[On the contrary,] what an excellent thing it is to exercise rulership over people, provided it is done rightfully and legitimately; but where is this rightfulness and legitimacy to be found?'"* The exalted Sultan assumed it with rightfulness and lawfulness, and he wielded it in the manner of powerful and mighty monarchs. Another tradition (*ḥadith*) relates that when [the Persian emperor] Kesrā Parviz passed away, the news reached the Prophet. He asked, "*Whom have they appointed as his successor?" They replied, "His daughter Burān." He said, peace be upon him, "A people who have entrusted the governing power over themselves to a woman will not prosper.*"[93] This is the most ample proof that a realm requires a courageous and capable man of authority; if this is not the case, there is nothing to choose between a man and a woman. Kaʿb Aḥbār has said, "The relationship between a ruler and his subjects is analogous to a fully-pitched tent which is erected round a single central pole, and its guy ropes are kept taut and secured by means of tent pegs. The tent of Islam is royal power; the supporting pole is the king, and the guy-ropes and tent pegs are the subjects. Now when one looks at this carefully, the foundation is the supporting pole that upholds the tent. Were it to become weak and fall, that would be the end of the tent, the rope and the peg."[94] Nushirvān has said, "Don't reside in a city which lacks an incisive and powerful ruler, a fair judge, [Gh 380] a continuously-assured supply of rain, a skilful physician and which has no flowing stream. Even if all these things are present but there is no incisive ruler, everything will be in vain." *These things revolve round the ruler like a sphere round a pivot; the pivot is the ruler*".[95]

A just and beneficent monarch has appeared; may he always continue in power and be firmly established! And if a mighty and commanding prince from the stock of Maḥmud and Masʿud has ascended the throne, there is no cause for wonder. Yaʿqub b. [F 486] Leyth was the son of a coppersmith, and Bu Shojāʿ ʿAżod al-Dowla va 'l-Din was the son of Bu'l-Ḥasan b. Buya, who fled as a rebel to the Samanids from the midst of the Deylamites, and by dint of his own mettle and firm resolution, and through the grace of the divine decree of God Most Mighty, he turned from the state of being a rebel to becoming a king. Then his son ʿAżod, through his lofty resolution and bold spirit, became even more powerful than his father and kinsmen, and he wrought those deeds and attained those achievements which have been set forth in the *Ketāb-e Tāji* of Bu Esḥāq al-Ṣābi.[96] They also recount many tales of Bu Moslem, the leader of the ʿAbbasid's successful bid for power, of Ṭāher Dhu'l-Yamineyn and of Naṣr b. Aḥmad amongst the Samanids. God, the Most Exalted One, has said, in regard to Saul (Ṭālut)—*and He is the most veracious of those who speak—"And He increased him amply in knowledge and bodily strength.*"[97] Whenever the care and solicitude of the Creator Most High come into play, He makes evident virtues and acts of greatness, and out of the ashes He kindles a blazing fire.

While engaged in this History, I asked the jurist Bu Ḥanifa Eskāfi to compose an ode concerning the passing away of Sultan Maḥmud, the accession to the throne of Amir Moḥammad and the seizure of the kingdom by Masʿud, and this he did in a remarkably eloquent fashion.[98] It induced me to surmise and speculate to myself that, if, without the encouragement of a reward and the prospects of a monthly stipend, Bu Ḥanifa could compose such an ode, to what sublime heights of eloquence might he soar if only a monarch should happen to look favourably on him! *The augury proved true!*[99] What I had intimated in my heart, the Divine Pen had already decreed! Before he had ascended the royal throne, the exalted Sultan Ebrāhim had seen several books penned by Bu Ḥanifa, [F 487] and he had appreciated both his fine calligraphic hand and his turns of phrase and took them as favourable omens for his release (i.e. from captivity). When he attained the throne, he sought out Bu Ḥanifa and asked him to compose verses for him. He composed a panegyric ode and was duly rewarded, and he asked for another one immediately afterwards. Other poets, too, after having remained for seven lean years without recognition or recompense [Gh 381] or largesse, were now duly rewarded.[100] Bu Ḥanifa became a favourite and composed many an eloquent ode, one of them being the following: (Ode)[101]

1. May the Omniscient Lord (*rabb-e ʿalim*) bestow a hundred thousand benedictions upon Ebrāhim, who is a purveyor[102] of divine mercy!

2. The sun of the lords of the seven climes, through whom this anciently-established splendour has been renewed!

3. To keep the garden of his praise freshly verdant, the showers of magnanimity became perennial.

4. The nightingale of the arts descended into the garden, and a breeze came from the orchard of glory.

5. Although owing to the vicissitude of the world, the unique pearl had to remain a long time enclosed in its shell,

6. God be thanked and praised that all those difficulties disappeared, and all ended well![103]

7. From the heavens of virtue, Jam appeared, and the accursed demon departed hobbling and crawling on all fours.

8. The lion (meaning here Sultan Ebrāhim) showed its teeth and revealed its claws, and the bull of dissension turned sickly and ill.[104]

9. What effect could the magic of Pharaoh have, when this staff of the one who spoke with God (*kalim*, i.e. Moses) became a dragon?[105]

10. The person who has savoured the majesty of Solomon (Soleymān) does not overpraise the throne of Belqis.[106]

11. The ruler knows that he depends on the Shaper of Things (i.e. God) and attaches no credence to almanacs and astrologers.

12. He has no cause for regret or remorse, for he remains temperate even when roused to anger.

13. His own good judgement serves him as his vizier, and his own well-tempered nature, his constant companion. [F 488]

14. O king, emperor and lord! A word in your ear, precious as a strung pearl!

15. The king will not be short of victorious conquests if he does away with sensual distractions.

16. If you wish affairs to proceed according to the desires of your heart, first exercise patience before giving vent to your heart's desires!

17–20.[107]

21. Let us see our opponent's opening gambit, and let us see what Fate has in store.

22. Take up the sword and put aside the wine, if you have heard the adage that "kingship recognizes no lineage."[108]

23. If you combine the pen and the sword, you will not be deprived of power over the seven climes (i.e. the whole world).

24. Do not place guilt or blame at other people's doors; do not see others as the source of your hopes and fears.

25. Whatever befalls us, good or bad, is at the behest of a beneficent God.

26. A man must be awesome and strikingly lethal like a viper, not a harmless silvery fish (*shim*), all tinsel and show.[109]

27. He should not be an eel,[110] half-hearted and contrary, neither fish nor snake. [F 489]

28. Regard an inherently base man with greatest contempt, even though everyone considers him lofty in status.

29. The habits and customs of this bunch of oppressors (*ẓalum*) fit exactly those of the fire-eating bird (*ẓalim*), if you look well enough.[111]

30. For he who is consumed by the infernal fire of his carnal soul has no helper or aid, human or divine.

31. A pithy dictum is better than a long-winded discourse; do not seek pearls in a mine or silver at sea.[112]

32. Be assertive and impetuous, like the demons: the very qualities that brought Satan up to the firmament.[113]

33. So long as there are beauties in this world, tall and erect, and so long as their tresses cascade down in curls,[114]

34. May you be radiant and robust, in fine shape, while your ill-wishers suffer a painful punishment![115]

35. May your battlefield always be filled with famed champions, as is, in the season of the Pilgrimage, the corner of the wall![116]

36. Be like your grandfather (i.e. like Maḥmud) and like your father's grandfather (i.e. like Sebüktegin),[117] compassionate to your intimates and to the masses of people, both high and low, alike!

Also by him:[118]

1. Blessed be those pure, shining cheeks like silver and for those two black locks of yours, with that [sickle] shape of two *jims*![119]

2. Scant justice would I have done to the range of your beauty, had I sung your praises a whole week long. [F 490]

3. You see that figure, like a proud cypress in a vision, with the hand of nature arranging a harvest of flowers on a silver base.[120] [Gh 383]

4.[121]

5. I am your lover, yet have nothing to show for it; for a man of high aspirations, poverty is a great trial.

6. In your face and your limbs, you resemble the moon (*māh*) and a fish (*māhi*); has anyone seen a moon smoother and more slender than the silvery fish?[122]

7. People cavil at your uniqueness and your two-facedness; but is not the one who has two faces a rose,[123] and is not the one who is unique a pearl?

8. No wonder if your tresses never come to rest (i.e. are tossed about), when what deranges them is that pearl-like dimple behind your ears.[124]

9. Do not rob me of my senses; is it not sufficient that in your wake, wise men are ensnared and die by your tresses?

10. Your lovely eyes would have never looked so fearful and downcast, had you not instilled fear into them through those pitch-black tresses of yours.[125]

11. Who do they think they are, those tresses of yours, that they should induce fear into your eyes, or who are you[126] to inculcate fear into anyone?

12. You would never be so bold and brash again were you to hear the name of the ruler of the seven climes, [F 491]

13. The emperor of Iran, the Amir of the Arabs and the Shah of the Persians![127] Best be brief: say, the Sultan of the World, Ebrāhim!

14. He who, like his forbears and father before him, you will find engaged in perpetual remembrance of and homage to the Wise Lord God.

15. A monarch in the people's hearts, and pious devotee in his own heart; when a monarch is like this, a kingdom cannot become weak!

16. No virtue in the world ever becomes apparent until men resolve to set their hearts upon it.

17. He is a seeker after God, patient and forbearing, faithful confidant of his own heart's secrets, victorious in battle and powerful, but merciful towards those he has put to flight.

18. His lofty resolution is like the heavenly sphere, and his bounty a shooting star, if covetousness in the aged or the young be compared to the accursed Satan.[128]

19. Guiltless of any crime, small or great, for thirteen years he bore the injustice of accursed fate.

20. If a person remained confined for thirteen years within paradise, that paradise would appear like hellfire to him.[129]

21.[130]

22. For thirteen years the king of kings remained in prison, bereft of all the blessings of this world, with patient endurance as his sole companion.

23. Although he suffered much at the hands of abject folk,[131] it was God Himself who preserved him from the evil of His creatures.[132] [F 492]

24. Just as God bestows kingly power on a person, He also takes it away; then why does the current proverb say, *"kingly power has no lineage"*?[133]

25. Emperor, Shah, Amir, King, Dispenser of Justice! After this, why should the drum be beaten under the rug?[134] [Gh 384]

26. Listen to whoever has advice to offer, and pay no heed if the person giving advice is like myself (i.e. the poet), pure at heart but a simpleton.

27. O wise Shah, learn wisdom even from ignoramuses, since through aberrant strokes of the pen (*taḥrif*) a man's written hand becomes clear and straight.

28. Revive the custom of Sultan Maḥmud with a strong sword, for through using the message and the letter (i.e. through mere diplomacy) the adversary does not go away.[135]

29. Shoulder the sword, and do not ask about yesterday and its eve if you wish your fame to extend far and wide.[136]

30. Make a display of power at the outset, and then afterwards conduct yourself with forbearance; forbearance which does not come from power does not become a forbearing man.[137]

31. Who is the man, from amongst the Tajiks (*tāzek*)[138] or the Turks, in this great centre of the court circle who has not in his heart a love (i.e. for the Sultan) rather than for gold and silver?

32. With such aged men—no, I take that back—rather, with such young-hearted men will the affairs of Khorasan speedily become regularized.[139]

33. That which your fine nature promises to fulfil, no emperor or amir or leader ever did before.

34. What matters if Moses (*kalim*) was deficient in speech (*kalām*),[140] he who was able to change his staff into a serpent.[141] [F 493]

35.[142]

36. Today, your slanderers have gone to ground and are silent, while yesterday they bathed in glory and held forth[143] as if they were King Dābeshlim.[144]

37. A man who has neither inborn merits (*gohar*) nor acquired skills (*honar*) can only use silence as his cover, in the manner of a penniless man making do with debts.[145]

38. Give thanks, thanks to the Lord of the World, who freely bestowed on you, without any mediation, this anciently-established kingdom!

39. Neither this nor that person, nor any aged person or young one, did anything, nor was it because of the changes coming round with each new year or any astrological computation (*taqvim*).

40. On the contrary, everything came from the decree of the Lord of the World; the decree came from the Lord of the World, and obedience from the subjects.

41. As long as people say that the Martyred Sultan was, from his lofty intentions, endowed with a better nature than all other kings,[146]

42. Live in happiness and joy, and drink wine from the hand of a beloved one[147] with such exquisite lips.[148]

43. Your foe is injured and battered and in fetters! He has become heartbroken, and through sickness at heart, infirm.

44. Make your kingdom prosperous and flourishing through justice and joyfulness! May that person who does not wish you to become great never prosper and flourish! [F 494]

These two odes containing so many moral examples and pieces of counsel have been set down. Such honest and blunt advice must be proffered repeatedly to exalted and blessed monarchs so that it may be written down. Mighty rulers must be impelled to construct an edifice of noble deeds, for although the intention itself is engrained in their natures, it will be awakened and aroused [Gh 385] by external prodding and wise counsel. Truly indomitable and resolute monarchs have always made a treasury out of wise words.[149] The one nearest to us in time is Seyf al-Dowla Abu'l-Ḥasan ʿAli.[150] It should be observed that, since he was so stout-hearted and capable, and since Motanabbi had given his all in eulogizing him, what magnificent style the poet could achieve! For so long as Arabic speech exists in the world, his words will never be effaced but appear fresher each day, and the very name of Seyf al-Dowla has remained alive because of him, as he has said in his own verse: (Poetry)[151]

1. *O my two friends, I do not see but a single real poet* (i.e. himself)*; how many claims do they* (i.e. other, pretended poets) *make, while I make odes.*

2. *Do not be amazed: swords are many, but today there is only one Sword of the Dynasty* (Seyf al-Dowla).[152]

3. *His noble nature unsheathes him in battle, while his habit of liberality and mercy sheathes him.*

4. *And when I saw that people are inferior to him in rank and status, it became clear to me* [153] *that Fate tries people and separates the true coin* [F 495]

5. *The most worthy of persons to wield a sword* (or: *"to be called 'Seyf'"*) *is the one who smites men's necks, and the one most worthy of command is the one who makes light of disasters.*

6. *The most wretched of God's lands is that of the Byzantines* (al-Rum)*; none there can deny your glory.*

7. *You launched raids upon it until you left it, with the eyelids of those even beyond al-Faranja sleepless.*[154]

8. *The lofty fortresses on the mountain peaks, are encircled by your cavalrymen, tight necklaces round the Greeks' necks.*[155]

9. *The one who leads continuous raids, whose swords do not leave their necks, except when the Seyḥān is frozen over.*[156]

10. *So that not one of them has been left, except those whose deep red lips and well-rounded breasts have preserved them from the sword blades* (i.e. the womenfolk).

11. *The Patricians are weeping continuously over them in the darkness of the night, while we regard them as things cast aside in the market, of no value.*

12. *This is what fate has decreed for people whose destinies it rules; the calamities of one group are benefits for another.*

13. *But because of the nobility of your dashing attacks, you are loved like a benefactor amongst them despite being their killer.*

14. *You have carried off lives to such a number that, if you were to gather them together, the present world would be filled with rejoicing that you were going to live for ever.*

15. *You are the incisive sword of kingly power, and the one wielding it [through you] is God; you are the banner of religion, and God is the One raising it ready for battle.*

16. *I am full of love for you, O sun and full moon of the age, even though Sohā and the Farqads may blame me regarding you.*[157]

[F 496]

17. *That is because your excellence is outstanding, and not because life with you is pleasant and unstressful.*[158] Gh 386]

Had he not possessed these virtues, how would Motanabbi ever have had the courage to describe him thus, since great men cannot stomach mockery and chop people's heads off for it! As long as the world continues to exist, monarchs will do mighty deeds and poets will relate them in verse. And one must realize the illustrious nature of this mighty dynasty of Sultan Maḥmud and the manner in which ʿOnṣori has eulogized it, as shown by some eloquent odes of his which I have included in this History.[159] It is clearly and obviously evident that people will see exploits like those of Sultan Maḥmud (*āthār-e maḥmudi*)[160] from this great Sultan Ebrāhim, so that the cavaliers of poetry and prose will enter the arena of eloquence and display such virtuoso performances that they will put preceding generations of poets in the shade. "*God Most High will facilitate that through his grace and His power and will make it easy. Indeed, He is the One all-powerful to do that, and that is of little account for God.*"[161]

I have also set down just after these sections what Daqiqi has composed, so that when the readers of this History reach this point and realize this, they may derive benefit. After that, I shall go back to the history of the reign of the Martyr Sultan Masʿud so that a fresh start may be made from that point which I had reached and had propelled my pen, if the Almighty God so wills. Daqiqi says: (Poetry)[162]

1. With two things one seizes a throne,
One is silken, the other saffron in hue:

2. One is a piece of gold, with the king's name inscribed (i.e. a coin),
The other is iron, tempered in Yemen.

3. Whoever covets a kingdom
   Needs a spur and a nod from heaven itself

4. And a way with words; a liberal hand;
   A heart given to love, yet adept at revenge.

5. For as a quarry, kingly power can elude,
   The raging lion; and the soaring eagle.

6. Two things can bring it down:
   An Indian sword, and gold, dug from a mine. [F 497]

7. Seize the kingdom with the sword, and bind its feet with dinars, if you can, [Gh 387]

8. Whoever is blessed by fortune, sword, and gold,
   And is upright and straight as a spear, and of royal lineage.[163]

9. Must also possess wisdom, generosity, and courage,
   For when has Fortune given away a kingdom for free?

Now this ode too has been recorded. If we live long enough, we old men will witness many further praiseworthy exploits, as has already become clear from the deeds and the demeanour of this mighty monarch in this short while; for a perfectly formed and translucent blossom on a young plant tells us well enough how good the fruit will be. And I, Bu'l-Fażl, if I live long enough in this all-devouring and deceitful present world to pursue my account of the deeds of this dynasty and the glorious era of this present monarch—may he live for many years!—will, when I reach his reign, seize the opportunity and in his name[164] turn this royal brocade into a cloth of gold. *Go Most High is the One who grants success in people's intentions and belief in His beneficence and grace!*

[The end of the seventh volume] [F 498]

[The beginning of the eighth volume]

The remainder of the year 424 [early May–25 November 1033]

I had already set down the history of this year in the seventh volume up to the point when the Martyred Amir Masʿud sent ʿAbd al-Jabbār, the son of Khᵛāja Aḥmad b. ʿAbd al-Ṣamad, on an embassy to Gorgān together with the household attendant (*khādem*) and the litter in order to bring back Bā Kālijār's daughter from the latter's harem to this monarch's. That day when I wrote down this episode was a day of rejuvenation at this exalted court, as I have already recorded,[165] and I was diverted from continuing the History; now, however, I am returning to the orderly sequence of the history.

Letters kept arriving from Ray conveying the message that "Ṭāher the secretary, the counsellor and administrator at Ray and those adjacent regions, is sunk in revelry, wine-drinking and all that goes with it.[166] The disgraceful state of affairs has reached such a point that, on one day, when the roses were in full bloom, Ṭāher held a festival of the scattering of rose petals on a scale such as no king ever has, with dinars and dirhams mingled amidst the rose petals strewn about. Tāsh and all the senior commanders were with him, and he distributed largesse to everyone. When they went back, his drunken comrades, together with his personal gholāms and intimates, threw off all self-control and shame, [Gh 388] and their antics became so extravagant that he ordered gold and silver drinking vessels to be brought in and he had them secured to a silken cord which he wore round his waist like a sash, and he placed on his head a crown of intertwined myrtle leaves decorated with red roses and began to caper about. His boon-companions and [F 499] gholāms also danced in a frolicsome manner, wearing crowns on their heads. The next day, this matter became public knowledge and the talk of the town, with outsiders and natives speaking about it. If these reports should reach the enemies of the realm and they realize that the supposed counsellor and adjutant of the region's finances and direction of affairs is behaving like this, and that the Commander-in-Chief Tāsh and others are aping him in merry-making, singing and dancing, what respect or dignity will there be left? All this will only lead to further troubles and headaches. This abdication of responsibility had inevitably to be reported, for any cover-up would have been harmful. It is for the exalted judgement to ordain the best course."[167]

The Amir became very downcast, but said nothing at the time. The next day, when the public audience was over, he kept back the Vizier and my master Bu Naṣr and said, "Bring those letters which had been sealed." They were brought, and he consulted with these two in private and they aired their views. The Amir said, "I had known about Ṭāher's arrogance and ineptitude, and it was a mistake to send him there." The Vizier replied, "No damage has so far been done. Letters of censure and rebuke should be written detailing his misdemeanours and castigating him for his deeds so that he doesn't do anything like this again, and takes a solemn oath not to indulge in wine-drinking for a year." The Amir said, "This is just what should be done, and Bu Naṣr should write, but thought must be given to appointing another regional counsellor and administrator. Who should we send?" They replied, "If the exalted judgement sees fit, we shouldn't make a change on the basis of one erroneous action of his." The Amir said, "You don't know the situation in those lands whereas I do. They're a bunch of people who have little love for the Khorasanis. What is required there is to have as awe-inspiring and substantial a presence as possible. In that case,[168] things will run smoothly, otherwise they will hold us in contempt, and all law and order will be swept aside." They replied, "The lord knows his servants at the court. A man of some substance and stature is needed there. Bu'l-Qāsem b. Kathir has recently come from Herat and has an impressive reputation. Bu Sahl Ḥamdavi is likewise a sagacious and competent person. Bu Sahl Zowzani has endured a lengthy period of tribulation, and is also an old servant of the lord and is a well-known figure. ʿAbdus likewise has acquired a good reputation and high standing. These whom I have just named are the most eminent of the lord's servants. [F 500] The lord can now consider them and can appoint whomever his judgement and heart settle upon."

The Amir said, [Gh 389] "Bu'l-Qāsem b. Kathir has not yet settled the affairs of his previous appointment.[169] It is necessary to hold an accounting of him and bring it to completion, since Aḥmad b. Ḥasan never accomplished this; when this accounting of him is settled, we will ordain whatever our judgement deems should be done for him. Bu Sahl Zowzani is not fit for any kind of office, great or small, save as a malicious talebearer and a fount of corruption and havoc. Aren't those acts of treachery which he wrought in regard to the Khwarazm Shah, and in other matters, enough? ʿAbdus is needed here. Bu Sahl Ḥamdavi is suitable for this post, since he is both sagacious and also competent and experienced, and he has filled important offices." The Vizier replied, "The lord has thought this out well; no-one else will do."

The Amir called out to the attendant who used to guard the entrance to the court and gave orders for Bu Sahl Ḥamdavi to be summoned. Following the royal command, he came in, went forward and sat down. The Amir said, "We have tested you in all sorts of things, and we have found you to be sagacious, competent and worthy of trust. The governance of Ray and the surrounding regions is of the utmost importance, and it is beyond Ṭāher's capacity," and he explained Ṭāher's recent conduct, and then went on to say, "We have chosen you for the post. Go back and get ready for departure, and we shall set out the necessary orders." Bu Sahl kissed the ground and said, "My own preference would have been to have performed some service here at the exalted court, but it is not for us servants to choose; it is for the lord to command. If the lord's judgement deems fit, let me sit down together with the Vizier and Bu Naṣr, and have my say about this. I will write out the contractual agreement (*movāżaʿa*) and will ask for all that is needed to make affairs run in an orderly fashion—since [F 501] from what I have heard, that office is in disarray."[170] The Amir said, "That will be exactly the right way to proceed." All three sat down together in a private conclave and did this. The discussion went on till a very late hour, and they discussed and covered all the important issues and then dispersed.

Bu Sahl Ḥamdavi wrote out a contract, covering all aspects and with their conditions exactly delineated, just as he knew how to write, for he was a man of considerable ability and experience. Bu Naṣr Moshkān formally presented it to the Amir. The Amir wrote his responses to it in his own hand, partly because it would enhance Bu Sahl's status and partly because[171] he was thoroughly in command of all the details of the case and could do justice to all its various aspects. He added his signature and device to it, and it was brought to Bu

Sahl Ḥamdavi, together with forty-odd other letters bearing the royal signature and device [Gh 390] which I, Bu'l-Fażl, wrote out in their entirety, my master having done the drafts of those. The Amir ordered a robe of honour for him of the quality made up for viziers, the complete outfit of the robe of honour including also a belt, a litter, ten Turkish gholām cavalrymen, 100,000 dirhams and a hundred pieces of clothing; and he ordered that his official mode of address should be "The Sheykh, the Mainstay" (*al-Sheykh al-'Amid*.)[172]

The Grand Vizier Aḥmad b. 'Abd al-Ṣamad took offence at this mode of address, and summoned me, Bu'l-Fażl. He reproached my master and showed his dismay, and gave me a long verbal message. I came back and delivered it. Bu Naṣr was a man of great dignity, attentive to decorum and very good at showing due courtesy and respect to people. So he said, "Only fools would get up on their hind legs and show their displeasure openly in such a case. For if the Sultan decides to raise up a stable boy to the rank of vizier, one should still devote oneself to maintaining one's respect for the Sultan's majesty and his exalted decree, rather than be pre-occupied with the person appointed, whether the latter be a nonentity or not." Yet although he used to be careful to observe limits like these, he was tenacious in the extreme [F 502] and on no account would he allow aspersions to be cast against him or against his Divān. He said to me, "Tell the Grand Vizier that I have known the lord, the Grand Vizier, for a very long time, and regard him as an eminent person of great wisdom and administrative capability, for had he not been so, he would not have attained that exalted rank. For out of so many outstandingly capable men whose names had been mentioned—and he knows well that they are all great figures, of high status and have held pre-eminent positions in the service of sultans—the Amir's choice fell on him. It may be that the customs and manners appropriate to serving royalty do not enter into the Vizier's calculations, since he has not been engaged in the service of kings and has not observed their customary ways and manners of doing things at close quarters, for he has been dealing with subordinates rather than with them directly. Nor can one say that he could have acquired the requisite knowledge from books, since in such matters it is one thing to peruse a book and another to see things for oneself. This Sultan of ours is today the marvel of the age, particularly in composing and commissioning letters and in devising official forms of address. The form of address for this Bu Sahl has been expressly enunciated by the Sultan, to the effect that one must write the title "*ʿAmid*," since we are greater than the Buyid house and our servant the Vizier is superior to the Ṣāḥeb [Ebn] ʿAbbād. The Grand Vizier knows full well that the Amir is right in saying this. And if the Vizier looks at it judiciously, Bu Sahl Ḥamdavi in his youth had golden trappings for his horse bestowed on him by a monarch like Maḥmud and was head of the Divān for the capital Ghaznin and those regions of India [Gh 391] adjacent to it. Also, for a long while he was the assistant of a vizier like Aḥmad b. Ḥasan, and in the time of Amir Moḥammad, when the latter ventured to secure the throne for himself, Bu Sahl became vizier and donned the robe of honour as a vizier. The Khwarazm Shah Altuntāsh wrote letters to him, and the Khᵛāja should know himself what he had written, [173] as I am not aware of the contents. To be fair, he must admit that if I, who am head of the Chancery, and who authorise the official titles, had devised this form of address for Bu Sahl, [F 503] no-one would have faulted me since I would have prescribed what he in fact deserved; so it is hardly fair to reproach me for this when the order has in fact come from the lord, the monarch, himself. The Vizier is still new in these matters; perhaps with the passage of time he will know me better. Although this is how things stand, in no way do I wish to treat the Grand Vizier's commands lightly in this matter. If he should write a note on this topic, I will convey it to the exalted court session, or if he should give a verbal message, I will pass that on as well."

I conveyed this message to Khᵛāja Aḥmad. He pondered for a while and then said, "Khᵛāja Bu Naṣr is right in this matter. It would be unwise to discuss this matter openly at the exalted court. It is also vital that Bu Sahl should not hear of it lest he feel offended by me. I hope that the Khᵛāja Bu Naṣr will not withhold such pieces of good advice from me in the future, for everything he says will be *taken to heart and is deserving of thanks.*" I went back and repeated these sentences to my master, and he was very pleased. The next day the two of them talked about it face-to-face, and that was the end of the matter.

On Tuesday, 6 Jomādā II [/9 May 1033], after the court session, Bu Sahl Ḥamdavi put on the robe of honour, came into the Amir's presence and kissed the ground. He presented the Amir with a bejewelled collar, and he was given a seat. The Amir said, "May it be blessed!'

and he gave Bu Sahl a ring with the Sultan's name engraved on it, saying, "This is the ring for the province of Western Persia, and we have entrusted it to you as our deputy in those lands, and after our own commands, the troops and the subjects must act in accordance with your ordinances in all matters involving the welfare and interests of the province. You must tackle that job with a stout heart." Bu Sahl replied, "I obey the command and will strive hard and seek the help and favour of God the Exalted One for success in fulfilling your trust in me." He kissed the ground, and went back to his house, and all the great men went to visit him and paid their due respects in a handsome manner.

The next day, the Amir [Gh 392, F 504] held court, and after this held a private session with the Vizier, Bu Sahl Ḥamdavi and Bu Naṣr Moshkān. The Amir said to Bu Sahl, "Last night we gave some thought to the matter of Ray and Western Persia (Jebāl-e ʿErāq), and it appeared to us that it would be best to send our son Saʿid with you, along with a lavish display of pomp and glittering splendour, in such a way that he will stand for and reflect our authority, and you can act as his regional counsellor and administrator and handle all transactions, deciding on demotions and promotions and legislative decrees. Our son will take his cue from you, and all this will be done with an impressive aura of authority." Bu Sahl said, "The exalted judgement is the highest of judgements, the lord is best informed about conditions there and issuing commands is the lord's prerogative. But if I may, I will speak forth according to what knowledge I possess and what I have personally witnessed and know, and then will follow the exalted command."

The Amir said, "You must give your opinion in full, since we place great trust in your wise counsel." He replied, "May the lord's life be prolonged! The situation in Ray and Jebāl is very different now from what it was when the lord had left them. Many troubles have surfaced there, and the officials sent out there have not been impressive in their display of power, as has become all too apparent; for otherwise, there would have been no need to despatch me personally. Ray and Jebāl are hostile territory with little love for people from Khorasan. Securing control of Ray drained all the resources of the Samanid house, until Bu'l-Ḥasan b. Simjur negotiated a truce between his own masters the Samanids on one side and the Buyid house on the other, and for a time, hostilities and open warfare ceased.[174] The Son of Kāku, who at present holds the governorship of Isfahan, Hamadan and part of Jebāl, is a cunning and artful opponent. He has both financial resources and troops, and the guile and craftiness to go with it. The situation in Ray and Jebāl will never become settled and ordered as long as we do not teach him a lesson, so that either he faces the requisite punishment and relinquishes his governorship, or else he toes the line and sends his son to the exalted court as a hostage, [F 505] becomes obedient and submissive, and delivers promptly the substantial annual tribute imposed upon him. The neighbouring rulers will take the hint and behave themselves. But with Ṭāher, Tāsh and that bunch of theirs, busy as they are with wine-drinking and merry-making and oblivious to their surroundings, nothing can of course be done. When I myself reach Ray, I shall stay there for a month and then lead an expedition against Isfahan and the Son of Kāku; and until I have dealt with him adequately, I shall not be able to attend to Ray. If the royal prince is to be with me, in no circumstances shall I deem it safe to leave him behind at Ray, [Gh 393], since I cannot place any trust in the people of Ray, and would have to take him with me and keep an eye on him at all times. When I go to face the enemy, I will not know the outcome, whether it be peace or war. If it is peace, so much the better; but if it is war, many of your servants, myself included, may lose their lives in the course of duty, and I would be concerned about the royal prince's welfare, bearing in mind that in making his way to Nishapur from that distant spot he would be faced with innumerable enemies.[175] If the lord sees fit, the title of governor of Ray and Western Persia can be bestowed on the prince and I can go as his deputy and pronounce the *khoṭba* in his name. I will remain for a month at Ray so that the financial officials and tax collectors can get to work and so that I can deal with the matter of Tāsh and organise the army stationed there, as well as the army accompanying me from the court, and march against the Son of Kāku, fully prepared and equipped. We shall settle the matter with him in the appropriate manner, either through peace or by war, and return to Ray with the task accomplished [F 506] and shall then inform the lord. At that point, the royal prince can set out in a proper and correct fashion and come to Ray without any worries lurking in the mind. This is how I see things; the exalted judgement will know best what to do."

The Amir asked the Grand Vizier and Bu Naṣr for their opinion. Aḥmad replied, "It's the most appropriate decision, no other is suitable and it should be put into effect." Bu Naṣr said, "Although this is not my own métier,[176] well, I find the sweet smell of victory and the conquest of Isfahan in these words!" The Amir laughed and said, "My view was exactly the same as Bu Sahl expressed, and it's the only correct way. We have a powerful army at Ray; do we need additional troops? It is necessary to choose financial officials and tax collectors from amongst the men here at court." Bu Sahl replied, "Even though there is a large army there, I should be sent from here fully equipped and armed, with a further army, so that my presence induces an impression of power and prestige in the minds of friend and foe alike, and also so that the Son of Kāku and the others may know that, emanating from the direction of Khorasan, there exists an unbroken chain of troops, thus instilling terror into their hearts." The Amir said, "That's a good idea. You know the leaders and senior commanders of the army. Make out a list and choose, and we shall appoint them." Bu Sahl asked for an inkstand and paper, and these were brought from the Chancery, and he began to write. He asked for the son of Arslān Jādheb, and pointed out that not only had he a good reputation but also that he had his own body of men and was himself a formidable warrior. This was granted. Bu Sahl further asked for two of the outstanding palace senior officers (*sarhang-e sarāy*), together with 200 daring and warlike palace gholāms who were at the threshold of manhood,[177] and was given these. He then said, "May the lord's life [Gh 394] be prolonged! We shall need five choice male elephants and five female ones for breaching walls and smashing through gates.[178] They may well come in useful if we have to besiege the defenders of a town." This too was granted. From amongst the financial officials, Bu Sahl asked for Bu'l-Ḥasan Sayyāri, Bu Sa'd b. Ghassān and 'Abd al-Razzāq [F 507] the accounting official, and assent was given.

The Amir said to the Vizier, "Go along to the Divān and make all the arrangements for the army and the financial officials, while we give orders regarding the gholāms and the elephants, so that he may depart for Ray on the first day of Rajab, since we intend, whatever happens, to set off ourself for Herat on the third or fourth of Rajab. In that way, we shall not have to worry further about Ray and Western Persia."

They departed from the Amir's presence, and the Vizier spent that day in the Divān till the time for the evening worship, and the senior commanders were summoned and the troops' pay and allowances were issued. He ordered them to get their arms and equipment ready so that they could go with Bu Sahl to Ray. They went back and got busy with getting their arms and equipment in order. The Amir summoned the major domo of the palace and the secretary for the gholāms, and he selected 200 gholāms, most of them just past pubescence, and all of them choice, bold and well-trained in handling their weapons. Their names were listed, and they were brought into the Amir's presence, with two senior officers who had an impressive record, and he manumitted them all. They were given their pay and allowances and extra rewards, and allotted fine horses. The senior officers were given robes of honour and standards and were ordered to go to Bu Sahl. The elephants were also selected and were brought to him. Bu Sahl was rushing about making preparations and collecting together great amounts of equipment and arms and getting things in order. He had twenty gholāms of his own and purchased fifty or sixty more before he set off for Ray.

ʿAbd al-Jabbār, the Grand Vizier's son, arrived with the bride (i.e. Bā Kālijār's daughter) and the stipulated tribute, having successfully exacted all the demands and having concluded a satisfactory contractual agreement with Bā Kālijār; and the Amir was very favourably impressed by him. He ordered that the envoys from Gorgān should be received that very day with due decorum. The womenfolk of the leading citizens of Nishapur, including those of the mayor, the judges, the religious lawyers, the notables and the financial officials, were taken in well-arranged litters to where the litter bearing Bā Kālijār's daughter had been stationed, about half-a-parasang from the town, and the Gorgānis, including her household retinue, were brought into the town in a courteously ceremonial fashion. The palace and the pavilions of Ḥasanak had been adorned and decorated at the Amir's behest as if they were the loveliest stretches of the garden of Paradise.[179] [F 508] They set down the litter there, and many women, including the bride's nurses and faithful personal attendants, servants, [Gh 395] slave women and girls, were likewise installed there, and the womenfolk of the notables of Nishapur returned homewards. That night, Nishapur became just like day because of the candles and torches. The eunuchs of the Sultan's harem sat down in their places at the door of the harem, and a large number of infantrymen were stationed as sentries at the portals of the palace, together with a chamberlain and his numerous staff. Countless things had been ordered and prepared at the exalted command, and these were sent into the inner quarters of the palace. Round about midnight, everyone belonging to the Sultan's harem came there from Shādyākh.[180]

The next day, the Amir gave orders that a large quantity of gold, jewels and other rare and precious things should be brought there. There were sumptuous festive gatherings and the womenfolk of the leading citizens of Nishapur were all conveyed there. They offered their presents and dined there, and then they returned home, but the bride, who remained inside the litter, was shielded from all. At the time for the night worship, the Amir mounted and rode from Shādyākh with a large escort from his retinue, 300 of the personal guard of gholāms, all mounted, and 300 gholāms on foot, at the front of the concourse, and five palace chamberlains. He came to Ḥasanak's pavilion, went inside the palace which housed the harem with ten of the household eunuchs, since it was lawful for them to see the womenfolk of the harem. These eunuchs and gholāms took up residence in the barrack rooms which surrounded the perimeter of the palace, originally built by the vizier Ḥasanak to accommodate five or six hundred of his personal gholāms. The royal sun caught sight of the moonlike beauty of the bride, and the very reflection of his radiance added lustre to the Gorgānis' pride and dignity, and the whole affair proceeded in an excellent manner, as God Most High had foreordained. Those outside the inner sanctum of the harem have no business to concern themselves with such matters, then or now, and it would be wrong of me, too, in this case to write down my reminiscences.

[F 509] The Amir spent the next day too enjoying himself in the seclusion of the harem quarters, and on the third day, towards daybreak, he went to Shādyākh. When it was daylight and he held court, the courtiers and retainers came to offer their obeisance, and Khᵛāja Bu Sahl Ḥamdavi and those men designated to accompany him came into the royal presence dressed in their travelling clothes, and took their formal leave. The Amir spoke encouraging words to them and awarded them renewed marks of favour. They set off towards Ray after the Friday worship on 1 Rajab of this year 424 [/2 June 1033].

This eminent figure, Bu Sahl Ḥamdavi, did many varied things when he was at Ray, some praiseworthy and some reprehensible. At times, the populace of Ray followed his orders and at others they acted wilfully, following their own personal inclinations, until he and his entourage finally rejoined the monarch in Nishapur before the disaster of Dandānqān befell. [Gh 396] I shall devote a separate section of this History to these events in which they can be set down and clarified, bearing in mind the fact that Bu Sahl and others were far away from us, having gone to a distant land.[181] The same goes for the section on Khwarazm. Out of these two sections, I shall first take up the matter of Khwarazm and shall relate how Hārun, son of the Khwarazm Shah Altuntāsh, openly proclaimed his rebellion and how ʿAbd al-Jabbār, son of the Grand Vizier Aḥmad b. ʿAbd al-Ṣamad, went into hiding.[182] For in these two sections there are many unusual and remarkable points.[183] For now, I shall carry forward in its proper sequence the History on which I was engaged, and shall do what is required.

On 2 Rajab [/3 June] Bā Kālijār's envoys and eunuchs who had come from Gorgān with the bridal litter were given suitable robes of honour. A very splendid robe of honour, such as is given to governors, was entrusted to them for Bā Kālijār, and on the next day, Sunday, 3 Rajab [/4 June] they set out for Gorgān. They had brought with Bā Kālijār's daughter such an amount of things, [F 510] specifically intended as the outfit for a new bride, as were unbounded and limitless in extent; it would be difficult to detail them all. I, Bu'l-Fażl, heard from Zarrin, the female musician and singer—this woman was very close to Sultan Masʿud, such that she became like a female doorkeeper guarding the interior of the palace and conveying the Sultan's various verbal messages to the members of the harem—and she was saying that the bride had a ceremonial resting place resembling an ornamental orchard, and it had been brought as part of her bridal outfit. Its floor surface was made up of silver planks fitted and interwoven with each other, with thirty golden trees arranged on it with leaves of turquoise and emerald and bearing all kinds of rubies[184] as its fruit; and the Amir was highly delighted when he saw it. Arranged round those trees twenty pots for narcissus had been placed, and all the sprigs of sweet-smelling herbs put there were made out of gold, silver and many kinds of jewels. Around these silver pots for narcissus[185] were placed golden platters all filled with amber and pastilles of camphor. This is the description of just one item of the bridal outfit, and the remaining items can be imagined by analogy. [Gh 397]

At the end of this month of Jomādā II, Khᵛāja Bu'l-Ḥasan 'Aqili was afflicted by a malady, and something appeared on his back[186]—*we seek refuge in God from the like of that!* The Amir sent physicians to him, but what can a physician do against one's allotted fate? On Monday, 4 Rajab [5 June 1033] he died, God's mercy be upon him!

An account of the rare and remarkable and events that newly occurred at Nishapur in the summer of this year

Amir Mas'ud one day held a court session. After the time of the dawn worship, a letter had arrived from the postal and intelligence agent of Ray to the effect that "The Turkmens are seething with discontent, and have changed their tune since they have heard news that the son of Yaghmur has come down from Balkhān Kuh into the steppes with an army in order to avenge the death of his father and the rest, and they may cause trouble [F 511] at any time. Because of this, the Commander-in-Chief Tāsh and Ṭāher are worried and have said that the situation needs to be reported to the Sultan. I have relayed this information so that this matter may be appraised." I, Bu'l-Fażl, was standing in attendance, since it was my turn of duty, and my master Bu Naṣr had not yet arrived. The Amir ordered me to send someone to fetch Bu Naṣr. I speedily despatched the door-keeper and Bu Naṣr came at once, it being nearly dusk. The Amir talked with him privately until it was almost evening, and he came back at the time of the evening worship and said, "Know, O Bu'l-Fażl, that a plan has been adopted which will beget much harm." Then he said to me *sotto voce*, "If the Amir asks whether Bu Naṣr has gone back home, tell him that 'He took away some paper so that what had to be written out could be written.'"[187] After his departure, the Amir summoned me and said, "When did Bu Naṣr leave?" I replied, "At the time of the evening worship, and a supply of paper was taken with him." He said, "Write a note to him on your own behalf and tell him that he should write out tonight the drafts of those letters which we commanded to be written but he shouldn't do the fair copies, so that tomorrow we can peruse the drafts and make a decision on this matter in conjunction with the Vizier. Then we shall decree what needs to be done." I went back, wrote out the note and sent it off.

The next day, when the court session broke up, he had a private session with the Vizier [Gh 398] and Bu Naṣr until the late morning, and then they arose. There was a summer house (*dokkān*) on the edge of the verdant garden; the two of them sat down just by themselves and talked at length, and then Aḥmad went to his Divān. At that summer house, amongst the trees, a *maḥfuri* carpet[188] was laid down for Bu Naṣr, and he summoned me. I went to him. He gave me a draft written out and addressed to Ṭāher the secretary and said, "A very compact, confidential note must be written out." The instruction to Ṭāher was, "We have decided that the Khᵛāja ʿAmid Bu Sahl Ḥamdavi should be sent with a strong military force and a senior commander of high repute, and he will be coming [F 512] hot on the heels of this letter. On 5 Rajab [/6 June] we intend to head for Herat, and when we reach there safe and sound, a body of Turkmens there will be arrested and their baggage and impedimenta will be taken to Ghaznin. You, Ṭāher, must also secretly adopt this same ruse and, on the pretext that you wish to hold a muster and inspection of the troops (*ʿarż*), seize them all.[189] Bu Sahl Ḥamdavi will also have arrived there, and his instructions on this topic are to be followed. For this vital message, a matter of the utmost importance, this slim note is further endorsed by the application of our device and motto,[190] and a courier has been secretly instructed to conceal it in his horse's saddle-felt or inside the lining of his boot, wherever he sees best to hide it. He has with him a letter, with the royal signature and emblem, written as an open document concerning the affairs of that region and on a large-sized sheet of paper, so that it may ostensibly appear that he has come on those matters." There was another letter containing information about a vital matter[191] affecting Ray and Jebāl.[192] I, Bu'l-Fażl, made the finished copy of this slim, compact note and that of the large letter. My master took them to the royal presence, he affixed the royal signature and emblem to both of them and he brought them back. A courier from amongst the trusty retainers was brought, and he was given a fine horse and a present of 2,000 dirhams, and this confidential note and the open letter were entrusted to him. My master told him what to do with the slim, confidential note, and how he was to deliver the large, open letter. I wrote out for him the letter officially attesting his authority as a royal plenipotentiary,[193] and the courier set off. Bu Naṣr went [Gh 399] into the Amir's presence and informed him of what he had done. The Amir then arose and [F 513] went into the private quarters of the palace, and drank wine there in private.

Bu Naṣr came back to that summer house on the edge of the garden and sat down on his own. He said to me, "Write down a letter from myself to my steward in Guzgānān and [Rebāṭ-e] Karvān[194] instructing him that he should, as soon as he reads this letter, place on the market my flock of 10,000 sheep which he has in his care, both full-grown sheep and lambs, and sell them at the going rate (*be-narkh-e ruz*), turn the proceeds into gold and silver coinage and remit it to Ghaznin. I wrote out the letter, and he endorsed it in his own handwriting. It was put in a pouch and placed in the despatch bag for Guzgānān, the neck of the bag closed with a ring and sealed and sent off.

My master remained sunk in thought for a long time, and I was asking myself what the Amir's order concerning the arrest of the Turkmens at Ray had to do with selling these sheep at the current market price at Rebāṭ-e Karvān. He said to me, "You must be wondering about the matter of the Turkmens and their seizure, and my letter giving instructions for the sheep to be sold?" I replied, "By God, by the lord's soul and head, that's exactly what I was thinking." He said, "Know that this idea of seizing the Turkmens is an unwise decision and an ill-judged plan, for in no way will it be possible to seize three or four thousand horsemen. Before the Sultan receives the letter from Ray informing him how and with what stratagems they were able to seize the Turkmens, he will make a rash and hasty move and order a bunch of them to be seized at Herat and the rest, with their baggage and impedimenta, driven off. This will incite the main body of the tribe, who are on the move with their baggage and chattels, and the news will reach Ray and the Turkmens there will also rise, Yaghmur's son will descend from Balkhān Kuh with a further, formidable band of cavalrymen and they will all band together, make forays into Khorasan, and rustle away all the livestock they find there and wreak havoc. I looked ahead and gave instructions that my sheep should be sold so that although [F 514] they may be sold at a very low price, at least I shall get something and won't let them be rustled off for nothing. For this erroneous course of action has been embarked upon; the Grand Vizier and myself have spoken at great length and have spelt out what the outcome would be, but to no avail. This lord is the opposite of his father in resolution and grit.[195] His father was [Gh 400] headstrong but far-sighted; if he made an unwise decision, and declared his firm intention to carry it through, it could be attributed to his despotic nature and regal hauteur. However, if someone explained to him the pros and cons of that matter, he would at first fly into a rage, make a great scene and hurl abuses at him; but once he had reflected on the situation he would revise his decision and return to the right path. This monarch is of a different stamp. He is behaving in a wilful fashion not tempered by subsequent reflection.[196] I don't know where all this will end." He said this and went home.

I said to myself, "This man is very farsighted, but perhaps such an outcome won't happen." But indeed, it happened exactly as he had thought, since the plan for seizing the Turkmens at Ray did not work out and they slipped away, as I shall recount, and came to Khorasan from the direction of Ray. They inflicted much damage, as is well known, and drove off most of the livestock in Guzgānān. I was having a meal with my master in Ghaznin a year later, and they had set down a very plump lamb. He said to me and to Bu Naṣr b. Ṭeyfur, who had been Commander-in-Chief for the Shāhanshāhis.[197] "How do you find the lamb?" We replied, "Superlatively fat and juicy." He said, "It came from Guzgānān!" We looked at each other. He laughed and said, "This lamb was bought out of the price I received for those sheep which were sold at Rebāṭ-e Karvān," and he related the story which I set down.

Also during this summer, the story of Aḥmad b. Ināltegin, the Commander-in-Chief in India, took a new turn. An important figure was driven into rebellion through unjust measures, and it was this, which, after of course the decree of God Most High, instigated the tumult in Khorasan [F 515] and led to the access of power for the Turkmens and the Seljuqs; for every event has a cause. The Grand Vizier Aḥmad b. Ḥasan [Meymandi] was on bad terms with this Aḥmad b. Ināltegin, because, as I have explained previously, Aḥmad b. Ināltegin had pursued claims concerning Aḥmad b. Ḥasan's goods and effects at that time when these goods of his were being sold by auction.[198] Aḥmad was equally on bad terms with the Judge from Shiraz, because on several occasions Amir Maḥmud had said that the Judge was a suitable choice for the vizierate. When Aḥmad b. Ināltegin was setting off as Commander-in-Chief of India, Aḥmad b. Ḥasan had put it into his head that he should pay no heed to the Judge from Shiraz, saying, "You are the Commander-in-Chief in India by virtue of the Sultan's command, and the Judge has no jurisdiction over you. You should not therefore let him dupe you [Gh 401] into being his subordinate." Aḥmad b. Ināltegin left in a confident mood buoyed up by these instigations, and he did not care two hoots about the Judge in regard to the question of the supreme command of the army.

This Aḥmad was a courageous man, and they used to call him the spitten image (lit. "sneeze") of Amir Maḥmud, whom he closely resembled.[199] There was some talk and speculation concerning his mother, the circumstances of his birth and Amir Maḥmud. There had been a state of friendship existing between that monarch and his mother; but the Almighty God alone knows the truth. Also, he[200] had well adopted the manners and habits of Amir Maḥmud in the way he comported himself in public and how he spoke. When he arrived in India, he had with him a number of bold and daring gholāms with a splendid array of arms and equipment. A quarrel arose between him and the Judge from Shiraz regarding the office of Commander-in-Chief. The Judge asserted that the office of Commander-in-Chief should be given to 'Abdallāh b. Qarategin[201] and that he should be under his overall authority. Aḥmad said, "On no account shall I serve under him. The Sultan invested me with this office, and [F 516] I have always been more prominent and enjoyed more prestige than 'Abdallāh, and he and the rest are to go forth under my banner." That arguing became protracted. The garrison at Lahore and the ghāzis[202] took Aḥmad's side and, by way of infuriating the Judge, he went off with the ghāzis and made off for a distant place. The Judge sent off swift envoys with a complaint about him. These envoys reached Bost at a time when we were about to set out for Herat and Nishapur. Amir Mas'ud asked the Grand Vizier Aḥmad b. Ḥasan for his advice, He replied, "Amongst them all, Aḥmad b. Ināltegin is the best person for the office of supreme commander. The answer must be sent back to the Judge that 'You are the official in charge of finances; why should you concern yourself with the function of Commander-in-Chief and the affairs of the army? Aḥmad will himself do what is necessary and collect the land tax and stipulated tribute from the Indian princes[203] and then go on raiding expeditions, and substantial wealth will accrue to the treasury. This in-house feuding between our servants[204] must cease.'"[205] The Amir approved of these words, and a reply along these lines was written out.

Aḥmad b. Ināltegin felt very secure and confident, since the Vizier had ordered a letter to be written telling him what the Judge from Shiraz had said [Gh 402] and how they had responded. He marched out with the ghāzis and the army of Lahore and exacted the whole of the land tax from the Indian princes. He paused for a while and then crossed the Ganges (Gang) river and proceeded down the left bank until he unexpectedly came up against a city called Benares (Banāras), which came within the province of Gang.[206] No Muslim army had ever penetrated as far as there. It was a city two parasangs by two parasangs in size with plenty of water about.[207] It was too perilous for the army to stay there any longer than from the time of the dawn worship to that of the afternoon, and it was not possible to plunder more than three markets: those of the cloth merchants, of the perfumers and druggists, and of the jewel merchants. The troops amassed a great fortune, since they all had their share of gold, silver, perfumes and aromatic substances, and jewels, [F 517] and returned well satisfied.[208]

The news of the success of this great raiding expedition nearly drove the Judge mad. He sent off swift messengers who reached us at Nishapur, and they let it be known that "Aḥmad b. Ināltegin took a vast amount of wealth from the tribute that was stipulated from the Indian princes and the land tax payers, and concealed the greater part of the money collected and only sent a small portion to the exalted court. My confidential agents had secretly accompanied him, without his knowing, as well as agents of the Overseer of the Realm and the postal and intelligence officer. They have noted down everything that he exacted, and this has been sent to provide the exalted court with a true picture and to prevent any attempts at deception by this treacherous fellow. Furthermore, Aḥmad had secretly sent emissaries to Turkestan by way of Panjhir in order to purchase Turkish gholāms for him.[209] So far, seventy odd gholāms have been brought and others are following closely at intervals. He has gained the support of all the Turkmens here and has alienated them from the court, saying, 'I am Maḥmud's son,' and has left the people in the dark about his intentions. We, as your servants, have brought these matters to your attention by way of giving sincere counsel; the exalted judgement will know best what to do."

These letters affected the Amir's thinking and made a deep impression, and he instructed my master Bu Naṣr to keep them concealed so that no-one should become aware of them. Following immediately after this, bearers of good tidings arrived, with letters from the Commander in India, Aḥmad b. Ināltegin, and from the postal and intelligence officer of the army, conveying the news of the victory at Benares, to the effect that "A most formidable enterprise was accomplished: the army has become enriched and a vast amount of wealth has been extracted (i.e. from Benares), together with the land tax taken from the Indian princes; and several elephants have been acquired. We wrote these letters from Indrabedi[210] and we are now heading for Lahore with a joyous heart." And what had happened was narrated in detail ...[211]

[The Year 425
(/26 November 1033–15 November 1034)]

[Gh 403, F 518] ... and they buried that young man.[1] The Amir was most distressed, for Satï was a praiseworthy and courageous young man, of fine stature and appearance and possessed of ability. His only defect was an addiction to wine-drinking, and he yielded up his life because of it.[2]

Worse was to follow. Mischief-makers and intriguers secretly wrote a letter to his brother Hārun, the new Khwarazm Shah, and told him that "The Amir commissioned a treacherous assassin to throw your brother down from the roof and kill him, and they will deal with all the sons of the former Khwarazm Shah (i.e. of Altuntāsh) in the same manner, one by one." Hārun had himself become rather ill-disposed towards the Grand Vizier Aḥmad, son of ʿAbd al-Ṣamad, and was put out by the presumptuous behaviour and impudent manners of the latter's son ʿAbd al-Jabbār. When the letter reached him, he, having been already to some degree duped by Satanic misapprehensions, was filled with malicious thoughts and grew suspicious. He embarked on a course of humiliating ʿAbd al-Jabbār for no good reason, treating him in a contemptuous fashion and impugning the soundness of his judgement. In the end, the matter reached the point that he came out in open rebellion, and ʿAbd al-Jabbār was compelled to go into hiding out of fear for his life, and both of them were destroyed in the process. A full account of these happenings with be given in that section of this History which will be devoted to Khwarazm, and, everything about them will be related there, if God wills.[3]

On Friday, 4 Jomādā II [/26 April 1034], before the time for the worship, the Amir graciously bestowed on the Grand Vizier [F 519] a robe of honour as a token of his satisfaction with him, since the Vizier was about to set out for Tokhārestān and Balkh. The reason for this was that the districts of Khottalān had become disturbed because of incursions by the Komijis[4] into the region. He was similarly ordered[5] to proceed to Valvālej and Panj-āb,[6] and that the military governor of the districts should join up with him, so that they could direct their efforts [Gh 404] to that important task and eradicate those rebellious elements. The Amir personally gave words of encouragement to him and praised him. The Grand Vizier went back to his house, and the great figures of the court came to pay respects and to offer their congratulations to him in a very complete manner; then, after the worship, he set out accompanied by four generals, ten field officers and a thousand fully armed and equipped cavalrymen. The head of the Chancery appointed the religious lawyer Bu Bakr, son of Mobashsher, to act as postal and intelligence officer of the army and to go with him (i.e. with the Grand Vizier) at the Amir's behest.[7] Letters were written to all the leading figures of the state[8] bidding them give ear to the Vizier's commands, and Bu Bakr was also ordered to write to the Sultan each day concerning what the Vizier considered wise policy and what was conducive to the welfare of the kingdom. The Vizier travelled along by the Bazh-e Ghuzak road.[9] I shall set forth subsequently, in its appropriate place, the notable deeds wrought by this master, as the precepts of historical writing demand. The next day, the Amir went to the Garden of a Hundred Nightingales[10] for a week's stay , and all the necessary equipment and supplies were transported there.

Meanwhile, successive letters kept arriving warning that Aḥmad b. Ināltegin had returned to Lahore along with the Turkmens, and many unruly elements from Lahore, and all sorts of rabble, had gathered round him, and that if his activities were not promptly curbed, the crisis would become protracted, since every [F 520] day his might and strength were increasing." The Amir was at this time at the Garden of a Hundred Nightingales. He held a private meeting with the Commander-in-Chief and the leading figures and courtiers, and sought their opinion on what measures they should adopt for suppressing this unruly and rebellious subject's outbreak, so that the Amir's mind would be set at rest on this score forever. The Commander-in Chief said, "When Aḥmad b. Ināltegin fled before him,[11] he did not have much military strength left, and whichever commander may be appointed to march out and confront Aḥmad will be able to cope quite easily, since there is at Lahore a large army (i.e. of loyal, regular Ghaznavid troops). If the lord gives his assent, I can depart within a week, despite the extremely hot weather (i.e. on the north Indian plains)." The Amir said, "It would be most unfitting to send you off on such a relatively small-scale venture, since there is trouble of various kinds in Khorasan. Disturbances and strife have also broken out in Khottalān and Tokhārestān, and although the Vizier has set off there and will deal adequately with the matter, once Mehragān is over, it will be incumbent upon us to go to Bost or to Balkh, and you must accompany our battle standard. We shall send out a commander, and that should be sufficient." The Commander-in-Chief said, "It is for the lord to command, and there is a body of commanders here in the exalted session, and others in the court at large; which of his servants does he instruct to go?" Tilak[12] the Indian said, [Gh 405] "May the lord's life be prolonged! I myself will go and perform this act of service so that I may discharge my obligation of rendering thanks for the lord's favours and rewards. Moreover, I am from India, and it is the hot season, and I shall be better able to travel within that land. If the exalted judgement sees fit, he will not deprive me of this honour." The Amir praised him for coming forward so eagerly, and he asked those present for their opinion. They replied, "This man has gained a great reputation and is fit for any mission, since he possesses retainers,[13] armaments and manpower of his own, and if he receives additional support from the exalted command, he will be able to see this matter [F 521] through to a successful conclusion." The Amir said, "Go back home and I will think about this affair." They went back home.

The Amir had said to some of his close confidants in the harem quarters of the palace, "None of those leading persons had the courage to take up the challenge or, indeed, showed any stomach for it, so that Tilak felt embarrassed by it all and stepped forward." He secretly sent ʿErāqi the secretary[14] to Tilak with a most heart-warming message and said, "We did realize what you said today and what you intend to do. What you said was not at all pleasing to the assembly gathered there in our presence. Now that you have taught them a lesson, we shall ensure that you succeed in your pledge: tomorrow we shall appoint you to this command and will do all that is possible and furnish you with plenty of financial support, troops and arms, so that you can accomplish this task on your own and dislodge the rebel[15], without having recourse to any help from them (i.e. the reluctant and carping courtiers), and no thanks to them, and you will gain further renown. For these people do not like it when we elevate someone to prominence, and they prefer it if we appear perpetually in need of their support without in any way putting themselves out. They have expressed a great deal of dismay at the sight of your promotion. Now you must persevere in the pledge that you have given so that you may leave. A blunder[16] has been made thanks to their words and intrigues, but what is done is done."

Tilak kissed the ground and said, "If this were beyond my capabilities, you would not have seen me display such boldness in the lord's presence and in such a distinguished gathering. At this present moment, whatever needs to be requested for this matter I will request, and I will draw up a document[17] so that it can be laid before the exalted judgement [F 522] and I can speedily depart and that wretched one can be overthrown." 'Erāqi came and explained the situation, and the Amir said, "That's a very sound course of action; the document should be written out." 'Erāqi threw himself heart and soul into this work, and he submitted for the Amir's opinion the document in which Tilak had set forth in detail his requests. [Gh 406] The Amir gave him carte blanche,[18] saying that when he passed by Pazh-e Pazhān,[19] he would do everything regarding confirming the role of the Indians. He gave a message to the Head of the Chancery (i.e. to Bu Naṣr Moshkān), delivered verbally by 'Erāqi, that the investiture patent and other documents for Tilak should be written out. In such circumstances, Bu Naṣr always endeavoured to do his best to carry our meticulously everything which the lords of the throne commanded, lest any criticisms and imputations should be directed at him. Whatever required writing out was done. The great men at the court cavilled at Tilak's appointment, *but it was a stroke of luck for him, a case of an unlikely person obtaining a high position,*[20] and this man was the cause of Aḥmad b. Ināltegin's being killed, as I shall set forth in its appropriate place. However, first I shall fulfill the requirements of history writing and shall set forth the circumstances and the achievements of this Tilak as they were, from the very start up to the time when he attained this high dignity; for much benefit is gained from recording such things.

An account of Tilak the Indian's position and career

This Tilak was the son of a cupper[21] but possessed an attractive appearance and physical presence, an eloquent tongue and a good hand for writing both the Indian (*hendavi, hendui*) and Persian languages.[22] He had spent a long time in Kashmir, serving as an apprentice and assistant, and had learnt something of trickery, the art of blandishment and legerdemain,[23] and from there [F 523] came to Bu'l-Ḥasan the Judge from Shiraz. The latter made him his confidant, since every master who saw him became inevitably enchanted by him. He filled a financial post under the Judge, appropriated a sum of money and overreached himself.[24] The Judge ordered a general restraint to be imposed on him.[25] Tilak used a stratagem so that his case was brought to the notice of the Grand Vizier Aḥmad b. Ḥasan,[26] on the grounds that the Vizier could redress the Judge's malicious and excessive act, since Khᵛāja Aḥmad and the Judge were on bad terms with each other. The Vizier sent a letter with the Sultan's signature and device by hand of three swift-riding troops (*kheyltāshs*), and against the Judge's wishes, they brought Tilak to the court. Khᵛāja Aḥmad b. Ḥasan listened to Tilak's plausible account[27] and managed [Gh 407] by a clever stratagem to convey a note from Tilak to Amir Maḥmud in such a way that the Amir did not realize that it was the Vizier's own work. The Amir ordered the Vizier to listen to what Tilak had to say, and as a result the Judge got into great trouble.

When these machinations were over, Tilak became one of the close circle of trusted confidants of Khᵛāja Aḥmad. He used to act as a secretary and translator for the Vizier in regard to the Indians, exactly as Birbāl[28] did in our Divān, and he began to prosper. I, Bu'l-Fażl, used to see him standing there (i.e. not amongst the secretaries, who had seats) since, apart from secretarial work and translating, he used to convey and bring back verbal messages. He conducted himself extremely well. When the Vizier suffered those trials and tribulations, which I have already described,[29] Amir Maḥmud sought out his retainers and secretaries in order to pick out from amongst them those suitable for service at the court. He took a liking to Tilak, and the latter began to work with Bahrām the translator. He was younger than Bahrām and more eloquent—the kind of person Amir [F 524] Maḥmud liked—and so he flourished. He secretly performed valuable acts of service for Sultan Masʿud (i.e. when the latter was still only the heir to the throne), since he brought all the Katur[30] Indians and a part of those from the outside palace service[31] into Masʿud's allegiance; and he did these deeds, fraught with great danger, while a monarch like Maḥmud was on the throne.

When Shah Masʿud arrived in Balkh from Herat, and the affairs of the realm had become settled, and Suvendharāy, the Commander-in-Chief of the Indian troops, was no longer alive,[32] the monarch showed favour to Tilak, bestowed upon him a gold-embroidered robe of honour, placed a gold collar encrusted with jewels around his neck, and gave him a contingent of cavalry. He became a person of importance, was awarded the right of having a small camp enclosure and a ceremonial parasol. A small drum used to be beaten when he went forth, the drum which was the customary privilege of the senior commanders of the Indians. Added to this was a standard with a crescent-shaped finial (*monjuq*), *and so on and so forth*. Finally, his status rose so high that he sat amongst the notables in private sessions and consultative deliberations until the time when, as I have already related, he proposed to take on the matter of Aḥmad b. Ināltegin and bring it to an end. His good fortune and the favour of Fate carried that work forward and he was successful. *Every affair has its cause, and men follow each other in succession.*[33] Such concatenations of events are not deemed incredible by the wise, since men are not born with fame and status at birth but attain it gradually, with the proviso that they should leave behind a good name as a memorial.

This Tilak turned out to be a quick-witted fellow with praiseworthy qualities, and the fact that he was a cupper's son did not impede his advancement throughout his life. However, had he enjoyed, along with his own spirited nature, wisdom and resolution [Gh 408] inherited merit through a fine pedigree, he would have excelled even more, since having both descent from a noble lineage and self-acquired nobility go well together.[34] But a person of noble lineage is not worth a tittle if he has not learnt any true knowledge, self-control[35] and courtesy, and can only boast about his father's deeds.[36] The poet has well said: (Poetry) [F 525]

1. *If only you had said in regard to acquired nobility* (ḥasab) *what you said in regard to nobility inherited through noble ancestors* (nasab),[37] *you would have spoken truly, but what bad progeny they gave birth to!*[38]

With regard to this concept of the man with nobility acquired through deeds and the one with nobility acquired through birth, I called to mind a poem in *rajaz* metre and several lines of poetry,[39] and I have set them down:

1. *The soul of ʿEṣām gave lordship to ʿEṣām, and taught him to attack and advance boldly in battle,*[40]
2. *And it made him a heroic monarch.*

[There is also] what another poet said regarding a man with nobility acquired through birth (ʿeẓāmi), *but who is foolish and stupid:*

1. *When a man lives his daily life with the bones* (ʿaẓm) *of a dead man* (i.e. with nobility acquired from his ancestors), *those bones are alive* (i.e. conveying the innate nobility) *when the man is dead.*
2. *He says "My father built for me a house* (beyt), *and then I pulled down the building and did not build it up."*
3. *The man whose lineage* (beyt) *is a lofty house* (beyt), *and he then demolishes it, has no lineage because of that action.*[41]

I have thus read that a man of obscure origins came to Yaḥyā b. Khāled b. Barmak at his public session. All kinds of men were present, some noted for an array of qualities and skills and some who were obscure. The man began to speak, scattering jewels of eloquence and cleaving open pearl shells of spell-binding words. Some of those in the audience who were of noble birth took umbrage at this and said, "May the Vizier's life be prolonged! Alas for such a man! If only he were of noble birth!" Yaḥyā laughed and said, "*He is thoroughly noble by birth!*", and he raised this man up in his service and he became one of the outstanding men of the age. There are in this present age of ours some people of noble ancestry, having horses and fine accoutrements, luxurious clothing, ceremonial cloths[42] and fine saddle coverings who, when they come to deliver a speech or display their virtues, remain stuck like a donkey on an icy stretch, [F 526] and the gist of their talk is to say "Our forefathers were such-and-such and did such-and-such actions." What is remarkable is that people of high excellence and talent are made to suffer through these people's slanders and self-conceit. *God is the One who vouchsafes sufficiency!* [Gh 409]

When the matter of the letters and the instructions for Tilak had been prepared, Amir Mas'ud ordered an extremely splendid robe of honour to be prepared for him, so grand an outfit that it even included large kettledrums and a banner. Tilak donned the robe of honour, and the Amir was most encouraging and gracious towards him. The next day, Tilak mustered his troops for a parade and came to the Firuzi Garden. The Amir mounted his steed and the Indian troops filed past. There were numerous cavalrymen and infantrymen with a full array of weapons and equipment, and there also filed past those cavalrymen of the palace troops who had been detailed to go with him, a contingent with fine arms and equipment, since the Judge from Shiraz had written that there were a host of well-armed people in India, and it was necessary to send out a commander of high reputation.[43] Tilak dismounted, kissed the ground and remounted. The horse designated for the Commander-in-Chief of the Indian troops was sent for, and he departed on Tuesday, 15 Jomādā II [/7 May 1034].

At the time of the afternoon worship on this day, the Amir came back to the Royal Palace[44] in the town. The following day, he went to the White Palace, and for three days he engaged in festivities, played polo and drank wine. Then he came to the Maḥmudi Garden; the furnishings and impedimenta were fetched, and he remained there till the middle of Rajab [/5 June]. From there he proceeded to the citadel of Ghaznin, and the field officer Bu 'Ali the castellan, acted as his host. He arrived there on Thursday, 23 Rajab [/13 June] and stayed there for four days; for one day he was the guest of the field officer, who was the castellan, and the next day the garrison there were the Amir's guests. The following day he went into a private session. It was said that he secretly gave orders regarding [F 527] the treasuries, since they were about to leave (i.e. for Bost and Khorasan). He had a drinking session[45] with his boon companions and the musicians and singers, and on 1 Shaʿbān [/21 June] he came back to the old Maḥmudi Palace in the town.

On Tuesday, 5 Shaʿbān [/25 June], from early morning onwards, after the court session, the Amir engaged in a wine-drinking party with the boon companions on the dais of the audience hall. There was a gholām called Nushtegin Nowbati,[46] one of those gholāms whom Sultan Maḥmud had brought back at the time when he had a meeting with Qadïr Khān; he was a handsome gholām, like a (hundred thousand) painted picture(s), for one more attractive and with a more agreeable form than him had never been seen. Amir Maḥmud had ordered that he should be kept within the body of gholāms who were most close to the Sultan, since he was still a child, and he had intended to have him brought up as a challenge and rival to Ayāz, who displayed more boldness and capriciousness than beauty[, and he died at Pushang].[47] When Maḥmud died, his son Moḥammad brought this Nushtegin into prominence at that time when he came to Ghaznin and assumed the throne, and he made him his food taster [Gh 410] as well as the server of wine cups, and lavished great wealth on him. When the period of Moḥammad's rule came to its end, his brother Sultan Masʿud raised this Nushtegin to such prominence that he entrusted to him the governorship of Guzgānān. The normal practice for a gholām who had become a member of the ruler's intimate circle was to have one eunuch as his attendant; for Nushtegin, two eunuchs were appointed who used to be with him night and day on alternate shifts, and the eunuch Eqbāl of the Golden Hands, who was the major-domo of the palace, would take care of all his interests.

By chance it so happened [F 528] that the boon companion Bu Noʿeym—perhaps through hearing tales of this Turk's beauty—had become besotted by him and would often glance at him furtively in wine-drinking sessions. This monarch Masʿud had been observing that[48] and kept it in his mind. This day, it so befell that Bu Noʿeym's head was befuddled from the effects of the previous night's wine-drinking, and the Amir likewise. The Amir gave a bunch of gillyflowers and white lilies to Nushtegin and said, "Give it to Bu Noʿeym," and Nushtegin gave it to Bu Noʿeym. Bu Noʿeym pressed his fingers into Nushtegin's hand. Nushtegin exclaimed, "What improper deed is this, to press your shameless fingers into the hand of the Sultan's gholāms!" The Amir was enraged by this—and only God, His mention is exalted, knows what went on in the Sultan's mind, since a king's inner thoughts are beyond one's comprehension—and he said to Bu No'eym, "Have you come to us to seduce our gholāms!"[49] Being by nature bold and brazen, Bu No'eym returned a rough answer, saying, "When did the lord ever see such things from me? If he has had enough of me, he can make up a more palatable excuse than this!"

The Amir grew extremely angry, and gave orders for Bu No'eym to be seized and dragged away by his feet and held prisoner in a cell. He said to Eqbāl, "Whatever this shameless dog possesses, immoveable property and moveable property alike, I have bestowed in its entirety on Nushtegin." Minions went along, entered his abode and sequestered all his possessions and valuables. At the time of the afternoon worship on this day, Eqbāl came into our Divān, accompanied by Nushtegin, and took letters and authorization documents with the royal device and motto for the seizure of all Bu No'eym's possessions and estates in Sistan and other places, and these were entrusted to Nushtegin's representatives.

Bu No'eym remained in dire straits for a very long time, during which the income of those estates went to Nushtegin. But at last, an opportunity for intercession occurred; the Amir relented and gave orders for Bu No'eym to be transferred from the citadel back to his house. Subsequently, he summoned him, gave him a robe of honour and showed him favours. He restored to him his estates, and he ordered that he should be given a present of 10,000 dinars so that he might acquire luxury goods, gholāms and herds, since all that had been taken away from him. I heard that, from time to time, [F 529] the Amir would say to Bu No'eym in a wine-drinking session, "Won't you look at Nushtegin?", and he would reply, "I didn't come to much good from that one occasion of looking [Gh 411] for me to do it a second time!", and the Amir would laugh. No-one ever saw or read about a king more noble-minded and merciful than he, God's mercy be upon him!

Subsequent to that, the Amir gave to this Nushtegin the job of Keeper of the Royal Inkstand in addition to the two posts he already had. He became a very prominent figure, so that when something of a young beard became visible on his handsome face, and he developed a manly physique, he moved up to become the commander of armies, prompting people to recite the verses of Ṣābi[50] composed when Mo'ezz al-Dowla, the Amir of Iraq, sent his Keeper of the Royal Wardrobe, Tegin, as commander of an army: (Verses)

1. *A young child, with the waters [of youth] gleaming from his cheeks, and the wood [of his slim body] still tender.*
2. *He has almost the form of young virgins, so that his breasts might be expected to swell.*
3. *They have girded on a sword at the slender part of the waist where a sword belt is tied, and a belt which is drawn round him.*
4. *They have made him commander of an army, but may the body of troops and their leader both perish!*

Subsequently, Bu Noʿeym and Nushtegin Nowbati had eventful careers and witnessed the usual vicissitudes of life which are the human lot. These will be related in their appropriate place, and what is mentioned here is sufficient.[51]

On Saturday, 16 Shaʿbān [/6 July 1034], the Amir went forth on an organised hunting expedition.[52] For more than a week, men had gone out to collect together a corvée for driving game, and it had been driven, and a great amount of game had come and excellent hunting was had. The Amir came back to the Maḥmudi Garden on 27 Shaʿbān [/17 July]. The head of the Divān of [F 530] Khorasan, Bu'l-Fażl Suri b. Moʿtazz,[53] arrived from Nishapur. He was given an audience and paid his respects, making an offering of a thousand Nishapuri dinars and laying before the Amir a highly-precious bejewelled collar. The Amir came back from the Maḥmudi Garden to the Old Palace of his father in the town on Saturday, [1 Ramażān/20 July]. On the first day of the month of Ramażān they began the fast.

On the third day of the month of Ramażān [/22 July] the presents that the head of the Divān of Khorasan had assembled were brought forward as offerings, amounting to 500 loads,[54] presents similar to those I had witnessed Ḥasanak bringing for Amir Maḥmud in that year when he came back from the Pilgrimage to Mecca and arrived in Balkh from Nishapur. There were such great quantities of clothing, rare and precious things, gold and silver objects, gholāms [Gh 412] and slave girls, musk, camphor, amber,[55] pearls, *maḥfuri* and *qāli* carpets,[56] fine cotton cloth (*kish*) and various kinds of luxury goods amongst these presents of Suri that the Amir and all those present remained struck with amazement, for he had managed to pick the most rare and precious objects from all the towns of Khorasan, from Baghdad, Ray, Jebāl, Gorgān and Ṭabarestān, with wines and victuals of the same calibre. That portion of the presents made up of gold coins was placed in purses of red and green silk, and the silver coins placed in purses yellow in appearance.[57]

I heard from Bu Manṣur the accounting official, who was a man trustworthy, of unimpeachable integrity,[58] noble spirit and perspicacious judgement, and who told me that "The Amir ordered that the presents should be secretly valued, and they were estimated at four million dirhams' worth. The Amir said to me, Bu Manṣur, 'What a fine servant this Suri is! If only we had two or three other servants like him, we would have accrued much benefit!' I replied, [F 531] 'Yes, it's just as you say,' and I didn't have the temerity to add that one should ask the people of Khorasan, both noble and humble, what hardships they have undergone in the producing of such an array of gifts, and that the true consequences of this venture would only become apparent later.'"

And Bu Manṣur's words turned out to be correct. For Suri was ruthless and tyrannical. When he was given a free hand over Khorasan, he destroyed the notables and local leaders, extracted large sums of money, and afflicted the poor and weak with his oppression. Out of every ten dirhams that he took he gave the Sultan only five. These notables were brought to destruction, and they sent envoys and wrote letters to Transoxania, and made complaints to the leaders of the Turks,[59] which made them incite the Turkmens (i.e. to take over Khorasan). Likewise, the poor and the weak raised up supplications to God, His mention is exalted. The agents of the postal and intelligence service did not have the courage to send a true report of Suri's doings, and the Amir would not hear a word against him, and seemed only concerned with those lavish presents of his until Khorasan was in truth lost through his tyranny and extortion. When that disaster occurred (i.e. the Ghaznavid defeat at Dandānqān), Suri came with us to Ghaznin. In the time of Mowdud's rule, he became the head of the Divān in the capital Ghaznin, and was up to the same tricks as in Khorasan, but it did not work, and he was restrained. Eventually he died in the citadel at Ghaznin, as will be related in its appropriate place. May the Almighty God show mercy, for his fate now rests with a Fair and Compassionate Judge! [Gh 413]

It may be that he will be saved by a balance of his deeds, for along with his acts of oppression he was a man who did many charitable acts and was assiduous in performing the worship. There are praiseworthy works of his at Ṭus, including at the shrine of ʿAli b. Musā al-Reżā, peace be upon him. Bu Bakr b. Shahmard, the adjutant and counsellor of the eunuch Fāʾeq Khāṣṣa,[60] had erected buildings there, and Suri ordered many extensions [F 532] to be built. He erected a minaret and purchased a valuable estate as a permanent endowment (*vaqf*) for the shrine. At Nishapur, he constructed an open ground for communal ritual worship[61] unsurpassed by anything previously designed by any ruler or notable; that monument is still there. A rivulet runs through the quarters of B[/M]olqābād and Ḥira,[62] a source of frequent flash floods in spring, which caused much trouble for the local God-fearing inhabitants. Suri ordered the banks to be reinforced with stones and fired brick and obviated that suffering. He established endowments for these two works so that they should not fall into disrepair. He also ordered important constructions to be made at the frontier post of Farāva and at Nasā.[63] All these exist and must be taken into account, but my earnest belief is that an abundance of such good work still does not compensate for an act of injustice inflicted upon the poor and the weak. The poet has expressed this admirably: (Poetry)

1. *Like a woman who steals pomegranates from the orchard of her neighbour; she offers them when visiting the sick, and aspires to be virtuous.*[64]

To steal a loaf from one's neighbour in order to give it to another is not legally admissible, and will not in the end bring a reward. I do not understand what these upstarts see in this present world that they summon up all their efforts and gather together a bunch of tawdry things, and shed blood and fight over it, only to let it slip away easily from their hands at the end when they take their leave of this world and while still pining for it. May God, His mention is exalted, bestow the gift of wakefulness and awareness through His grace and kindness!

At the end of Suri's tenure of office, Bu'l-Moẓaffar Jomaḥi went to Nishapur as postmaster and intelligence officer on Amir Masʿud's order. (This distinguished man has been referred to and described in several places in this History, and the Grand Vizier Aḥmad, son of ʿAbd al-Ṣamad, had much affection and respect for him.)[65] The Vizier secretly gave him instructions to report back impartially and without fear about [F 533] what Suri was up to, and he used to do this, and Suri went after his blood. In the end, his despatches made an impression on the Amir's mind, and he began to write more bluntly to the Vizier. On one occasion, he had sent some verses to the Vizier, and I saw them and wrote down these two or three verses that I remembered. The Vizier deftly arranged it so that the Amir heard these verses of Bu'l-Moẓaffar, for they had been intended for him, and they served their purpose. They are these: (Poetry) [Gh 414]

1. O Amir, look towards Khorasan, for Suri is up to his tricks and snares![66]
2. If his ill-omened hand is allowed to roam for long, he will make prolonged trouble for you.
3. On whatever mission you may send Suri, he will return like the bad shepherd, not with the flock but with the branded carcass.[67]

The final outcome of that was that enemies came and seized Khorasan, as will be explained in detail later.[68]

This affair has reminded me of a very remarkable and instructive story which I thought I ought to write down in order to show that there are many instances similar to that of Suri's—this so that readers may gain some further insight, even though it will prolong the narrative.

Story

I have read in the historical accounts of the caliphs that, when the Barmakid house was in the ascendant, and when the Commander of the Faithful Hārun al-Rashid called Yaḥyā b. Khāled, who was his vizier, "Father," and raised up Yaḥyā's two sons Fażl and Jaʿfar to high office, [F 534] as is well known and recorded in books, a man of the ʿAlids rebelled and seized Gorgān, Ṭabarestān and the entire mountainous region of Gilān, and his movement grew very strong.[69] Hārun was alarmed and disquieted because he had read in books that the first sign of a breach in the fabric of the ʿAbbasid caliphate would be that an ʿAlid rebel would appear in the land of Ṭabarestān. He summoned Yaḥyā b. Khāled al-Barmaki privately and told him, "A serious problem has arisen, and it is not one of the type that a military commander can resolve; either I shall have to go myself or else you yourself or one of your sons, Fażl or Jaʿfar, must go." Yaḥyā said, "It is unseemly for the Commander of the Faithful to lead an expedition against every rebel[70] who pops up. I myself remain here at the lord's side to make plans for troops and for finance, but my offspring Fażl and Jaʿfar are there for the lord to command; what does he ordain?" He said, "Fażl must go, and he must be given the governorship of Khorasan, Ray, Jebāl, Khwarazm,[71] Sistan and Transoxania so that he may govern from Ray, and despatch deputy governors [Gh 415] to the towns and deal with this rebel either through war or else win him over by peaceful measures. Fażl's requirements and troops must be made ready, so that tomorrow he may don a robe of honour, set out the day after tomorrow and take up his position at Nahravān[72] until a complete array of troops, [F 535] supplies and equipment reach him." Yaḥyā said, "I will carry out the command;" and went back and prepared everything.

He said to Fażl in private, "O my son, this is a momentous affair which the Caliph has ordained for you and an extremely exalted degree to which he has raised you as a denizen of this present world, but it entails a dire punishment in the next world, since it involves the necessity of overthrowing a descendant of the Prophet, peace be upon him. But in order to remain in this lord's favour, we have no choice but to obey, since we have many enemies and we are suspected of being sympathetic towards the ʿAlids."[73] Fażl replied, "Don't worry, I shall persevere, even at the expense of my own life, in order to ensure a peaceful end to this affair."

The next day, Yaḥyā and Fażl came into the Caliph's presence. Hārun al-Rashid bound together a lance and battle standard for Khorasan in Fażl's name, and they were given to him, together with the investiture patent for the governorship of Khorasan. He donned a robe of honour, and went home with a very large escort. All the great figures of the court went to him and presented their respects and congratulations to him. The next day, he set out and reached Nahravān.

He halted there for three days until 50,000 cavalrymen, commanders and senior officers joined up with him. Then he moved off, came to Ray and encamped there. He despatched an advance force (*moqaddama*), with 20,000 cavalrymen, by the Donbāvand (Damāvand) road to Ṭabarestān,[74] and sent out the remaining troops with other commanders to various parts of Khorasan. Then he despatched envoys to the ʿAlid Yaḥyā, and used conciliatory measures until Yaḥyā agreed to peace terms, on condition that Hārun would send back to him an agreement for safe conduct (*ʿahd-nāma*) in his own hand, written on that document which Yaḥyā the ʿAlid would personally write down. Fażl reported back Yaḥyā's terms, and Hārun al-Rashid agreed to them and was very pleased with the arrangement. Yaḥyā sent a document by an envoy who was one of his trusted confidants. Hārun wrote on that in his own handwriting, and the judges and the professional witnesses attested it, and after that, oaths were administered verbally. Yaḥyā was reassured by that, and went to Fażl and was most nobly treated. He then went on to Baghdad, where Hārun welcomed him cordially and [F 536] bestowed much wealth on him. Fażl went on to Khorasan and stayed there for two years, and awarded great amounts of largesse to visitors and poets at his court.[75] He then sought permission to stand down, and this was granted. He came back to Baghdad, and Hārun showered boundless favours and generosity upon him.

The story of what subsequently happened to that ʿAlid would take too long to relate, and my concern here [Gh 416] is with other matters. Fażl brought the usual customary presents for al-Rashid.[76] After this, al-Rashid so decided that he would send a governor to Khorasan, and his choice fell on ʿAli b. ʿIsā b. Māhān.[77] He asked Yaḥyā [b. Khāled] for his opinion. Yaḥyā answered that ʿAli was a bully and a tyrant, but that it was for the lord to decide. (A deterioration in the position of the house of Barmak had set in, with cracks already visible.) Rashid, in a display of anger towards Yaḥyā, sent ʿAli, son of ʿIsā, to Khorasan. ʿAli began to exercise his powers and set about exacting wealth in excessive quantities without anyone having the courage to divulge his actions in public. Confidential agents of the postal and intelligence service wrote letters to Yaḥyā, and he would bide his time and use various ploys so that he might drop something about that in Rashid's ear, or he would get one of those who had suffered ʿAli's tyranny to make an impromptu appearance before the caliph and plead his case.

But it was to no avail whatsoever, and matters reached such a stage that Rashid took an oath pledging that anyone coming with a grievance against ʿAli would be redirected to ʿAli himself.[78] Yaḥyā and the rest were reduced to silence.

ʿAli brought ruin and desolation to the regions of Khorasan, Transoxania, Ray, Jebāl, Gorgān, Ṭabarestān, Kerman, Isfahan, Khwarazm, Nimruz and Sistan, exacting limitless sums. From the wealth thus collected he made an offering of presents to Rashid which was unequalled before or after him. Those presents arrived at Baghdad, and a list of them was shown to Rashid. He was highly delighted [F 537] and remained filled with wonder. Fażl, son of Rabiʿ, who was the Great Chamberlain, nursed an animosity towards the house of Barmak and was supporting ʿAli b. ʿIsā. Rashid asked Fażl, "What should be done regarding the presents that have arrived from Khorasan?" He replied, "The lord should take up his seat on a vantage point, and he should make Yaḥyā, his sons and other servants sit or stand there so that the presents may be brought forward. The house of Barmak will be mortified and it will become clear to all and sundry, high and low, how treacherously they have behaved; for the amount of presents brought by Fażl b. Yaḥyā from the whole province of Khorasan was less than what a local governor might bring from a single town, and now ʿAli is sending such lavish presents by contrast!" This suggestion was most pleasing to Rashid, [Gh 417] since he had taken a dislike to the house of Barmak, and the time of their ascendancy was nearing its end.

The next day, he came to the elevated gallery overlooking the square and sat down there. He made Yaḥyā and his two sons be seated, while Fażl b. Rabiʿ and another group, and a crowd of people, stood there. Those presents were brought into the square. There were a thousand Turkish gholāms, each bearing in his hands two multicoloured garments made from Shushtari, Isfahani, *saqlāṭun* silk and *molḥam* brocade,[79] and beautiful Turkish brocades, as well as other materials. The gholāms stood there with those garments. After them came a thousand Turkish slavegirls, each one bearing in her hand a golden or silver goblet filled with musk, camphor, amber, other kinds of perfumes and aromatics, and other rarities from the various towns; then a hundred Indian gholāms and a hundred very pretty Indian slavegirls dressed in valuable fine muslin garments. The gholāms bore Indian swords of the most exquisite kind, and the slavegirls carried thinly-woven muslin cloths in very fine baskets woven from (?) bamboo (*qaṣab*). Along with them, five male and two female elephants were brought in, [F 538] the male ones with coverings of brocade and gold and silver dangling ornaments,[80] and the female ones with litters made with gold, and girths and accoutrements set with jewels. Twenty horses were brought in after the elephants, with gold saddles, shoed with gold and with equipment set with the jewels of Badakhshān[81] and with turquoises, these being horses from Gilān.[82] Then 200 Khorasani horses with brocade horse cloths, and twenty [hunting] eagles and twenty falcons.[83] Then they brought in 1,000 camels, 200 with pack saddles and with headstalls covered with silk, the pack saddles having brocade coverings laid over them, and the rest of their accoutrements and coverings highly decorated, [and] out of them, 300 camels with litters (*maḥmal*) and frameworks in which to convey women (*mahd*), and with twenty of these frameworks made of gold. There were 500,300 pieces of rock crystal of every kind; 100 yokes of oxen; twenty extremely expensive jewelled collars; 300,000 pearls; 200 pieces of imperial Chinese porcelain,[84] made up of platters, cups, etc., each one of such superlative workmanship, and 2,000 other pieces of porcelain comprising drinking-cups, large beakers, porcelain wine jars, both large and small, and various other kinds; and 300 pieces of hangings,[85] 200 *qāli* carpets and 200 *maḥfuri* ones.[86]

When all these various bounties and luxury articles reached the square and the Caliph's presence, a jubilant, concerted shout of the *takbir*[87] arose from the troops, barrel-shaped drums were beaten and trumpets sounded, all that in a manner never before heard, seen or remembered. Hārun al-Rashid turned towards Yaḥyā the Barmaki and said, "Where were all these things in the time of your son Fażl?" Yaḥyā answered, "May the Commander of the Faithful's life be prolonged! In the time of my son's governorship, these things [Gh 418] were in the houses of their owners, in the towns of Western Persia and Khorasan." Hārun al-Rashid was stung by this reply, and the gifts turned sour on him. Looking sullen and out of humour, [F 539] he rose and left the stand. They carried those objects away from the court session and the square, and conveyed them to the treasuries, palaces and stables. The Caliph remained very downcast at those words of Yaḥyā, for Hārun al-Rashid was an intelligent man and he realized the full extent of their implications.

When Yaḥyā returned home, his sons Fażl and Ja'far said to him, "We are your obedient servants, and it is not for us to pick faults with our father's words and judgement, but we were very alarmed at those untrimmed and forthright words which you said to the Caliph. They should have displayed more forethought, and you should have been more tactful and gentle." Yaḥyā replied, "O my sons! We are has-beens,[88] and our time is approaching its end, and after God's decree, it will be you who will be deemed the cause of the forthcoming misfortunes. But while I am still at my post, I have no choice but to speak out for justice, and I will not indulge in flattering words and deceit, for one cannot alter the decree of Fate by means of lying words and skulduggery. As the saying goes, '*When one's time come, the attempt to evade it can be the cause of death*'.[89] Tonight my words will be going through the mind of this hard-hearted man, and doubtless tomorrow he will talk about them and will want a clear decision. I will let you know happens. Go back, and don't worry."

They went back very downcast, since they were young and inexperienced, whereas the old man, Yaḥyā, was wise in the ways of the world. He ate a pleasant meal with his boon companions, and then went into the inner quarters of his residence for a period of privacy. He called for music-making, a singing girl and wine, and set about drinking. There was a book entitled "The subtleties of the devices and stratagems of capable people"[90] which he sent for, and he was sipping his wine slowly and listening in a leisurely frame of mind to the songs, the bowing of instruments and declaiming, and was reading his book until the remainder of the day and half the night had gone by. Then he said to himself, "I've got the measure of this affair!", and went to sleep. He arose at dawn and went along to the court session.

When the public audience was over, Hārun al-Rashid had a private word with Yaḥyā. "O Father," he said, [F 540] "yesterday you directed at me such harsh words; what was the occasion for such talk?" Yaḥyā replied, "May the lord's life be prolonged! True and just words may well be harsh, and [Gh 419] in former times, such words as these used to be praised. Now, times have changed, for such is the working of the deceitful present world that it never allows things to remain the same; and although my detractors have turned the lord against me, and I can detect signs of disapproval and changed attitudes, nevertheless, while I am still in active service, I shall not refrain from offering my sincere advice and will not behave in a disloyal and ungrateful manner." Hārun said, "O Father, don't talk like this and poison your heart with doubts and fears, for your status and that of your sons have remained exactly as they were; and never stop offering us sincere advice, be it harsh or gentle,[91] for it all comes as equally pleasing and acceptable to us. The words you uttered yesterday have made a powerful impression on our mind. You must explain them fully so that the true situation may be ascertained."

Yaḥyā rose to his feet, kissed the ground, sat down again and said, "May the lord's life be prolonged!" I can set forth today a detailed exposition of part of yesterday's words, and the greater part may be set forth tomorrow in more detail." Hārun replied, "Very good!" Yaḥyā said, "The lord has given a free hand to ʿAli, and he does whatever he likes, and our spies and informers do not dare to report back what goes on there, for he killed two men whom I had secretly planted there (i.e. to report on ʿAli's misdeeds). He reduced the subjects in Khorasan to a state of destitution, uprooted the influential and important classes, seized estates and lands, and reduced the lord's troops to indigence. Khorasan is a very important frontier region, with enemies like the Turks close at hand. You should not pay heed to these presents that he sent, since he has only sent two or three dirhams out of every ten which he has seized; rather, you should focus your attention on the problem that, at any moment now, a disturbance may occur which may prove intractable. For the people of Khorasan [F 541] will despair of the caliph and will raise their hands to God, His mention is exalted, and will stage a great revolt and turn to the Turks for help.[92] I fear that the situation may reach such a point that the lord will have to go personally to suppress the outbreak and that, for every dirham that ʿAli, son of ʿIsā, has sent, an expenditure of fifty dirhams or more will be necessary in order to suppress that uprising. I have said what I know to be true and have thus fulfilled my duty; it will be for the lord to command. I will give a clearer exposition and explanation of the topic tomorrow." Hārun al-Rashid said, "It's just as you said. O Father, may God reward you with kindness, what needs to be done in this regard will be done. Come back tomorrow and show us what you have said." Yaḥyā went back much encouraged, and recounted what had happened to his sons Fażl and Jaʿfar, and they too became happy.

Yaḥyā sent a messenger and summoned ten of the richest jewel merchants of Baghdad, [Gh 420] and said, "The Caliph requires thirty million dirhams' worth of jewels, of the rarest and costliest available." They answered, "This is most welcomed. Through the lord's auspicious rule and his justice, if someone asks for thirty million dinars' worth of jewels, this amount exists in Baghdad. The ten of us have the amount which he desires, and yet more still." Yaḥyā said, "May God bless you! Go back home, and come to the court tomorrow with the jewels so that you may be brought into the Caliph's presence, and what the exalted judgement ordains is requisite, shall be done." The jewel merchants went back, and came the next day to the court with caskets of jewels. Yaḥyā sought a private audience for them with Hārun al-Rashid. This was granted, and they were brought into the Caliph's presence with the jewels, which they displayed to his approbation. Yaḥyā gave them a written receipt for twenty-seven million dirhams; Hārun al-Rashid had his emblem and motto affixed to that, and he said, "Go back home so that it can be decided what should be done in this matter, and then go to Yaḥyā tomorrow, so that he can conclude the deal according to our instructions." The jewel merchants went home and the caskets of jewels were locked and had seals placed on them, and they were placed in the treasury. [F 542]

Hārun al-Rashid said, "O father, what's this you have done?" He answered, "May the lord's life be prolonged! Keep the jewels safely till tomorrow; I will extract the receipt [from the merchants] and tear it up, and the owners of the jewels will not dare to say anything. If they should come to the lord with their grievance, they should be referred to me and I will deal with them." Hārun said, "We can do this, but how can we justify ourselves when we stand for judgement in the open plain on The Day of Resurrection in the presence of God, His mention is exalted? Such conduct would induce both our own subjects, as well as strangers visiting this city, to take flight, and we would become infamous throughout the whole world." Yaḥyā said, "In that case, the situation of ʿAli b. ʿIsā is on the same footing in Khorasan, as I have shown. If the lord does not consider it permissible that ten people should complain of his injustice and be left in a distressed condition, why does he consider it fair for many millions of Muslims to be rendered distressed by one governor of his and for them to offer up imprecations against him?" Hārun said, "You have spoken well, O Father, and you have explained the situation clearly. Transfer the caskets to your house, and give them back to the owners of the jewels. I know now what needs to be done regarding this tyrant ʿAli b. ʿIsā." Yaḥyā returned home, and the next day the jewel merchants came along. He ordered the jewel caskets to be given back to them, with their locks and seals intact. The sale was declared null and void and the receipt was taken back. He said, "This sum of money is not available for spending just now. When the taxation from Egypt and Syria comes in, these jewels will then be purchased." They called down blessings on his head and returned home.[93]

This episode remained in Rashid's mind and he kept wondering [Gh 421] how he could dismiss ʿAli. Meanwhile, the ascendancy of the house of Barmak had come to its end, and Hārun brought about their downfall, as is well known.[94]

Rāfeʿ b. Leyth b. Naṣr b. Sayyār, who had been made governor in Transoxania thanks to ʿAli b. ʿIsā, began a rebellion in Transoxania and attracted many men of substance from Merv to join him. He himself had a considerable army, and many people from Transoxania also flocked to join him.[95] The whole of Khorasan became filled with rebellion and strife. Several military expeditions [F 543] despatched by ʿAli b. ʿIsā were defeated, till affairs reached the stage that he sought help from Hārun. Hārun sent a powerful army under Harthama b. Aʿyan[96] to reinforce [ʿAli b.] ʿIsā, and secretly instructed him—giving him an investiture patent for the governorship of Khorasan in his own handwriting—to seize him unawares, clap him in bonds, get justice for the subjects in Khorasan for his activities, and then send him back to Baghdad. He was then to set about dealing with Rāfeʿ's revolt until it should be satisfactorily settled either by war or by a peace agreement. Harthama set out, and at Merv managed to catch ʿAli unawares and seize him. He stripped him of everything he possessed and then sent him to Baghdad, in bonds, under the custody of one of Rashid's own attendants, and took over *de facto* control of Khorasan. Rāfeʿ's revolt was growing stronger every day, and Harthama was unable to suppress it, until it became necessary for Rashid, whose life was nearing its end, to drag along there his frail body, with a numerous army and with his son Ma'mun commanding his vanguard. While on the road to there, he exclaimed on several occasions, "Alas for the house of Barmak! It is only now that I recall Yaḥyā's words, 'The caliphs never appointed a vizier like Yaḥyā.'"[97] His final fate was that Ma'mun went to Merv and established himself there, and sent an army with Harthama against Samarqand; and when Hārun al-Rashid reached Ṭus, he passed away there.[98]

This story has come to its end. Although the insertion of stories like these stretches out the narrative, I bring in such tales for they yield many a beneficial point for the readers to apprehend. Enough said!

On Sunday, 9 Ramażān[99] of the year 425 [/28 July 1034], a traveller[100] arrived from Khwarazm bringing a slim, confidential message sewn into [the cover of] a waterbottle, from the postal and intelligence officer of that province. He had entrusted just five [Gh 422] lines to the traveller, to the effect that [F 544] it was necessary to enquire of him, the traveller, about the state of affairs. The traveller repeated the postal and intelligence officer's verbal message, "My mission, to inform on the situation here, has become mortally dangerous. ʿAbd al-Jabbār, the Vizier's son, fearing for his own life, has gone into hiding. They are searching for him but cannot find him since he has a secure hiding place. Hārun (i.e. the son of Altuntāsh) has become tyrannous and is preparing an army. He is buying up a great number of gholāms and horses and intends to attack Merv. The followers of the Grand Vizier have all been arrested and their property and finances sequestrated. However, the *khoṭba* remains as it is,[101] for Hārun is not in open rebellion. He maintains that 'ʿAbd al-Jabbār is haunted by his own shadow and has taken to flight on account of his own high-handedness and oppressive ways.' I, as postal and intelligence officer, have been allowed to keep my position and I work for them. Whatever I write will be according to their wishes and this should be understood. The General Bāytegin, Aytegin the Cupbearer, Qalpāq, Hendovān and most of the former senior commanders of Sultan Maḥmud are all opposed to doing this, but what can they do? They cannot succeed against all the troops and cavalrymen. If this province is regarded as being of any value, something must be done, for things are deteriorating day by day. So ends my report for your information."

When Amir Masʿud became apprised of this state of affairs, he became troubled in his mind. He had a private meeting with Bu Naṣr Moshkān and there was much talk. It was decided that the traveller should be sent back and that a letter should be written to the commanders urging them to provide Hārun with wise counsel and to restrain him in order to avoid any calamity or disorder until the arrival of the royal banner in Khorasan, when the necessary measures to deal with this situation would be enacted. The decision was taken that the Amir should affirm his intention of making a move to Bost and from there a journey to Herat, and he ordered a letter to be written to the Khᵛāja Aḥmad b. 'Abd al-Ṣamad concerning these matters, asking him what his views were on this important affair, [F 545] and asking him to do whatever was necessary and write a personal letter (i.e. to Khwarazm). Bu Naṣr sat down privately, and the confidential letters for Khwarazm were written out, in a very slim format, and the Amir affixed his emblem and motto to them all. The traveller was given a handsome gift of money, and he set out for Khwarazm. Whatever was necessary in these matters was written to the Vizier. There will be a chapter specially devoted to the affairs of Khwarazm, dealing with them in a much fuller way than this; here I shall not venture into detail.[102] [Gh 423]

On the fifteenth of this month [/3 August 1034], letters arrived from Lahore with the news that Aḥmad b. Ināltegin had come there with a large force and that the Judge from Shiraz and all the local men of eminence[103] had retired to the fortress of M.n.d.k.k.v.r.[104] There was continuous warfare, districts were being devastated and there was perpetual chaos and mayhem.[105] The Amir was plunged deep into thought, since his mind was occupied by events on three fronts: because of the "'Erāqi" Turkmens; because of Khwarazm; and because of Lahore, for this reason which I have just explained.

Letters also arrived from Nishapur with the news that, exploiting Suri's absence, the people of Ṭus and Bāvard were planning an attack (i.e. on Nishapur) and that Aḥmad b. 'Ali b. Nushtegin, who had fled from Kerman and had arrived there with those troops that had accompanied him, was preparing to combat them.[106] The Amir instructed Suri that he should return soon to Nishapur, and Suri expressed his obedience.[107] On [Wednesday,] the nineteenth day of this month [/7 August] he was given a very splendid and fine robe of honour.

On Tuesday [1 Shavvāl/19 August], they celebrated the Festival of the Ending of the Fast. The Amir ordered sumptuous celebrations to be held, and after that, a festal spread had been laid out, and he ordered wine to be served at the banquet to the courtiers, retainers and troops, [F 546] and they returned home in a very drunken state. The

Amir himself had a wine-drinking session with his boon-companions, but he did not display much good cheer because his mind was much occupied with several other problems.[108] Confidential letters, of the highest importance, arrived from Lahore to the effect that Aḥmad b. Ināltegin would have occupied the citadel,[109] had it not been for the news that Tilak the Indian had prepared a powerful army of all kinds of troops and was heading in his direction. The hapless Aḥmad lost his nerve, and differences appeared among his army. While still engaged in the wine session, and having read the confidential missives, the Amir ordered that a letter should be sent to Tilak the Indian and that the confidential missives should be included with the letter, and he gave instructions that an attack on Aḥmad should soon be launched. The Amir affixed his emblem and motto and added a section at the foot of the letter in his own handwriting, couched in trenchant language and imbued with the regal tone that was his hallmark. The official form of address for Tilak at this time, on documents emanating from our Divān, was "The Trusted One" *(al-Moʿtamad)*. The letter was sent off quickly. [Gh 424]

On Thursday, 18 Shavvāl [/5 September 1034] a letter arrived from Gardiz that the Commander-in-Chief Ghāzi, who had been incarcerated there, had died. I heard that he had been kept in the citadel most benignly, with only light bonds. Someone secretly came to the castellan of the fortress and said, "Ghāzi is plotting to escape. A strong knife has been brought in to him, and at night he is digging a tunnel and spreading out the earth from it beneath the curtaining in his room so that it cannot be noticed, and he keeps the tunnel hidden by day." So the castellan went to him at night unexpectedly and saw the earth, the knife and the tunnel. He upbraided him, "Why have you done this? There's nothing lacking in the way in which you are comfortably held." He answered that he had committed no crime, but others envious of him had prevailed upon the lord Sultan and turned the latter's heart against him. He had harboured hopes that the exalted gaze would look on him with favour again, but when [F 547] he received no recognition, and his imprisonment became prolonged, he plotted a way out, in the usual manner of prisoners and other wretches. If he had secured his freedom, he would have thrown himself before the lord, and the latter would necessarily have shown mercy towards him. The castellan transferred him from that cell to another cell and kept a closer watch on him, and ordered that the tunnel should be firmly blocked up with bricks and earth. He reported the incident (i.e. to the Amir) and the reply came back that Ghāzi was innocent and that he would experience the royal favour at an appropriate time. It was necessary to keep his spirits up, and he should be well looked after. Ghāzi was cheered up by these words, and he would have experienced the Amir's favour, but the fateful decree of death, from which there is no escape for any human being, came down and he died, God's mercy be upon him. He was a fine commander.

An account of the return of the royal envoys from Turkestan with the travelling throne (*mahd*) bearing the bride, and the envoys from the Khāns who came with them

It was almost four years since our envoys, the boon-companion Bu'l-Qāsem Ḥaṣiri and the Judge Bu Ṭāher Tabbāni, had left Balkh for Turkestan in order to conclude an agreement with Qadïr Khān, and to seek a daughter of his for Sultan Masʿud and a daughter of Bughrātegin for the prince Amir Mowdud. They had concluded the agreement and made the marriage contracts. Qadïr Khān died and Bughrātegin, the eldest son and the designated heir, succeeded to the Khanate of Turkestan, [Gh 425] assuming the honorific title of Arslān Khān.[110] This led to an interlude of uncertainty; time passed and the envoys remained there for a lengthy period. Letters of congratulation on the new ruler's accession and of condolence for the recently-deceased Khān went from the court here (i.e. from the Ghaznavid capital) *according to the usual custom on such occasions*. When the matter of Turkestan and the succession to the Khanate were settled, our envoys were despatched home with their mission fulfilled. Arslān Khān sent his own envoys with them, and the brides[111] were brought. As fate would have it, the bride designated [F 548] for the prince Mowdud, passed away. Shāh Khātun, Qadïr Khān's daughter, who was intended for Sultan Masʿud, was duly brought. When they reached Parvān, the Judge Bu Ṭāher Tabbāni died there. Various stories are told regarding the manner of his death. Some people said that he died after a violent attack of dysentery. Others said that he was served with some roasted fowls which were poisoned; he ate of them and died as a result. *Only the Almighty God knows the unseen.*[112] There are many secrets which will be revealed on the Day of Resurrection, "*on that Day when neither wealth nor sons will profit a man, except he who comes to God with a sound heart.*"[113] I consider it an act of utmost foolishness that anyone should commit the treacherous act of spilling the blood of Muslims[114] for the sake of securing status and the meretricious gains of this world. *May God, His mention is exalted, preserve us and all the Muslims from what is forbidden, from greed and from following our own fancies, through His favour and the amplitude of His grace!*

On Friday, 19 Shavvāl [/6 September 1034],[115] they decorated the town of Ghazni in the same grand style that it was decked out in that year when this Sultan arrived here from Western Persia on his way to Balkh and assumed the throne. So many bridal platforms and arches had been erected and so many embellishments created that it was beyond one's powers of description, for she was the first bride that had ever been brought here from Turkestan, and the Amir wanted the Turks (i.e. Arslān Khān's envoys) to see a spectacle whose like they had never witnessed before. When the envoys and the bride reached Shajkāv,[116] the order reached them to the effect that they should halt and stay there. The boon-companion Khᵛāja Bu'l-Qāsem came to the court at that moment. He saw the Sultan and [F 549] received much favour, since he had endured great hardship and distress. The Sultan saw him alone, except for the Head of the Chancery, Bu Naṣr Moshkān, who was also present, and their private audience lasted almost till the time of the afternoon worship. Then Bu'l-Qāsem returned home.

The next day, Monday, 21 Shavvāl [/8 September], the holders of court offices, the commander of the police guard and the official assigned to look after the visiting envoys, went with led horses [Gh 426] and brought back the Khān's envoys. The entire town was bedecked with decorations, and there was a most lavish display of pomp and ceremony. When they saw the envoys, such an amount of coins was scattered forth, dinars, dirhams and everything else, at Afghān-shāl, in the Rasula (?) square[117] and in the markets, that the envoys remained struck with wonder. They were brought in and set down, and food that had been prepared was brought forward. At the time of the afternoon worship, all the womenfolk of the important men and the eunuchs went out to meet and to greet the bride, and from Shajkāv onwards those people had been swollen by the addition of a great throng, the like of which, so people said, could not be recalled. The palace had been decorated and adorned to such an extent that the two women, Zarrin and ʿAndalib,[118] related to me that never at any time had the Amir made and commissioned a display and effort on that scale, and this at a time when all the jewels and state regalia were still intact, may this empire endure for ever![119] For several days the town was decorated and bedecked: the populace was making merry, the notables and prominent people were disporting themselves in various ways, and wine-drinking went on until these festivities came to an end. After a few days, [F 550] when the envoys had on several occasions come to the sultan's court session, and when the agreements had been concluded and made firm at this end, and after enjoying feasting, wine-drinking and polo games, and tasting the grandeur of the occasion to the full, they were despatched back to Turkestan with a fine send-off and in a very contented and happy state. Exceedingly fine letters were written on these matters, and are registered and set down in the volume that I compiled. If I were to include them here, the narrative would have become very lengthy. This History is becoming overstretched as it is, and I realize that I may be regarded as long-winded and wearisome, but I want to do full justice to this great house of the Ghaznavids, and for that I have today only my pen; at all events I am doing my duty.

On Thursday, 25 Shavvāl [/12 September 1034] envoys arrived from Nishapur, with letters from Aḥmad b. ʿAli b. Nushtegin, and the military governor of the town, with the following encouraging news:

Since time immemorial there has been bad blood[120] between the people of Nishapur and those of Ṭus, and when Suri decided to go to the capital and set off, the God-forsaken rabble seized the opportunity, and a great number of evil and ill-intentioned people came, bent on plundering Nishapur.[121] By chance, Aḥmad b. ʿAli b. Nushtegin had arrived there via the Tun road,[122] in flight from Kerman. Out of a feeling of shamefulness and disgrace,[123] he had halted there, [Gh 427] but a letter had come to him requiring him to proceed to the court. But before he could depart, these God-forsaken ones came to Nishapur. Aḥmad was a stalwart warrior and had led his troops on many an occasion. Moreover, he was exceptionally adept in equestrian skills, polo playing and the *ṭabṭāb* game.[124] [F 551] He therefore prepared himself for this challenge. The Ṭusis came via the road through the mountain pass of Kharv,[125] Poshanqān[126] and Khālanjuy.[127] There was a multitude of them, the greater part of them on foot and with no proper formation, being led by a commander from Bāvard[128] who was one of the hapless remaining survivors of the ʿAbd al-Razzāq family.[129] They were running and hurrying along, with a great deal of tumult and clamour, and it was as if all the caravanserais of Nishapur had thrown their doors open and the town left without protectors and defenders so that this bovine brigade from Ṭus[130] might be able to concentrate on their task, load themselves up with plunder and then go back home. When the lion-hearted Aḥmad b. ʿAli b. Nushtegin became aware of this and saw them in such disarray, he told his troops, "I have been watching them; they are digging their own graves. Follow my orders closely, and don't do anything rash." They replied, "It is for you (as the commander representing the Amir) to command, and we will follow." He said to the masses of the common people, who numbered over 20,000 and who were armed with clubs and stones and the odd weapon, "Take care not to move from your places, and back me up by making a great clamour, for if a group of you decides to advance heedlessly, the Ṭusis will seize their opportunity and the Nishapuris will lose heart if some of our folks are killed."[131] They answered, "We'll do as you say." They remained in their place, and [F 552] sent up a great clamour so that one would have said that it was the Day of Resurrection.

Aḥmad held 300[132] cavalrymen concealed in an ambush within an area enclosed by walls and he instructed them, "You must be ready and on the qui vive, and listen to my orders. When the Ṭusis get close, I [Gh 428] shall go out to encounter them, will engage them in a brief skirmish,[133] and then turn round and take to flight so that the poor wretches will press on more eagerly and will think that I have been routed. I will be gently drawing them away further and further on until they go past your positions[134]. When they get past, I shall turn round and stand my ground. Once the battle becomes intense and you hear the trumpets, drums and clamour of the Nishapuris, you should pour out from your hideouts. God, His mention is exalted, will help us to triumph, for I know that, with this strategy I have devised, victory will be ours." They replied, "We'll do it."

Aḥmad returned from the place chosen for the ambush, and went back a good distance, as far as that open stretch which is on the way to the square of 'Abd al-Razzāq. He arranged his infantry and cavalry in their formations of a right, a left, a centre, the wings and a rearguard. He had fifty cavalrymen with first-class mounts in his vanguard, and he sent out a scouting party. Shouts of "God is most great!" and the voices of the Qor'ān-reciters rose up, and a mighty clamour arose in the town. Towards the time of the midday worship, a very numerous horde of the Ṭusis poured in like ants and locusts. From their midst, 300 horsemen of all kinds, and five or six thousand armed footsoldiers cut loose[135] and rushed forth, while the rest held back. Aḥmad slowly moved forward with his 400 cavalrymen[136] and his 2,000 infantrymen and went past that point where the ambush had been set up. He found that his advance guard had engaged in fierce fighting with the Ṭusis' forward scouts. Then the two main armies came together in a hard-fought, hand-to-hand (lit. "beard-to-beard") combat, and they remained closely engaged for a while. There were casualties on both sides, [F 553] as well as countless numbers of wounded. Meanwhile the Ṭusis were receiving reinforcements.

Aḥmad gave the order to his infantrymen, having pre-arranged with them that they should fall back and gradually retreat. When the Ṭusis saw that happening, they advanced more boldly. Aḥmad was fighting with them and falling back till he knew that he had gone back a considerable distance beyond the place of the ambush, and then he stood his ground in a very stout fashion. The fresh and unused cavalry and infantrymen who had been stationed there in the rear, now joined up with him. The fighting grew fiercer. He ordered that the trumpets should be blown and the drums beaten all at once, and that the masses of the populace should all at once raise a great cry, such that one might say that the earth was rent open. The fresh and unused cavalrymen came out of their hideouts, trumpets were blown and a great battle-shout went up. The Ṭusis were attacked from front and rear; their battle order [Gh 429] crumbled, they fell into disarray and were terror-stricken. They turned in flight and impacted with the others who were still coming up to the place of battle, and were each only concerned with saving his own skin. With their spirits elated, the Nishapuris went after them and killed so many that the numbers of dead were limitless and incalculable. Because of the intensity of their defeat and their terror of the Nishapuris, they so feared for their lives that they hurled themselves into the vineyards and gardens, throwing down their weapons. The Nishapuris were going into the vineyards and gardens, seizing them by their beards, dragging them out and chopping off their heads. It got to the stage that five or six women were seen on the gardens below who were herding along before them twenty-odd Ṭusi men and were smacking them as they went along.

Aḥmad b. ʿAli b. Nushtegin, with the pick of his cavalry, pursued those God-abandoned souls as far as Khālanjuy, three farsakhs from the town. They killed vast numbers of them, took many of them captive, and came back from there to the town at the time of the evening worship, victorious and triumphant, with much plunder and many beasts of burden and weapons. The next day, he gave orders for gallows to be erected, and [F 554] many of the Ṭusis were hanged and gibbeted there, and the heads of others who had been slain were collected together and placed at the foot of the gallows, while those considered too weak and feeble were set free. The Ṭusis were awestruck, and from then on did not dare to nurture any ambitions regarding the Nishapuris.[137]

The Amir was delighted at Aḥmad's exploits, and thus the stain on his reputation, acquired through his flight from Kerman, was removed.

An account of the affairs of Kerman and the routing of the army which had been stationed there

One story inevitably leads to another, and the events in Kerman and the reasons for the rout have to be explicated and related, for this is what the writing of history demands.

At that time when Amir Masʿud came from Herat to Balkh, he had sent an army under the general, the Keeper of the Royal Wardrobe,[138] to Makrān. The enterprise had been a great success; Bu'l-ʿAskar became firmly ensconced on the throne there, order was achieved in that province, and the populace began to enjoy peace and tranquillity. It was at this same period that secret agents who were in the province of Kerman reported to Amir Masʿud that evildoers were wreaking mischief and that the ruling power there, the Amir of Baghdad, was not redressing their grievances because [Gh 430] he was wrapped up and incapacitated by troubles of his own.[139] The Amir's lofty resolution incited him to secure the annexation of that province, especially as Kerman bordered on Sistan; moreover, all the lands from Ray and Isfahan as far as Hamadan were under his obedience and were clients of this empire. There were discussions at Balkh on this matter with the Grand Vizier Aḥmad, son of Ḥasan, and they were engaged in this debate for some days, until at last it was decided that Aḥmad b. ʿAli b. [F 555] Nushtegin should be appointed governor and Commander-in-Chief, with Bu'l-Faraj Pārsi as his adjutant and counsellor of the army and in charge of finances and tax-collecting. Investiture patents for those offices were drawn up and were adorned with the royal signature and emblem. Exceptionally fine formal presents were bestowed: for the governor, a belt, a two-pointed hat, kettledrums, a standard, five elephants, and a complete outfit of other arms and equipment commensurate with these; and for the adjutant and administrator of the army, a saddle and trappings adorned with gold and a sword with its belt. Aḥmad b. ʿAli donned the robe of honour. Preparations were made, with a most impressive display of military strength. The Amir sent for the register listing the army's strength (*jarida-ye ʿarż*), and the Head of the Army Department came along. Four thousand cavalrymen were detailed to go with him, 2,000 of them Indians, 1,000 of them Turks and 1,000 of them Kurds and Arabs, together with 500 infantrymen of every kind. A letter was written to the head of the financial administration of Sistan for him to muster and equip 2,000 infantrymen from Sistan; and the salaries of these troops (i.e. of the main army) and the ones of those troops (i.e. the Sistani infantrymen), was to be paid out by Bu'l-Faraj out of the revenues frøm Kerman.

When these preparations were completed, the Amir mounted and rode out to the open country; and this army, with its senior officers wearing their gold belts and with full equipment, passed before him in review. They were fully armed and fitted out, and the Amir gave further verbal instructions to the governor Aḥmad b. ʿAli, the adjutant and counsellor of the army, and the senior officers. They took their formal leave and departed. They seized Kerman, and the bunch of Deylamite ruffians who were there took to their heels, and the governor and army adjutant and counsellor established effective control; the populace was contented and began to hand over taxes.

The Amir of Baghdad, who had enjoyed friendly relations with the late Amir Maḥmud and was in touch with him through diplomatic correspondence and missions, was hurt and offended by this episode and sent an envoy to Amir Masʿud with a strong message of protest. The reply went back from Sultan Masʿud, "That province, Kerman, adjoins our own territory on two sides. It was in a neglected state, and the subjects came seeking help against the evildoers. It was incumbent upon us to bring deliverance for the Muslims and, moreover, the Commander of the Faithful has sent us an investiture patent, instructing us to annex any such province that we see bereft of a lord or redresser of grievances."

The Amir of Baghdad [F 556] reproached the Caliph about this affair and conveyed his dismay. The Caliph gave the answer, "This debate must come to an end. Our very own backyard, Baghdad, Kufa and the Savād, are not kept in a peaceful enough state [Gh 431] for you to be entitled to speak about Kerman." The matter was closed. The enmity remained, but the Buyids were afraid of attempting to regain Kerman since our troops were gathering strength on the other side of Hamadan and they feared that Baghdad too might slip out of their hands.[140]

A period of time elapsed, and signs of weakness and vulnerability began to appear in Khorasan, Khwarazm and elsewhere. The Turkmens grew more powerful, and also, our own people in Kerman (i.e. the soldiers and financial officials) were taking too many liberties and going beyond accepted norms of behaviour, until the local populace became desperate and were crying out for redress. A few of them went secretly to the Amir of Baghdad's vizier, the Son of Māfanah,[141] bearing letters from the notables of Kerman seeking assistance and saying, "These Khorasani troops are off their guard and are preoccupied with their misdeeds. A contingent of cavalry should be sent, with an awe-inspiring commander, in such a way that the populace themselves join in the task, so that we might be delivered from the oppression of the Khorasanians and cast them out."

Ebn Māfanah and the Amir of Baghdad's army commander came unexpectedly with 5,000 cavalrymen, and en route a further 5,000 irregular troops (*del-angiz*)[142] joined up with them. They came upon Kerman unawares and entered it from two sides. At Narmāshir[143] a fierce battle took place, and the subjects joined in *en masse* against the army of Khorasan. Aḥmad b. ʿAli b. Nushtegin had fought well, but the Indian troops flagged and turned in flight, and the morale of the rest was shattered. Aḥmad was forced to retreat. He travelled along the Qāyen road to Nishapur with a detachment of troops from his personal guard and from the Sultan's army; another group made its way to Makrān. The Indian troops went to Sistan, and thence to Ghaznin.[144]

I, Bu'l-Fażl, had gone [F 557] to serve the Amir in the Garden of the Hundred Nightingales. I saw the senior officers of those Indian troops who had arrived there. The Amir had ordered them to be lodged in the great building where the Chancery has its seat. The court official[145] Bu Saʿid was bringing to them harsh, condemnatory messages from the Amir. Matters came to such a pitch that one message came with the order that they were to be beaten with canes.[146] Six of the most senior of the commanders slashed themselves with their daggers,[147] so that blood began to flow in that abode. I myself, Bu Saʿid and others left the house. This news was brought to the Amir, who said, [Gh 432] "These swords ought to have been wielded in Kerman!" He chastised them a great deal but in the end forgave them. After that, chaos and confusion took hold of the affairs of the realm, and it was never again possible to send an army to Kerman. Aḥmad b. ʿAli b. Nushtegin also came back, but felt ashamed and miserable, and it was not long before he died.

An account of Amir Masʿud's departure from Ghazna for the vicinity of Bost, and thence to Khorasan and Jorjān

When it was time to leave—the affairs of Khorasan, Khwarazm, Ray, Jebāl and other regions being as we have set forth—Amir Masʿud decided on an itinerary which would take him to Bost and then from there to travel to Herat; and from the central and focal position of Herat in Khorasan, he would then be able to see what he should decree regarding different issues. Amir Masʿud bestowed on Amir Saʿid a robe of honour and entrusted to him the capital Ghaznin, with the arrangement that he was to reside in the citadel at the Government

Headquarters and to preside over public hearings of grievances and receipt of petitions there, and the field officer Bu ʿAli the castellan was to be with the prince as his counsellor and adviser[148] for affairs of the state. He sent other amirs who were his sons, [F 558] with their household retinues, eunuchs and servants to the fortresses of Nāy and Diri.[149] He gave a robe of honour to Amir Mowdud with the intention that he should accompany him. He ordered letters to be written to Tilak to the effect that he should pursue with even greater effort the operations against Aḥmad, son of Ināltegin, which he had so zealously undertaken, having expelled the latter from Lahore and having brought forth the Judge (i.e. the Judge of Shiraz) and his supporters from the citadel, so that the Sultan's mind might be once and for all freed from any worries regarding the affair of Aḥmad b. Ināltegin. [He also ordered letters to be sent] to the vizier Aḥmad b. ʿAbd al-Ṣamad with instructions that when he had finished his business in Khottalān and Tokhārestān, he was to await orders to proceed to the royal court wherever the exalted banner might be.

When he had dealt with these important matters, the Amir set out from Ghaznin on Saturday, 26 Shavvāl [/13 September 1034]. On 7 Dhu'l-Qaʿda [/23 September] he arrived at Teginābād and spent seven days there. Only once did he drink wine, for his mind was pre-occupied with problems on several fronts. From there he came to Bost on Thursday, [Gh 433] the seventeenth of this month [/3 October] and installed himself in the Pavilion in the Plain of Logān. Many additional gardens, buildings and pavilions had been built there.[150]

Important letters arrived from Khorasan with news of the Turkmens and their incursions into the fringes of Merv, Sarakhs, Bādghis and Bāvard, and the excessive amount of harm inflicted by them, and of the impotence of the local officials and the military governor to oppose and restrain them. Suri had written, "If the lord, God forbid, doesn't head for Khorasan speedily, there is a danger of its being lost, for they are secretly receiving help from ʿAlitegin. Also, Hārun from his base in Khwarazm is doing his utmost to encourage them in their evil ways, and it is said that he has secretly arranged with ʿAlitegin that Hārun should move from Khwarazm towards Merv while ʿAlitegin makes for Termez and Balkh, and they should meet up with each other." The Amir became extremely perturbed when he received these pieces of news.

On Wednesday, the last day of this month [/16 October], he set off from Bost. En route, messengers arrived with a letter from Tilak that the deluded rebel Aḥmad b. Ināltegin had been killed [F 559], his son taken captive, and the Turkmens who used to be in his service had returned to obedience. At this news, the Amir became very joyful, and a heavy load was lifted from his shoulders. He ordered drums to be beaten and trumpets sounded, and the messengers to be given robes of honour and largesse; they were paraded round the army encampment and received great sums of money. The letters from Tilak, the Judge of Shiraz and the postal and intelligence service agents gave the following account:

"Tilak came to Lahore, and several Muslims who had allied themselves with Aḥmad were arrested. He ordered their right hands to be cut off. This open display of punishment and manifestation of power terrified those people who had joined up with Aḥmad, and they were seeking quarter for themselves and were dissociating themselves from him. The collecting of taxation and finance became organised and settled. Tilak, with a fully-armed and equipped force, and reinforced by a large horde of troops, mostly Indians, pursued Aḥmad closely. In the course of this pursuit, there were skirmishes and close engagements. Aḥmad experienced God's abandonment of him. Tilak was using blandishments and deceptions with Aḥmad's followers, and they were coming over to his side. There was a very fierce battle in which Aḥmad stood firm, but he was beaten and took to flight. The Turkmens deserted him en bloc and sought a pledge that they would not be punished (*amān*), which Tilak gave to them. Aḥmad, together with his personal guard and some others most closely implicated in his rebellion, 300 cavalrymen in all, fled. Tilak pursued him relentlessly. He had written letters [Gh 434] to the rebellious Indians, the Jāts,[151] for them to close the road against this God-forsaken one and for them to be on their guard, saying that, 'Whoever brings him alive, or his head, to me, I shall give him 500,000 dirhams.' For this reason, the world had become for Aḥmad constricted and cage-like, and his men began to go their own way. The end of his affair was that the Jāts and all kinds of other infidels were hot in pursuit of him. One day, he came to a river, being mounted on an elephant. He tried to get across. The Jāts, numbering some two or three thousand cavalry and infantrymen, attacked him, he having less than 200 cavalrymen left with him. He plunged into the river. The Jāts rushed in from two or three directions, mainly because they coveted the fine array of goods and belongings that he had with him. When they got near him, he tried to kill his son with his own hands, but the Jāts prevented this. His son was mounted on an elephant. [F 560] They dragged him off, and launched arrows and wielded short spears[152] and swords against Aḥmad. He struggled valiantly to defend himself but in the end they killed him and cut off his head. As for the retainers who were left with him, some were killed and others were taken as prisoners; and a great amount of money and valuables fell into the hands of those Jāts. Their chief immediately sent messengers to Tilak, who was not far away, and they gave these good tidings. Tilak was filled with great joy. Representatives of his came to a meeting and had discussions with the aim that Aḥmad's son and his severed head should be sent to Tilak. There was talk about the sum of 500,000 dirhams. Tilak said, 'You've acquired a great amount of wealth plundered from this man's possessions. It was a notable act of service that you did for the Sultan, and you will receive the benefits from that; now you must be compliant.' Twice the envoy had to go to-and-fro and seek instructions. They eventually agreed on 100,000 dirhams. Tilak sent the money, and they brought Aḥmad's head and his son to him. He turned back towards Lahore with his mission accomplished and so that he might put in order the remainder of affairs and, after that, hasten towards the exalted court as speedily as possible, *with the permission of the Almighty God*."

The Amir ordered congratulatory responses to be sent, and he heaped favours and praises on Tilak and the other commanders. The envoys were sent back and Tilak was ordered to return to the court bringing the head of Aḥmad b. Ināltegin and the latter's son. Such is the end of those guilty of treachery and rebellion![153] [Gh 435] From the time of Adam to this present day, it has always been the case that no servant has risen in revolt against his master without losing his own head; since this is set down in books, I shall not dwell on it at length. The Amir ordered that letters about this event should be written to men of eminence and notables, to the distant provinces of the empire and to client princes, and he sent off messengers, for indeed it was a great victory.[154]

The Amir reached Herat on Thursday, 15 Dhu'l-Ḥejja [/31 October 1034], and on Wednesday, the twenty-first of this month [/6 November] he set off from Herat on the road to Pushang with the aim of proceeding to Sarakhs, and he reviewed the army there at Pushang. They had brought Moẓaffar b. Ṭāher, the chief tax collector and local governor (*'āmel va za'im*) of Pushang, in bonds. [F 561] The head of the Divān of Khorasan, Suri, had made false insinuations about him, and had enlisted allies like Bu Sahl Zowzani and others hoping to bring about his downfall (for Bu Sahl had been rehabilitated through the exalted favour, and he had come back to the court and taken up his role as a boon-companion[155]). As the inexorable workings of fate would have it, at that very moment when Moẓaffar's case was being brought up, the Amir, may God sanctify his spirit, was feeling extremely harassed and very irate, since letters had arrived with news of the Turkmens and their depredations. The Amir cried out in vexation, "This pimp Moẓaffar must be strung upside down!"[156] A somewhat stupid-minded palace chamberlain called Khumārtegin T.r.sh.k,[157] who was a former retainer of Sultan Maḥmud, and who had been a man of courage and manly qualities, came out and mentioned these words of the Sultan. Suri's followers and all those who were enemies of Moẓaffar seized the opportunity offered by these words, and speedily handed over 1,000 dinars to this chamberlain. Without referring the case back to the Amir, the chamberlain ordered that Moẓaffar b. Ṭāher should be strung up from one of the trees growing by the side of the palace; he was hanged from it, and gave up the ghost.

Khᵛāja Bu Naṣr Moshkān was in the Divān. He became highly distressed at this news, and he summoned the Commander of the Guard and Moḥtāj,[158] and spoke to them most severely and upbraided them, saying, "This is no minor matter which has occurred. The Sultan may give orders when he is carried away by anger; in such cases, there should be a period of delay, for the man Moẓaffar was not a common thief." They replied. "A chamberlain appeared and gave this order. We were wrong not to refer this matter back and enquire about it further. Fate [F 562] has now wrought its work; what does the Khᵛāja ordain?" He replied, "What can I ordain? The Amir is bound to hear about this, and I cannot possibly know what he may ordain." They went away shaken and mortified.

The Amir's original anger subsided, and he decided to have some food, and he summoned Bu Naṣr. In the midst of the meal, [Gh 436] the matter of Pushang came up. The Amir said, "What excuse is this presumptuous cur putting forward?"—he meant Moẓaffar—"for the oppression which he has inflicted on the poor folk of these regions?" Bu Naṣr answered, "May the lord live for ever! How is Moẓaffar going to say anything ever again and how can he speak?" The Amir said, "What's the reason for this and what's happened to him?" Bu Naṣr looked towards the Commander of the Palace Gholāms, Begtughdï. Begtughdï said, "May the lord live for ever! Moẓaffar was hanged according to the exalted command." The Amir said, "What are you saying?", and he let out a loud exclamation and stopped eating. The commander explained further. The Amir became furious and said, "It's very remarkable that people can be killed as easily as this, especially a man like Moẓaffar! You are the Commander, and you were in the palace; why did you agree to this, and why didn't you inform us about it?" He answered, "May the lord's life be prolonged! I am the Commander of the Palace Gholāms and have very heavy responsibilities; apart from these, I don't concern myself at all with anything else and I don't say anything about other matters arising at the court. I only heard about this man after they had killed him."

The Amir rose from the table irradiating anger and washed his hands. The Commander Begtughdï was summoned and given a seat. The Amir said, "Summon this palace chamberlain," and he was summoned, quaking with fear. He said, "O dog, why was this man killed?" He replied, "The lord said so-and-so, and I assumed it was what he genuinely wanted." He said, "Seize him!" The household servants seized him. He said, "Take him outside the tent and administer 1,000 strokes of the stick [F 563] as if he were a mere slave until he confesses exactly how this happened." They bore him out and started beating him. He confessed, and the Amir became fully informed about the story of the money (i.e. the bribe paid to have Moẓaffar hanged). He was carried away by intense anger against Bu Sahl and Suri. The Commander of the Guard and Moḥtāj were summoned. The Amir said, "Why did you kill Moẓaffar?" They replied, "The lord's command arrived by word of a chamberlain's mouth." He said, "Why didn't you refer back once again and make enquiries?" They replied, "That should have been done; we'll do so in future. The Amir said, "If it wasn't for what this palace chamberlain has said, I would order your heads to be cut off. Just now, each of you must receive 1,000 strokes, so that after this you will be more careful." Both men were taken away and beaten.

The Year 426
[/16 November 1034–4 November 1035]

[Gh 436, F 563] The first day of the year fell on a Saturday.[1] The Amir reached Sarakhs [Gh 437] on 4 Moḥarram [/19 November].[2] The camp enclosure and the large tent had been erected on the bank of a large stream,[3] and there were plenty of troops in the army encampment.

On Sunday, the ninth of this month [/24 November], a letter arrived from the postal and intelligence officer of Ray announcing the death of Bu'l-Ḥasan Sayyāri, God's mercy be upon him. He held the office of head of the Divān there, a most capable and worthy man. The Amir ordered a letter to be written to Sistan, where ʿAziz Pushanja was in charge of the collection of taxes (*mostaḥeththi*), commanding him to proceed to Ray and take up the office of head of the Divān there.[4] A letter also went to Khᵛāja Bu Sahl Ḥamdavi, the civil governor[5] of Western Persia notifying him of this arrangement.

During these two or three days, confidential letters arrived from Khwarazm with the news that Hārun was making preparations for a march on Merv. The Amir forwarded those secret letters to the Grand Vizier [F 564] Aḥmad b. ʿAbd al-Ṣamad, and a confidential response arrived here from the Grand Vizier,[6] which I deciphered. He had written: "Although I was busy with the affairs of Khottalān and Tokhārestān, I took in hand the matter of Khwarazm and the God-forsaken wretch Hārun, since that is our most serious and pressing problem. Thanks to the blessed fortune of the exalted realm, the matter is now mostly rectified, although much gold had to be expended for that end. Plans have been finalized so that, on the day when the accursed Hārun decides to set out from Khwarazm for Merv, those ten gholāms who have pledged their allegiance to my own trusty agents, will overwhelm him and dispose of him at once. After his death, his schemes will be scotched, and his plans will come to nought. My son ʿAbd al-Jabbār will come out of his hiding-place, ready for action, and take control of the city [of Khwarazm].[7] He will refurbish the army with weapons and a distribution of money, since the greater part of the troops are men of Sultan Maḥmud and of Altuntāsh and are on my side. I have done all that was humanly possible. Let us now see what happens and what God Most High has decreed. These ten gholāms are the ones closest to Hārun, and have already several times endeavoured to carry out the deed, but to no avail, since Hārun remains within his palace at all times and is for ever on the watch, and he never rides out for an outing in the open air or for hunting or for polo-playing, being fully occupied with preparations for the attack on Merv. God willing, this over-reaching, luckless soul will not achieve his wish and the curse brought down on him for his rebellion will bring about his own downfall."[8]

When I decoded the encrypted message[9] and wrote out a clear and comprehensible copy,[10] Khᵛāja Bu Naṣr read it at the time of the afternoon worship and was highly delighted, and he went to render service at court. After the formal audience and when the court session broke up, the topic of Aḥmad b. Ināltegin [Gh 438] was raised, and everyone [F 565] had something to say; and they also began to talk about Hārun and Khwarazm. The General Bu'l-Nażr said, "Hārun's case is akin to that of Aḥmad, and we should have some news to arrive at any time now." The Amir said, "*The favourable omen is the true one,* and God willing, it may well turn out as you say." Bu Naṣr gave the transcribed version (*tarjama*) of the message to the Turk who acted as Keeper of the Royal Inkstand. The Amir read it and folded it up,[11] and it was given back to Bu Naṣr. They discussed matters for a further hour. The Amir made a sign, and those present went home. Khᵛāja Bu Naṣr had also returned but he was summoned back again, and they remained closeted together in private talk till the time of the evening worship. He then returned and came back to the tent. He summoned me and said, "The Amir was highly delighted at the coded message that came, and he said, "My decision was that we should proceed to Merv; but if the matter of Hārun is settled and done with, we must make for Nishapur, so that we may restore some order to the unruly and chaotic state of Ray and Jebāl, and so that the people of Gorgān may forward the taxation due." I replied, "May the lord's life be prolonged! Whether the matter of Hārun is settled and done with—and, God willing, it will be settled very soon, since there are already signs pointing that way—or whether it drags on, my best advice would be that the lord should proceed to Merv—for these Turkmens have spread throughout the fringes of that province and are now concentrating the greater part of their strength on the regions of Balkh and Tokhārestān—so that they may be dealt with and cut off from their support and resources in Transoxania; for secret agents in Bokhara and Samarqand have written that others bent on mischief are preparing to cross the Oxus. When the exalted banner is near to Balkh and the Oxus, being at Merv, which is the central point of Khorasan, all these threats of instability will be dispelled." The Amir said, "That's exactly so. At all events, let us now remain here for some days at Sarakhs so that we may see how things develop." And in matters like these, Bu Naṣr was the most far-sighted and perspicacious person in the world. May God Most High have mercy on all [F 566] who have passed on, *through His kindness, His grace and the breadth of His benevolence!*

On Sunday, 15 Moḥarram [/30 November 1034] the Commander-in-Chief ʿAli b. ʿAbdallāh[12] came to the army encampment and saw the Amir, and reported on what he had done in the course of his mission away from the court.

On Wednesday, the twenty-sixth of this month [/11 December], a letter arrived from Balkh announcing the death[13] of the General Begtegin, son-in-law of the Commander-in-Chief, who held the offices of castellan and governor of Termez. He had performed many an important service in the time of Amir Maḥmud, in that he captured the Commander-in-Chief of the Shāhanshāhis (i.e. the Buyids), Bu Naṣr b. Ṭeyfur, in the rural district of Nishapur and brought him to Ghazna.[14] In the time of this [Gh 439] present monarch, he displayed praiseworthy acts of service at Teginābād in the matter of Amir Moḥammad, Sultan Masʿud's brother, as I have previously mentioned.

Now, as Fate would have it, a strong detachment of Turkmens came into the fringes of Termez and did a great deal of damage and plundering in Qobādhiyān,[15] and drove off the livestock. The General Begtegin, well-equipped and with a full array of troops, pursued them. They fell back before him and entered Andkhud and Mila.[16]

Begtegin was driving them on relentlessly. He caught up with them in the neighbourhood of Shoburqān and battle was joined from mid-morning till the time of the two worships (i.e. the afternoon and evening ones). There was fierce fighting[F 567] and many men were killed, mostly Turkmens, and in the end, those God-forsaken wretches fled the field and took to the desert. Begtegin went after them. His close retainers said, "The enemy has fled in a battered and bruised state; it would be imprudent to pursue them further." But he defied them, for his decreed span of life had come to its close. He came upon a group of the most battle-hardened of the enemy, and fierce fighting was renewed, for the fugitives were fighting for their lives. Begtegin came up against one of their cavalrymen. He sought to attack him, and raised himself up in the saddle; a gap appeared in his mailed coat exposing his lower abdomen. One of the Turkmens suddenly shot an arrow that struck him there. He stood his ground while in pain, and with much exertion and great difficulty pulled out the arrow without letting his followers know, until it became too painful to bear and he turned back. When he reached the camp which had been made along the road, they opened up a silk brocade covering from a beast which was being led along, lifted him down from his horse and laid him down to rest. He died, and the army came to Shoburqān and buried him there. When, after three days, the Turkmens heard about this disaster, they came back.

The Amir was saddened by this news, for Begtegin was a fine commander. He immediately summoned the Commander-in-Chief ʿAli b. ʿAbdallāh[17] and reviewed the situation with him. ʿAli replied, "May all our lives be offered up as a sacrifice in the lord's service! Although the Grand Vizier is there, Tokhārestān and Guzgānān up to the banks of the Oxus are now bereft of a military commander; a commander with a mighty army must unavoidably be sent." The Amir said, "The Commander-in-Chief must go with an army and hem in these brutish camel-drivers[18] and inflict a drubbing on them, and [F 568] then proceed to Balkh." He replied, "I'm at your service; when should I go?" He said, "The day after tomorrow; given the importance of this news, [Gh 440] one should depart with alacrity." ʿAli expressed his obedience, kissed the ground and went back. Those men who were previously appointed to go with him and had come during the course of this week were re-appointed for this task (i.e. for ʿAli's army). On

Friday, the twenty-eighth of the month of Moḥarram [/13 December 1034], ʿAli came to render service and saw the Amir, and departed for Guzgānān. In accordance with the exalted command, Khᵛāja Bu Naṣr appointed the secretary Bu Sahl Hamadāni as officer for the army in charge of intelligence and the conveying of messages, and he departed with the Commander-in-Chief.[19] ʿAli accomplished that commission well, since he was prudent by nature and knew how to lead and manage an army in campaigns. He subjugated those ruffian camel-drivers and imposed contractual agreements upon them, and then headed for Balkh, leaving behind a formidable and awe-inspiring impression. The next day, Saturday, two mounted messengers brought a letter from Merv, sent by the Sultan's special servant (*khāṣṣa*) Nushtegin,[20] with the words "A detachment of Turkmens, fleeing before the victorious army,[21] came here from the direction of Sarakhs. When I got news of this, I rode off, fully armed, with my personal gholāms and the army, and caught up with them. A fierce battle ensued, lasting from the time of the midday worship till nightfall, until they finally took to flight towards the desert of Dah Gonbadān.[22] It would have been imprudent to pursue them into the desert at night. When news arrived the next day that they had made a clear break,[23] I came back and ordered an awesome display of might and power, and the heads of those slain, about 200 in all, were stuck up on poles as a dire warning, and twenty-four of their most doughty warriors, who were captured in the fighting, have been sent forward for the royal judgement to pronounce on their disposal." The Amir was drinking wine [F 569] when this good news arrived. He gave orders for the messengers to be given robes of honour and presents of largesse, and they were led in a triumphal parade accompanied by the sound of trumpets and drums. At the time of the afternoon worship on that day, while he was in a wine-drinking feast, he ordered the captives to be thrown down for trampling before the elephants in front of the large tent. It was a day for striking terror, and the news of it spread far and wide.

On Monday, 8 Ṣafar [/23 December 1034], the Grand Vizier Aḥmad b. ʿAbd al-Ṣamad came back victorious and with much booty. Great deeds had been accomplished by him on the borders of Khottalān and Tokhārestān. He had restored peace and calm to those regions, and a great display of power and prestige had been made there. In accordance with the royal command that he had received, he had entrusted the regions to the Great Chamberlain Bilgetegin, and had returned home, and was met by a welcoming party in a most worthy manner. When he came into the Amir's presence, he was received very warmly before the whole court, followed immediately afterwards by a private audience.

The Head of the Chancery was also present at this session. I heard from him that the Amir said to the Vizier, "Thanks to the persistent and valiant efforts of the Vizier, the situation in Tokhārestān and Khottalān has become settled, and God willing, the matter of Hārun too will soon reach a satisfactory conclusion. The Turkmens fled in terror and departed, and the majority of them [Gh 441] dragged themselves to Farāva from the vicinity of Bāvard and Nasā. A powerful army under the Master of the Royal Stables Böri, and several generals and senior commanders of high renown, went in pursuit of them. ʿAbdus is acting as adjutant, counsellor and executive officer (*kadkhodā'i u moshir u modabber*) of that army. Suri has likewise been ordered to proceed along the road to Ostovā[24] with the General Qadïr and the military governor of Nishapur and Ṭus, fully equipped and armed, and to join up with this army (i.e. that of Böri); and they are not to turn back from pursuing the enemy until the latter takes refuge in the Balkhān Kuh range. Suri has taken with him all necessary supplies of food and fodder and equipment necessary for a desert campaign. We have ourselves decided to proceed to Merv and spend this winter there so that everything becomes settled and order is restored completely. What does the Vizier [F 570] say about this?" Aḥmad replied, "This is the only correct solution. Through these measures, Khwarazm can be recovered and these Turkmens cleared out of Khorasan; moreover, they will not dare to cross the Oxus (i.e. to invade Khorasan again)." The Amir said, "Return to your places now; we can give these plans further thought, for we are going to be here for a few more days yet." They went back. The Vizier went to his tent, and the people of prominence, notables and courtiers went to render service and to offer their greetings to him.

On Sunday, 14 Ṣafar [29 December 1034], Ṭāher the secretary, Bu'l-Moẓaffar Ḥabashi the postal and intelligence officer, and several others, were brought back from Ray by swift-riding *kheyltāsh*s, but without being manacled.[25] They were held at the entrance of the large tent and camp enclosure, mounted on mules and in litters,[26] and the Amir was informed. He ordered that they should be held in the guard tent. All of them were held captive there. At the time of the afternoon worship, the Amir held court. After the court session, the secretary ʿErāqi went to and fro with verbal messages between the Amir and them. The final outcome was that Bu'l-Moẓaffar was given a thousand lashes on a flogging frame. (He was a most capable and noble-minded individual and a very close friend of the Head of the Chancery, Bu Naṣr Moshkān, but the latter did not dare to breathe a word in mitigation because the Amir was so enraged.) After Bu'l-Moẓaffar, four of Ṭāher's financial officials and others of his followers were likewise given a thousand strokes. He also ordered that Ṭāher should be lashed, but pleas for leniency and intercession [Gh 442] were made by all and sundry until he forgave him the beatings. Ṭāher was taken to India and held captive in the fortress of Giri,[27] and the rest were taken to the town of Sarakhs and held there in the prison. Bu Naṣr spent much effort [F 571] in the case of Bu'l-Moẓaffar so that he would be well treated in jail. He remained incarcerated for a year, and then a favourable opportunity was sought and intercession made until he was freed. Ṭāher fell out of favour with the Amir and his reputation was tarnished, so that he was never given a post again and died out of office. *We seek refuge in God from reversals of fortune!*

On Wednesday, 17 Ṣafar [1 January 1035], after the court session, the Amir had a private meeting with the Vizier, the Head of the Chancery, retainers and courtiers. Khᵛāja Ḥoseyn, the palace intendant,[28] was also there. They discussed the forthcoming move, and it was decided that they should proceed to Merv, and having reached that decision, the meeting ended and they dispersed. Khᵛāja Ḥoseyn, the palace intendant, put in hand preparations for the journey, and on the twentieth of this month [/4 January 1035] he set out for Merv in order that he might give commands for extensive supplies of food and fodder to be assembled so that there should be no lack of these when the victorious banner should arrive there. Three days after his departure, the Amir gave orders for the camp enclosure to be erected on the road to Merv at a distance of three parasangs from the army encampment. The festival of Sada[29] was approaching. The royal camels and those of the entire army were brought into the open plain, and they began gathering tamarisk branches so that Sada could be celebrated before they set out on the journey. They brought the tamarisk branches they had gathered to the plain, where there was a large stream, filled with snow,[30] and piled snow up on it until it became as high as a citadel. They constructed quadrangular arched edifices (*chahār-ṭāq*), of great height, out of wood and filled them up with tamarisk branches, and they collected more tamarisk branches for there was an abundance of it which grew on a huge mountain [nearby]. They also provided many eagles and pigeons and whatever would add to the glitter and splendour of this night.[31] [F 572]

I heard from Khᵛāja Bu Naṣr as follows: The Grand Vizier said to me, "What are the odds and probability that the arrangements to go to Merv are still on and running smoothly?" I replied, "Until the Amir actually sets out, we can't be sure." He said, "Why all these doubts and speculations when the camp enclosure[32] has already been set up on the way and the palace intendant has gone ahead?" I replied, "Both the camp enclosure and the palace intendant can be brought back again. There's no point in putting one's heart into this venture until we have covered at least one or two stages on the way to Merv."

Sada came along. On the first night the Amir installed himself under an awning which had been put up on that river bank. The boon-companions and musicians and singers came along, [Gh 443] and the wood pile was set on fire. (I heard later that the flames of that fire could be seen from about ten parasangs away.) They released pigeons smeared with naphtha, and began to let run wild beasts smeared with pitch[33] and set alight. It was a Sada whose like I never saw again, and the whole affair ended up in joyful celebration.

The next day, the Amir did not hold court. On the day after that, he held a private session after the public court session, with the Vizier and the prominent figures and pillars of state, and said, "I set my mind on our going to Merv, but now I have thought the matter over. The royal special servant Nushtegin is there with a well-equipped army. He attacked a detachment of the Turkmens and they fled before him. We shall send a further contingent of cavalry to join up with him as reinforcements. Suri and ʿAbdus went to Nasā with a powerful army, and the Commander-in-Chief ʿAli to Guzgānān and Balkh. The Great Chamberlain is in Tokhārestān with an army. These armies are close to each other. As for ʿAlitegin, he has made a pact with us,[34] and the others would not dare to make a move against us. [F 573] As I see it, the correct course is to proceed to Nishapur so that we can be near to Ray and make our presence felt and resolve the current entanglements and difficulties. The people of Gorgān will be stricken with fear, and they will forward the stipulated tribute due for the last two years." The Vizier replied, "The correct view is what the exalted judgement envisages." Bu Naṣr did not breathe a word. The Generals Begtughdï, Sübashï[35] and Bu'l-Nażr did not feel bold enough to comment on such matters, especially now that the Vizier had spoken in these terms.[36]

The Amir gave orders that a letter should be written to the palace intendant Ḥoseyn instructing him to return and for the great marquee to be brought back. They obeyed the order and went back. Two swift-riding *kheyltāsh*s were designated, the letter was written, and they speedily mounted and rode off. Bu Naṣr said to the Vizier, "Did the Grand Vizier observe how they would not allow a sound scheme to go forward?" He answered, "I saw that. All this is the secretary ʿErāqi's doing, as I have learnt, but now is not the time to say anything. At any rate, we shall go along to Nishapur where the Amir will halt a while. Then if we see that this ʿErāqi has managed to persuade the Amir to go to Gorgān and Sāri purely for his own selfish motives, so that the people of that province should witness his splendour and luxurious trappings and his closeness to the Amir, and the Amir makes preparations for going, I shall expound in a forthright manner the erroneousness of this journey, and I shall abjure all responsibility for it. For ʿErāqi has taken leave of his senses; he says anything which comes into his mind, and this lord takes it all in, since ʿErāqi has made him believe that there is no-one who gives better advice than him. In truth, thanks to him, Khorasan and Western Persia will be lost, as I can well see." [Gh 444]

The attendants brought back the grand marquee[37] and set off in the direction of Nishapur. On Sunday, 27 Ṣafar [11 January 1035], the Amir, may God be pleased with him, left Sarakhs, and he arrived at Nishapur on Saturday, 4 Rabiʿ I [/17 January] and encamped at Shādyākh. The year was a dry one, and the winter had gone by to the extent that around twenty days of the month of Bahman[38] [F 574] had elapsed before the first snow, some four fingers deep, fell at Nishapur. Everyone was amazed at this, and later the effects of this drought became apparent; I shall relate its strange and remarkable manifestations.

On the third day after the arrival at Nishapur, the Amir held a private session with the Vizier and the great men of state. Bu'l-Ḥasan ʿErāqi stood near the throne, and there was talk on all sorts of topics. The Amir said, "I won't tarry here longer than a week, since Khorasan has been pacified, the Turkmens have gone off to Hell and the army is on their tail. In this way, the supply of food and fodder will remain intact here in Nishapur until we return in the summer. Suri will come back here soon and will see to any other matters. It is said that at Dehestān ten *mans* of wheat can be had for a dirham, and fifteen *mans* of barley for the same sum. We will go there, and that food and fodder can be consumed freely, there will be plenty to eat for the army and they will escape the rigours of the cold,[39] and we shall be near Khwarazm and Balkhān Kuh. ʿAbdus and the army will hear that we are in Dehestān and will take comfort from it. The news will also reach Ray and Jebāl that we have set off from Nishapur for that region; Bu Sahl, Tāsh and the garrison who are there will be much heartened. The Son of Kāku and other rebellious elements will be forced to toe the line. Tāsh can go as far as Hamadan, for he will face no resistance or opposition there. The gold and the clothing which have been collected together at Ray can be brought back to the court. Bā Kālijār is to send the tribute of Gorgān, stipulated according to the agreement and owing for the last two years, together with the presents and, moreover, he is to come and render service. If he decides to play up, we will perforce go to Setārābād, and, if needs be, also to Sāri and Āmol since it is only a short distance.[40] It is said that there are a million people in Āmol; if one dinar is taken from each person, there will be a million dinars, and clothing and gold will also be acquired. All this will be straightened out within three or four months. When we get back to Nishapur some time after Nowruz, if desired we can spend the summer there, and Suri and the subjects can get together everything necessary in the way of food and fodder. We have decided on this course of action, and we shall undoubtedly go. [Gh 445, F 575] What is your opinion about this, and what do you say?"

The Grand Vizier Aḥmad b. ʿAbd al-Ṣamad looked at the gathering there and said, "You are the leading men of the army; what do you say?" They replied, "We are obedient servants, who are brought here to fight wars, wield our swords and add more provinces to the empire; whatever the lord Sultan commands, we will slavishly follow even unto death. This is our brief; questions of what should be done and what should not be done, of what is fitting and what is not fitting, fall into the domain of the Khᵛāja, since he is the Vizier, and are no business of ours."

The Vizier said, "Although Aḥmad b. Ināltegin has been overthrown, India is in turmoil. From here to Ghaznin is a long way, and it is unwise to turn our back on Ghaznin and India. Also, there have been rumours going around that ʿAlitegin has passed away and has yielded up his soul to the Almighty, and this rings true to me since I have heard that he has died from an illness that he was suffering from.[41] He was a shrewd, crafty and experienced man, and he knew how to deal tactfully with each side. The Turkmens and Seljuqs were the backbone of his military power, and he used to keep them on his side by the power of his words and through the silver in his purse, for he knew that if they broke away from him, he would become weakened.[42] Since his death, the reins of government in that province have fallen into the hands of his two feeble children, and from what I have heard, the relations between the Seljuqs on one side and the two sons and ʿAlitegin's commander-in-chief Qunush[43] on the other, are not good. In all likelihood those enmities will intensify and the Seljuqs will no longer be able to stay there. They cannot head for Khwarazm since, as arranged and as already put in motion by me, by now Hārun will have set out for Merv and will have been killed, those regions will have become disturbed and Shāh Malek[44] will have made his way there, he being a fierce enemy of the Seljuqs. They will have nowhere to go but Khorasan. I fear that they will come to Khorasan out of necessity, for they will have heard about the present situation here of the horde of Buqa, Yaghmur, [F 576] Köktāsh and the rest, who are their dependants (*chākerān*). If at that point, God forbid, things happen thus, and the lord is absent, the situation will become very long-drawn out. The correct course of action is what the lord had pondered over first, before the exalted judgement decided against it, that he should go to Merv. I have set forth what I know according to the extent of my knowledge; the final command rests with the lord."

The Amir said, "My special servant Nushtegin is at Merv with a fully-equipped army, and there are two powerful commanders with armies at Balkh and in Tokhārestān. How will it be possible for the Turkmens of the Oxus river region to attack Merv and to emerge from the desert? The successors of Altuntāsh are busy on their own sorting out their affairs. There is no other sound course of action for us but to go to Dehestān until we see how things go in Khwarazm." The Vizier said, "It can't be anything but auspicious!"

The Amir said to the General Sübashï, "The camel-drivers must be instructed not to take the camels to more distant places for pasturing, since we intend to depart within five days' time, and we want a senior commander to remain here with Suri's deputies so that when Suri arrives, they can join up with him to gather together food and fodder for our return. The rest of the army will go, in its entirety, under our own banner." Sübashï obeyed the command. He then said to Bu Naṣr Moshkān, "Letters must be written to Merv and Balkh instructing them to be vigilant and to keep watch over the entry points into the desert and the crossing-places over the Oxus with great care. For we are going to head for Dehestān so that, from that region, we may be facing towards Khwarazm, Nasā and Balkhān Kuh, and the Turkmens may be scared off en bloc from Khorasan, and all our sources of worry may disappear." He said to the General Begtughdï, the Commander of the Palace Gholāms, "Get the palace gholāms properly organised and ready, leaving the invalids and the sick here in the citadel. The rest are to go, fully equipped and armed, with our banner, [F 577] likewise the horses which are to be led." They arose and departed.

I heard from Khᵛāja Bu Naṣr Moshkān, who said: When we had gone back, the Amir summoned me on my own, and talked to me in private, saying, "You didn't say anything on these topics!" I replied, "May the lord's life be prolonged! It was a lengthy session, and everyone said what he knew. I am a secretary by profession and do not go outside my own field." He said, "Yes, indeed, but for a long time now you have been involved in important matters of state, and I am well aware of the fact that whatever my father used to do, and whatever decision he used to make, when everyone had had their say and had gone back home, he would discuss with you, since you possess a clear judgement and such unique regard and selfless concern for the welfare of the state." I answered, "May the lord's life be prolonged! If what they have told the lord concerning the position in Dehestān, Gorgān and Ṭabarestān and the availability of food and fodder, gold and clothing there turns out to be true, and nothing untoward occurs in Khorasan, this is an excellent course of action, and one of great value and benefit. But if there is the possibility that some crisis may occur in the future—*we seek refuge in God [from such a happening]!*—and those desired ends may not be achieved, it would be a better and sounder policy to reconsider these plans. I shall say no more, for I do not want to give the impression that I am interceding on behalf of Bā Kālijār and the people of Gorgān. False rumours are rife at court implying that I am an advocate for that group and am their spokesman. I swear to God that I am not, nor ever have been, and have never had any other goal but the welfare of the realm. [Gh 447] The matter of the Gorgānis can be satisfactorily settled by means of messages containing sound advice and by sending an envoy, unless there is some other aim in view." The Amir said, "We do have other intentions, as you have heard at several court sessions, and we have to make this expedition." I replied, "May the God Most High crown this expedition with good results and complete success!" and I went back.

The Vizier was waiting for me, having heard the news that the Amir had had a private meeting with me. When I arrived, he said, "You were there a long time." I recounted to him what had happened. [F 578] He said, "The plan of this ʿErāqi has been assiduously implanted in the Amir's head; it was made firm at Sarakhs; and here at Nishapur it is being nurtured by this same ʿErāqi and is made to look even more delectable by the day. You will see what the outcome will be and what I am apprehensive about.[45] Although things are the way they are, I am going to write a memorandum (*roqʿat*) and will speak out more clearly, but no-one but you should present it to the Amir." I answered, "I'll do that, but it won't do any good." The Vizier said, "I shall do what is incumbent upon me, so that when the time comes and he feels remorseful about this expedition—and by God, he *will* rue the day, for he has insisted upon it purely out of obduracy and sheer wilfulness—he will not be able to say that no-one pointed out the pitfalls of this way; and I want you personally to pass on this message so that you can be my witness. I know that he will take it badly—he already regards me with disfavour, and I will descend even further in his estimation and he will revile me—but I consent to it and will never refrain from giving sound advice." I said, "The lord has spoken well; this is what religion, faith and our sense of gratitude to the Amir decree." I went off to the Divān. He had ordered letters to be prepared for Merv, Balkh and other places, and these were written out and sent off.

The next day, when the royal audience was over and the Vizier was about to depart, the Amir said, "We are still set on leaving the day after tomorrow." The Vizier said, "May it be an auspicious day, and may all your desires be fulfilled! In this context, I have written a memorandum, and have also given Bu Naṣr a verbal message. If the exalted judgement sees fit, he will present them to you." The Amir indicated his assent and they departed. The Vizier gave that memorandum to Bu Naṣr. It was expressed in a most comprehensive manner, replete with sound advice. In a forthright manner he had written: "It is not the place for servants to tell their lords that they should do such-and-such a thing, since great and noble lords can do and can ordain whatever they wish; but it is incumbent upon a servant who has secured such a position as I have—thanks to the lord's confidence in me [F 579]—not to withhold sincere advice on any matter. Yesterday there was discussion about this journey to Dehestān, and the exalted judgement made the decision that we should set forth. The army commanders [Gh 448] in that state audience said that no matter what the command was, their task was necessarily to carry out the orders, unquestioning obedience being the pillar of their profession.[46] But when they came out with me, they told me in private that they regarded the journey as an unsound venture and absolved themselves of any direct responsibility for it. What is being presented to the exalted judgement stems solely from good will and a desire to offer sound advice, so that if—God forbid!—anything should go wrong, the lord will not say that, amongst our servants, not one showed us the pitfalls of this way. However, it is for the lord to issue commands for anything he may ordain, and servants have no alternative but to obey."

Bu Naṣr said, "This memorandum is most trenchant and thoroughgoing; what verbal message shall I deliver with it? The Vizier replied, "It depends on how it is received by the Amir, for it should be pitched accordingly and should adhere to the written missive." He went and delivered the memorandum. The Amir read it through carefully twice and then said, "What's the verbal message?" Bu Naṣr said, "The Vizier says, 'I strive to observe the rules of decorum, but here I had to speak at length and to speak openly. As long as I am involved in matters of state, I shall express and expound what I know to the full extent of my knowledge. Everything is written down in the memorandum. The final point is this: I say that it is unsound policy to travel to this region and to leave Khorasan neglected, with so much turmoil and so many rebellious elements and troublesome opportunists about there. For the rest, it is for the lord to command.'" The Amir said, "These words of the Vizier don't add up to much. Khorasan and the approaches to it are full of troops; the 'Erāqi Turkmens have fled, having been driven back to Balkhān Kuh with the army hot on their heels. It is clear how far we are from Dehestān and Gorgān, and whenever we wish we can get back to Nishapur within a fortnight." [F 580] Bu Naṣr said, "This is exactly the case, and it is for the Sultan to give orders; but servants, most notably the Vizier, have a duty to say their piece." He replied, "Just so."

The Amir left Nishapur for Gorgān on Sunday, 12 Rabi' I [/25 January 1035] travelling via the Esfarāyen road.[47] On the way it felt bitterly cold, with very strong winds, especially up to the head of the Dinār-e Sāri valley[48] (we were travelling in the month of Esfandārmodh),[49] and I, Bu'l-Fażl, was feeling so terribly cold while riding my horse that when we reached the head of this valley I felt as if I was not wearing anything at all, in spite of the fact that I had taken all precautions and was wearing quilted trousers stuffed with feathers[50] [Gh 449] and a jacket of red fox fur, and had donned a rainproof coat.[51] When we came to the Dinār-e Sāri pass and entered the valley—the distance having been only two parasangs—those winter clothes suddenly felt burdensome and heavy upon me (i.e. because of the sudden rise in temperature). When we came out of the valley I saw the whole world covered with narcissus, violets, and all kinds of aromatic plants and greenery, with countless trees densely packed together on the plain as far as one could see.[52] Truly, no more pleasant region than Gorgān and Ṭabarestān exists, but it is very plague-ridden, just as Bu'l-Fażl Badi' has said:[53]

> *Jorjān! What has let you know what Jorjān is!—A mouthful of figs and speedy death!*[54]*—When a carpenter sees a Khorāsāni, he makes [for him] a bier made according to his size!*[55]

The Amir arrived in the town of Gorgān on Sunday, the twenty-sixth of the month [F 581] of Rabi' I [/8 February 1035]. He passed by the tomb of Qābus which is on the road,[56] and camp was made at a place on the other side of the town at a place called Moḥammadābād, on the banks of a large river.[57] As he was travelling on the road from one side of the town to the other in order to make camp there, one of the troops of the Ghaznavid army who was of servile birth (*mowlā-zāda*)[58] had stolen a sheep. The aggrieved owner came before the Amir and poured out his grievances. The Amir reined in his mount and told the troop commanders, "I want you to bring this *mowlā-zāda* here immediately." They rode off, and by the decree of Fate and by the arrival of the man's allotted term of life, they brought back the soldier in question—and the man was in receipt of a pay allotment[59]– still in possession of the sheep which he had stolen. The Amir said to him, "You've got a pay allotment?" He answered, "Yes, I have, amounting to so much and so much." He said, "Why did you steal a sheep from the people of a district which is a province of ours? If you were in need of meat, why didn't you pay for it with silver? You have drawn your pay allotment, and you can't be destitute." He answered, "I did wrong." He said, "You are certainly going to witness the reward of those who commit crimes." He ordered him to be hanged from the city gate of Gorgān, and he gave the man's horse and trappings to the owner of the sheep. A proclamation was made that "This will be the reward of anyone who oppresses the subjects of these regions." Because of this, a great sense of awe and fear was generated.

The shepherd (i.e. the ruler) is able to maintain his flock (i.e. the subjects) through such means as this. For a monarch who does not give out largesse[60] or does not, moreover, mete out punishment at the appropriate time, will face rack and ruin. [Gh 450]

The story of how the Just Amir Sebüktegin administered exemplary punishment

I heard the following account from Khᵛāja Bu Naṣr. One day, the Khwarazm Shah Altuntāsh [F 582] recalled an incident while the conversation was about the affairs of monarchs and their conduct, and the fact that they should display their authority promptly or else face trouble, and he said that he had never seen a man like the Just Amir Sebüktegin for meting out justice, bestowing largesse and showing administrative ability (*kadkhodā'i*), and for displaying knowledge and all the customary practices of kingship.[61]

He continued, "It happened at that time when the Amir Sebüktegin went to Bost and overthrew Bāytuz and his partisans[62] through his well-attested use of cunning stratagems, and that province was cleared of all his opponents. One day, he was inside the main tent of the camp enclosure during the noontide heat on the plain of Bost. I, together with nine others of my comrades, belonged to that group of gholāms who were never out of his sight, day and night, for a single hour, and we used to take turns to stand on guard in pairs. Someone with a grievance came to the entrance of the camp enclosure, groaning and wailing volubly. It was my turn to be on duty, and I was outside the large tent with my comrade. I was armed with my shield, sword, bow and battleaxe. The Amir called out to me. I went into his presence. He said, 'Bring in that man who is complaining so loudly.' I brought him in. The Amir said to him, 'What's your grievance?' He replied, 'I am a poor man and I possess only a date palm. An elephant is being held by the date palms, and its keeper is carrying off all my dates gratuitously. I beseech you, O God, may the lord attend to my cries!' The Amir mounted his steed immediately, and we two gholām cavalrymen rode off at his side, with the complainant going before us to show the way. When we came to the date palms, by a remarkable stroke of fortune, we found the elephant keeper with the elephant tied up beneath the date palm, and he was cutting down the dates. He was unaware that the Amir was standing there some distance away and that the Angel of Death had arrived to seize his soul. The Amir spoke to me in Turkish,[63] saying, 'Remove the string from your bow, climb up to the elephant and from there on to the tree, and hang the elephant keeper with the bowstring.' I went off. The wretched fellow was busy cutting down the dates. When he heard me coming, he looked round. Before he could make a move, I had come upon him and seized him, and I was about to put the bowstring round his neck and strangle him. He was fighting desperately for his life now, and I was in danger of being hurled down by him. The Amir saw this, rode forward and shouted at the fellow. When he heard the Amir's cry [F 583] he was stunned and became all weak and feeble, and I finished him off. [Gh 451] The Amir ordered a rope to be brought, and the elephant keeper was securely tied to the end of it and hanged. He gave the man who had been aggrieved 1,000 dirhams there and then,[64] and he bought the date palm from him. This made a deep and awesome impression, with the result that during the entire period of his rule, I never saw or heard anyone, in any place, bold enough to seize a single apple unlawfully from anyone else. On several occasions we went to Bost, and the elephant keeper was still there gibbeted on that tree.[65] In the end, they cut the rope and the corpse fell down from there."[66] By means of such exemplary punishment, it is possible to keep a whole world under control.

Bā Kālijār and his entire retinue of Gorgānis had left their lands and properties with all their wealth and possessions and had gone towards Sāri, fully armed and prepared.[67] He had taken with him Anushirvān b. Manuchehr, together with the notables and leading commanders like Shahrāgim and Mardāviz[68] and other stout warriors, with whom Bā Kālijār was connected. The next day, when Amir Masʿud arrived, a group of the senior commanders of the Arabs, with their cavalry host—it was said that they numbered 4,000 riders—came to the court, and the Amir welcomed them and showed them favour, and gave the commanders robes of honour. The military strength of the Gorgānis depended entirely on these Arabs. They remained attached to the court and, indeed, the survivors of them are still here in Ghazna. Bā Kālijār, it was said, seized upon this occasion as an opportunity to get rid of them because he had been under their control [F 584] and subject to their importunities.

The office of head of the Divān of Gorgān was given to Saʿid Ṣarrāf, who had been adjutant and counsellor to the Commander-in-Chief Ghāzi.[69] He donned the robe of honour and went to the town of Gorgān and began to exact wealth. They were seeking out and going through the houses and the property of those who had fled, and seizing whatever they found. But only a small amount was finding its way to the treasury, and the greater part of it they appropriated for themselves, as is the norm in such cases.

An envoy arrived from the son of Manuchehr and Bā Kālijār, with the verbal message that "The lord of the world has come to his own province, and we as his servants proffer our obedience. The reason for not coming earlier was that it would not have been possible for appropriate hospitality and service to be offered, and we would have been filled with shame. We took up our residence at Sāri, awaiting the exalted command, so that, as far as is within our power, we might render any service which may be ordained." He gave the answer that "It has been resolved and decided that we should go to Setārābād and establish ourselves there, since the climate there is more clement. From there, whatever needs to be ordained will be ordained," and the envoy was sent back with this message. [Gh 452]

About ten days later, throughout which we had been drinking wine, the Amir had a private session with the Vizier and the leading men of state, and he came to the decision that Amir Mowdud should remain in this encampment with 4,000 cavalrymen from every (ethnic) group, together with their senior commanders, with the General Altuntāsh as the commander of this detachment; and all were to follow the instructions of the prince Mowdud. He also decided that 2,000 of these Arab cavalrymen who had come over to his side[70] should go to Dehestān under the command of the Master of the Royal Stables, Böri, accompanied by 3,000 royal cavalrymen, half of them Turks and half of them Indians. These likewise were to be under the supreme command of Mowdud. The private session came to an end, the army departed to Dehestān [F 585] and the Sultan gave all the necessary instructions to his son.

On Sunday,[71] 12 Rabi' II [/24 February 1035], the Amir set off from Gorgān. From here to Astarābād[72] was a distance of two stages along a road called "Eighty Bridges" (Hashtādpol), with thick forests stretching as far as the eye could see and flowing streams. That year, the heavens did not vouchsafe any rain, for had there been a single downpour, the Amir would have had to return. Not only is the road narrow, but the ground in that locality is soft, and the streams and water channels innumerable; if it should rain just once during a week, several days would be required for an army of only modest size to be able to get through, and an army of the size that this monarch possessed would have found it impossible. But since it had to be that Fate had decreed that great trouble should appear in Khorasan, the divine foreordaining was such that, in a region where it rains continuously, no rain should fall, so that this monarch was easily able to travel along this road with an army of this magnitude and come to Āmol, as I shall relate.

On 13 Rabi' II [/25 February] the Amir came to Astarābād. They had pitched the great tent high up on the Sāri road side of the city, on a very tall and broad mound,[73] a most pleasant spot overlooking the entire region of Sāri lay beneath it. The camp enclosure and the divāns had all been set up below this mound. Buqi the watchman of the army,[74] was of a most pleasant and witty disposition, a good mimic and player of the pandore (*ṭonbur*), and much appreciated by the Amir and the leaders of the army. He told Bu Naṣr, "At the time when the Commander-in-Chief for the Samanids, Tāsh, having been defeated by Bu'l-Ḥasan Simjur, came to Gorgān, and the Buyid house and the Ṣāḥeb Esmāʿil [Ebn] ʿAbbād, granted to him these regions, he erected a large tent on this mound.[75] I, Buqi, was in my prime then and acted as watchman for the army. Tāsh passed on, [F 586] the Simjuris passed on and Sultan Maḥmud likewise passed on, and now this lord has come and a tent has been set up here; I am afraid that the time [Gh 453] of my own passing has come. The poor fellow took this as an omen, and it came true, since he fell ill the next day and died during the night, and was buried there. Certainly, he had travelled thousands of parasangs, most of them with Amir Maḥmud in India. He was a tough and courageous individual and I saw him at assaults on fortresses, where he dashed forward and suffered many wounds from stones and all sorts of missiles; he confronted many perils and scored many successes. By the end of his life he had reached ninety-three years, and he died here in his bed! *No soul knows in which land it is to die.*[76] Bu Esḥāq has well said: (Poetry)

1. *A heedless one oft falls asleep, and is placed in his grave niche without ever having felt ill.*

2. *O you who places the corpse in its grave, the grave speaks to you, but you have not been aware of it!*[77]

On the day after next, from dawn onwards the Amir indulged in wine-drinking on top of this mound. It was the season for citrons and oranges, which were visible from the mound, hanging in large quantities from branches in the gardens below.[78] He gave orders that great amounts of citrons and oranges and branches laden with fruit should be picked and brought up. They arranged them all round the tent on the height and bedecked that place as if it were the garden of Paradise itself. He summoned the boon-companions and the singers and musicians also came, and wine-drinking got under way. In truth, it was indeed a most pleasant and happy day!

The order came to my master Bu Naṣr to bring the incoming letters to the Amir, [F 587] and he brought forward the gist of the letters.[79]

When the Amir had finished reading them, he took Bu Naṣr back to the wine-drinking party. In the course of that, the Amir said to him, "Buqi has passed away." My master exclaimed, "May the lord endure for ever, and may he continue with a household with royal power and youth until all we servants of his have passed away in his approval and service, since our wellbeing and salvation lie in that! But the lord should bear in mind that Buqi has passed away, and I cannot think of a single person in the entire army who could replace him." The Amir made no response and did not follow up and act upon the wider implications of Bu Naṣr's words, namely, that satisfactory replacements could no longer be found for other persons either. Verily, Bu Naṣr was speaking the truth there. The like of Buqi will never appear again, and one can safely say that, if the whole world were combed, a watchman like Buqi would not be found. However, the important thing is to endeavour to fulfill one's goal and acquire worthy men, for those who have inherited them effortlessly tend to lose them easily. In this book I have already described Sultan Maḥmud's [Gh 454] directions and commands regarding the training of his men and there is no need for repeating them here. As a consequence, he could always rely on the support of competent men. I have merely expatiated on these few points in the context of wardenship (*pāsbāni*) as they may be of some use.

A further embassy arrived here from Bā Kālijār and others, and they brought the verbal message that "We are obedient and faithful servants. The roads to Sāri are narrow and difficult; the exalted stirrup should not trouble itself to proceed further. Let whatever the Amir desires be enunciated, and it shall be brought forward to his presence with all obedience and effort." The reply was given that "It is our desire to proceed to Sāri in any case, so that we see these regions for ourselves. When we have reached there, whatever needs to be ordained will be ordained." The envoys returned home.

It was the day of Nowruz.[80] On 21 Rabi' II [/15 March 1035] the Amir set out [F 588] for Astarābād and arrived at Sāri on Thursday, the twenty-sixth of this month [/10 March]. The next day, Friday, the General Nushtegin Valvāleji was sent with a detachment of troops to a village which had a fortress, with an old man from the notables of Gorgān in charge of it, so that the fortress might be subdued. Bu'l-Ḥasan b. Delshād the secretary, was designated to go with him as postal and intelligence officer of the army, this being Bu'l-Ḥasan's first ever appointment. This fortress was in close proximity to Sāri and had no strong defences. They set off and swiftly took it in a day and returned at once. According to what Bu'l-Ḥasan related to Bu Naṣr, there had been much disorderly behaviour and much plundering, though very little of it had reached the royal treasury. Thus although Bu'l-Ḥasan was new to the job and by no means established in his position, he had managed to unearth the disreputable conduct that had been going on and to disclose it[81] in the exalted court session, thereby impressing the Amir and acquiring a reputation as an upright and solid person. Shorn of his property and wealth, this old man, the defender of the fortress, was brought to the court in a parlous state, accompanied by his aged wife and three daughters. The Amir was filled with remorse; he treated him kindly, asked his forgiveness and sent him back home. I must unavoidably set down such happenings, for they widen one's awareness and understanding and ensure that this History is following its true path, [Gh 455, F 589] for one should not, when writing history, indulge in suppressing, perverting or exaggerating the matter in hand.[82] If Nushtegin Valvāleji wrought evil, he tasted it himself.[83]

On Sunday, 1 Jomādā I [14 March 1035], the Amir left Sāri for Āmol. The roads that we had gone along and others that we followed were all very narrow, allowing only two or three riders to ride alongside each other at a time. To left and right, uninterrupted expanses of forest stretched up to the mountains, with swift-flowing rivers through which not even elephants could wade. We came face-to-face with a large wooden bridge along this road, over a most remarkable river with a course winding like a bow. The army was only able to cross that bridge with great difficulty, for although the water [F 590] was not all that deep, the ground along it was such that every beast that set foot there sank in it up to its neck, thus providing that land with its own natural defences. They encamped here since it was on the road to the town and there was an abundance of pasture, and plenty of room for a large army to encamp there.

Three envoys arrived from the ʿAlid Nāṣer, the leading citizens (*moqaddamān*) of Āmol as well as the populace, bringing the news that "When the Son of Manuchehr, Bā Kālijār, Shahrāgim and the rest heard that the Sultan was marching towards Āmol, they left hurriedly towards Nātel, Kājur and Ruyān, hoping to exploit the narrowness of the terrain at Nātel to engage the victorious royal army in skirmishes there. But if they are unable to hold on to their position there, they will cross over the pass of Kalār, since they are travelling light, and will flee into Gilān.[84] I, the servant Nāṣer and other leading citizens and the populace are all obedient servants of the Sultan and have stayed put here awaiting the royal command." He answered, "The land tax of Āmol is remitted. The populace should remain in their places, since we have no concern with them; the aim is to get hold of the fugitives." The envoys returned home with this message.

The Amir pushed on rapidly and reached Āmol on Friday, 6 Jomādā I [/19 March 1035]. More than 500,000 to 600,000 [Gh 456] men had come out to greet him, all looking fresh and neat, robed in fine clothes.[85] I did not see anyone without a head shawl of cloth from Shaṭā, Tavvaz or [F 591] Tostar[86] or embroidered with thread, or without a piece of cloth made up into a waist wrapper;[87] they said that this was their custom. The Amir turned from the town's open space for worship[88] on to the road with a detachment of the royal gholāms, and travelled along the edge of the town and encamped on the other side of it, some half a parasang away, where the tents had been erected. The Commander of the Palace Gholāms Begtughdï, with his troops and the rest of the army, formed up and went into the town, and from there came to the army encampment. The *janbāshiyān* (?)[89] had been placed on duty, with the result that no-one suffered the loss of a single dirham, and the people offered up prayers for the Amir, for they had never before seen such a well-equipped and disciplined army. I, Bu'l-Fażl, had gone into the town before the parade of the army and I found it a most pleasant town, with all the booths and shops open and the people cheerful and carefree. I shall relate later how things developed and what havoc those instigators of evil wrought, with the result that the paradise of Āmol became a hell.

The next day, the Amir held court, and afterwards had a private session with the Vizier and the great men of state, and said, "I am going to lead an expedition in person to Nātel." The Vizier said, "The Gorgānis should not be allowed the compliment of being pursued by the lord himself, for there are, God be praised, many an illustrious commander here for the task." The notables there joined in affirmation, "What use are we if the lord has to hazard his valuable self in undertaking this alone?" The Amir replied, "The right course is this. The Vizier is to stay here with the baggage and look after things, and Bu Naṣr Moshkān is to be with him to deal with the correspondence. The General is likewise to stay here and is to take the necessary precautions for all sorts of eventualities. A strong detachment of gholāms, amounting to 1,500 men, is to come with us, together with 8,000 first-rate cavalrymen, the cream of selected units (*tafāriq*), ten elephants, [F 592] machinery and equipment for reducing fortresses and 500 camels for conveying the armoury.[90] Go back, sit down in the domed tent,[91] and get all these things prepared, since I intend to depart tomorrow night whatever happens. ʿErāqi the secretary is to come with us, but the boon-companions and other men are all to remain here." Those present went back and did what he had ordered.

When half the night had gone by, the Amir mounted his steed on the night of Sunday, 8 Jomādā I [/20–1 March 1035] and went forth in the vanguard. [Gh 457] Large kettledrums were beaten and this detachment of palace gholāms set off. Behind them came the rest of the army, detachment after detachment, fully armed and prepared for action. The next day, at the time of the midday worship, they reached Nātel, having covered the distance of two stages of the journey without a break.[92] They found that the Gorgānis had made a stand there and had prepared for battle, not knowing that the Sultan had come in person. There was a fierce battle, as I shall subsequently describe in detail. On the Tuesday, during the mid-morning, on 11 Jomādā I [/24 March], three palace gholāms arrived with the good tidings of victory, and brought with them the Amir's drawing-ring[93] as a token of the veracity of this, straight from the victorious battle field, whence they had been sent off at a gallop by the Amir and given two horses each. They gave the drawing-ring to the Commander of the Palace Gholāms, the General Begtughdï. He took it and kissed it, stood up and then kissed the ground. At his orders drums were beaten and trumpets blown, and a great clamour arose from the army encampment; the three palace gholāms who had brought the news were paraded in public, and those prominent figures who were present, such as the Vizier, the General Bu'l-Nażr and others, exhibited their gratitude and lavished large sums in celebrating the occasion.

At the time of the afternoon worship they encamped, and a letter giving thanks for the victory was written to the Amir [F 593] from the Vizier, the General and the court personnel. The Head of the Chancery, Bu Naṣr Moshkān, wrote it out—it was a truly remarkable letter, leading the Vizier to aver that he had never seen a letter on the subject of a drawing-ring couched in such terms—and within the text of the letter Bu Naṣr had inserted this verse of Motanabbi: (Poetry)

1. *The secret of your eminence is known only to God, and what the enemies say [about you] is a kind of delirious raving.*[94]

I myself had the draft of this letter in my master Bu Naṣr's own hand, but it too was lost, in the manner which I have already mentioned in several places in this book. The Commander Begtughdï deputed two palace gholāms and two of his own gholāms to deliver this letter.

At the time of the evening worship, the detailed account of the victory[95] arrived. It was in the handwriting of the secretary 'Erāqi, having been dictated by the Amir himself, in the following terms:

"When we left Āmol, we rode all night and cut through thickets so dense that even a snake would have found it hard to slide through them, and the next day, at the time of the midday worship, we reached Nātel. We had travelled with great haste, so that when we encamped, our troops kept on arriving all through the night, and half of it had elapsed before everyone had arrived, since two stages had been covered in a single journey. The next day, Monday, spies came and told us that the Gorgānis had conveyed their baggage and impedimenta with the Son of Manuchehr out from the town of Nātel and had made an army encampment on the far side of the town, had pitched tents and had left the heavy impedimenta and troops unfit for service with the baggage. Bā Kālijār and Shahrāgim, with large numbers of their best and most battle-hardened cavalrymen and infantry, accompanied by their commanders and champion warriors, had come to this side of the town. There is a very narrow bridge there [Gh 458] which is the sole crossing point, and they seized this—the level ground the other side of the bridge is even narrower than on this side.[96] They intended to give battle at that bridge, [F 594] since there is only a single track surrounded by forests, rivers, marshy pools and water channels. They talked it over and decided that, if they should be defeated, the cavalry would make its way back from these narrow places, and fifty of the choicest infantry from Gilān and Deylam would guard the bridge and strive hard and persevere until they had made sure that their own side had managed to retreat from the battlefield and had escaped,[97] for there were many treacherous obstacles and tight spots, and they could not be overtaken there.

Having learnt all this, we decided on our response and issued the necessary measures to tackle this matter. We put on a coat of mail, mounted a female elephant, and weapons were placed in the litter with us. We gave orders for the large kettledrums for battle to be beaten, and gholāms, one group of cavalrymen and a larger group of infantrymen, stationed themselves round our elephant. A group went forward, driving in front of themselves a large and most powerfully-built elephant noted for its pugnacious and aggressive nature. We pushed onwards, with a large force of cavalry and infantry behind us. When we reached that flat terrain and the bridge, the Gorgānis advanced with a substantial body of cavalry and infantry. A fierce and determined battle was joined. The difficulty that we had to face was that there was insufficient elbow-room for the army in those narrow straits. It did not therefore matter if one had a hundred thousand cavalrymen and infantry or five times as many, it would have amounted to the same thing.[98] Had it not been thus, the Gorgānis would not have dared to tarry for even an hour, since they would have been wiped out at a stroke by a single detachment of our troops.

A number of their cavalrymen, together with a numerous force of infantry, launched a fierce attack. They had as their commander a rider with his face covered, who was well versed in the tactics of [F 595] feigned retreat and then return to the fight.[99] It so happened that a javelin[100] reached our litter and elephant, and the palace gholāms pressed the enemy back with their arrows. We ourselves fought fiercely, and they fought fiercely. They wounded and painfully afflicted with their arrows and javelins the male elephant of ours which was in the forefront of the engagement, so that it turned around in agony and headed towards us, and was trampling down every one of our men that it found in its path, while the enemy followed on behind, encouraging it forward with their loud clamour. Had this male elephant reached us in this fashion, it would certainly have charged at our own female elephant and an irreparable disaster would have occurred, [Gh 459] for if a male elephant receives such wounds and turns around in the midst of a battle, it does not spare anything in its path. By a stroke of good fortune, in this rushing back it passed to the left, to the edge of the plain where there was a deep rivulet (naghol, for b.gh.l. of F 595. n.6; Ravāqi, op. cit., 47) with shallow water in it. The elephant driver was a most agile and experienced man, and he drove the elephant into there, and by the grace of God he deflected its damage and affliction from us and our troops in those narrow places, and all were profoundly grateful.

The champions from amongst the gholām cavalrymen, the dashing *kheyltāsh*s and the infantry fought fiercely against the enemy. From the ranks of the leaders of the Gorgāni troops, one appeared in front of us. From the back of the elephant we dealt him a blow with our mace so that he fell from his horse from the thrust of that blow, and the gholāms rushed in to finish him off. He cried out to us and asked for quarter, saying [F 596] that he was Shahrāgim. We gave orders for them to take him off his horse.[101] When the Gorgānis saw him taken captive, they turned round in flight, and before they could get back to the bridge, the champion warriors of the palace gholāms killed large numbers of them and took many of them prisoner. Unlimited numbers of their troops fled left and right within those bounds and were either killed or drowned.

At the site of the bridge there was an immense throng, and a fierce battle took place. The opposing troops fell on each other, and many were killed on both sides; we, in our entire life, had never seen such a battle. The Gorgānis held the bridge until towards the time of the afternoon worship and displayed fierce resistance so that our infantry could not get through from any direction. In the end, the cream of our infantrymen pushed forward in pursuit of them with shields, spears, bows and all sorts of weapons, and they sent up a hail of arrows so that the sun's light was obscured. They strove valiantly until the bridge was taken. They managed to do this because five or six of the battle-hardened Gorgāni infantrymen acted as leaders,[102] sought quarter and were granted it, and came over to our side. Once the bridge was cleared, our vanguard dashed forward speedily and we followed on. A few of our cavalrymen came back to us and reported that ever since[103] Shahrāgim had been taken prisoner, the Gorgānis had all taken to flight, and had left to us the army encampment, tents and everything they had, including even their large cooking pots with the food cooked in them. We ourselves encamped there, since there was no other spot [Gh 460] suitable for camping. The cavalrymen who were still fresh went after the fugitives and captured large numbers of infantrymen of all kinds.[104] As for the leading figures, the commanders and the cavalrymen, they had all fled precipitately. The way was still very narrow, and the pursuing troops had to come back. What happened [F 597] has been set forth in detail, so that the exact happenings of the occasion may be put on record. We ourselves are proceeding back to Āmol in such a manner that, God willing, we shall be there very soon."

On Saturday, 12 Jomādā I[105] [/25 March 1035] Amir Mas῾ud returned to Āmol in a fine form and in a triumphant state. He chose a different place to halt this time and gave orders for the camp enclosure and the great tent to be erected there, and he dismounted in an auspicious manner. He said to Bu Naṣr, the Head of the Chancery, "Letters announcing our victory must be sent to the various lands by means of couriers bearing the good tidings." These were written, and the *kheyltāsh*s and palace gholāms went off. On the Friday, he held a court session with great pomp and splendour. The ῾Alid and the town notables had come along en bloc to render service. The Amir said to the Vizier, "Go and sit in the domed tent and have the ῾Alid and the town notables seated there, for we have a verbal message for them." The Vizier went to the domed tent and arranged for the group to be seated. The Amir decided on a wine-drinking session and it was all arranged, and boon-companions and the singers and musicians were in attendance.

Bu Naṣr returned home, having expended much effort on despatching letters announcing the victory with their couriers. It was my spell of duty to be there in the Chancery. A domestic attendant came and summoned me. I went into the royal presence, up to the throne, bearing the inkstand and paper. He motioned me to sit down and I did so, He said, "Write down as follows: The sum of money which is to be collected from Āmol and Ṭabarestān, and what Bu Sahl b. Esmā῾il is to collect, comprises a million dinars in the gold coinage of Nishapur; 1,000 sets of Rumi and other varieties of clothing; 1,000 *maḥfuri* carpets and *qāli* carpets; and 5,000 pieces of fine cotton cloth." I wrote this down and then arose. He said, "Take this document [F 598] to the Vizier, and give him our message to tell those people that they must see to it that our orders are obeyed with alacrity so that there is no need for an official collector[106] to be sent in and for assignments of money due to be written out for the troops[107] and for our demands to be extracted by sheer force." I took the document to the Vizier, and presented it to him privately and conveyed the verbal message. He smiled and said to me, "You'll see, they'll have these regions burnt and uprooted and much infamy and disrepute will accrue from this, and they won't find 3,000 dirhams! [Gh 461] What wickedness! If they turn all Khorasan upside down, they won't get this kind of money and material! But the Sultan is occupied with wine-drinking, and has said these words with his own luxurious living, wealth and treasuries in mind and as his yardstick."

Then he turned towards this 'Alid and the notables of Āmol, and said, "You should know that after the Gorgānis drew their swords against their lord, and became rebellious outcasts, they will not set eyes on this region again. A strong and prominent commander will come here, in the same way as was sent to Khwarazm, in order to secure these regions and so that you become relieved of these afflictions." The Āmolis offered up prayers profusely. Then he continued, "You know that the lord Sultan has expended a vast amount of money to bring the army here and drive away these oppressors. An appropriate financial offering from these regions is therefore required."

They replied, "We are obedient subjects in regard to what is in our power to pay, since these regions are sparse in resources and the people poor. The amount of money due from us since earlier times, according to the customary practice, has been 100,000 dirhams from Āmol and Ṭabarestān, and the corresponding amount to this of *maḥfuri* and *qāli* carpets. If a greater sum than this is demanded, the populace will suffer greatly. What does the Grand Vizier now ordain?" The latter replied, "The Sultan has ordered a document such as this to be drawn up, and he has given Bu'l-Fażl such-and-such a verbal message," [F 599] and he showed the document and explained the terms of the message, saying, "I will show some consideration, so that this amount which is written down in the document may be taken [also] from Gorgān, Ṭabarestān, Sāri and all the other places, and so that you in Āmol may not suffer an inordinate amount of hardship." When the Āmolis heard these words, they were transfixed and mortified, and they said, "We can't offer an immediate answer to these words, but no-one has the means to hand over this amount of money. If the Vizier will permit, we will go back and speak with the people at large." The Vizier told me, "Tell the Sultan what you heard." I went off and told him. He gave the answer, "Good! They'll go back home today and return ripe for plucking[108] tomorrow. This money must be collected very quickly so that we don't have to remain here for long." I came back and recounted what I had been told,[109] and the Āmolis went back filled with great distress. The Vizier likewise went home.

The next day, the Amir held court, and afterwards had a private meeting with the Vizier, and said, "We must find a means of getting this money today." The Vizier replied, "May the lord's life be prolonged! I am overjoyed[110] at the prospect of well-filled coffers. But this is a substantial amount, and yesterday the men from Āmol were most unresponsive; what does the lord command?" He said, "The amount that had been decreed in the document is recoupable from Āmol alone. If they assent to it willingly, all well and good; but [Gh 462] if not, Bu Sahl b. Esmāʿil must be sent to the town to thrash it out of them,[111] according to their means (*yasār*)." The Vizier came back to the domed tent and pressed hard on the Āmolis—and far fewer men[112] had come than the previous day—and told them what the Sultan had said. The ʿAlid and the Judge said, "Yesterday we called together a meeting of the people and explained this situation; a very great lamentation rose up, and naturally, they didn't respond to the demands and went away. It appears that last night [F 600] many people fled from the town, but we could not bring ourselves to flee, for we have committed no crime and remain obedient subjects. Now it is for the Sultan and the Grand Vizier to ordain, and he can give orders appropriate to the situation."

The Vizier knew that the situation was exactly as they had described, but it was not opportune to say anything to the Amir. He summoned Bu Sahl b. Esmāʿil and passed these notables on to him, and he sent them to the town. Bu Sahl set up a divān and began exerting strong pressure on the people. Those who fell into his hands gave information about those who had fled, since one does not find any town without that sort of thing going on and people evil enough to betray each other and act as informers. The cavalrymen and infantrymen were going along, seizing people and bringing them in. The assignments of money for the troops' salaries were put into operation by Bu Sahl ʿEsmāʿil. They wrought havoc on the town, and did whatever they wanted and arrested whom they wished. The Divān in its operations was like the Day of Resurrection. The Sultan was unaware of all this, but no-one dared to set forth what was happening and to tell him the truth. As a result, in the space of four days, 160,000 dinars came to the army (i.e. as part of their salaries), although they had seized well in excess of twice that amount, resulting in great tribulation[113] as well as ignominy, to the extent that seven or eight months after that, it was ascertained that people complaining of tyranny had gone from this town to Baghdad and had raised cries of complaint at the court of the caliph and, it was said, they had also gone as far as Mecca, *may God protect it*; for if the people of Āmol are weak and powerless, they are also articulate and stubborn, and they had good reason for speaking out! All that criminal behaviour and burden of sin was to be laid at the door of Bu'l-Ḥasan ʿErāqi and the others; but the Amir ought to have ordered firm action[114] to be taken in such matters as these. It is very hard for me to write down such words, [F 601] but I have no choice; there should be no equivocation in history. If those persons who were with us then at Āmol should read these sections impartially, they would aver in all fairness that what I have written is a faithful account.[115] [Gh 463]

The Amir occupied himself here constantly in merry-making and wine-drinking. On Friday, 28 Jomādā I [/10 April 1035] he went to Alhom on the shore of the Sea of Ābaskun.[116] Tents and awnings were set up there, and they drank wine and caught fish. They saw the ships of the Rus,[117] which appear in all places and pass by, without anyone ever being able to get their hands on them, since it is well known that any ship can make for any of the ports they hold.[118] This place Alhom is only a small town; I did not see it myself, but Bu'l-Ḥasan b. Delshād, who had gone there, told me all this.

On Monday, 2 Jomādā II [/14 April], the Amir returned to the army encampment at Āmol. The majority of its population had taken to flight and were hiding in the forests. Meanwhile, a man who was the General Begtughdī's purveyor of *foqqāʿ* [119] had gone to get some snow and ice.[120] On his way, at the edge of the forest, was a village. He laid his hands on a maiden there with the intention of dishonouring her, but her father and brothers quite rightly prevented him. They put up a fight with this purveyor of *foqqāʿ* and his companions, and the purveyor was struck by a javelin. He came back and told the Commander Begtughdï, and succeeded in kindling his wrath. The next day, without seeking royal authorization, Begtughdï mounted an elephant [F 602] and rode along to that village and the nearby forests with a detachment of royal gholāms. Much plundering and killing ensued, to such an extent that it was reported that they had massacred several figures revered for their asceticism and piety while they were sitting on their prayer rugs, clasping their copies of the Qorʾān. All who heard about this reviled them bitterly. The news reached the Amir. He appeared most distressed and heaped violent reproaches on Begtughdï, since the Amir had become full of remorse for everything that had happened in this region, and he kept on upbraiding and fulminating against the secretary Bu'l-Ḥasan. But other sinister elements had been at work,[121] for when we returned, we had to face grave and dire twists and turns of fortune.

During this week, important secret letters arrived from Dehestān, Nasā and Farāva with the news that marauding Turkmens [Gh 464] had emerged once more from the desert and were heading for Dehestān. Amir Mowdud had written that "I have sent out large detachments of cavalry as scouting parties in all four directions, and have ordered that the she-camels and the mares of the royal herd[122] should be brought closer to Gorgān, and that the number of horsemen keeping watch over the herds should be doubled or trebled."[123] The reply letters went back that they were to remain on guard and that the exalted banner was coming back presently.

On Tuesday, 3 Jomādā II [15 April 1035] an envoy arrived from Bā Kālijār, and he had sent his son with the envoy. He sought to offer excuses for the warfare which had taken place, asked for forgiveness and said, "One of my sons is already occupied in rendering service at the lord's portal in Ghaznin, but he is far away from me, hence unable to intercede on my behalf, so his brother has come to render service. It befits the solicitude and kindly feelings of the lord that he should show mercy, so that this ancient house of the Ziyarids [F 603] should not become prey to the designs of enemies."

The envoy and the son were brought before the Amir, were welcomed and given lodging and hospitality. The Amir sought the advice of the Vizier and the great men of state. The Vizier said, "The wisest course appears to me that this son should be given a robe of honour and should be sent back with the envoy in a happy and contented state—since we ourselves face momentous affairs—until the time when we can see how affairs turn out, and then, in the light of our personal and direct observation, a decision can be reached about these regions (i.e. Gorgān and Ṭabarestān). At all events, he will not abruptly slip away from our hands." These words were very acceptable to the Amir, and an answer to the letters, couched in favourable terms, was written out. This son was given a fine robe of honour, as was likewise the envoy, and they were sent back in a handsome manner.

It was on the sixth of Jomādā II [/18 April], a Friday, that a letter arrived from Balkh with news of the death of 'Alitegin and of the accession to power of his eldest son over those lands (i.e. of Transoxania).[124] The news was a matter of concern to the Amir, for the control of affairs had fallen into the hands of inexperienced youths.[125] He was anxious that no rash or impetuous action should occur. He ordered that letters should be written to the Commander-in-Chief 'Ali Dāya regarding this matter, instructing him to go to Balkh, assume control of the roads and take complete precautions lest any crisis occur. He further ordered that letters should likewise be sent to Termez, to the castellan of the fortress there and to the field officers Bā Naṣr and Bu'l-Ḥasan.[126] The castellan at this time was Qotlogh (text, *khotlogh*), a former retainer of Sultan Maḥmud, an affable character but alert and cautious. Two swift-riding couriers were nominated [Gh 465] to convey letters to Bokhara containing expressions of condolence and accession greetings for 'Alitegin's son, *as befits such occasions*. They were to travel speedily and to bring back accurate information; if this inexperienced youth contemplated some untoward action, it might be that this letter would shame him into desisting. The form of address for him [on the letter] was set down as *"The Excellent Amir, Son" (al-Amir al-Fāżel al-Walad).*[127]

Although this letter went off, this young viper[128] had seized the opportunity presented by his father's death and the Sultan's absence from Khorasan, and he was hearing that there was considerable disturbance and turmoil. Hārun, the God-forsaken rebel, had been reported as preparing[129] to come to Merv with a large army in order to seize Khorasan. [F 604] These two young men made an agreement with each other and made preparations for Hārun to come to Merv and for the sons of 'Alitegin to plunder Chaghāniyān and Termez, and from there to travel by the Qobādhiyān[130] road to Andkhud and join forces with Hārun. ʿAlitegin's sons ransacked Chaghāniyān, and the governor there, Bu'l-Qāsem, the Sultan's son-in-law, fled before them and took refuge among the Komijis.[131] Having laid waste to Chaghāniyān, they came to Termez by the Dārzangi road.[132] They had regarded the fortress of the garrison at Termez as a ludicrously easy prey. They sent Üker[133] with a battle standard and 300 cavalrymen to the fortress gate, believing that upon his arrival, the fortress would straightaway fall into their hands, either by force or peacefully, so that they might plant their putrid battle standard[134] on the fortress's roof. *One's conjecture may be a wrong one or it may hit the mark*;[135] they were unaware that there were walking into a lion's den. Suffice it to say that when they reached the citadel, those valiant lions opened up the gate and bellowed out, "Welcome! If you have any valour, step inside and visit the inferno[136] of our fortress!"

The forces of ʿAlitegin's sons thought that it was going to be a piece of cake[137] and that it was a simple affair. But as soon as they went forward, the cavalry and infantrymen of the fortress flew at them and within a short time seized a group of them and made them captive. The rest of them fled in a rout back to ʿAlitegin's son. They reproached Üker, but he replied that "The pot is still there simmering. We just had a little taste of it; you are welcome to try it out for yourselves!" They heaped execrations on Üker, and called him an impotent fop.[138] The trumpets were sounded, and Tun.sh,[139] the Commander-in-Chief, [Gh 466] advanced in the vanguard, with the rest of his forces following on after him. The whole army surrounded the fortress and encamped there.

I heard from ʿAbd al-Raḥmān the reciter and singer,[140] who had made his way from the devastating of Chaghāniyān [F 605] to Termez, and he related that the forces of ʿAlitegin's sons had several clashes with the defenders of the fortress and were defeated in every single bout, and were at the end of their tether and livid on account of the savage invective that the womenfolk of the Sagzis were hurling at them.[141] One day, Üker, who was a commander of high prestige and who possessed 1,000 cavalrymen, decided to attack the fortress. He went forward on foot bearing a broad shield. Bā Naṣr and Bu'l-Ḥasan b. Khalaf[142] said to the man operating the ballista,[143] "We'll give fifty dinars and two sets of clothing if you can knock down Üker."

He got ready a stone weighing five or six *man*s, observed for a while, took thought and then drew back the cords of the ballista. The stone was hurled forward and struck Üker on the middle of his body, and he immediately gave up the ghost. (At that time, a man would be hit on the head with a single stone from the ballista weighing five *man*s and would die without uttering a further word.) When Üker fell to the ground, a great cry arose from the enemy troops, since he was such an eminent figure. His retainers fell on him and bore him away. The impact of the incident broke the back of the army of ʿAlitegin's sons. The Ghuri who operated the ballista received the gold and the clothing. The sons of ʿAlitegin had received the news that the God-forsaken Hārun had been killed and that the Commander-in-Chief of the Ghaznavid army had reached Balkh. They turned back from Termez *with their tails between their legs*[144] and went back to Samarqand through the Iron Gate.[145]

A swift courier arrived with a confidential letter from the postal and intelligence officer of Ray, Bu Naṣr Beyhaqi, brother of Amirak Beyhaqi. It came from him and not from his predecessor because Bu'l-Moẓaffar Ḥabashi had been dismissed from the office of the *barid* and replaced by Bu Naṣr. In the time of Amir Maḥmud, this noble-minded man had been intendant of the palace for this monarch Prince Masʿud, and he performed many an important and dangerous mission [F 606] and many laudable acts of service. He is a valiant man, and an old friend of mine. After we lost control of Ray, this Khᵛāja went through a turbulent phase, with many ups and downs, which will be recounted later in this History. At the present time, in the year 451 [/1059], he is here in Ghaznin in the protective shadow of the lord of the world, the Great Sultan Abu'l-Moẓaffar Ebrāhim b. Nāṣer Din Allāh [Masʿud], may God perpetuate his rule.

The confidential letter went as follows, "The Commander-in-Chief Tāsh Farrāsh received a drubbing from the Son of Kāku's advance force." The answer went back, "Greater alertness and care must be taken in affairs. We have finished with the matter of Gorgān and Ṭabarestān, and are now coming from Āmol by the Damāvand road [Gh 467] to Ray, since there is no serious concern to keep us back in Khorasan." We wrote this with the aim of instilling fear into our enemies in those regions and intimidating them, for in reality we were facing such an important array of problems in Khorasan that it had driven from our minds all concerns about Ray and the Son of Kāku. I shall speak about the affairs of Ray and Khwarazm sparingly and in dribs and drabs, since there will be two comprehensive and richly detailed chapters about the state and affairs of both those regions, as I have already mentioned previously. For those desiring an annalistic recital of historical events, this should suffice.

On Sunday, 22 Jomādā II [/4 May 1035], the Amir departed from Āmol. The stay here had lasted forty-six days. On the road, he saw men of the palace infantry bearing along several of the Āmolis in bonds. He asked who these people were. They replied that these were men from Āmol who had not handed over any money from the stipulated taxation. He said, "Let them go free, and cursed be that man who thought up the plan of coming here." He gave orders to an army commander to see to it that nothing was taken from anyone and that they were all set free, and this was done. It rained steadily along the road, and both the men and their beasts suffered greatly. [F 607]

On Wednesday, 3 Rajab [/14 May], while we were on the road, a letter arrived with the news that Hārun, son of the Khwarazm Shah Altuntāsh, had been killed and that the army that had been sent to attack Merv had returned to Khwarazm. The Amir was overjoyed at receiving this news and lavished much praise on the Grand Vizier Aḥmad b. ʿAbd al-Ṣamad, since Aḥmad had devised this stratagem, as I have previously mentioned, and the ungrateful one was overthrown. The poet Maʿrufi Balkhi[146] has expressed it eloquently, (Poetry)

1. The one who disavows the begetter of his blessings is akin to the one who denies religion; exert yourself strenuously to kill the one who denies![147]

May the Almighty God seize all those who do not acknowledge bounties bestowed on them, *by the right of Moḥammad and his house!* The Messenger [of God] has said, *"Fear the evil of a person to whom you have done good"*,[148] and the words of the Bringer of the Divine Law are right. The great scholars are referring to such a person as that within the context of this saying, namely, *O you who have no innate qualities* (aṣl)!, for those of pure birth never forget to show fitting gratitude for the benefits from their patron and benefactor. It thus happened that, when Hārun set out from Khwarazm, [Gh 468] and was at a spot four parasangs from the town where he was about to encamp, twelve gholāms who had been suborned to kill him came along, attacked him with their swords, battle axes and maces, and hacked that ungrateful dog to pieces. The army fell into a turmoil and returned homewards. Those are remarkable tales which I shall set forth in that separate chapter which I have promised;[149] this amount will be sufficient here.

On Saturday, 6 Rajab [/17 May], news arrived of the death of the Great Chamberlain Bilgetegin, God's mercy be upon him. When the Commander-in-Chief 'Ali Dāya reached Balkh, the Great Chamberlain came to Nishapur according to the royal command, and from Nishapur to Gorgān. The greater part of the Arabs of Gorgān who had gone over to the Ghaznavid side[150] were entrusted to him to bring back to Nishapur. As soon as he reached there, [F 608] he died; *"No soul knows in which land it is to die."*[151]

On Monday, 8 Rajab [/19 May], the Amir reached Gorgān. The weather was very hot, and particularly so there, since it is known for its hot climate,[152] and the beasts became weak and lethargic, since at Āmol and on the journey they had eaten only rice stalks.

I heard from Khvāja Bu Naṣr Moshkān, who said: The Amir was bitterly regretting the fact that he had gone to Āmol for he was now witnessing its dire consequences. He summoned me for a private session, and there were just the two of us. He said, "Why did we do such a thing! God's curse rest on this wretch 'Erāqi! Nothing was achieved, the army got nothing and I have heard that the local populace had been badly abused." I replied, "May the lord's life be prolonged! The Vizier and the rest of us servants were saying as much, but it was not possible to protest any further against the exalted judgement, for it would have been misconstrued (i.e. that they were going beyond their rank and station and were showing disobedience). As for the exalted judgement's words, 'What advantage was there in coming to these regions?', it could be said that it certainly brought benefits to someone else (i.e. to Bā Kālijār, see below). But it would be wrong to go over this account again, since people will get the idea that these words have been spoken by way of deprecation."[153] He said. "Your words are all weighty and serious, and not said out of *Schadenfreude* and frivolousness, and you have shown a care for our welfare; by our life and head, speak without reservations!"

I replied, "May the lord's life be prolonged! Bā Kālijār has gained a great deal from this affair. He was considered a weakling and one lacking in authority amongst his troops and his people; the lord seized the powerful figures, at whose hands he had suffered, and has them in his custody. The commanders of the Arabs with their mounted followers, who did nothing but cause him trouble and drain his purse, have been removed from those regions and he is now free of them. [Gh 469] Because of the manifold acts of oppression which Bu Sahl b. Esmāʿil inflicted on the populace, [F 609] they can now appreciate Bā Kālijār and his rule. But all this can be easily attended to, may the lord's life be prolonged, and can be rectified with a modicum of attention and care, for Bā Kālijār is a prudent person and an honest servant, and it will only take a single letter and envoy to bring him back into the fold. We are hopeful that, through the favour of God Most High, no crisis will occur in Khorasan through this period of the Sultan's absence." The Amir said, "This is exactly the case," and I went back.

However, they[154] prevented Bā Kālijār from being won over and appeased after so much enmity and mistrust,[155] and they said, "A tax collector and a military governor must be appointed here." They did not know that once the power of the exalted banner was far away from those lands, Bā Kālijār would return; the subjects, who had been afflicted by misery and had been the victims of our tyranny, would give him their support; the tax collector and military governor would ineluctably and of necessity have to leave; and all honour would be lost.[156] Bu'l-Ḥasan b. ʿAbd al-Jalil, was appointed head of the Divān and counsellor and administrator of the army, with a strong detachment of troops, so that he might remain there when the exalted banner returned to Nishapur.[157]

When affairs became settled on this wise, "*the supreme calamity*"[158] was that, at the time of the afternoon worship on that day when the Amir arrived in Gorgān, elated at the news about Khwarazm and the overthrow of the God-forsaken one, Hārun—and rightly so, because a great disaster had been averted—he embarked on a session of wine-drinking and drank all through the night, and then, following his father's practice, there was no court session the next day, and everyone left the court. Despite the hot weather, the decision was made to stay in Gorgān for two weeks. After the midday worship, Khᵛāja Bu Naṣr summoned me, and we began eating lunch. Two riders of Bu'l-Fażl Suri came in, two-horse troopers from the daredevil riders (*div-sovārān*) of Farāva. They came forward and gave the appropriate greetings. Bu Naṣr said to them, "What news is there?" They replied, "We've come from Nishapur in two and a half days, and have taken fresh horses all along the route and have ridden fast at a gallop (*be-monāqala*) without a pause for rest by day or night and only halting briefly for a bite of food, since [F 610] these were our orders from the head of the Divān; but we don't know who instigated it." The Khᵛāja stopped eating, and sat them down to eat, and he took the letters. He opened the purse containing them and started to read, and he seemed extremely troubled and began to shake his head in dismay. I, Bu'l-Fażl, realized that some calamity must have occurred. Then he said, "Saddle the mount." He washed his hands and sent for his cloak. We got up. He said to me, "Follow me to the court." [Gh 470]

Those riders were given lodging, and I went along to the court. The court was deserted, and the Amir had been drinking wine well into the day and had then gone off into a sleep. Bu Naṣr told me, when we were alone, that "A large body of the Seljuq Turkmens crossed the Oxus and, taking the road through the desert of Dah Gonbadān,[159] have passed by the vicinity of Merv and finally reached Nasā. They have sought the mediation of the head of the Divān, Suri, asking him to act as an intercessor with the Sultan and that Nasā should be given over to them, on the basis that one out of their three commanders should come to the exalted court and render service there,[160] and they themselves should be considered as an army ready to perform to its utmost any service which it might be commanded. O Bu'l-Fażl, Khorasan is lost! Go to the Grand Vizier and give him this news."

I went back and found him risen from his sleep and reading a book. When he saw me he said, "May it be good news!" I replied, "May it be so." He said, "I know that the Seljuqs have entered Khorasan." I replied, "That's so," and I sat down and told him the situation. He exclaimed, "*There is no might or power except with God, the Exalted, the Mighty One!*"[161] He went on to say, "Lo, this is the result of going to Āmol and of the secretary 'Erāqi's plan! Have a mount saddled!" I came out, and he mounted. Bu Naṣr came from his Divān to see him and they talked together confidentially, with no-one else there except myself. He gave him Suri's letter. [F 611] He had written, "Ten thousand horsemen of the Seljuqs and the Yināliyān[162] came from the direction of Merv to Nasā. They cleared from their path the Turkmens who were in that vicinity, and another group of Khwarazmians,[163] and did not provide them with other quarters, not seeing any occasion for this. The letter which they had written to me I have sent enclosed with this letter, so that the exalted judgement may peruse it."

The letter ran thus: "*To the lofty presence of the exalted Sheykh, the Master, the Sayyed, our lord Abu'l-Fażl Suri b. al-Mo'tazz, from the slaves Yabghu,*[164] *Ṭoghrïl and Dāvud, clients* (mavāli) *of the Commander of the Faithful.*[165] It was not possible for us slaves to remain at Bokhara in Transoxania. While 'Alitegin was alive, we enjoyed a mutually harmonious and friendly relationship, but now that he is dead, we have to deal with his sons, both young and inexperienced, and with Tun.sh, 'Alitegin's Commander-in-Chief, who has control over them and the kingdom and the army and with whom we have had many an acrimonious encounter, so that we could no longer remain there. Khwarazm fell into a very disturbed state with the killing of Hārun, and it was not possible for us to move there. We have come for protection to the Lord of the World, the Great Sultan, the Dispenser of Favours, so that the Khᵛāja, Suri, might act as a mediator [Gh 471] and might write to the Grand Vizier Aḥmad b. 'Abd al-Ṣamad and intercede with him, since there is a bond of friendship between him and us. Every winter, the Khwarazm Shah Altuntāsh used to allot us, our families and our beasts a place within his province until the springtime, and the Grand Vizier used to act as intercessor. If the exalted judgement sees fit, we can be admitted as submissive vassals in such a way that one of us three leaders [F 612] could be serving at the exalted court, while the others could undertake whatever task the lord may command, and we shall be able to shelter beneath his mighty shadow.[166] The districts of Nasā and Farāva, which border the desert, could be bestowed on us so that we may deposit our baggage and impedimenta there and feel free from cares and worries. We will not allow any evildoer from Balkhān Kuh, Dehestān, the fringes of Khwarazm or the regions adjacent to the Oxus to cause trouble, and we will drive away the 'Erāqi and Khwarazmian Turkmens. If, God forbid, the lord does not give us a favourable answer, we do not know what will happen to us since we have no place on earth and there is nowhere left for us. We did not dare to write anything directly to that august court, given its overpowering splendour, so we wrote to the Khᵛāja in order that he might bring this matter to a conclusion in a masterful fashion, *if God, Most High so wills.*"

When the Vizier read these letters, he said to Bu Naṣr, "O Khᵛāja, until now we were dealing with mere sheep herders, and look how many headaches *they* created for us and how the troubles are still with us. Now we face commanders set on seizing provinces. I did protest vociferously on many an occasion that it was unwise to come to Ṭabarestān and Gorgān, but the lord paid no attention. A wretched fellow like 'Erāqi, who doesn't know his right hand from his left, paraded a whole bunch of lies and false promises but nothing came of it for it was all hopeless and futile. Peaceful provinces like Gorgān and Ṭabarestān fell into turmoil and became ruined, and their loyal subjects turned into rebels, and Bā Kālijār will adopt a devious way from now on; and in Khorasan a crisis of this magnitude has occurred. May God Most High cause this affair to have a happy outcome! Now despite this, they won't allow matters to proceed on the right course; they will provoke and stir up these Seljuqs, and one can imagine what the result will then be." He continued, "This is too important to be neglected for an instant; we must inform the Amir." Bu Naṣr [F 613] said, "He has been drinking wine all night up to almost noon, and is now enjoying his sleep." He replied, "This is no time for sleeping! He must be informed and told that an important matter has come up, and he must be woken up!" [Gh 472]

I, Bu'l-Fażl, was sent to the Amir's private servant Āghāji Khāṣṣa,[167] and I spoke with him. He went into the camp enclosure, stood there, and made a coughing noise to attract attention. I heard the Amir's voice calling out, "What's the matter?" The personal servant answered, "Bu'l-Fażl has come, and is saying that the Grand Vizier and Bu Naṣr have come to the domed tent and must see the lord, since something serious has occurred." He said, "All right," and he got up. I offered up invocations for his well-being. The Amir sent for a pitcher and water, washed himself, and came out of the camp enclosure into the tent. He summoned them both for a private audience. I remained standing there. The letters were read out, and he was extremely disturbed by the news and heaped curses on 'Erāqi's head. The Grand Vizier said, "The divine decree is working out its course; 'Erāqi and the rest are mere instruments for this. The lord ought to give matters more thought before he embarks upon putting them into effect. Now that this situation has arisen, efforts must be made so that it does not become drawn out." He said, "What's to be done?" The Vizier replied, "If the exalted judgement sees fit, the Generals Begtughdï and Bu'l-Nażr should be summoned, since there is no top-level Commander-in Chief (*sepahsālār*) here, and there should also be present the General Sübashï, who is held in very great esteem, together with others whom the lord may think appropriate to summon, both men who bear weapons (i.e. Turks) and Persians (i.e. civilian advisers),[168] so that the matter may be discussed and a decision made." He said, "That's a good idea."

They came out, and attendants went along and summoned the commanders. People began to assemble according to the usual procedure. At the time of the afternoon worship, he held court. He kept back the Grand Vizier Aḥmad b. ʿAbd al-Ṣamad, the Head of the Army Department Bu'l-Fatḥ Rāzi, the Head of the Chancery Bu Naṣr Moshkān, and the Generals Begtughdï, Bu'l-Nażr and Sübashï. From amongst the boon-companions, Bu Sahl Zowzani was summoned, [F 614] since from time to time he used to summon him and give him a seat in such privy sessions. All sorts of views were aired and debated. The Amir said, "This is no small matter. Ten thousand Turkish horsemen, with many leaders, have come, planted themselves in the midst of our province with their avowed grievance that there is no place of refuge left for them, while in truth, it is we who have become afflicted. For our part, we shall not allow them to settle on the land and grow in size and strength,[169] for one must remember what mischief and trouble were brought by those Turkmens whom my father allowed in and brought over the river and gave a place within Khorasan where they lived as camel herders (*sārbānān*). We cannot allow these people, whom the Vizier says are lusting after territory, [Gh 473] to remain there and to take their ease there. The wise course is for us personally to lead an expedition from Gorgān, together with the palace gholāms and the most select troops of the army, travel by the route of Samangān which comes out between Esparāyen and Ostovā,[170] and emerge at Nasā and attack them as fiercely as possible so that they are totally destroyed and wiped out."

The Vizier said, "The wise course of action will be what the exalted judgement thinks." The Head of the Army Department, the Head of the Chancery and Bu Sahl Zowzani all concurred with these words. The Vizier said to the Generals, "What do *you* say?" They replied, "We are servants. Our business is making war, and we put into effect the commands we are given and wield our swords in order to frustrate the enemy; the direction of public affairs is the Vizier's job."[171] The Vizier said, "At all events, it is necessary to make enquiries about the present state of the road." [F 615] Several men who were familiar with that road were immediately brought in. They enumerated three possible routes. One of them was through the desert passing by Dehestān, most arduous, with no water or pasture, and the other two were even rougher and most uneven. The Vizier said, "I will offer what good counsel I know, and then it will be up to the lord to command. The mounts of the one-horse troopers and those of the palace gholāms had been for the most part existing on a diet of rice straw during the long sojourn at Āmol. Since we have come back here, they have been able to graze on grass.[172] From here to Nasā conditions are as have been delineated above, rough and rugged. If the lord were to set off personally and were to press on in haste, the mounts would lag behind and the selected and seasoned troops from the army[173] which come up for action will have only a small reserve of strength left, whereas the enemy will be well rested and prepared and will have stout mounts. Great care must be taken to avoid any mishap and consequent loss of honour and prestige, for the lord's setting off in his own precious person is no small undertaking. The other point is that these Turkmens have become quiescent and they have made no obvious trouble; they have written to Suri in these terms and have shown submissiveness. It would be best, so it seems to me, to send a favourable answer to Suri and ask him to tell these country folk (or, "chieftains"?)[174] that they should not worry since they are welcome here (lit. "have come into their own land") and are under our authority and protection; we were setting out for Ray, and when we reach there, whatever is deemed necessary and whatever seems beneficial for their interests, will be ordained. This letter will go off, the lord will leave here for Nishapur in an auspicious state, the mounts will have time to draw breath and recover their strength, and the position of these newly-arrived ones[175] will become more clearly known [Gh 474]—then, if need be, and if it appears the correct course that they should be ejected from Khorasan, a powerful contingent from the army under an alert and experienced commander can go with a fully-equipped force and put an end to their affair, [F 616] for there will be a loss of prestige if the lord leads an expedition against them in person, especially if the attack is launched from here. I have set forth how the situation appears to me; it is for the lord to command."

Those who were present all agreed that this was the correct view. It was accordingly decided that, within three days, the journey back to Nishapur would be made. The Amir ordered Bu'l-Ḥasan b. ʿAbd al-Jalil to be summoned to this court session. He came in, and received the command to proceed to the town of Gorgān with five senior commanders (*moqaddamān*) chosen from the *sarhangs*, a general officer (*ḥājeb*) and 1,000 cavalrymen, and he was to be the army's administrator and adjutant. This was in order to see what Bā Kālijār would do regarding the taxation he was obliged to hand over; then at that point the Amir would ordain whatever his judgement deemed necessary; the discussions about this went on for some time. Bu'l-Ḥasan was taken along to the Royal Wardrobe; he donned a robe of honour and came into the royal presence with the senior officers and the general officer. These were likewise given robes of honour. They went back, and after leaving the court drew up their troops in order and went off towards the town.

On Wednesday, 10 Rajab [/21 May 1035], swift couriers arrived from Khwarazm and brought the news of the killing of the Grand Vizier's son ʿAbd al-Jabbār and of his family and entourage. After Hārun was murdered, ʿAbd al-Jabbār had acted hastily and had immediately emerged from his hideout, had mounted an elephant and had appeared at the open ground before the Government Headquarters. The other son of the Khwarazm Shah, who was called Khandān, together with the eunuch Shakar and their gholāms had fled.[176] By an unfortunate combination of circumstances, the eunuch Shakar came with a force of gholāms to the open space before the government headquarters on some matter, and confronted ʿAbd al-Jabbār, who hurled insults at him. Shakar told the gholāms, "Let him have it!" (*dehid*). They waded in with their bows and arrows and their battle axes and killed ʿAbd al-Jabbār, together with his two sons, a cousin of his and over forty of his retainers. They brought back Khandān and set him up as Amir.[177] (A detailed account of these happenings will be given in the section on Khwarazm.)[178]

The Vizier held a commemorative session and sat in formal mourning, and all the notables and great men went to him.[179] I saw how courageous he was, [F 617] for no tears flowed from his eyes. In all things that define a man's greatness he excelled, and in this case too, he showed great fortitude and was applauded for it. Indeed, it is exactly as if the poet had him in mind when he composed this verse, (Poetry)

1. *People weep over us, but we do not weep over anyone; indeed, we have harder hearts* (lit. "livers") *than camels.*[180]

The Amir sent to him his boon-companion, the religious lawyer ʿAbd al-Malek Ṭusi, with a verbal message of condolence. [Gh 475] This religious lawyer was an eloquent and wise person. When he delivered the message, the Vizier rose to his feet, kissed the ground and then sat down again, saying, "May I, my children and all the members of my family be the ransom for a single hair of the lord's head! The happiness of servants lies in their devoting their lives to doing the lord's will." All men are made in the same mould,[181] and no-one acquires a good reputation erroneously.[182] This refusal to display grief is reminiscent of how ʿAmr, son of Leyth, behaved, and I shall relate what I have read about it so that it is included here; *God is the One most knowledgeable what is right!*

The story of ʿAmr b. al-Leyth, the ruler in Khorasan, and his serene composure on hearing the news of his son's death

One year, ʿAmr b. al-Leyth returned from Kerman to Sistan at a time when his son Moḥammad, who was known by the epithet of "the chivalrous youth of the army" (*fatā 'l-ʿaskar*),[183] a most virtuous and unblemished youth, had grown to maturity and was ready for appointment to office. By chance, while crossing the desert from Kerman, this youth was afflicted by paroxysmal pains[184] when they were five stages' travel away from the capital of Sistan,[185] and it was not possible for ʿAmr to halt there. He left his son there with physicians, trusty retainers, one secretary and a hundred swift camel-riders. He told the chief of the camel-riders that swift riders should be sent off one after the other [F 618] and that the secretary should write down what the patient was doing, what he ate, what he said, and whether he was sleeping or not sleeping, so that ʿAmr might be aware of everything which was happening, until it could be known what God Most High had decreed.

ʿAmr came to the city and installed himself in the private quarters of the palace and sat there alone on his prayer mat on a bare floor,[186] and stayed there day and night on that very floor and without a pillow beneath his head. The camel-riders kept on arriving, twenty to thirty times in the course of a day and night, and what the secretary had written was read out to him, and he wept and lamented and gave away large sums of money as alms. He went on thus for seven days and nights: fasting by day and breaking his fast at night with a piece of dry bread on its own, and he grieved bitterly and often. On the eighth day, towards dawn, the chief of the swift camel-riders came in, bearing no letters, for the son had passed away and the secretary could not bring himself to write down the news of his death and had sent the chief of the camel-riders instead, hoping that ʿAmr would realize what had happened. When he came into ʿAmr's presence, he kissed the ground but he had no letter with him. ʿAmr said, "The child has died?" The chief of the camel-riders replied, [Gh 476] "May the lord live for many more years!" ʿAmr said, "*Praise be to God!* Praise be to the Almighty Lord, for He has put into effect everything He has willed and whatever He wills shall be done! Go away, and keep this to yourself." He himself arose and went to the bathhouse. He had his hair combed out and attended to. He came back, rested and went to sleep. After performing the worship, he summoned the major-domo of the palace. He came in, and he gave him these orders: "Go, and prepare a great feast, and get ready for tomorrow 3,000 lambs and what goes with them, wine and the vessels, and musicians and singers." The major-domo went back and everything was got ready. ʿAmr instructed the chamberlain, "Tomorrow there will be an open court session. Inform the troops and the populace, high-born and lowly alike." [F 619]

At dawn the next day, he sat on his throne and held court. A lavish feast had been laid out, and after the court was finished they embarked upon it. Wine was served, and musicians and singers got to work. When the feast was about to end, ʿAmr b. Leyth turned towards the leading figures, the retainers and the troops stationed at the court, and said, "Know that death is a certainty. For seven days and nights we were taken up with the illness of our son Moḥammad. We did not have any sleep, food or rest lest he die. But it was the Almighty God's will that he should die. If it were possible to bring him back, we would sell our dearest possessions to have him; but this way is barred to mankind. Since he is dead, and we know that no dead person ever comes back, lamentation and weeping are sheer folly and are best left to women. Return to your homes, carry on happy and normal lives, since it is unfitting for monarchs to indulge in formal mourning." Those present offered up prayers for him and returned home.

Men's resolution becomes firmer through stories like this, and the weak and ignoble also benefit according to their own capacity.[187]

Amir Mas'ud set out from Gorgān on Thursday, 11 Rajab [/22 May 1035] and reached Nishapur on Monday, 22 Rajab [/2 June], and took up quarters in the Garden of Shādyākh. On Sunday, 28 Rajab [/8 June], Aḥmad b. 'Ali b. Nushtegin died at Nishapur. *For every term of life there is a written document.*[188] One can say that, with his passing, equestrian skill, polo-playing, proficiency at the *ṭabṭāb* game[189] and other skills of this kind, were effaced. When the Amir reached the town, he threw himself enthusiastically into making preparations for the army so that he might despatch it to Nasā. The Turkmens had become quiescent so that they might see what was going to happen. The letters from the courier service informers of Bāvard and Nasā were to the effect that, "From that time when we had left Gorgān till we arrived at Nishapur and took up residence there, no acts of destruction[190] and oppressive behaviour have taken place; [Gh 477] the greater part of their baggage and impedimenta has been plundered and carried off by Shāh Malek, [F 620] and their morale has reached a low ebb. What has been left to them they keep with themselves, and they have transported it to the fringes of the desert. They are being extremely alert and watchful day and night, preparing themselves for either peace or war. They have been somewhat reassured by Suri's response, but still remain very apprehensive about the future. The Seljuqs and Ināliyān are out on horseback every day from early morning till towards noon, stationing themselves on an eminence, and secretly making plans because, since they have heard that the exalted banner has set out on its way to Nishapur, they are very fearful." Khᵛāja Bu Naṣr laid these letters before the Amir. The Amir left off drinking and was feeling very worried, and rued the day when he had embarked on this journey that had produced nothing from Ṭabarestān except infamy and had brought Khorasan into its present state. Meanwhile, ʿErāqi no longer had the temerity to pronounce on matters of state in the Amir's presence.

There was also a most remarkable and astonishing development: the Amir became suspicious of the Grand Vizier Aḥmad b. ʿAbd al-Ṣamad, despite his many meritorious and devoted acts of service and his wise strategy culminating in the assassination of the God-forsaken Hārun, and he regarded the Grand Vizier's son ʿAbd al-Jabbār as the prime instigator of Hārun's rebellion. Moreover, the Vizier's calumniators spread around the false idea that, in the context of the Seljuqs' entering Khorasan, the Vizier had been engaging in some sort of covert communication with the enemy, meaning by this the occasion of the Seljuqs' entering Khorasan.[191]

I heard from Khᵛāja Bu Naṣr, in the course of a private conversation which he had with Bā Manṣur b. Ṭeyfur[192] and myself, in which he said, "The Almighty God knows that this Vizier is upright and honest and a fount of sincere advice, and is innocent of all such allegations as these. But monarchs tend to form ideas of their own and one cannot always fathom what they think and what goes on in their minds. I, Bu Naṣr, by reason of the fact that my whole professional life, from youth up to this very day, has been with them, [F 621] have a more clear understanding of their ways, and I think that it is the working of ineluctable Fate that had made this lord of ours so suspicious of the Vizier, to the extent that he opposes any correct decision or wise counsel, on whatever topic, that comes from the Vizier. *When the inevitable decree comes along, a man's sense of vision becomes blind.*[193] On several past occasions, he had this master under scrutiny and entrusted him with important missions. He appointed him to lead substantial armies towards Balkh, Tokhārestān and Khottalān, while secretly he appointed a spy and informer (*movakkal*) over such a distinguished commander. The Vizier was fully aware of this but turned a blind eye to it, and it did not stop him from offering wise counsel. Now when the matter of the Seljuqs has arisen, and the Amir is depressed and worried on this account, and is preparing [Gh 478] to send an army to Nasā, he held a private conclave on this topic; there was a wide-ranging discussion, but to whatever the Vizier said, the Amir returned a dismissive and scoffing answer.

"When we went home, the Vizier had a private conversation with me and said, 'You see what's happened to me? By the Almighty God, this is a strange business! A son of mine like 'Abd al-Jabbār, together with many of my retainers, had to lose their lives for the sake of Khwarazm before this lord could realize that, in the matter of Khwarazm, I was blameless! I don't have a sufficient supply of sons and retainers to squander away on every occasion when he becomes suspicions and has fanciful delusions, just so that he may realize or not realize that I am guiltless. But the case of these Turkmens is even more bizarre: Regardless of everything else, why should I be attracted towards them? Is it so that—after having kissed the ground before me and my hands (i.e. after having previously acknowledged their own subordinate position)—if they do manage to enhance their stature, they should make me their vizier! At all events, at this moment when I am the vizier of a monarch like Mas'ud b. Maḥmud, I would not stoop to become vizier to a bunch of people who have done much obeisance to me in the past! Since I am in such a plight, how can I have the heart and the determination, how can I strive with my hands and feet, and how can I offer sound advice and counsel?'"[194] [F 622]

"I said, 'May the lord's life be prolonged! Things are not like this. You should not let your mind dwell on such situations, for bitterness and rancour are not appropriate at a time when such important issues have arisen.' He replied. 'O Khᵛāja, are you trying to pull the wool over my eyes? I'm not a small child. Didn't you see how many barbed words were bandied about today? For a long time now I have been noticing this and ignoring it, but now it has gone too far.' I said, 'Would the Vizier regard it as appropriate if I should raise this state of affairs with the exalted lord?' He replied, 'It won't be any use, because they have poisoned this lord's mind. If, on some occasion, there should be talk on these topics, and if you can faithfully set forth wise counsel such as you are well able to do, and what you know of me, then it will be appropriate, and you will have performed a magnanimous act.' I said, 'Good!'

"It so happened that the Amir had a private session, and there was talk of Balkh, 'Alitegin's sons, Khwarazm and the Seljuqs. I said, 'May the lord's life be prolonged! One should not let important matters pile up, and it is regarding these issues as insignificant that has brought upon us these current worries and anxieties. There should be a let-up in this pleasure-making for a while, there should be a concentration on affairs and there should be consultation with the Vizier.' The Amir said, 'What are you saying? All this is the Vizier's doing because he's not frank with us.' He stood his ground [Gh 479] and began to reel off complaints about the Vizier, that such-and-such happened regarding Khwarazm, and his son did so-and-so, and that now he's brought in the Seljuqs!

"I replied, 'May the lord's life be prolonged! The Vizier had a lengthy session with me yesterday concerning this matter, and has spoken at length (i.e. about this animosity on the Sultan's part) and was exceedingly despondent. I asked him whether it would be appropriate to convey these words to the exalted court session? He said, "If there should be talk, it would be appropriate to mention it, provided you explain matters as coming from yourself." If the command is now given, I will set forth these matters.' He said, 'Good, carry on!' I embarked on recounting *in toto* everything that the Vizier had said. He pondered deeply for a while, and then he said, 'Indeed, he is telling the truth, for he sacrificed his entire household, [F 623] his own son and his retainers, for the sake of Khwarazm, and in all sincerity he took the right measures to bring about the downfall of that deluded Hārun.' I answered, 'Since the lord knows that this is the case, and this man is his vizier, and the lord further knows that he has successfully accomplished several commissions entrusted to him and that he has expended life and limb and wealth and possessions in serving you, what is the advantage of regarding him with ill favour and treating him with suspicion? For the bad effects of that will rebound on the lord's affairs, and how can the Vizier who is suspected of ill will exercise sound judgement in his work? For he would be led to believe that whatever he thinks or says would be misconstrued. He won't say anything except what may pass as palatable at that moment, and thus real issues will not be addressed and the interests of good governance will be ignored.'

"The Amir said, 'It's just as you have said, and until now, no disloyalty to us on this man's part has been evident; but they have filled our ears with tales about him and are still doing so.' I said, 'At this moment, the lord is facing many important matters. If the exalted judgement deems fit, this man's heart should be won over again and anyone making unwarranted remarks against him should be firmly rebuked, so that the Vizier's confidence is restored and his devotion rekindled, and so that the lord's affairs do not become impossibly entangled but run smoothly instead.' He said, 'What should we do about this?' I replied, 'If the lord sees fit, he should be summoned to a private audience and be made to feel appreciated.' He said, 'We will feel too self-conscious for that' (May God, He is exalted and magnified, forgive that great monarch! It can be said that no more noble or more forbearing ruler than him may be found.)[195] I said, 'What, then, would the lord suggest as the best course?' He answered, 'You must go to him at the time of the afternoon worship with a verbal message from us, and must say whatever you consider will be appropriate [Gh 480] and will have the effect of reassuring his mind. We ourself will also have a face-to-face talk tomorrow, so as not to leave any grounds for his feeling resentful and under suspicion. [F 624] When you get back, you must see us and give us a full account.' I said, 'If the exalted judgement sees fit, 'Abdus, or some other of the lord's intimates whom the lord considers appropriate should accompany me, for two men are better than one.'[196] He replied, 'I know what you're thinking, but we have no need to appoint anyone to keep an eye on you. Your honesty and general concern for our interests are firmly established and known to us.' He spoke many a kind word, so that I felt overwhelmed and embarrassed. I took my leave and went home.

"At the time of the afternoon worship, I went to the Vizier, told him everything that had transpired and I gave him the message, replete with heartwarming words. When it ended, the Vizier rose, kissed the ground, sat down again and wept, saying, 'I shall never forget my indebtedness to this monarch's lordly status for bestowing upon me such an exalted office, and so long as I live, I shall not be sparing of my advice, service or concern and care. But I hope that the words of my foes, and those envious of me, will not be listened to, and if I commit any error, I should be told about that and the Amir himself should rebuke me for it and not let it fester within his own heart. In so far as I am being regarded with suspicion and have thus become apprehensive and prevented from doing my work, it has a deleterious impact on day-to-day state affairs, and that being the case, what can one say about important matters?' I replied, 'The lord, the Grand Vizier, should take great heart and recover his equipoise, for if, after this, any act of double-dealing and hypocrisy is on foot, responsibility for it should be laid at Bu Naṣr's door.' I cheered him up, went back, and recounted to the Amir in its entirety what had taken place, and I added, 'If the exalted judgement sees fit, soothing and encouraging words should be addressed to the Grand Vizier tomorrow in a private talk, since what he hears directly from your exalted presence will have an altogether different impact on him.' He said, 'I'll follow your advice.'

"The next day, after the court session, he had a private talk with the Vizier, since the courtiers [F 625] had gone back home. He summoned me, Bu Naṣr, and he talked extensively with the Vizier in a very encouraging way, so that no resentment or suspicion remained in the Vizier's mind. It was vitally necessary for me to say these words so that these matters could be brought into the open and resolved, for without the Vizier, things will not go well."[197] We[198] replied, "This is exactly the case," and offered up prayers and invocations for him, praising his devoted work for the welfare of the realm. [Gh 481]

When Amir Masʿud came to a firm decision to send a powerful army, under a prestigious commander, to Nasā, he had a private session with the Vizier, the Head of the Army Department, the Head of the Chancery, Bu Sahl Zowzani the boon-companion and the Generals Begtughdï, Bu'l-Nażr and Sübashï. A minion went off, and the notables, the field officers, the generals and those holding administrative charges in the provinces[199] were summoned, such as the General Nushtegin Valvāleji, the Master of the Royal Stables Böri and others. When they were all present, the Amir said, "We have now been here for several days; the army has had a rest and the beasts have drawn breath. Although the letters from our informers in Nasā and Bāvard indicate that the Seljuqs are overawed and are not harassing the local population, however much we ponder over these matters, it cannot be right that 10,000 Turkish horsemen should remain in our midst. How do we solve this?"

They all looked at each other in silence. The Vizier said, "Give your opinions, for the lord's words are directed at you, and you have been summoned here for this important matter. The situation is exactly as the exalted judgement has envisaged: either Khorasan should be cleared of these people and the whole lot of them hurled back to the far side of the Oxus, or else they must enter the lord's service, in successive groups, and be obedient, and their chiefs must send a hostage (or: "hostages")[200] to the exalted court." Begtughdï said, "It is well-known that the late Amir [F 626] of his own free will brought a group of Turkmens into Khorasan, and what depredations they wrought and are still wreaking! These are merely following in their footsteps. A foe never becomes a friend,[201] and the remedy for them is the sword. Arslān Jādheb said this, but no-one listened to him, and things happened as they did."[202] The other prominent figures said the same. Agreement was reached that an army would go to Nasā under an experienced commander. The Amir said, "Whom shall we send?" They said, "If the exalted judgement sees fit, we will sit down outside with the Vizier, and this affair can be properly arranged through verbal messages." He replied, "Good!"

They went back. Bu Naṣr Moshkān was going to and fro, and there was much discussion until a decision was reached that there should be ten commanders, all senior officers of the army stationed at the court (*moqaddamān-e ḥasham*),[203] and their chief should be the General Begtughdï and the administrator and adjutant Khᵛāja Ḥoseyn b. 'Ali b. Mikā'il.[204] A force of 15,000 cavalrymen, from all ethnic groups, was to be got ready plus 2,000 palace gholāms. Begtughdï said, "I am a servant who obeys orders, but it has been said that too many cooks spoil the broth.[205] Several eminent commanders have been put up from the army [Gh 482], comprising a group of the former commanders of Sultan Maḥmud and some recently promoted to senior positions (*bar-kashidagān*) by the lord, inexperienced youths. There should be one single chain of command directly from the Commander-in-Chief.[206] I am a man getting on in years, with my faculty of sight and my body impaired, and I cannot see properly. There must be no divided counsels in the supreme command; grave defects will arise from that and the lord will consider me responsible for them."

The Amir answered, "No-one out of these commanders will dare to deviate from your orders and go beyond them." [F 627] Some of those present did not approve of Begtughdï's going as commander, and they said, "It's just as this old man says; this enterprise mustn't be spoilt," but the Amir said, "Begtughdï must go without fail," and so it was finally settled that he should go. All those who had been there went back, so that those who were to go on the expedition could get things ready. In private, the Grand Vizier said to Bu Naṣr, "I am most concerned about this military expedition, but I daren't say a word lest it be misconstrued." Bu Naṣr asked, "Why is this?" He answered, "There is a most inauspicious conjunction." (He was very knowledgeable about astrology.) Bu Naṣr said, "I am likewise unhappy; I don't know anything about the stars, but this much I do know, that it is better to take into the fold a horde of strangers, who have found their way to this land and who are behaving in a submissive manner, than to drive them away and alienate them. However, since the lord and the group of commanders see it thus, there's nothing for it but to keep silent until we see what Almighty God has decreed." The Vizier said, "I have to speak out; if my words go unheeded, I shall have absolved myself of responsibility." And he did speak out, but it was to no avail, since the decree of Fate had come down and such a decree cannot be challenged.

The next day, the Amir mounted and went out into the open plain which lies before the Garden of Shādyākh. He halted there, and the troops were counted off with the tip of a whip,[207] and everyone there agreed that there was a sufficient number to conquer the whole of Turkestan and that the 2,000 palace gholāms there, all fully equipped and armed, would be sufficient for the whole world. The Amir bestowed much favour on the Commander of the Palace Gholāms, the General Begtughdï, and showered him with compliments, and he told all the prominent figures and senior officers, "This man is your commander and our representative. All of you should give ear to his instructions, for his ordinances will be on a par with our own commands." All of them kissed the ground [Gh 483] and said, "We will obey the commands." The Amir rode back. Platters of food had been set up, and all the prominent figures, senior officers, retainers and troops stationed at the court were given places to sit [F 628] and eat. When they had finished, the Commander Begtughdï and the other senior officers who were appointed for this campaign received robes of honour. They came into the royal presence, offered up service, and then went back. The next day, Thursday, 9 Shaʿbān [/19 June 1035], this army set out for Nasā, with a complete panoply of arms, equipment and matériel. The Khᵛāja Ḥoseyn b. ʿAli b. Mikāʾil was with them, and he had with him large amounts of clothing and gold so that he might reward, according to the amount and extent of their service, those who on the day of battle should acquit themselves well and whose worth he could discern. Two elephant keepers with two elephants were appointed to accompany them so that, since the commander had an elephant as his personal mount, Ḥoseyn too should ride an elephant on the day of battle and be able to observe the battle scene for himself.

On Friday, the tenth of this month [/20 June], the Amir ordered that the duty of delivering the *khoṭba* at Nishapur should be entrusted to Master Abu ʿOthmān Esmāʿil b. ʿAbd al-Raḥmān Ṣābuni, may God have mercy on him.[208] This man was the unique one of the age in every branch of learning and skills, and especially in sessions where the arts of preaching and of eloquence were displayed. People saw his expertise in this as being at such a pitch that even the finest orators would admit defeat when confronted by him. On this day, he delivered a very fine *khoṭba*. The Judge Abu'l-ʿAlāʾ Ṣāʿed, may God enfold him with his mercy, took offence at this procedure, and sent messages to the Amir that tampering with the status quo and well-established laws was unfitting.[209] The answer came back that he appreciated such a view, so that the Judge should not take umbrage.

At the time of the afternoon worship on Tuesday, 21 Shaʿbān [/1 July], a confidential despatch arrived from the intelligence agent who was with the conquering army to the effect that "The Turkmens were defeated at the first onslaught when the army's vanguard made contact with them, with the result that there was no need for the centre, right wing and left wing of the army to join battle. Around 700 or 800 men were killed and decapitated on the spot, a large number were taken prisoner and a great amount of plunder carried away." Immediately the report arrived, court attendants [F 629] went as harbingers of the good news to the houses of the notables. They made known this report, and were amply rewarded for it. The Amir ordered trumpets to be blown and drums beaten for the reception of the bearers of the good news. He summoned the boon companions and the musicians and singers. They came, and struck up playing and singing. He ate and drank all night until it was day, and much rejoicing and merry-making went on, since it was several days since wine had been drunk and the month of Ramażān was approaching. The Amir's carousing induced everyone else to rejoice, and they all made merry in their own homes.

At dawn, a report arrived to the effect that "The Sultan's army [Gh 483] suffered a devastating defeat, and everything they had with them, matériel and equipment, had fallen into the enemy's hands. The Commander Begtughdï's gholāms got him down from the elephant, and they set him on a horse and quickly led him away. The *kadkhodā* Khᵛāja Ḥoseyn b. ʿAli b. Mikā'il was captured, since he was mounted on the elephant and could not get to a horse. The army is retreating in several different directions."[210] Immediately this report arrived, the duty secretary informed Khᵛāja Bu Naṣr. Bu Naṣr had a house at Moḥammadābād near to Shādyākh. He came to the court straightaway. When he read the letter, which was very brief, he became extremely perturbed and plunged into grief. He asked what the Amir was doing. He was told that he went off to sleep at dawn and that in no way would it be possible to get him awake till towards noon.[211] He wrote a note to the Vizier describing to him this situation, and the Vizier came, and the retainers, the troops stationed at the court and the great personages started to come along as was the usual practice. When I, Bu'l-Fażl, reached the court, I found the Vizier, the Head of the Army Department, the Head of the Chancery, Bu Sahl Zowzani, Suri the head of the Divān of Khorasan, the General Sübashï and the General Bu'l-Nażr sitting by themselves at the gate of the Garden, the gate being locked against them since there was no-one living in the Garden. They were all deep in sorrow because of this disaster and were talking about it, but did not know [F 630] exactly how it had all happened. Towards noon, they wrote a note to the Amir and described the dreadful calamity. This missive of the courier was placed inside the folds of the note. A household servant took and delivered it. He brought back the answer, "No-one is to go back home, for there will be fresh reports from hour to hour, since there are riders expressly stationed along the road. After the worship, there will be a court session and the matter can be discussed there." The rest of the courtiers were sent back home, while these leading figures stayed at the court.

Towards the time of the midday worship, there arrived two riders of Farāva, Suri's retainers, men from his dare-devil riders, on their horses and fully armed, hot from the battlefield with all possible speed, men who had been through a battle.[212] They were brought in and questioned closely about the situation: how was it that the original letter told of the Turkmens being killed and routed, while the next letter reported the enemy's success and victory?

They replied, "This was God's doing, and it never entered anyone's mind that the enemy, gripped by fear, without weapons, lacking strength and devoid of resources, would be able to bring mayhem to an army of such great strength with such effortless ease. However, and if truth be told, this fiasco would not have occurred if they had obeyed the orders of the Commander Begtughdï; [Gh 485] but they did not obey them, and they all did whatever they liked, since there were so many commanders about. At the outset, they were acting prudently and keeping careful watch, and the journey between each stage was done in proper formation, with the centre, the right section, the left section,[213] the wings, the reserve treasury (*māya-dār*), the rearguard and the advance guard going along in correct formation. When they came upon the tents (i.e. of the Turkmens), they saw a cluster of them, empty, with a number of beasts and sheep herders. The Commander said, 'Proceed carefully and keep your formation—for the enemy are lying in wait on the fringes of the desert and have prepared ambushes—so that no mishap occurs and our scouts can go forward and reconnoitre the situation.' They disobeyed the order, [F 631] and it so happened that when the scouting party moved on, the mass of the troops plunged into those tents, with their tent furnishings[214] and emaciated sheep, and killed plenty of people indiscriminately.[215] This was the basis for that first report that the Turkmens had been defeated.

"When the Commander saw their predicament and the futile foray, he was forced to move forward with the army's centre, they all became intermingled and the pre-arranged orderly formations were abandoned,[216] especially when they reached that village where the enemy lay in ambush and had got ready to deliver battle. They now gave battle. Khᵛāja Ḥoseyn was mounted on the elephant. The battle proved to be of the fiercest kind, for the enemy dug their heels in and showed firm resolve, and things did not turn out the way we had thought, namely, that the enemy would flee at our first charge. Moreover, the day became extremely hot, the desert sands were smouldering in the heat, and the troops and the animals were suffering from thirst and beginning to wilt. There was water to the army's rear. Some of those commanders with no battle experience said, 'We should let the army fall back in a leisurely and smooth fashion as part of a feigned retreat and hit-and-run stratagem,[217] till it reaches the watering-place.' They did not have sufficient foresight to realize that such a retreat would appear as a flight, and the rank-and-file could not work out in their minds just what the intention was. Without the Commander being aware of what was happening, they fell back. When the enemy saw that, they thought it was a flight, and they burst out of their ambush positions and plunged into the fray with great ferocity. The Commander Begtughdï remained there in a state of perplexity, with a weak faculty of sight and utterly powerless, on top of his she-elephant. How could he retrieve that situation, given that the army was following its own whim and when the enemy [F 632] had emerged, powerful and in control of the situation? When the enemy encircled the elephant, his personal gholāms brought him down from it and set him on a horse, and fighting their way through the enemy lines, bore him off, otherwise he would have also been taken captive. And what a refreshing water and restful encampment that turned out to be! No-one was able to go to anyone else's help, and every man sought to save his own skin. [Gh 486] Wealth, valuable equipment and matériel in those large quantities fell into the hands of our opponents. Our men all fled, each group by a different route. The two of us were friends. We waited until the Turkmens stopped harrying our troops and went back, and we felt safe again. We rode all night, and now we have arrived. No-one has reached here before us, and the truth is just as we have related. The head of the Divān (i.e. of Khorasan, meaning Suri) appointed us and eight of our comrades from this army to bring back news. We do not know what has happened to our comrades or where have they got to. If anyone should come up with a different account, he should not be listened to because it was our task in the army to find out how things were going on and to obtain all the news. Alas that an army so great and so well equipped as this should be destroyed because of dissensions amongst its leaders! But such was the divine decree."[218]

When the great men and the commanders heard these words, they were plunged into deep gloom that an army so great and so well equipped should have perished so gratuitously. Khᵛāja Bu Naṣr dictated to me, Bu'l-Fażl, what he had heard and it was written out. The Amir held court after the worship, and then a private conclave was held. The notables sat down, and the talk went on till the time of the evening worship. The Amir read the document just written out, and discussion ranged over all sorts of topics. The Vizier reassured the Amir, saying that "It was in accordance with the divine decree, and ever since the world has existed, things like this have occurred, and [F 633] this sort of thing has happened to great armies on many occasions. May the lord be preserved for ever, since through the lord's continued existence and that of his empire, all critical situations can be retrieved!" The Head of the Army Department said, "After the decree of the Almighty God, this defeat has been caused by the lack of co-operation between the army's commanders." Everyone expressed more or less the same sentiments, some putting it more delicately and some more bluntly.

When they had gone back, the Vizier said to Bu Naṣr, "You were very silent and said nothing; then when you did speak, it was like the stone from a mangonel which you had hurled at a glass house." He replied, "What can I do? I am a man who uses blunt words and I cannot rein in my choleric nature. This lord did not listen to me when I conveyed your reservations (i.e. the Vizier's doubts about the whole expedition), and this calamitous event had to happen. As long as I live, the bitter taste of this will not leave me, for nothing had prepared me for such a happening within this mighty empire. First I refer to the lord, to the Grand Vizier's response, and then to that of the others present: out of solicitude and concern for the lord's well-being and in order not to rub salt into the wound,[219] they spoke soothing words, and I too kept nodding my head in agreement and approval, [Gh 487] since there was no other way out. The Amir kept on pressing me, saying, 'Bu Naṣr, what do *you* have to say on this?' and he kept on insisting. What could I do except to tell the truth and offer him a piece of sound advice so that he might perchance refrain from acting wilfully and attend to matters of state instead in a more informed manner?" They all said, "*May you receive your reward from God!* You spoke most aptly then and you speak justly now," and they all returned homewards.[220]

Afterwards, I asked Khᵛāja Bu Naṣr, "What were those words that caused such a commotion amongst those present?" He replied, "All of them were uttering fawning and beguiling words, and were making light of the momentous affair which had happened, as people do in such occasions.[221] [F 634] Seething with anger I was of course not saying a word, but the Amir would not have it and insisted that I spoke. I said, 'May the lord's life be prolonged! Although matters of warfare are not my métier and I said nothing, either at the time when the army was despatched or at this present time when a great calamity has befallen; but now, since the lord is insistent, it would be discourteous of me to hold my tongue. I am sick at heart, and would that I had died before seeing this day!' The Amir said, 'Speak plainly and without reservation, for we have no cause to doubt the sincerity of your counsel.' I said, 'May the lord's life be prolonged! Merry-making and pleasurable pursuits must be laid aside for a while. He should keep a personal eye on the army, and he should reject those economies which the Khᵛāja, the Head of the Army Department, is advocating, thinking this to be an act of service which he is doing, and he should make it his business to ascertain the feelings of the troops and look after their interests, for it was through the use of brave men of valour that the late Amir could amass such great amounts of wealth. Unless the troops are cherished, men will come along and—God forbid!—carry off the wealth, and all sorts of perils will loom ahead. I know that these words of mine will not please the lord; truth is a bitter pill and sound advice is unpalatable. But there is no other way, and loyal and concerned servants should always be forthright in offering advice.' The Amir said, 'It is exactly as you said, and it is clear to us that you have our best interests in mind.' All aspects of the matter were discussed, and it was decided that an envoy should be sent to the Turkmens, something which should have been done before all this so that we would not now face such an humiliation. I myself, Bu Naṣr, am in no way in agreement with this policy, and I don't know what the outcome will be. *God is the One who gives sufficiency, through His grace!*" [F 635]

On Friday, 23 Shaʿbān [/13 July 1035], a letter arrived from Ghaznin announcing the death of [Gh 488] Bu'l-Qāsem ʿAli Nuki, the father of Bu Naṣr, who is today, in the fortunate time of the Exalted Sultan Abu'l-Moẓaffar Ebrāhim b. Nāṣer Din Allāh Masʿud, Chief Overseer and Head of Intelligence for the Realm (*moshref-e mamlakat*). The Amir had during these two years given the office of headship of the postal and intelligence system, which Bu'l-Qāsem held, to Ḥoseyn b. ʿAbdallāh, and the office of the oversight of Ghaznin was entrusted to Bu'l-Qāsem in exchange for it. This was not due to any apparent act of disloyalty on Bu'l-Qāsem's part, but rather, because Ḥoseyn asked for appointment to the postal and intelligence system. He was the son of the Head of the Chancery for Amir Maḥmud and had acted as vizier at Herat for this lord, Masʿud, during his father's time. Mas'ud felt he could not refuse him, and gave the office of the postal and intelligence system to him, and the office of the oversight of Ghaznin—which was the more important office—to Bu'l-Qāsem. I have no choice but to give an explanation of circumstances like these so that I may do justice to the great men and elders of this great house and may fulfill the duties of pledging fidelity and friendship which I owe to them.

After this, the fugitives began to drift in, arriving by all sorts of routes, downhearted and filled with shame. The Amir ordered that they should be reassured and consoled and that what had happened should be attributed to the divine decree. But the senior officers were confronted directly by the Amir's harsh reproaches for the way they had disobeyed the Commander-in-Chief, and they begged for forgiveness. I heard the General Nushtegin Valvāleji say, in the presence of Khᵛāja Bu Naṣr, that he alone lost over two million dirhams. The Commander Begtughdï also arrived, and gave his own first hand account of the events to the Amir, saying, "If the leading commanders had not disobeyed, I would have conquered the whole of Turkestan with this army." The Amir replied, "We have become fully aware of the situation, [F 636] and your own service and good intentions are clear to us." The palace gholāms likewise arrived back, battered and benumbed, but mostly on horseback.[222]

This was the first great setback (lit. "weakening," *vahn*) which this monarch suffered, and after this there was setback after setback, till at the end he was martyred and departed from this deceitful world with much pain and regret, as I shall explain in all its detail in its appropriate place, if the Almighty God so wills.[223] How could he have repelled the decreed Fate once it came down, since it had been foreordained[224] that the Seljuqs should reach that status? *God does what He wills and pronounces judgement as He wishes!*[225] Political power is entirely the result of a conjunction of favourable happenings.[226] One should read books about people's deeds and conduct[227] and historical accounts and realize that there have been in the past many remarkable occurrences and unusual events, so that one does not at once rush in to cavil at this mighty monarch, and attribute weakness to him, even though [Gh 489] he could have a strong streak of arbitrary behaviour (*estebdād*) and there were lapses of judgement in his policies. One should recognize all that as coming from God, His mention is exalted, for no human being intends evil against himself.

After this battle took place, all the Amir's talk was about this topic. He commiserated with the Head of the Army Department Bu'l-Fatḥ Rāzi, and behaved kindly with the army, showing concern for them and looking after their interests, especially those soldiers who had gone off on the campaign to Nasā, since most of them had lost their weapons and equipment and their mounts.

The month of Ramażān came in and the fast began. Letters arrived from the confidential agents who were lying low at Nasā.[228] They had written that such large quantities of equipment, furnishings, animals, gold and silver, clothing, weapons and luxury goods fell into the Turkmens' hands [F 637] that they were dumbfounded, as if they could not believe what had happened. When they found themselves in a secure position, they held a council, and the leading men, commanders and elders sat down together within a large tent and held discussions. They said that they had never imagined or expected that such a thing would take place and that they could not take the credit for it, and they said that "It was not we who defeated this great army, but it was merely that we were protecting ourselves. It was due to their own recklessness, and the will of God Most High, that such events took place so that we were not wiped out at one fell swoop but, on the contrary, so much wealth and equipment fell into our hands without premeditation; and we thus went from rags to riches. Sultan Masʿud is a great monarch and there are none like him in Islam. A catastrophe such as this befell this army of his through a want of good advice and a lack of leadership (*bi-sālāri*). But he possesses many commanders and plenty of troops. We should not delude ourselves by what happened, and we should send an envoy and adopt a subservient approach and offer apologies and to reiterate that what we are saying is exactly what we said previously. How could we avoid fighting back when they attacked our homes and our persons?[229] Let us see what answer comes back, so that we can then see how to proceed."

When the Amir had perused these letters, he felt less apprehensive, and he discussed them with the Vizier in private. The Vizier said, "It is not a suitable course of action[230] [to maintain] that 'whatever they do, we should never parley with them except by the sword'. It was unwise to despatch the army. On these matters, [Gh 490] Bu Naṣr is my witness, since I had spoken with him; but [F 638] since the Amir was in an ill humour and foolhardy words were being bandied about, there was no course but to remain silent until one could see what the turn of events would be after this."

Directly on the heels of these confidential letters from the secret agents, an envoy arrived at the court from the Seljuq Turkmens, an elderly and eloquent religious scholar of Bokhara. He had a letter addressed to the Grand Vizier, which was written in a very humble and deferential tone. It said, "We were unwise to approach Suri as a go-between and intercessor, for he is impetuous and did not follow the right path and consider correctly what the consequences would be. He inevitably persuaded the lord Sultan to send an army against us. God forbid that we should have had the boldness to rise up against the victorious army,[231] but when they swept down like wolves on a flock, while we were under a promise of protection (*zinhāriyān*), and they attacked our homes, womenfolk and children, what alternative was there to repelling them in order to save each our own precious skin?[232] We remain, here and now, pledged to the words which we had said at the outset, and what happened can be considered as the working of the evil eye which came about without our desiring it. If the Grand Vizier sees fit, by virtue of the fact that he has accommodated us in Khwarazm in the time of the Khwarazm Shah Altuntāsh, when his hospitality towards us created its own bonds of loyalty,[233] he will intervene in this affair and act as intermediary, and will mollify the lord Sultan's heart in such a way that our excuses will be accepted, and this representative of ours will be sent back with a letter of reply, in such a manner that our minds may be thereby set at rest and there will be no more cause for recriminations. If the Grand Vizier should send a trusty envoy from his own retainers to accompany our own envoy, that would be even better, for he will hear our words and see for himself that we are mere servants who seek nothing but good."

The Grand Vizier read this letter and listened to the envoy's verbal message, which corresponded to what was in the letter but which was more comprehensive. He gave orders for the envoy to be given suitable lodging and hospitality, and retailed to the Amir this state of affairs in its entirety in a private session where they were joined by the leading figures at court. The Amir [F 639] did not regard with disfavour this attempt at a rapprochement, and they accordingly decided that the Judge Bu Naṣr Ṣini should be sent back with this scholar of Bokhara so that he might go and hear the words of the Turkmen leaders, and if there was no trickery, and the discussion was open and frank, and he was able to bring back a clear report of what they had said, he would request envoys to be sent with him, and they would discuss matters openly and freely and a correct mode of procedure would be established so that they would all feel reassured. They came back from the Amir's presence with this decision adopted. The Vizier and the Head of the Chancery sat down together privately, and they explained to the Turkmens' envoy that a great deal of effort [Gh 491] had been exerted in order to win over the Sultan's mind and to persuade him to accept these excuses, and that this envoy, Ṣini, who was one of the trusted retainers of the Ghaznavid court, should be sent back fully informed and cognisant so that the present turmoil could be attended to and good order restored.

I have to give an account of this man Ṣini, so that I may fulfill the requirements of the History. This person was *a shrewd and practical man*,[234] not exactly erudite, but not given to blandishments and trickery either.[235] His father had been a tutor to Amir Maḥmud when the latter was a child and had taught him the Qorʾān, and he had acted as leader of the worship for the Just Amir Sebüktegin. But then he had had a fit of ill temper and had gone off to Turkestan, and had taken up residence there in Özkend, where he had been entrusted with various posts by the late Ilig.[236] [F 640] Amir Maḥmud had secretly managed to employ him as an agent and informer there, and he had proved extremely useful on that score. For these two reasons (i.e. his father's tuition of Prince Maḥmud and his role as a secret agent among the Qarakhanids), Bu Naṣr Ṣini had a secure position in the Sultan's favour. At the end of Amir Maḥmud's reign the post of the oversight of the court[237] was entrusted to him, and Ṣini put the office on a firm basis. At the beginning of his reign Amir Masʿud retained him in this post, but his arrogant and prickly nature proved too much for the Sultan, and he gave the post to the overseer Bu Saʿid and appointed Ṣini to the local governorship (*zeʿāmat*) of Ṭālaqān and Merv.[238] He sent his son there to act as his deputy, and he himself accompanied us on all our journeying. The end came in Mowdud's reign. Bu Sahl Zowzani who resented him had him incarcerated in a fortress in India, having plotted against him till he was dealt with, and he died there.

They relate the manner of his death in several different ways: through poison in [the effervescent drink] *foqqāʿ*, in wine, or in roasted meat or testicles.[239] Only God Most High can know the truth; and no-one remains of those people involved. There will be a resurrection and an impartial accounting, and a just and omniscient Judge, and much filth and wickedness at present concealed beneath this earth will come to light! May God Most High vouchsafe salvation, *through the right of Moḥammad and all his house!*

The Amir ordered a handsome present of money to be given to the Judge Ṣini, and he summoned him and told him in person the message on these lines, in the presence of the Vizier and the Head of the Chancery. He went back and made preparations for departure. The aged envoy from Bokhara was given a present of money, and the Vizier summoned him [F 641] and said to him everything that had to be said by way of reply to the messages. They, Ṣini and the Bokharan, set off from Nishapur on Thursday, 2 Ramażān [/11 July 1035],[240] and Ṣini remained there for a while. We had despatched swift couriers [Gh 492] with Ṣini; these now arrived back with letters embracing all the issues under discussion, and replies went out until an agreement was arrived at. Ṣini arrived back in Nishapur on Wednesday, 19 Shavvāl [/27 August]. He had with him three envoys from the Turkmens, one each from Yabghu, Ṭoghrïl and Dāvud, accompanied by the scholar from Bokhara.[241] The next day—they were sent to the Vizier's Divān, and much discussion went on, and time passed until the hour of the afternoon worship. There were discussions with the Amir by means of verbal messages between the two sides. Finally, it was decided that the government of Nasā, Farāva and Dehestān should be given to these three leaders. A robe of honour, an investiture patent and a standard were to be sent for each of them, and Ṣini was to go back in order to present the robes of honour to them and to administer an oath to them that they would be obedient to the Sultan and carry out his commands, and would content themselves with these three governorships. It was further agreed that when the Sultan should go to Balkh, and when they themselves felt secure, one out of these three leaders there was to come to the court and enter the Sultan's service.[242] The court official charged with receiving and entertaining envoys performed his duties well and made them feel comfortable.

My master prepared the drafts for the investiture patents, and I myself wrote out the fair copies from them: Dehestān in the name of Dāvud, Nasā in the name of Ṭoghrïl and Farāva in the name of Yabghu, and the Amir affixed his emblem and motto to them. Letters were written from the Sultan, and these leaders were formally addressed as "chieftains" (*dehqān*).[243] Three robes of honour were prepared of the quality fit for governors, comprising a two-pointed hat, a standard and a sewn robe, these in the same style as we wear; a horse, saddle ornaments and a belt set with gold, these however in the Turkish style; and uncut pieces of cloth of all kinds, thirty pieces for each one of them. The following day, the Amir summoned the envoys, and the robes of honour and presents of money were handed over to them.[244] On the Friday, after the worship, on the twenty-first [F 642] of Shavvāl [/29 August], Ṣini and these envoys set out from Nishapur to Nasā. The Amir appeared less apprehensive, and he set about merry-making and wine-drinking after a long stretch of abstinence.

During this week letters arrived from the Commander-in-Chief ʿAli b. ʿAbdallāh and the postal and intelligence officer of Balkh, Bu'l-Qāsem b. Ḥātemak, to the effect that "When ʿAlitegin's sons heard that the Commander Begtughdï and our army had come back from Nasā with their hopes dashed, they planned for a second time to launch an attack on Chaghāniyān and Termez. They had covered two or three stages from Samarqand when the news reached them that the governor of Chaghāniyān, the Amir Bu'l-Qāsem, had collected together a strong force composed of the Kanjina[245] and the Komijis, and that the Commander-in-Chief ʿAli had arrived in Balkh with a substantial army and was planning to cross the Oxus river. [Gh 493] On hearing this, they aborted their plans and went back."

The reply went out that "The problems with the Seljuq Turkmens who were installed at Nasā have been resolved and they have pledged their obedience, realizing that the developments that led to the General Begtughdï's return[246] was not on account of their own skills. As an act of grace on our part, they have received robes of honour and governorships, and they have become quiescent, and one of their leaders is going to come for service at court. We will remain at Nishapur until our envoy returns. Mehragān is near. After Mehragān, we shall come to Balkh via the Herat road in order to spend the winter there, and a response to this act of presumptuousness (i.e. on the part of 'Alitegin's sons) will be given, *with the permission of the Almighty God*."

Monday,[247] 16 Dhu'l-Qa'da [/22 September 1035] was Mehragān. The Amir [F 643] took his place early that morning to celebrate the festival, but did not drink wine. Coins for scattering and presents were brought along on a limitless and incalculable scale. After the worship, he set about wine-drinking, and the rites and customs of Mehragān were carried out in their entirety, in a very fine fashion and with all their ceremonial details.[248]

Ṣini arrived back from the Seljuqs. In a private session with the Vizier and the head of the Chancery, he confided that "It would be wrong to give the Sultan the wrong impression. Now that I have been to them, I have seen that these people have bloated and exaggerated ambitions, and it appears that much mischief has been instilled into them. Although they have submitted to agreements, I personally have no faith whatever in them. I heard that in private they have been contemptuous and scoffing, and have thrown down the two-pointed hats and trampled them underfoot. It is incumbent on the Sultan that he should defer the journey to Herat so that no disaster occurs. I have said my piece and performed my duty."[249] The Vizier replied, "What impossible words are you saying? They have dismantled and taken out the camp enclosure, and he wants to leave tomorrow. But it is one's duty to inform the Sultan of all this. If he does set out, he should certainly place a strong army here, and they should remain here as a garrison." He gave Khᵛāja Bu Naṣr a verbal message for the Amir about this. Bu Naṣr went off and spoke with the Amir.

The Amir answered, "Surely they are unlikely to rebel, and if they do, measures to deal with them will necessarily be put into action, for it is no longer possible to remain here since the question of food and fodder has become very acute. The General Qadïr with a force of cavalry and 1,000 horsemen from various sections of the army (*sovār-e tafāriq*)[250] must be left at Nishapur with Suri, the head of the Divān, who also has a large number of troops. There is an army at Sarakhs, and [F 644] another one likewise at Qāyen, and we shall leave a strong contingent at Herat also. All of them should be told to follow the head of the Divān's instructions, [Gh 494] and if need should arise, and if he should summon them, they should join him quickly. From Balkh, inasmuch as we are continuously reading the letters from secret agents concerning the situation of this group of the Turkmens, further measures will be ordained,[251] since the distance is not great. The Vizier must be informed so that he may put into effect today what we have commanded, for we shall depart without fail tomorrow." Bu Naṣr came and spoke with the Vizier, and they got everything ready.

Amir Masʿud set off from Nishapur on the next day, Sunday, 19 Dhu'l-Qaʿda [/25 September 1035],[252] and came to Herat on the last day of the month (i.e. 30 Dhu'l-Qaʿda/6 October). From Herat he went out on Sunday, 6 Dhu'l-Ḥejja [/12 October][253] along the road to Bavan and Bagh[shur][254] and Bādghis. He was in high spirits travelling along this road, and was busy with wine-drinking and with hunting. The commander Tilak came into the royal presence at Marv al-Rudh and rendered service, having returned victorious from combating the deluded rebel Aḥmad b. Ināltegin. He had with him a well-equipped army and many senior officers, with a battle standard and ceremonial parasol. T.m.k the Hindu accompanied Tilak, and was like a second Tilak. The Amir heaped favours on him, spoke eloquent words of praise and gave him hopes of further benefits, and likewise showed favour to the commanders of the Indian troops. He stood on an eminence as the Indian troops of the army, cavalry and infantry, slowly filed past him, and it was a fine army. The elephants, amounting to fifty-five, which had been taken as tribute from the Indian princes (*takkorān*), were paraded in front of him. The Amir was very impressed by this army. On the fringes of Guzgānān, he said to the Khᵛāja Bu Naṣr, "Masʿud b. Moḥammad b. Leyth has turned into a worthy young man. [F 645] He did praiseworthy service in the region of Ray, and we found him faithful and reliable in all that we commanded him. He should be given a place in the Chancery." Bu Naṣr replied, "I will do this, and he is deserving of this act of favour." He was brought into the Divān.

The History of the Year 427 [/5 November 1035–24 October 1036]

[Gh 494, F 645] The first day of Moḥarram fell on Wednesday.[1] On Saturday, the fourth of this month [/8 November 1035], the Amir entered Balkh. It was the first day of the month of Ādhar,[2] and he took up his quarters in the Palace [Gh 495] of the Gate of ʿAbd al-Aʿlā. On Monday, the sixth of this month [/10 November], he came to the Great Garden, and the quarters[3] and the divāns were installed there, for they had prepared and arranged the place well and it was within a most pleasant and spacious location.

The governor (*vāli*) of Chaghāniyān[4] came to Balkh on the very day that the Amir had arrived, and received a warm welcome and was given befitting accommodation and copious amounts of food and delicacies. On the next day, he came to render service, saw the Amir, and was greeted with many marks of honour and favour, and then returned to the same palace which had already been prepared for him. Several times in the course of the day, Bu ʿAli, the official in charge of the reception and entertainment of envoys, would go to him bearing gifts and favours and presents and offering his services, as instructed by the royal command. The gifts that the governor of Chaghāniyān had brought, comprising horses of noble breed, Turkish gholāms, falcons and hawks,[5] hunting cheetahs[6] and specialities of those regions, amounting to a large quantity, were brought into the Amir's presence and the whole array made a highly favourable impression on him.

On Thursday, 9 Moḥarram [/13 November 1035], a great and splendid feast had been prepared. They brought mounts [F 646] and fetched the governor of Chaghāniyān. There was polo-playing, and then they sat down at a feast and drank wine afterwards, and the day ended most enjoyably. On Wednesday, 15 Moḥarram [/19 November] the governor of Chaghāniyān donned a very splendid robe of honour, such as is given to governors. Many other favours were also bestowed on him, since this noble-hearted man was related to this lofty house through marriage to a royal lady.[7] (The ruler (*ḥākem*) of Chaghāniyān is still alive at this moment, the year 451 [/1059], but his life is in ruins for he did not show adequate self-control and discretion. The Khᵛāja Ra'is ʿAli b. Mikā'il was with him in Chaghāniyān.[8] But enough said; this should suffice here.)[9]

When the governor of Chaghāniyān donned the robe of honour, he was presented to the Amir and he performed the rites of service. The Amir bestowed many marks of honour and favour on him, saying, "Your Amir[10] has suffered much at the hands of these upstart sons of ʿAlitegin, who do not know their place and their status. When the news reached us, the Commander-in-Chief was sent with an army, and we have come here in order to rectify matters. The governor must return to his home region with blessings and auspiciousness, and gather together his supporters until a prestigious commander with a powerful army is despatched from here and crosses the Oxus. The two forces (i.e. of the governor and of Masʿud) can link up together so that these opportunist mischief-makers can be overthrown." The governor affirmed that he would follow this course of action and rendered service and went back. He was taken to the portico (*ṭārami*)[11] in the Garden and given a seat there. The Vizier and the Head of the Chancery came there, and they renewed his agreement of fealty to the Sultan and administered a further oath, and returned him to his residence.[12] At the time of the afternoon worship he mounted and set off for Chaghāniyān. [Gh 496]

On Sunday, 26 Moḥarram [/30 November], the Amir went to the Vale of Gaz[13] [F 647] for hunting, together with his personal entourage, the boon-companions, and the musicians and singers. On Sunday, 3 Ṣafar [/7 December] he came to the Great Garden. The next day a messenger with the by-name of Öge[14] and the given name of Musātegin arrived from the sons of ʿAlitegin, accompanied by a scholar of Samarqand. The official in charge of hospitality for envoys conducted them into the town and offered them hospitality and lavish gifts. After three days' rest,[15] they were brought into the royal presence. The Amir said nothing since he was annoyed with those who had sent them. The Vizier enquired, "How did you leave the Amirs?" Öge was unable to say anything, but the religious scholar spoke out in an eloquent fashion, saying, "We have come as a delegation offering excuses, and the Mighty Sultan will surely accept them out of his magnanimity; for our Amirs are only youths, it was persons of bad character and evil intentions who impelled them to make an incursion into this region."[16] The Grand Vizier said, "The lord of the world looks at intentions and motives and not at actions,"[17] and they were conducted to the portico. The Amir had a private session with the Vizier and the head of the Chancery regarding this matter. The Grand Vizier said, "May the lord's life be prolonged! Khorasan, Ray, Gorgān and Ṭabarestān are all in turmoil. The lord recalled Bu'l-Ḥasan b. ʿAbd al-Jalil from Gorgān with the army, and some sort of contractual agreement was concocted with the Gorgānis—a wise move, since it enabled Bu'l-Ḥasan to return without losing face. The sons of ʿAlitegin are hostile to us to a certain extent;[18] it is better to be conciliatory than to have them as sworn enemies. The wisest course seems to me that the excuses of these young men should be accepted and an agreement made such as existed with their father." He replied, "That's a good idea! You must go to the portico and put this into effect."

The Grand Vizier and Khᵛāja Bu Naṣr came to the portico, and they scrutinized closely the letter from ʿAlitegin's sons. It was a letter couched in a most deferential manner, offering an apology for the episode of the attack on Termez and Chaghāniyān, in these terms: "An error was committed, and that person who [F 648] instigated it has received his just deserts. If the Mighty Sultan sees fit, let what took place be pardoned, so that the friendly relations inherited from our father may be renewed." The accompanying verbal messages were in this same vein. Bu Naṣr went to the Amir and retailed this information, and brought back favourable replies containing many an encouraging word. Their official escort conducted the envoys back to their lodging. The Vizier appointed [Bu Saʿd] Masʿadi for the embassy,[19] preparations for his mission were made, and the letter and the message to be delivered verbally were written out. The envoys of [the sons of] ʿAlitegin were each given a robe of honour and presents of money. The entire party departed.[20] A peace treaty was drawn up and an agreement concluded, so that calm and order could be restored. The governor of Chaghāniyān was brought into these arrangements so that there might be no further incursions into his territory.[21] [Gh 497]

On Sunday, 10 Ṣafar [/14 December 1035], the Amir gave the Vizier a robe of honour, one of very fine quality. On the same day, the commander Sübashï was raised to the position of Great Chamberlain, and a robe of honour, whose complete outfit included a standard, a crescent-shaped finial for its shaft, a drum (*ṭabl*), a large barrel-shaped drum with a curved body (*dohol-e kāsa*),[22] sets of clothing, pouches filled with silver and other things befitting such a rise in status. Both notables went back to their respective homes, where they were well rewarded with plenty of presents and gifts in recognition of the favours they had received.

The next day, Tilak was given a very fine robe of honour for the command of the Indian troops. When he came into the Amir's presence and offered service, the Amir said to the treasurer, "Bring in a collar which has been set with jewels." This was brought. The Amir took it, and summoned Tilak to come forward, and he placed that collar round his neck with his own august hands, and spoke many a kind and congratulatory word concerning the acts of service that he had rendered over the affair of Aḥmad b. Ināltegin, and Tilak went back.

On Wednesday, the fourteenth of the month of Rabiʿ I [/16 January 1036],[23] a great feast had been prepared, a most elaborate endeavour, and seven festal spreads[24] had been set up on the great platform and throughout the grassy stretches of the Great Garden. [F 649] All the great men, retainers, courtiers and people from various groups[25] were brought there and set down at those festal spreads. Wine was handed out, and a splendid occasion got under way; and they made their way homewards from the feast in a drunken state. The Amir proceeded from the Garden to a summer pavilion there, and sat down to drink wine, and an excellent day drew to its close.

On Tuesday, the twentieth of this month [/22 January],[26] Bu 'l-Ḥasan ʿEraqi the secretary was given a robe of honour and a golden belt as Commander of the Kurdish and Arab troops, and his brother Bu Saʿid was also given a robe of honour so that he might act as his representative and deputy over this group and go with them to Khorasan until that time when Bu'l-Ḥasan could follow after him.

On Sunday, the twenty-fifth of this month [/27 January],[27] a letter arrived from Ghaznin announcing the death of Moẓaffar, son of Khᵛāja ʿAli b. Mikāʾil, God's mercy be upon him. He was a courageous, capable and effective man who acted as deputy to his father.[28]

Meanwhile swift couriers were arriving from the head of the Divān of Khorasan, Suri, and from the postal service and intelligence officer, with the news that the Seljuq Turkmens, and the ʿErāqi ones who had joined up with them, had renewed their activities and were sending out bands to every place in the districts. They were inflicting much suffering on the populace, seizing everything they came upon and causing a great deal of mischief. A letter arrived from Bost that a group of them had come to Farāh and Zir.kān,[29] and had driven off a large number of beasts. Letters likewise arrived from Guzgānān and Sarakhs with similar stories, [Gh 498] with a reminder that decisive measures were needed in this case, otherwise the province of Khorasan [F 650] would become devastated.

Amir Masʿud had a private session with the Vizier, the pillars of state, and the retainers and courtiers, and they exchanged views. They came to the decision that the Great Chamberlain Sübashï should go to Khorasan with 10,000 cavalry and 5,000 infantry and that the brother of Bu'l-Ḥasan ʿErāqi should remain at Herat with all the Kurdish and Arab troops until Bu'l-Ḥasan should arrive on his heels. All were to obey the instructions of the Great Chamberlain, and were to act in unison, taking each other's views and judgement into consideration. The head of the Divān of Khorasan, Suri, was to apply himself to the task of organising the troops' salaries so that the army should not be lacking in pay and provisions and that Khorasan should be speedily cleared of the Turkmens.

On Monday, 14 Rabiʿ II [/15 February 1036], the Amir mounted his steed and went out to the open plain. He took up his place on an eminence with the most impressive possible display of splendour, and with the prince, Amir Mowdud, the Grand Vizier and all the prominent men of state stood there rendering service. The cavalry and infantry were all well turned out, with a complete panoply of arms, and there were many choice and fearsome-looking elephants clad in body armour and with litters and pack saddles. The part of the army designated for Khorasan stood there in the general parade in separate units and in detachments according to each ethnic group (*ṭāʾefa*). The Great Chamberlain Sübashï had excelled in organising this ceremonial parade, which met with the Amir's approval, and likewise Bu'l-Ḥasan ʿErāqi and the senior officers for their part. The parade came to an end after the performing of the midday worship.

The next day at dawn, ʿErāqi's brother departed with the army of Kurds and Arabs, and on the day after, the Great Chamberlain Sübashï left with the army that had been designated for him to lead. The Amir gave orders that the post of counsellor and adjutant of the army and the task of sending back news from the army should be given to Saʿid Ṣarrāf. He received his instructions and went off in the tracks of the Great Chamberlain. The Amir had also decreed that a muster-master (*ʿāreż*) should be appointed for this army, a man steadfast and trustworthy and proficient in the functions of the Army Department, and to whom the salaries of the army could be given in the form of assignments[30] to be issued by him. He should also be capable of making decisions on his own and of appointing and dismissing,[31] for given the volatile situation in Khorasan, it would not always be possible to refer matters to the royal court. The choice fell on Bu Sahl b. Aḥmad b. ʿAli, and his master, the Head of the Army Department Khᵛāja [F 651] Bu'l-Fatḥ Rāzi, sent him into the Amir's presence. The Vizier praised him greatly, and the Amir ordered that instructions with the royal device and motto concerning his appointment should be written out. I myself, Bu'l-Fażl, wrote out the letter of appointment for him, and he also departed. He won much acclaim in this post. [Gh 499] When the Great Chamberlain suffered that calamity in Khorasan, as I shall relate, this noble-hearted man lost[32] a great sum of money and a vast amount of valuable equipment and baggage, and he fell into the hands of the Turkmens. They treated him with great harshness and he yielded up a further sum of money after being hard pressed and mulcted.[33] In the end, he was released and came back to the court. He is still alive at the time when I am writing this work, and is a strong pillar of the administration in the Army Department. Although it is true that he has not risen above the level of a subordinate,[34] as a consequence of that he has a carefree and untroubled life[35] and passes the time without being troubled by anyone, regardless of any changes at the top of the Army Department. His choice is the one favoured by all wise persons. He too departed, and joined up with the Great Chamberlain, and they all proceeded in the direction of Khorasan.[36]

On Thursday 9 Jomādā I [/10 March 1036] the Amir mounted and rode off to hunt on the outskirts of Marv al-Rudh. On Monday, the thirteenth of this month [/14 March], he came to the Great Garden. On Saturday, 17 Jomādā I [/18 March], he came back from the Great Garden to the Palace of the Gate of ʿAbd al-Aʿlā. The next day he left there to go lion hunting at Termez,[37] where he enjoyed seven days of excellent hunting before returning to the Palace. On Saturday, 1 Rajab [/30 April], he left the town of Balkh and travelled along the road to the capital Ghaznin. On Friday, the twenty-first of the month [/20 May], he reached the capital in a state of health and happiness, and took up residence in the Old Maḥmudi Palace at Afghān-shāl with blessedness.

The Masʿudi Palace had been made ready. In the later part of the morning he mounted and went there, [F 652] and made a close inspection of the entire place. He designated the houses for the officials, the barrack-rooms of the palace gholāms and the Divāns for the Vizier, the Head of the Army Department, the Head of the Chancery and the Intendant of the Palace, and then returned to the Old Maḥmudi Palace. The personnel bustled about on their various duties, straightening out their own individual places. The court attendants were laying out the royal carpets and furnishings and were hanging the curtains and drapes. It was a palace the like of which could not be found elsewhere, and no other monarch had ever ordered the construction of such an edifice. All was based on his own knowledge and architectural design (*handasa*), and he marked out with his own exalted hands the base lines of it, for in such matters, and most notably in the arts of geometry and architectural design, he was a marvel to behold. The palace took four years to build, and apart from the immediate expenses (i.e. money expended on wages and salaries for the skilled labourers), the corvées and forced labour levies came out at double that,[38] for I once heard the painter and architect (*naqqāsh mohandes*) ʿAbd al-Malek say in the presence of the field officer Bu ʿAli the castellan, "Seven times have I set down a million dirhams expended on wages and salaries." Bu ʿAli commented, [Gh 500] "I am aware that there has been twice as much on corvées and forced labour levies. All this was done with my knowledge." Today, in spite of the calamities which have since befallen, this palace is still a wondrous sight;[39] the buildings and gardens are proof enough. They have been making additions to the buildings over a period of twenty years, and of those buildings several parts have also fallen into disrepair.[40] [F 653] May this exalted capital and its celebrated buildings endure for ever, and also for the servants of the dynasty amongst its inhabitants, *through the right of Moḥammad and his house!*

On Tuesday, the twenty-fifth of the month of Rajab [/24 May 1036], the Amir came to this new palace and took up residence there. On

Monday, 9 Shaʿbān [/7 June], there took place the circumcision of several of the princes, the Amir's sons. A great celebration and an elaborate spectacle had been arranged, and disporting and amusement went on for seven days and nights. There were sessions for wine-drinking, and the Amir, celebrating both the circumcision celebrations and the last days of Shaʿbān[41]—since the month of Ramażān was near—toured the palace and the grounds, and indulged in the drinking.

Then they set about preparing for the month of fasting, and they began it on the Monday [1 Ramażān/28 June]. On Friday, the fifth of that month [/2 July], very important secret information arrived from Khwarazm, to the effect that "These regions have passed firmly under the control of Esmāʿil Khandān, son of the Khwarazm Shah Altuntāsh. All those gholāms who had killed his brother Hārun fell into his hands and were at once executed, and in the same way, whoever had followed the Grand Vizier Aḥmad b. ʿAbd al-Ṣamad, was killed, including the Vizier's other son, and the *khoṭba* was made first for the Commander of the Faithful and then for Khandān. The household servant Shakar[42] holds all affairs in his personal grip, and they have seized control and have blocked all the roads. There is a constant coming-and-going of envoys between the Turkmens and Esmāʿil's court."[43] The Amir became extremely concerned on hearing this news, and he ordered that Esmāʿil's brother Rashid should be held in custody at Ghaznin, but he ordained that the Khwarazm Shah's daughters should not be molested in any way.[44]

On the Wednesday, they celebrated the Festival [of the Ending of the Fast][45] attending meticulously to customary procedures and with great éclat. The retainers and courtiers were seated at the feast and served with wine. On Sunday, 5 Shavvāl [/1 August], [F 654] the Amir went off on a hunting expedition involving the rounding-up of game,[46] together with his close intimates from the army, the boon-companions, and the musicians and singers. A great deal of game had been driven for them to hunt down. Swift riding camels conveyed back to Ghaznin [the captured game as presents] for each person from among the great men of state.[47]

On Sunday, the nineteenth of the month [/15 August] the Amir came to the Garden of a Hundred Nightingales. On the next Sunday, 26 Shavvāl [/22 August], the secretary Bu'l-Ḥasan ʿErāqi, who was Commander of the Kurdish and Arab troops, set off for Herat via the Ghur route[48] with a very impressive array of equipment and matériel.

The General Sübashi had previously [Gh 501] gone to Khorasan with the army, and the mountainous regions had also become disturbed for this reason.[49]

On Saturday, 3 Dhu'l-Qa'da [/28 August], the Sultan's son Prince Majdud donned the robe of honour for the governorship and military command of India so that he might go off to Lahore, a fine robe of high calibre, fit for a prince and more particularly an offspring of such a monarch. He was given three generals, all clad in their official black robes. Accompanying him, Bu Naṣr b. Bu'l-Qāsem b. 'Ali Nuki went from our Divān to act as secretary,[50] and Sa'd, son of Salmān, to act as accountant,[51] while the field officer Moḥammad took over the function of making and unmaking appointments and other administrative decisions.[52] Drums, a battle standard, large kettledrums, and an elephant with its litter were to accompany the prince. The next day he came into the presence of his father in the Piruzi Garden, with his forces fully arrayed. The Sultan embraced him, and Majdud performed the rites of service, and took his formal leave and departed.[53] The Khwarazm Shah's son Rashid was brought along after him, in fetters, so that he could be held prisoner at Lahore.[54]

On Thursday, 8 Dhu'l-Qa'da [/2 September], a letter arrived from Ray brought by three riders bearing the good tidings that "'Alā' al-Dowla, the Son of Kāku, was driven away by the victorious army, and those [F 655] regions of Jebāl have now become peaceful. He had attracted a number of Turkmen cavalrymen from Khorasan to his side and had plied them with gold, but these had now returned to Khorasan by the Ṭabas road."[55] The Amir became filled with joy at the receipt of this news. Trumpets were blown and barrel-shaped drums beaten. The envoys were given robes of honour, paraded in triumph[56] and amply rewarded with gifts. Congratulatory responses were sent off, praising the Civil Governor of Western Persia, Bu Sahl Ḥamdavi, and the Commander-in-Chief Tāsh, and it was stated that "Our banner will certainly now travel to Bost, and thence we shall come to Herat and the situation there will be taken in hand." The envoys returned. I am not describing these military operations here lest the thread of the History be lost. An account of what had occurred at Ray and in Jebāl will all appear in a detailed section, extending from that time when Bu Sahl went out to Ray until he returned to Nishapur, and Ray and Jebāl were lost to us. In that section all events will be made clear and recorded.[57]

Saturday, 24 Dhu'l-Qa'da [/18 September] was the feast of Mehragān. The Amir installed himself for the festivities of Mehragān at the head on the dais of the New Palace in the portico. (The golden throne, the crown and all the vessels and utensils for feasting and wine-drinking sessions[58] were not yet ready, and the goldsmiths and gilders in the citadel [of Ghazna] were at work preparing them; it took a long time after this before they were ready. They were destined for another day, as will be recounted in its proper place.) The royal princes, [Gh 502] the retainers and the courtiers came into the royal presence, presented their own offerings and went back. Everybody was installed in an appointed place, according to their rank, on that great platform which extends to the left and the right of the palace. They began to bring forward presents, including from the governor of Chaghāniyān[59] and Bā Kālijār, the governor of Gorgān, for when Bu'l-Ḥasan b. ʿAbd al-Jalil returned from that region and disturbances occurred in Khorasan, the Amir considered it wise to placate Bā Kālijār and bring him back into the fold. An envoy arrived and a trusty confidant went from here, and a fresh contractual agreement was set in place. Although Bā Kālijār had been badly mauled and bruised, he now adopted a calm and conciliatory attitude, and he did not attempt [F 656] any further rebellion or commit any mischief. Presents were also brought from the governor of Makrān,[60] from the head of the Divān of Khorasan, Suri, and from other administrative and financial officials in outlying provinces of the empire. The time passed joyously until the proceedings came to a close.

Then the Amir arose and went to his private quarters in the small palace. He changed his garments and came to that winter residence with a dome[61] which is situated to the left of the platform of the court (no-one has ever seen such residences as those two, a summer one on the right and a winter one on the left; the houses are still standing—a clear and objective proof of my words—and may they long continue to exist! One should go along and see them for oneself) A plinth (*ādhin*) had been built against this house, and a very large and wide oven had been constructed there,[62] and the court attendants would climb up a ladder to supply and lay the firewood; the oven is still there. They set the firewood alight, and the gholāms assisting with the cooking came in with spits[63] and went about turning and roasting fowls on them, and they cooked eggs[64] and carried out everything necessary and appropriate for kings on the day of Mehragān, including roasting meats and roasting skinned and prepared lambs on the spit.[65] The great men of state came to the court assembly and the boon-companions likewise sat down in their places; they all began to eat heartily, [Gh 503] *polishing off their plates with their fingers,*[66] and wine flowed in many beakers, spouted vessels and bumpers. The musicians and singers struck up their music and singing, and it was a day such as a monarch like this would lay on. The Vizier used not to drink any wine, [F 657] and he went home after one or two rounds of wine had circulated. The Amir remained there till the time of the midday worship, long enough for the boon-companions who were not of the inner court circle[67] to take their leave. Then he came to the platform of the *nāʾebān*,[68] which is not far from the Garden. A celebration on a majestic scale had been prepared there, and the inner circle of boon companions, and the singers and musicians, came there; this lasted till the time of the afternoon worship, and after that they departed.

On Sunday,[69] 9 Dhu'l-Ḥejja [/3 October], and on the second day after that, they celebrated the Festival [of the Sacrifice]. The Amir came to that elevated structure (*khażrāʾ*)[70] which overlooks the review ground, facing towards the plain of Shābahār. He halted there, and the worship appointed for the Festival was performed,[71] and the ceremony of the ritually-slaughtered offering made accordingly. The Amir came down from the elevated pavilion, and he sat down at the great platform where a feast had been prepared. The retainers and courtiers and the notables were summoned to the feast, and wine was served as well,[72] and they were then sent back home.

The following day the Amir held court, and afterwards had a private session with the Vizier and the great men of state. After much debate, it was decided that the Amir should go to Bost, accompanied by the Vizier, so that, if necessary, the exalted banner could proceed to Herat, and if not, he could send the Vizier by himself. Orders were given to the prince, Amir Mowdud, and to the Commander-in-Chief, ʿAli b. ʿAbdallāh, that they should go with their personal retainers and a strong army of royal troops (*lashkar-e ... solṭāni*) to Balkh and take up their position there so that the whole of Khorasan would be garrisoned with mighty men and troops (*ḥasham*) from the capital.[73] They went back from the court and got everything ready for their expedition. [F 658] The next day, the Amir mounted an elephant and with his close retainers took up his position on the plain of Shābahār, and his dear son, the Commander-in-Chief and the fully-equipped army presented themselves before him in their battle formations (i.e. for the *ʿarż* or inspection). They passed before him, and these two eminent men, Mowdud and ʿAli b. ʿAbdallāh, and the senior officers performed the rites of service and departed for Balkh, having been given robes of honour before they set off. The Amir came to his palace with good fortune and a happy frame of mind.

A splendid robe of honour had been prepared for Amir Saʿid. He donned it and came into the royal presence. The Sultan lavished favour on him and gave orders that he was to stay at Ghaznin in the palace of the [former] Grand Vizier Abu'l-ʿAbbās Esfarāyeni at the village of Āhangarān.[74] At the citadel, the field officer and castellan Bu ʿAli was granted a robe of honour and [Gh 504] given orders that he was to be in charge of the royal son's affairs and those of Ghaznin. This year, the Sultan ordered the jurist Nuḥ to act as a companion to the prince. Nuḥ is a man whose worthiness is universally acknowledged today and is a friend of mine; I have set forth this much about him and, following the rules and customs of history, I shall have more to say about him later as events unfold. [75] Khᵛāja Moḥammad b. Manṣur b. Moshkān,[76] God's mercy be upon him, was likewise appointed as one of his boon-companions. The Sultan was always promoting this son in status and was extremely attentive to his comforts and luxuries and was most prodigal in bestowing upon him additional items of equipment, gholāms and arms, and retainers and servants, thus making it evident that he was his favourite son. But the father desired one thing and the Almighty God another, since the royal prince died in his prime of youth, as I shall subsequently relate; and it was, Mowdud who acceded to the royal throne after his father's death; and this lion cub exacted vengeance for the murder of his father, Masʿud. All have now passed on; may the Almighty God have mercy on them, and may He grant long life to the exalted Sultan Ebrāhim, *through the right of Moḥammad and all his house!*[77] [F 659]

When Amir Masʿud had completed these arrangements, the camp enclosure was set up on the road to Bost, and he set out from Ghaznin on Thursday, 13 Dhu'l-Ḥejja [/7 October], and entered Teginābād on Wednesday, the twenty-sixth of this month [/20 October]. He spent seven days there occupied in merry-making and wine-drinking, and then set off towards Bost. *God is the most knowing one!*

The History of the Year 428 [/25 October 1036–13 October 1037]

[Gh 504, F 659] The first day of Moḥarram fell on Monday. The Amir installed himself in the Pavilion in the Plain of Logān[1] on Thursday, 4 Moḥarram [/28 October 1036]. This palace is situated at one parasang's distance from Bost. Around the time of the midday worship, when all the troops formed a semi-circular formation to drive the game into one spot[2] (those regions abound in game) and when they had tightened their grip and closed in, the game was herded into the garden which lies in front of the palace. More than five or six hundred of the encircled game came into the garden, while out in the open plain a large number had been caught by means of hunting cheetahs and dogs.[3] The Amir sat in an elevated structure, shooting arrows from there, and the gholāms were running about in the garden and retrieving the fallen game. It was a very fine hunt. I had seen the same sort of thing done by Amir Maḥmud when he was also [F 660] here at Bost. A wild ass had been captured on the way and secured [Gh 505] by cords around its legs. He then ordered it to be branded with the name "Maḥmud"[4] and then released, since storytellers had recited and recounted[5] in his presence that Bahrām Gur used so to do.[6]

On Friday, 19 Moḥarram [12 November], two envoys from the Seljuqs were brought into the army camp, and provided with a good spread of food and hospitality. There was a scholar from Bokhara, an eloquent person,[7] and a Turkmen, thought to be closely connected with the Seljuqs. On the next day, Saturday [/13 November], the Amir held court with great pomp and display, and the envoys were brought into his presence, where they performed the ceremonial rites of obeisance. They were taken to the Vizier's Divān for a private session, which the head of the Chancery, Khᵛāja Bu Naṣr Moshkān, also attended. A letter had been written to the Vizier Khᵛāja Aḥmad b. ʿAbd al-Ṣamad, which entrusted its report to its accompanying verbal message. The verbal message was as follows: "Up to now, no mischief has been committed on our part. But it is well known that there are other Turkmens in Khorasan, and more are coming, since the routes from the Oxus and from Balkhān Kuh lie open. The territory bestowed upon us[8] is too small and insufficient in size to contain all our people (i.e. the Turkmens' families, etc.).[9] The Grand Vizier must intervene in the matter and request from the lord Sultan that these townlets on the edge of the desert, such as Merv, Sarakhs and Bāvard, should be given to us, with the arrangement that the postal and intelligence officers, judges and the head of the lord's Divān should remain in place, collect the taxation and hand it over to us as pay allotments so that we can be the lord's army and clear Khorasan of mischief-makers. If our service is required in Western Persia or any other place, we will fulfill our duty and [F 661] will set about any task, however difficult. The Great Chamberlain Sübashï and the army of Nishapur are to remain stationed at Herat; if they should attack us, we shall necessarily have to set about driving them off, with the concomitant loss of dignity and mutual respect. This is what we request; the exalted judgement has superior knowledge."

Bu Naṣr went away and reported to the Amir what they had said. He replied, "Send the envoys away, and the two of you come to me so that we can discuss this matter." The Vizier and Bu Naṣr went into the Sultan's presence. The Amir was in a great rage. He said to the Vizier, "This arrogation of authority and the barefaced demands and sheer arrogance of these people have exceeded all bounds; on the one hand, they have squeezed Khorasan dry,[10] and on the other, they are sending deceitful blandishments and honeyed words. These envoys must be sent back and plainly told that 'Between us and you lies the sword. Armies have been despatched to wage war, and we are now in process of leaving Bost and will go to Herat.'" The Vizier replied, [Gh 506] "So long as these people talk in this vein and remain quiescent, it is better not to discard the veil of dignified and formal respect. The wisest course seems to me that a reply containing both minatory and conciliatory words should be sent, so that some degree of affability is maintained. Then, if the lord so commands, I can go to Herat, and the Great Chamberlain and the whole of the army can subsequently come to Herat and deal with them, and resolve the matter through either peace or war. The lord will also be near us; if need arises, he can make a move." The Amir said, "This is good counsel. These envoys must be sent back on this wise. Khᵛāja Bu Naṣr is to write out on his own behalf what needs to be written. He is to wake them up from their delusions, and he is to say that, presently, you, Aḥmad, are going there to attend to the matter." The two of them went back, and they spent two or three days engaged in these [F 662] negotiations and discussions, until an agreement was reached with the envoys. A letter of reply together with a verbal message were handed over, and they were given robes of honour and presents of money and sent back to Khorasan on Thursday, 25 Moḥarram [/18 November].

On Tuesday, 1 Ṣafar [/24 November], a confidential letter arrived from the deputy of the postal and intelligence officer of Herat, Bādghis and Gharjestān with the information that "The Turkmen Dāvud, with 4,000 armed and equipped cavalrymen is leading an attack on Ghaznin by the road of Rebāṭ-e Razn (?), Ghur and Siyāh Kuh.[11] What has been bruited abroad recently has been set forth; only God Most High can know the truth of this matter." The Amir became highly perturbed at this news. He sent for the Vizier and said, "Nothing good will ever come of this crowd; how can an enemy ever turn into a friend? You must go to Herat with a fully-equipped army while we travel to Ghaznin, for in no circumstances can the seat of the empire be left unattended." The Vizier answered, "I obey the command, but this news doesn't sound genuine to me. We are well past Mehragān, and even a bird cannot make it in this season by the Rebāṭ-e Razn road to Ghaznin."[12] The Amir said, "What nonsense you're talking! When has the enemy ever been constrained by icebound conditions? Go at once, and prepare to depart, for whatever happens, I am going back to Ghaznin the day after tomorrow."' The Vizier went back. Those who had been privy to the discussion assembled together and sent a verbal message to the Amir through Bu Naṣr, saying "If, God forbid, this news *is* authentic, there will be other messengers coming. The lord should remain until further news comes along." Bu Naṣr went off [Gh 507] and delivered the message. The Amir said, "I agree. We'll remain for three days, but [F 663] the camels and the horses for the gholāms should be brought back from their present pasture grounds."[13] They said, "That's a sound course of action," and men were sent off to bring back the horses and camels.

There was much commotion in the army camp, and those who had amassed stocks of food and fodder now began to sell at low prices. Khᵛāja Bu Naṣr said to me, "Keep hold of your supplies of provisions, and purchase more, because this news is highly unlikely and goes against all one's reasoning and intuition. It has been said, *"Don't account as veracious any news which does not tally with one's sense and judgement."*[14] This lord of ours is an epitome of virtues and manly qualities, but his chronic obduracy (*estebdād*), casts a veil over his virtues." It happened exactly as he said. On Saturday, 5 Ṣafar [/28 November] another letter arrived, pointing out that "The earlier information was false, and the actual situation was that 150 Turkmen cavalrymen had passed through those regions and had themselves spread the news that they formed the vanguard of Dāvud's force in order to strike fear and avoid being pursued." The letter allayed the Amir's fears, the move to Ghaznin was cancelled and people's minds were set at rest.

On Monday, 7 Ṣafar [/30 November], the Amir rode out before daybreak to the bank of the Hirmand[15] river, together with falcons and hawks, hunting cheetahs, the retainers, boon-companions, and musicians and singers. Food and of wine were brought along. A great deal of game was hunted down, since they were occupied with the chase until towards noon. Then they halted on the bank of the river, where tents, and canvas shelters and awnings had been erected. They ate and drank, and enjoyed themselves thoroughly. As Fate would have it, after the [midday] worship, the Amir asked for some boats, and ten vessels were procured. They prepared one of them, the largest, for him to sail in. They had laid down coverings and drawn up the sails. He went on board with two boon-companions, a wine steward, two [F 664] cupbearers, a gholām and the Keeper of the Royal Weapons. The boon companions, the musicians and singers, the attendants and the rest of the party were in the other boats. All were caught unawares when suddenly they saw that, since the currents had gathered strength and the boat was full, it began to sink and break up. They only realized what was happening when the boat was about to go down, and a great clamour arose. The Amir stood up, and as luck would have it, there were other boats close by. Seven or eight men jumped out of them and secured the Amir, snatched him away from imminent danger and got him into another boat. He was severely battered, and his right leg was injured such that parts of the skin and flesh were sheared off. He had been very near to drowning, but God, [Gh 508] His mention is exalted, vouchsafed mercy after displaying His power. The joyful proceedings and rejoicing were to a great extent overlaid by that near-disaster.[16] *What joyful blessing is not tarnished by Fate?*[17]

When the Amir reached the boat, they steered the boats along and arrived at the bank of the river. The Amir, having arrived back from a visit to the next world (i.e. having narrowly escaped death), went into the tent and changed his clothes, for they were wet and soiled. He mounted and quickly came to the palace, since extremely unpleasant accounts had spread through the army encampment, causing a great deal of anxiety and alarm.[18] The notables and the Vizier came out to welcome him back and to provide an escort. When they found the monarch safe and sound, loud shouts of joy and invocations to God arose from both the army and the populace, and alms were given out in thanksgiving on an unprecedented scale. The next day the Amir ordered letters to be written to Ghaznin and the entire realm about the occurrence of this momentous and grave incident and the subsequent safe deliverance. He gave instructions that a million dirhams at Ghaznin and two million dirhams in the other provinces of the empire should be distributed to the deserving poor and the destitute by way of thanks for this deliverance. These were written out and confirmed by the royal signature and emblem, and envoys conveying the good news went off. On Thursday, 11 Ṣafar [/4 December], the Amir was attacked by a fever. A burning fever, [F 665] one causing delirium, raged to the extent that he was unable to hold court and remained secluded from people with the exception of the physicians and a handful of his male and female servants and attendants. Everyone was most perplexed and concerned, wondering what would happen.

On Wednesday, 17 Ṣafar [/10 December], an envoy arrived from the sons of 'Alitegin, a man called Alptegin, who was accompanied by the official preacher of Bokhara, 'Abdallāh Pārsi. The official escort assigned to the envoys went out with the holders of court offices and took with them saddled horses for the envoys and escorted them back to the army encampment with due decorum; they were lodged comfortably and plenty of delicacies and offerings were sent to them. The Amir was informed about the arrival of the envoys, and he sent a verbal message to the Vizier through the physician Bu'l-ʿAlāʾ saying, "Although we are feeling weak because of this illness, we have no choice but to show fortitude. Tomorrow we shall hold a public court session so that all the army may see us.[19] The envoys must be brought forward to our presence so that they can be publicly viewed. Then afterwards, plans will be made for sending them back." The Vizier replied, "The lord has spoken most aptly, for people are extremely worried and concerned, and much good will come out of the trouble that the lord is inflicting upon himself and the physical discomfort which he will have to bear. The next day, [Gh 509] the Amir sat down on his throne on the great platform at the head. The Vizier, the pillars of the state, the retainers and courtiers came to the court and were overjoyed to see the Amir, and they offered up their prayers and gave away large sums of money to the poor. The envoys were brought into the royal presence; they offered up their service and were conducted to seats. Amir Masʿud said, "How was our brother the Ilig when you left him?"[20] They replied, "Thanks to the auspicious rule of the great Sultan, he is well contented and prospering. So long as he is the recipient of the friendship and kindness bestowed upon him by the Sultan, [F 666] the Ilig enjoys ever-increasing happiness, fame and prestige. He sent us servants with the aim that friendship and accord might become greater."

The official escort of the envoys conducted them to the Vizier's Divān, and the Amir meanwhile had a private session with the Vizier Aḥmad ʿAbd al-Ṣamad, the Head of the Army Department Bu'l-Fatḥ Rāzi, Bu Naṣr Moshkān, and the Commander of the Palace Gholāms Begtughdï and the General Bu'l-Nażr. The power and prestige of Bu'l-Nażr had increased by many degrees, and he was directing all the affairs of the court as deputy for the Great Chamberlain Sübashï who, at the time of his departure from Balkh to Khorasan, had sought this arrangement from the Amir and had been granted it. The Amir said, "You must hear what these envoys have to say, and they must be sent back during this same week. Care must be taken to ensure that no-one has any contact with them without express permission. It is vital to keep a close watch on their attendants and retinue so that they don't get any inkling of my condition. I am unable to sit in court any longer than this. Summon Bu'l-ʿAlāʾ the physician and take him with you, so that, by means of messages, the matter may be entirely concluded today." They replied, "We'll do this; the lord suffered a great deal of pain and discomfort through holding this court, but it has brought great advantages." He said, "Yes, this is so."

All those at the meeting went back, and the Amir arose and returned to his private quarters. Bu'l-ʿAlāʾ came to the Vizier's Divān. My master took up and perused the letters and the transcriptions of the verbal messages. There was written, "We do not know how we shall be able to provide an excuse for that erroneous course of action which occurred,[21] given the fact of such royal solicitude on the part of the lord Sultan. Now, at this present juncture, when the state of friendship and accord has reached this high degree, we have three aims in mind, concerning which these envoys have been sent; once the agreement is concluded by the two sides and these three aims secured, all our desires will have been totally achieved. The first is that I should have my[22] status elevated by being honoured with a bride (*vadiʿat*) from that noble side (i.e. from the Ghaznavid royal house for the Ilig to marry). The second is that we should be deemed noble enough in rank[23] [F 667] to have a bride from our own side (i.e. a Qarakhanid princess) nominated for one of the Sultan's sons. [Gh 510] As a result of these arrangements, all territorial desires on the part of this realm, which is contiguous with the lord's empire, will be abandoned. The third aim is that, with the permission and the mediation of the Sultan, there should be an agreement and an exchange of correspondence between us and Arslān Khān, who is the senior figure and the Khān of Turkestan, so they may be convinced that the enmity has ended, and that the houses[24] have become united, and the reasons behind the feuds and open hostilities eradicated.[25] We sent these envoys with the verbal communications and the messages for this very reason. It befits the lofty resolution of the great Sultan that he should respond favourably to us over this, and that envoys from the exalted royal presence should accompany our own envoys so that we too may put into effect what has been sought. Thus when these aims have been achieved, our armies can cross the Oxus and join up and unite with the Sultan's armies and put out all this sedition and revolt. We will observe the royal command in this matter and, God willing, we will do our utmost to maintain unity in every way.

My master wrote down in his own hand this set of verbal communications and messages, and gave them to Bu'l-ʿAlāʾ the physician for him to take to the Amir. After an hour or two, he returned with the Amir's approval. The envoys were sent back to their lodging. Bu'l-ʿAlāʾ again went and came back, and told the Vizier and Bu Naṣr Moshkān, "The lord asks, What should we do in this case, and what is the wisest course of action?" They answered, "There is nothing unreasonable in young Yusof, son of ʿAlitegin's, requests, and some benefit will accrue to us if they are granted. First, we will be henceforth saved from any future headaches and mischief from his quarter; and second, he has troops, and it is possible that they may be of use to us.[26] This is how your servants see it; but the correct course of action is what the exalted judgement perceives as the right one."

Bu'l-ʿAlāʾ went off and returned with the response, the Sultan says, "What you servants say is very sound advice. All three of the requests should be granted, and letters of reply should be written out and an envoy designated to go back with their messengers." They noted down the names of some possible candidates for the Amir's consideration and gave the list to Bu'l-ʿAlāʾ to take back with him. The Amir chose ʿAbd al-Salām, the mayor of Balkh, [F 668] who was one of the royal boon-companions with some past experience of diplomatic missions. Khᵛāja Bu Naṣr returned home. The letters and the verbal messages were entrusted to ʿAbd al-Salām, and it was agreed that a sister of the Ilig should be given in marriage to the prince, Amir Saʿid, and from our side, a daughter of the Commander-in-Chief, the Amir Naṣr,[27] should be given to the Ilig. With these terms, the envoys set off on Tuesday, 23 Ṣafar [/16 December] with their requirements fulfilled.

Before the Sultan's illness had subsided, letters arrived from Bu Sahl Ḥamdavi, the civil governor (ʿAmid) of Western Persia, saying that "When the Son of [Gh 511] Kāku realized that he had come to an impasse and was not capable of waging a successful war, he sought to put forward excuses, and he is now asking for Isfahan to be given to him as a grant of territory in return for the handing over of its taxation.[28] Without the exalted command, I could not put this into effect. I have kept his envoy with me, and have forwarded the letters from the caliph's vizier, Moḥammad b. Ayyub,[29] to the exalted court and to myself, in which the vizier has interceded concerning this matter, seeking that this man, the Son of Kāku, should be retained in place. I await the exalted command regarding this affair so that action may be taken according to the royal command."

Bu Naṣr brought out, in his own handwriting, the salient points of these letters. Ever since the Amir had fallen ill, this was Bu Naṣr's usual practice, and from the large amount of business at hand, he would pick out items devoid of unpleasant news and would send them to the inner palace by me personally and I would give them to the Amir's personal servant Āghāji and bring back the answers without much fuss or ceremony and without seeing the Amir; until now when I brought[30] this résumé (i.e. of the letter from Bu Sahl Ḥamdavi), with its good news. Āghāji took it and bore it inside. Then an hour later he reappeared and said, "Bu'l-Fażl, the Amir summons you." I went into his presence. I found the room [F 669] had been darkened, with linen curtains hanging down cut into many strips and moistened with large bowls filled with ice on top of them.[31] I found the Amir there, seated on a throne, wearing a loose shift of Tavvazi cloth[32] and a scarf[33] round his neck, with a collar thoroughly impregnated with camphor, and Bu'l-ʿAlāʾ the physician seated there, below the throne. The Amir said, "Tell Bu Naṣr that today I feel well again, and in the next two or three days a court session will be held, since the illness and fever have completely gone. It is necessary to write a reply to Bu Sahl stating that this contractual agreement should be put into operation after making sure that no loopholes remain, and he is to make a deposition to this man that we have granted this contractual agreement for this second time out of respect for the intercession of the Caliph's vizier.[34] If after this he shows any sign of treasonable activity, his entire house will be uprooted and destroyed. An answer must also be written regarding this to the Caliph's vizier, according to the official protocol, and couched in felicitous terms. You are personally to bring that letter which is to be written to Bu Sahl so that I may affix my official emblem and motto, because there is another set of instructions to be communicated to you."

I went back and told Bu Naṣr what had happened. He was filled with great joy, and made prostrations to the Almighty God in thanks for the Sultan's recovery. The letter was written, and I bore it to Āghāji and I was allowed in and was thus fortunate enough for a second time to set eyes on the august lord. He read that letter, called for the inkstand, affixed the official emblem and motto and tossed it over to me, saying, "It should be given to two reliable swift-running couriers (*kheyltāshs*) so that they can go off speedily with Bu Sahl's own mounted messenger and bring back the reply. Also, an answer to the postal and intelligence officer of Ray should be written, stating that "We have decided [Gh 512] to come from Bost to Herat and Nishapur in order to be nearer to you, and so that your intended plans can be put into action more quickly and go forward in a more satisfactory manner." A letter should further be written to the head of the Divān [of Khorasan], Suri, to be conveyed by [F 670] these couriers, and instructions given that supplies of food and fodder for us in large quantities should be got ready at Nishapur and the staging posts,[35] since the illness that afflicted us is now over, and our banner will soon be on the march to resolve the present difficulties which have arisen in Khorasan. Come back here when the letters have been despatched so that I can give you a message I have for Bu Naṣr." I obeyed and went away with the letter with the official signature and emblem affixed, and I informed Bu Naṣr how matters stood. For his part, this truly worthy man and most capable secretary put pen to paper in good heart, and, having completed the task before the time of the midday worship, had the couriers despatched along with Bu Sahl's messenger. Then he wrote a note to the Amir setting forth all that he had done. He gave it to me, and I took it, was allowed entry into the inner palace and delivered it. The Amir read it and was pleased with it, and he told the household servant Āghāji to bring in the purses, and he said to me, "Take them! In each purse there is 1,000 methqāls' weight in gold pieces. Tell Bu Naṣr that these are the gold pieces that our father brought back from his expeditions against the infidels in India[36] when he smashed up golden idols and melted them down into pieces. They thus have a most licit pedigree as an untainted form of acquired wealth.[37] On all our journeys, some of this gold should be brought along with us so that when we wish to give alms and to ensure that these are paid from an unimpeachable source, we would be able to draw upon this supply. We hear that the Judge of Bost, Bu'l-Ḥasan Bulāni,[38] and his son Bu Bakr possess only a small property and suffer from financial constraint but refuse to accept anything from anybody. The father and son should each be given a purse of this gold so that they can acquire a small estate with this untainted money and live more comfortably, and [F 671] it will also give us the opportunity to show to some extent our gratitude for the blessing of our recovery and renewed health."

I took the purses and brought them to Bu Naṣr, and I explained what had happened. He offered up prayers and invocations and said, "This was a most appropriate deed by the lord. I have heard that there have been times when Bu'l-Ḥasan and his son have been in dire straits for the want of ten dirhams." He went back to his house, and the purses were taken along too. After the worship, he despatched a person to summon the Judge Bu'l-Ḥasan and his son, and they came. Bu Naṣr conveyed the Sultan's message to the Judge. He offered up prayers and invocations, and said, "This gift is a mark of great honour; I have accepted it and I have now given it back, since I have no use for it. The Day of Resurrection is very near, and I shall not be able to give an account for it. I am not saying that I could not well do with it, but since I am content with what I have, little though it is, what use to me is this burden and responsibility?" [Gh 513] Bu Naṣr said, "Praise the Lord, this is most strange! Does the Judge refuse the gold from the broken-up and splintered idols of the temples, gold which Sultan Maḥmud must have brought back[39] by the might of his sword from his expeditions, and regarded as untainted and thoroughly acceptable by the Commander of the Faithful?" He replied, "May the lord's life be prolonged! The case of the Caliph is something different, since he is the lord exercising temporal power over the Muslims. The Khᵛāja has accompanied Amir Maḥmud on his raids, whereas I have not, and I have no way of knowing whether those raids were conducted according to the custom of the Chosen One[40] or not. I won't accept this,[41] nor bear any responsibility for it." Bu Naṣr said, "If you won't accept it, give it to your disciples and to the deserving poor and destitute." He answered, "I don't know any deserving poor in Bost to whom I can give the gold. And besides, why should someone else take the gold but leave me accountable for it on the Day of Resurrection? I will never agree to take on this responsibility."[42] [F 672]

Bu Naṣr said to his son, "You take your share!" He replied, "May your Honour's life be prolonged! All things considered, I am still the offspring of the man who has spoken these words, and all that I know comes from him. Just one day of observing and learning from his conduct would have made it incumbent upon me to follow him for the rest of my life, let alone all these years when I have been constantly at his side. I am just as afraid of that reckoning, of that standing before God for judgement and that questioning, as he is! What little I have of worldly goods is lawfully acquired and adequate for me, and I have no further needs." Bu Naṣr said, "May God bless you both! You two are the very embodiments of true nobility", and he wept and sent them back. For the remainder of the day he was in a pensive mood and he kept on recalling this episode. Next day he wrote out a note to the Amir and told him what had happened and sent back the gold. This left a deep impression on the Amir.[43] I often heard that whenever he caught sight of anyone masquerading as a Sufi or spotted one of those tricksters with a finely-trimmed moustache[44] who try to ensnare people with their religiosity (lit. "having put on the skirt of hypocrisy and having worn the coarse garment of an impostor") but have hearts blacker than their own cloaks, he would laugh[45] and say to Bu Naṣr, "May the evil eye be far from the Bulānis!"

At this point a very remarkable and delightful tale has come to mind which I found in the chronicles of the ʿAbbasid caliphs and which I thought I should set down here.

The story of the Commander of the Faithful with Ebn al-Sammāk and [ʿAbdallāh] Ebn ʿAbd al-ʿAziz the two ascetics

One year, Hārun al-Rashid had gone to Mecca, *may God Most High protect it.* When [F 673] the prescribed rites of the Pilgrimage had been performed it had been said that there were two great ascetics there who never went near any ruler, one called Ebn al-Sammāk[46] and the other [Gh 514] [Ebn] ʿAbd al-ʿAziz ʿOmari.[47] He said to Fażl b. Rabiʿ, "O ʿAbbāsi,"—for that is how he used to address him[48]—"I have a desire to see these two pious men who shun the company of rulers, and hear them speak and learn about the way they live and their outward behaviour and inner nature; what's the best way to proceed?" Fażl replied, "It is for the Commander of the Faithful to decree and to state what he desires and wishes to be done so that your servant can make the necessary arrangements." He said, "My intention is that we should go to them in disguise and see how we find them both, for false ascetics[49] are recognizable by their love for the baubles of this present world." Fażl said, "That's a sound idea; what does the lord command?" he answered, "Go back, get ready two Egyptian asses and two purses containing 1,000 methqāls in gold, and dress as a merchant, and be here with me at the time of the night worship and I'll tell you what is to be done." Fażl went back, and got this all ready, and at the time of the afternoon worship came to Hārun. He found him dressed as a merchant too. The Caliph arose and mounted the ass, with Fażl on the other ass. He gave the gold to a man who knew where the houses of both of the ascetics were. They sent him on ahead with two envoys from the caliph's personal retinue, and they came along in disguise and without a torch or candle so that they would not be recognized.

First, they reached 'Omari's house. They banged on the door several times until a voice was heard saying, "Who is it?" They answered, "Open the door, it's someone who wishes to see the ascetic privately." A slave girl, one who had been bought for a low price,[50] came and opened the door. All three of them, Hārun, Fażl and the trusty guide, went in. They found 'Omari standing there performing the worship in a room with a threadbare mat and a lamp placed at the bottom of an ewer. Hārun and Fażl [F 674] sat down for a while until he had completed his devotions and greeted them. He then addressed them and said, "Who are you, and what brings you here?" Fażl replied, "It's the Commander of the Faithful, and he deems it a blessing to visit you." He said, "May God reward you with kindness! Why did he go to so much trouble? He should have summoned me and I would have come, since I am in his obedience and authority because he is the successor of the Prophet and obedience to him is incumbent on all the Muslims." Fażl retorted, "It was the Caliph's own choice that he should come to you." He said, "May the Almighty God make great his honoured status and prestige, just as he has recognized this servant's status." Hārun said, "Give us some spiritual counsel and words that we can take to heart and act upon." He said, "O you who have been appointed to guard the Almighty God's creatures on earth, know that God Most High has bestowed on you the greater portion of the earth so that by means of part of it you may redeem yourself from the flames of Hell. Furthermore, look in a mirror [Gh 515] so that you may see this fine face of yours and realize what a pity it would be to inflict the flames of

Hell on it. Watch over yourself and don't do anything that will make you deserving of the Most High Creator's wrath." Hārun wept and said, "Say on!" He continued, "O Commander of the Faithful, you will know that on the road from Baghdad to Mecca you passed by many burial grounds; man's return is to there. Go, and tend that other abode (i.e. the grave), for your sojourn in this house (i.e. the present world) is all too brief." Hārun wept even more copiously. Fażl said, "O ʿOmari, enough of your acerbic words! Do you realize who you're talking to?" The ascetic became silent. Hārun made a sign for their guide to set down before him one of the purses and said, "We wanted to free you from penury, so we have ordered this for you. ʿOmari said, "*There is no respite for a man encumbered with a family and relatives*,"[51] [F 675] and I have four daughters. If I did not have their care to think about, I would not accept it, since I myself have no need of it." Hārun arose, and ʿOmari escorted him to the door of the house until Hārun mounted and rode off. On the road he said to Fażl, "I found ʿOmari a moving and powerful speaker, but he nevertheless has an inclination towards this world. How strongly seductive are these dirhams and dinars! What a really great man it is who can turn his face away from such things! Let's go and see how we find Ebn Sammāk!"

They went along until they reached the door of his house. They rattled the ring on the door repeatedly until there came a voice, "Who is it?" They said, "We are looking for Ebn Sammāk." The person inside went away for a long time, and then returned and asked, "What do you want of Ebn Sammāk?" They said, "Open the door, it's very pressing business." [Then after this, a slave girl opened the door; they went in and sat down in darkness.][52] They were kept waiting on a bare floor for a while longer. Fażl called out to the slave girl who had opened the door to bring him a lamp. The slave girl came and told them, "Since this man purchased me, I have never seen him with a lamp." Hārun was astonished. They sent out their guide, and he tried his best and knocked on many doors till he brought a lamp, and the place was lit up. Fażl said to the slave girl, "Where is the sheykh?" She answered, "Up on this roof."

They went up on to the roof of the house and saw Ebn Sammāk performing the worship and weeping as he recited this verse, "*Did you then think that We created you only for Our sport?*",[53] and he repeated this and kept on reciting. Then he uttered the final salutation of the worship, since he had seen the lamp and had become conscious of people around him. He turned his face and greeted them with "Peace be upon you!" Hārun and Fażl responded with the same words. Then Ebn Sammāk said, "Why have you come at this hour [F 676] and who are you?" Fażl retorted, "It's the Commander of the Faithful [Gh 516] who has come to visit you, for he had expressed a wish to see you." He replied, "This required my assent, and if I had given it, then he could have come, for it is not right to confuse and distract people in this way." Fażl said, "It ought to have been thus, but now it's happened and is past. It's the successor of the Prophet, and obedience to him is a canonical obligation for all Muslims, and this includes you yourself, for the Almighty God says, '*Obey God and obey the Messenger and those of you set in authority.*' "[54] Ebn Sammāk said, "Does this caliph follow the path of the two Sheykhs, and by this figure of two I mean Bu Bakr and 'Omar, *may God be pleased with them*,[55] for his command to be equated with the command of the Prophet?" He replied, "He does follow in the same path." He said, "I am surprised to hear this, for in this holy city of Mecca, I see no signs of such conduct, and since there are no such traces here, it can be surmised what the situation is in other parts of the realm." Fażl stood there reduced to silence. Hārun said, "Give me a word of guidance, for I have come to hear your words and to become more spiritually aware." He said, "O Commander of the Faithful, fear the Almighty God, for He is One, He has no partner and needs no consort. Know that on the Day of Resurrection you will be made to stand before Him and there will be two possibilities: you will either be taken to Paradise or else to Hell, and there is no third place apart from these two abodes."

Hārun wept bitterly until his face and body were moist with tears. Fażl said, "O Sheykh, do you know what you are saying? Could anyone doubt that the Commander of the Faithful would go anywhere but Paradise?" Ebn Sammāk made no reply to this and ignored him, and he turned to Hārun and said, "O Commander of the Faithful, this man Fażl is with you tonight, but at the Day of Resurrection [F 677] he won't be with you. He won't be able to speak on your behalf, and if he does, they won't listen to him. Study yourself and have compassion on yourself." Fażl was filled with awe, and Hārun wept so hard that they were afraid he might faint and collapse. Then Hārun said, "Give me some water." Ebn Sammāk arose and brought a pitcher of water and gave it to him. When Hārun was about to drink, he said to him, "O Caliph, I adjure you by the right of your kinship with the Prophet, if this water was withheld from you, tell me how much you would pay for it?" He replied, "Half of the kingdom." He said, "Drink, and I hope you enjoy it!" After Hārun had set about drinking, Ebn Sammāk said, "If this water you have drunk cannot be discharged from your body, how much would you give to be able to pass water again?" He replied, "Half of the kingdom." He said, " O Commander of the Faithful, you should not be inordinately proud of a kingdom worth no more than a drink of water! But be that as it may, since you have taken on this task, dispense justice and show munificence to the Almighty God's creatures." Hārun replied, "I accept that," and he made a sign [Gh 517] that the purse should be brought forward. Fażl said, "O Sheykh, the Commander of the Faithful had heard that you are in straitened circumstances, and tonight this has been confirmed. He has commanded this gift of lawfully acquired money to be given to you; take it!" Ebn Sammāk smiled and said, "Heaven forfend! Here I am offering advice to the Commander of the Faithful so that he can keep himself away from the fires of Hell, while this man here is bent on hurling me into those very flames! Away, away with it! Take this fire away from my presence lest even at this very moment we, the house and the whole quarter should be consumed!," and he arose and went down from the roof. The slave girl came running out, saying, "O noble sirs, go back home, for you have caused this unfortunate old man much pain tonight." Hārun and Fażl left, with the guide bearing the gold. They mounted and rode off. All along the road, Hārun [F 678] kept on exclaiming, "Here indeed was a man!," and afterwards he used often to recall the story of Ebn Sammāk.

I bring in such stories as this hoping that readers may perhaps derive some benefit from them and that they may leave an impression on their hearts and minds. I now return to the historical narrative.

On Thursday, 1 Rabiʿ I [/23 December 1036], Amir Masʿud held a court session, a public one, since he had now fully recovered his health. The retainers and courtiers, and the common people of Bost, came into the royal presence and presented their offerings. The subjects offered up many prayers and invocations for him. They had brought with them many sacrificial animals for slaughter at the court, and this they did and distributed the meat, together with bread, amongst the poor. It was a joyful occasion, the like of which no-one could remember.

On Monday, the twelfth of this month [/3 January 1037], a letter arrived from Merv announcing the death of the royal special servant Nushtegin, who was the military governor of those regions. It contained his verbal testamentary disposition on his deathbed, saying that "Amir Masʿud had not manumitted him. Hence everything which he owned belonged to the Sultan. This must be made clear so that, if the Amir should think fit, he should manumit him and confirm his rights of property, and should validate and put into effect the charitable foundations (*owqāf*) that he had constituted. Second, his entire belongings by way of gholāms, luxury items, arms and equipment, and estates should all go to the lord. His gholāms are skilled and workmanlike, and he has taken a great deal of trouble to train them, and they are effective as a unit and should not be dispersed. There is a certain gholām, their senior commander, who is called Khumārtegin the Qorʾān-reciter and who has been brought up and trained by him personally. He is a man of wise counsel and trustworthy, and of singular valour and manliness; the Amir should retain him as their commander, for this will be sound policy."

The Amir freed the special servant Nushtegin and ordered that his charitable foundations should be validated and put into effect, and replies were written to his letters. His gholāms were taken care of and treated with much consideration, and Khumārtegin retained as their commander. [Gh 518] It was decreed that "They [F 679] should remain in their usual place so that the finance and tax director can keep on issuing their living allowances and salaries, and so that they can continue doing their stipulated tasks and duties until that time when we summon them, bestow them on one of our sons and entrust their care to him." The letters were authenticated with the Sultan's signature and device, and two *kheyltāsh*s bore them away.

On Thursday, the twenty-second of this month [/13 January], letters arrived from Khorasan with the news that "The Turkmens have dispersed themselves through the fringes of the realm and have plundered the town of Tun.[56] Bu'l-Ḥasan ʿErāqi, the commander of the Kurds and Arabs, spends his nights and days at Herat imbibing wine, and the local governor and tax collector Bu Ṭalḥa Sheybāni complains bitterly about him. He and the other notables and men of substance there are exasperated by his flippancy. He sent one of his gholāms with a detachment of Kurds and Arabs to drive away a group of Turkmens, but without any advanced planning or forethought, and it led to a fiasco with many of his men killed or taken captive by the Turkmens." The Amir became very despondent at this news and sent for the Vizier. They discussed all aspects, and it finally came to this that the Amir told him "You must proceed to Herat and stay there until the Great Chamberlain Sübashï and the whole army of Khorasan come to you. You should scrutinize them closely, their allowances and salaries should be paid out, and they should then go forth fully armed and equipped and engage the Turkmens and expel them from Khorasan by the sword. For nothing good will ever come from them, and everything that they promised and undertook up to this point was deceit, blandishment and trickery, since everywhere they went they left neither stock nor tillage.[57] Relieve this miscreant little wretch ʿErāqi (*ʿErāqiyak*) of command of the Kurds and Arabs, appoint over them two experienced commanders from among their own ranks, and entrust the whole body of them to the Great Chamberlain. Send ʿErāqi to the court so that he may experience what he has deserved, for we have lost Khorasan and Western Persia because of him and his brother. When you have reached there and assumed command, and have seen things for yourself, write letters back to us promptly and regularly, and we will be sending forth further instructions as the situation requires." He expressed his obedience and went back. He sat down with Bu Naṣr and they talked at length about these matters. [F 680] The next day the Vizier wrote out a contractual agreement. It was brought to the court, and Bu Naṣr laid it before the Amir in a private session, and there and then in the same session he wrote out replies as the Amir commanded and deemed fit, and these were validated by the affixing of the Sultan's signature and emblem.

On Tuesday, 5 Rabiʿ II [/26 January], the Grand Vizier was highly honoured with an array of most valuable gifts, including a male and female elephant, a mule, a litter and a hawk,[58] and a substantial number of Turkish gholāms. He came into the royal presence. The Amir spoke many a kind word to him, going so far as to say that "The Vizier is our father, and he is bearing the burdens which we should bear. He will relieve our mind of responsibility for this important matter,[59] [Gh 519] for his orders are on a par with our own commands."

The Vizier replied, "I am a servant, and I hold my life as a sacrifice for the lord's commands. I shall do everything in regard to this charge as is humanly possible in the task ahead." He returned home highly exalted and with a most stately retinue, and people lavished gifts and offerings upon him to an extent beyond anything they could recollect from the past.

A particularly warm and close friendship existed at this time between the Vizier and Khᵛāja Bu Naṣr, for he fully recognized Bu Naṣr's unique qualities, and he asked him to suggest a trusted member of the Chancery to accompany him and offer advice and expertise on the letters which required to be written back to the Sultan and so that he could also report back to the court on all [F 681] the Vizier's activities in different spheres. He ordered the scholar Bu Bakr b. Mobashsher to be appointed as secretary for this job, and Bu Naṣr gave him the necessary instructions. The next day, the Vizier set off for Herat in great splendour, with a full panoply of arms and equipment, and accompanied by about 1,000 cavalrymen.

On Monday, 25 Rabiʿ II [/15 February], the Amir went to Yomnābād and Meymand[60] for recreation and hunting. Khᵛāja ʿAbd al-Razzāq, the grandson of Ḥasan,[61] was his host there and served in his inimitable and elegant way, offering fitting presents,[62] while his stewards lavished food and presents[63] upon the royal entourage. The Amir lodged in those regal buildings at Meymand built by Khᵛāja Aḥmad b. Ḥasan, and then on Wednesday, 4 Jomādā I [/23 February] he returned to the Pavilion in the plain of Logān.[64] The next day a letter arrived with the news of the death of Satïlmïsh, the commander of Arslān.[65] The Amir had raised him up in status and had given him the military governorship of Bādghis by virtue of the fact that he had been treasurer in the time of Amir Moḥammad and had been the first person who had gone forth from Khorasan to meet Amir Masʿud and had brought with him a number of Arslān's gholāms, as I have previously mentioned.[66]

On Sunday, the eighth of this month [/27 February], Bu Saʿid b. Maḥmud b. Ṭāher, the treasurer [F 682] of Bost, died. He was a most noble and capable young man, and wise beyond his years. Khᵛāja Bu Naṣr used to spend a great deal of time with him and would say of him, "This young man will go far if he lives long enough and stops his habitual drinking, particularly as he mostly indulges first thing in the morning."[67] But he did not stop, and it was said that he died of this.

What a sorry tale this is! *"Indeed, God has troops of helpers, including honey!"*[68] He died at the end of his appointed span, and the remarkable thing was that, two or three days before he died, [Gh 520] he threw a very splendid party. He invited Bu Naṣr and a whole host of people. I was also there, and there was much revelry. This turned out to be his leave-taking, for three days later he made the journey from which no-one has returned. This line of verse of the poet can serve us as a memento: [Poetry]

1. *What do the Nights* (i.e. Fate) *show us, and what corruption have they brought?*[69]

2. *Every day we have to seek consolation for the death of someone dear to us.*[70]

His father Maḥmud b. Ṭāher was a man of some eminence, one of the treasurers of Amir Maḥmud, who enjoyed the Amir's full trust. He also died young. That monarch, in remembrance of what was due to the deceased, showered favours upon this noble son of his, and this noble-minded man, the son Bu Saʿid, attracted much public esteem and fame. Amir Masʿud had shown further consideration to him by extending his patronage to him, so that he became even more prominent. But he was not vouchsafed long life and passed away in his youth. [F 683] He had married into a great house, that of Bu'l-Nażr Rokhudhi,[71] an illustrious master and the most trusty of the Khwarazm Shah Altuntāsh's retainers, and an intimate of Amir Maḥmud. He left behind two sons, both capable and ready for service. Their maternal uncle, Khᵛāja Masʿud Rokhudhi, on two occasions acted as Head of the Army Department for two such monarchs as Mowdud and Farrokh-zād,[72] and he left behind many a praiseworthy deed and displayed much chivalry and liberality, as befits men of his noble nature and stature.[73] If he suffered tribulations from the vicissitudes of ignoble fate during the year 451 [/1059] and had to face harsh times, it would all end well; for if water finds its way down the bed of a stream once or twice, it will do so again. The ups and downs of fortune are a blessing in disguise. So long as one is alive and well, wealth and possessions can come and go, and the sufferings that men of true merit have to endure in such times is usually taken as a touchstone of their noble endurance rather than a piece of unalloyed misfortune.

I have set forth this section because here was the appropriate place for it and I shall have further dealings with this important figure and more to say on how he fared in his later posts, for before long Amir Masʿud would have promoted him and he would be engaged in important matters of state and would have his full share of success and misfortune. All this will be narrated, *in accordance with the will of God Most High*, in its proper sequence.

On Tuesday, 17 Jomādā I [/8 March], the secretary Bu'l-Ḥasan ʿErāqi, who had been dismissed from command of the Kurds and Arabs, came to the court. The Grand Vizier Aḥmad b. ʿAbd al-Ṣamad had sent him off with due decorum and respect but had appointed five cavalrymen to guard him. [F 684] The Amir did not allow him into the court but sent him to the secretary Masʿud b. Moḥammad b. Leyth [Gh 521] as if he was under house arrest. Everyone went to visit him, and they found him extremely downcast and apprehensive. In the end, Bu Naṣr spoke out for him—this man belonged to the ranks of the secretaries[74]—and interceded on his behalf until the Amir relented. He came forward and rendered service, and took up a place once again in the Chancery, but his reputation was tarnished, he was cut down to size and he no longer dared to speak above his station;[75] in the end he passed away, as I shall mention later on.[76]

On Sunday, the twenty-first of this month [/12 March], letters arrived from Bu Sahl Ḥamdavi and the postal and intelligence officer of Ray with the news that "The Son of Kāku's words and promises were all a pack of lies and a ploy and subterfuge to gain time. He has gathered forces from the outlying regions and they all came together. Elements of the Turkmen followers of Qïzïl and Yaghmur and those from Balkhān Kuh who had fled before the Seljuqs have also joined up with him, since the fellow has plenty of gold and large assets, with a well-filled treasury, and he has headed towards Ray with a well-armed and equipped force. What concerns us is that he knows full well that Khorasan is in turmoil because of the Seljuqs and that reinforcements cannot be sent to us. We are striving our utmost, and we shall see what God the Exalted One decrees." This made the Amir most apprehensive and he ordered the following response to be written: "The Vizier, the Great Chamberlain and the troops are in Khorasan to deal with this affair of the Seljuqs, and we too intend to go there. You must be resolute and face the challenge valiantly, for with this army that you have at your command you can conquer the whole of Western Persia." These replies went off with an agent of the postal service and also by swift couriers. [F 685] I shall describe these events in their entirety in the separate section devoted to the story of Ray; the above should suffice here.

On Tuesday, 29 Jomādā II [/19 April], the Vizier's letters arrived saying that "I am pursuing matters diligently. The tax collectors and financial agents of the various towns who had been summoned are arriving, with the required sums collected and brought in. The Great Chamberlain and the troops reached Herat. Bu Sahl b. ʿAli,[77] the deputy Head of the Army Department, is conducting an army review in a very thorough manner in my own presence and is giving out the pay in ready coins.[78] Once the army is fitted out and equipped and they march out against the enemy, I shall furnish them with advice on strategy and will do my utmost to succeed as the lord's servant. I am hopeful that, with God the Exalted One's favour, our aims will be achieved. The wise course is, in my opinion, that the lord should come to Herat once the Nowruz celebrations are over, and should spend the summer here [Gh 522]—since preparations have been made, and there is no need to worry about the question of food and fodder and other things—so that I can then go to Merv and the Great Chamberlain can go forth with an army against the enemy. In this way the Great Chamberlain will feel secure and encouraged from all sides and this revolt will be quelled and the matter of Ray and Jebāl, which has also become entangled and troublesome, will be straightened out and the lord will be relieved of all worries."

The Amir ordered the following reply to be written: "The Vizier is our deputy in Khorasan. Merv and the other towns are full of troops; why should our presence be needed at Herat? We will head for Ghaznin, for this is the best way. ʿAlitegin's sons are toeing the line, and there is no cause for worry in the region of Balkh and Tokhārestān. Our dear son Mowdud and the Commander-in-Chief ʿAli are there; should there be any need for further troops, [F 686] you should go to them for reinforcements." The replies, couched in these terms, went off.

I heard Bu Naṣr say at the time, "The right course was the one suggested by the Vizier, but this Amir will not listen, and he will not be deflected from his intention of proceeding to Ghaznin, since he has set his heart on that. But, God be praised, it is not Ghaznin which is in danger of being taken away from him! It is to Herat or Merv or Nishapur that he should go, and he should reside in Khorasan for a year or two so that perhaps this great convulsion can be treated. On several occasions I have also shown the Amir what the Vizier has written to me, and what he had written in even franker terms; but it was to no avail, for truly, the Almighty God Most High has ways and wishes that we, His servants, cannot decipher or unravel."

On 11 Rajab [/30 April], the Amir travelled from Bost towards Ghaznin and reached there on Thursday, 7 Shaʿbān [/26 May]. He arrived in the Maḥmudi Garden with the intention of staying there for some time, and began indulging in wine-drinking sessions and kept on carousing continuously, with no respite.

On Tuesday, 12 Shaʿbān [/31 May], the Prince Amir Mowdud, reached Ghaznin from Balkh, a letter having gone from Bost instructing him to make this move. He came to this rendezvous and received a warm welcome. On Tuesday, 19 Shaʿbān [/7 June], the Amir came to the citadel, where the *sarhang* Bu ʿAli the castellan had laid on hospitality. On Friday, the twenty-second of this month [/10 June], he came back to the New Masʿudi Palace. [F 687]

Before he could return from the Maḥmudi Garden, a letter arrived from the Vizier. It said, "The affairs of the army have been put in order, and it has gone out against the enemy with a stout heart. When the Turkmens realized that matters had been set on foot in a more determined manner, they withdrew en masse towards Nasā and Farāva so that not a single one of them remains in the regions of Guzgānān, Herat and these districts. The Great Chamberlain [Gh 525] went to Merv and set up camp outside it and sent out a military governor to every place, and taxes are being collected;[79] what should I do now?" The reply went out, "Since the situation is thus, the Vizier should come to Ghaznin via the Ghur road in order to see us and tell us in person what needs to be reported, so that decisions can be made on a more firm and informed basis."

The month of the fast (i.e. Ramażān) came in, and the Amir began his fast in the New Palace. Each night, the Princes, Amirs Saʿid, Mowdud and ʿAbd al-Razzāq, were in the Great Hall (*khāna-ye bozorg*), and with them, taking turns in attending, were the chamberlains, the retainers and the boon-companions. The Sultan, meanwhile, would end his daily fast and eat privately within the inner palace quarters.

On Saturday, 15 Ramażān [/2 July], the Vizier reached Ghaznin and saw the Amir, and there was a private meeting with him and the head of the Chancery which lasted till the time of the midday worship. The Vizier related everything that had happened and everything that he had done; the Amir was most pleased by it all and praised him with many congratulatory words. The Vizier returned home. The next day, they held another private session, and there the Vizier had said, "If the lord had come to Herat, not a single Turkmen would by now have been left in Khorasan; but perhaps [F 688] their God-given allotted time in Khorasan has not yet reached its end.[80] At all events, so long as the Great Chamberlain and the troops are stationed in those regions,[81] the Turkmens will not indulge in any mischief. But I am deeply concerned about the fate of Ray and of Bu Sahl and the army there, and all that gold and valuable clothing that they carry with them, faced as they are with an enemy like the Son of Kāku; for now that the exalted banner will not be going to Khorasan, one cannot know how they will fare." The Amir replied, "They will not give us any trouble, for there is a well-equipped army there with good commanders, and Bu Sahl knows his business. The Son of Kāku, the Deylamites and the Kurds do not have any stomach for war; I have seen them in action and tried them myself, and I am keeping an eye on the situation." The Vizier said, " God willing, may the lord's realm have nothing but good fortune bestowed upon it!"

On Monday, 17 Ramażān [/4 July], the Commander-in-Chief ʿAli also arrived from Balkh with his personal gholāms and close retainers, travelling light in accordance with the royal command which had been issued that he should leave the army behind at Balkh and come for consultation on his own. He saw the Sultan and was well received and returned home.

Monday was the day of the Festival of the Ending of the Fast (i.e. on 1 Shavvāl/18 July). A week before, the Amir had given instructions on the arrangement of the parades for this day. The troop formations and the display were of such calibre that even the aged men and elders confessed that they could not remember anything on that scale from times past. [Gh 524] There were large numbers of cavalrymen on the plain of Shābahār also.[82] The Amir sat on the great platform at the New Palace on a throne made of wood, since the golden throne had not yet been made. The palace gholāms, numbering 4,000 odd at this time, began to come in, and within that great palace they stood there in several lines. The Amir then held court, and the fast was officially broken by eating the morning meal. The palace gholāms began to make their way to the New Square, [F 689] and were standing there, making [83] the square and all the plain of Shābahār appear as if it had become a field of anemones.[84] After this, the Amir mounted his steed[85] and came to that eminence (*khażrā*) overlooking the square and the plain of Shābahār, and the special worship for the Festival was celebrated.[86] The Amir sat down to the feast in the Spring Pavilion that is situated on the right side of the platform. The royal princes, the Vizier, the Commander-in-Chief, the Amirs of the Deylamites[87] and the leading retainers were given seats at this spread and the rest of the people at other spreads. The poets recited verses, and after that, musicians and singers came in and bowls of wine were handed round, with the result that they all staggered back home from the feast in an intoxicated state. The Amir mounted and came to the gilded chamber on the roof where preparations had been made for a session for wine-drinking, and they set about enjoying themselves drinking.

The next day no court was held, but on the third day (i.e. on 3 Shavvāl/20 July), he held court. The gholāms of the royal special servant Nushtegin arrived from Merv under a senior commander called Khumārtegin, and also Nushtegin's counsellor and adjutant, the secretary Maḥmudak, and several men of his retinue, all of them in fine array and fully equipped. They came into the Amir's presence and received a warm welcome. He gave orders that the gholāms used to being quartered in barracks (*gholāmān-e vothāqi*) should be given accommodation separately in the Old Maḥmudi Palace and should be treated handsomely. The next day he summoned them to appear before him in a more private interview, and he kept back thirty of the choicest gholāms for himself and bestowed the remainder on his four sons Sa'id, Mowdud, Majdud and 'Abd al-Razzāq. He ordered 'Abd al-Razzāq's share to be many more times that of the others since the others already had many gholāms and he did not, and the Amir had intended to award him a provincial governorship.

Also during Shavvāl, the Amir went on an hunting expedition involving the rounding-up of game,[88] together with a group of palace gholāms, some troops, boon-companions, and singers and musicians. Some very good hunting was had, and they had a festive time on [F 690] the hunting ground itself[89] and drank wine. I myself was present at this hunting party, though Khᵛāja Bu Naṣr was not there. A great amount of game was brought back to Ghaznin on swift riding camels. The retainers, the troops stationed at the court, and the royal princes, accompanied the Sultan. *May God be pleased with them all!*

On Wednesday, the twenty-fourth of this month [/10 August], he returned to the Garden of a Hundred Nightingales, and on the next day he issued an order that the possessions and estates that the royal special servant Nushtegin had left behind should be thoroughly scrutinized in the presence of his counsellor and adjutant [Gh 525] and secretary Maḥmudak, and other supervisory agents, and that the charitable endowments for the building and upkeep of his tomb should be maintained exactly as they were. He bestowed his travelling equipment, including his tents, his main one and others, and a number of horses and camels, on his son Amir ʿAbd al-Razzāq, together with three villages, one in Zābolestān and two at Peshawar.[90] The rest was designated as crown property (*khāṣṣa*).[91] He bestowed Nushtegin's residence on the prince Amir Mardān Shāh, together with a great amount of furnishings and carpets and several pieces of silverware. What Nushtegin had left behind and the luxury items in his possession were beyond measure. The governorship of Merv, which was held by him, he gave to the General Begtughdï, Commander of the Palace Gholāms. An investiture patent was written out, and he sent there his counsellor and adjutant, Bu ʿAli Zowzani.

In the course of this week, there were talks with the Commander Begtughdï in order to arrange a marriage between the prince, Amir Mardān Shāh, and a daughter of Begtughdï. Bu Naṣr b. Moshkān delivered the message verbally, and Begtughdï insisted for a while that he did not have the capacity to receive such a great favour and he did not see how he could cope. Bu Naṣr spoke in an appropriately comprehensive and persuasive manner until Begtughdï consented, and they clasped hands and came to a verbal agreement for the time being until a royal command could be issued to conclude the wedding contract (*ʿaqd-e nekāḥ*). The Commander Begtughdï knew what he had to do and what had been intended. He embarked on the preparations there and then, and about a year afterwards the marriage contract was concluded with a ceremony [F 691] whose like I had never witnessed before at this court, and in such a manner that there remained no person high or low, of note or mere apprentice to some profession or trade, courtier[92] or doorkeeper, trumpet player or drum beater who did not receive some present from the Commander Begtughdï, ranging from 12,000 dirhams down to 5,000, 3,000, 2,000, 1,000, 500, 300, 200 or 100, this last being the minimum figure for a gift. Amir Mardān Shāh was brought to the Commander Begtughdï's palace, and the wedding contract concluded there. Dinars and dirhams were distributed to everybody. Begtughdï dressed Amir Mardān Shāh in a black silk brocade coat which was decorated with pearls, and put on his head a four-sectioned hat lavishly trimmed with gold and set with jewels. He placed round his waist a belt studded all over with jewels. There was an extremely valuable horse shod with golden horse shoes and having a saddle set with gold and its ornaments set with jewels. There were ten Turkish gholāms with horses and appropriate equipment for attendance, 10,000 dinars and 100 pieces of expensive clothing of every colour. When the marriage contract was completed, Amir Mardān Shāh was brought into the Amir's presence for the latter to see him, and they related to him the proceedings and what they had done, and Mardān Shāh went back to his mother.

Amir Mardān Shāh was still very young, being only thirteen years old. A long time afterwards, in the early part of the year 430 [/autumn 1038], the Commander Begtughdï's daughter was brought into this prince's private, women's quarters, [Gh 526] she being still very young. They were seated together, and the wedding was celebrated[F 692] on a scale whose like no-one could recall. The Amir gave orders for a breath-taking display to be made, since he was very fond of this son, and his mother was of noble lineage. I heard from Bu Manṣur the accounting official, who said, "I was busy for several days, with the assistance of several of my aides, drawing up the account for the wedding outfit and expenditure, and it amounted to ten million dirhams. I myself, Bu'l-Fażl, saw that account after the deaths of Sultan Masʿud and Amir Mardān Shāh,[93] and I was struck with wonder that one person could by himself provide and get together all that. I shall mention a few items: four golden crowns set with jewels; twenty golden dishes with the fruit on them made of a variety of jewels; twenty golden boxes for holding spindles encrusted with jewels; and a besom made of gold with strings of pearls as its bristles. I have described only a few samples, and mentioned just one item out of a thousand, but it should suffice, and from these one can imagine what the rest of the items could have been.

An account of the animosity that arose between Amir Masʿud and Bughrā Khān, and the Amir's despatching Bu Ṣādeq Tabbāni to Kāshghar and Ṭarāz in Turkestan with a message until the cause of the mutual ill-feeling was removed through the mediation of Arslān Khān

I have related how, in the time of the late Amir Maḥmud, Bughrā Khān, who had at that time the honorific title Yaghāntegin,[94] came to Balkh in the time of his father, Yusof Qadïr Khān, so that from there he might proceed to Ghaznin. He was coming as the Sultan's son-in-law, since the noble lady Zeynab, the daughter of the late Amir, [F 693] had been betrothed to him, and he was hoping, with our help, to seize Bokhara and Samarqand and their surrounding regions from ʿAlitegin, since he had already received from us encouragement in that direction. But he received the answer, "You must return home, for our plan is to attack Somnath now, and when we have accomplished that, and when you have taken over the khanate of Turkestan, then we can join forces and deal with this affair."[95]

The subsequent events have all been set down in a separate section of this work,[96] including how Yaghāntegin returned home from Balkh vexed and affronted; our own return from the expedition afterwards; the assumption of the khanate by the two sons of Yusof Qadïr Khān, Bughrātegin Soleymān and Yaghāntegin Moḥammad, and their coming to fight with ʿAlitegin when the latter's brother [Aḥmad] Ṭoghān Khān was overthrown; [Gh 527] the jurist Bu Bakr Ḥaṣiri's mission to Merv from here; and the subsequent war and the peace agreement and their return home, since Arslān Khān[97] did not want his brother Bughrā Khān[98] to share a border with us,[99] adding to Bughrā Khān's feelings of rancour and disappointment.

Afterwards, it was no longer possible for the lady Zeynab to be sent there, since Amir Maḥmud had died and Amir Masʿud succeeded to the throne. Within a year, Qadïr Khān had also died, and Arslān Khān Soleymān, the designated heir, became Khān of Turkestan. He allotted the whole of the provinces of Ṭarāz, Espijāb and their surrounding regions to his brother Bughrā Khān Moḥammad and awarded him this honorific title of Bughrā Khān.[100] There were ostensibly friendly relations between the two, but beneath the surface there was enmity.

As I have related previously, Amir Masʿud sent Khᵛāja Bu'l-Qāsem Ḥaṣiri and the Judge Bu Ṭāher Tabbāni, the kinsman of this Imam Bu Ṣādeq Tabbāni, [F 694] on an embassy to Arslān Khān and Bughrā Khān so that the marriage contract and the agreement might be renewed.[101] They set off, and remained there[102] for a long time until they completed their mission and came home with one princess, Qadïr Khān's daughter, who was intended as Sultan Masʿud's bride, and the other princess, Arslān Khān's daughter, as Amir Mowdud's intended bride. But the one intended for Amir Mowdud died on the way back, and the Judge Tabbāni likewise received the Divine Summons at Parvān. Bu'l-Qāsem, with a train of servants and the bride, arrived in Ghaznin and that wedding took place. Bughrā Khān had sent back with our envoys a chamberlain on a diplomatic mission, together with a scholar, and had sought that the royal princess Zeynab should be sent, and Arslān Khān had also spoken about the topic. She was about to be sent off when the Amir was informed that Bughrā Khān had been expressing some ill-disposed words on the subject of inheritance, maintaining that Zeynab should be allotted her share according to the law regarding the shares of sisters and brothers.[103]

The Amir was extremely offended by these words, and he sent back Bughrā Khān's envoy with fine promises for the future but with his immediate request unfulfilled. He wrote a letter of complaint to Arslān Khān and spoke of his displeasure at such churlish words. Arslān Khān reproached his brother for his rashness and his half-baked words. This made Bughrā Khān extremely embittered, and all was lost, for he now became genuinely ill-disposed towards both his brother and ourselves. The situation reached such a pitch that when the Seljuqs entered Khorasan and defeated Begtughdï, and the news of the defeat reached Turkestan, spies reported that Bughrā Khān had rejoiced at our loss and seemed pleased at their victory, for on the one hand he was on hostile terms with us, and on the other, Ṭoghrïl was a friend and erstwhile protégé of his. [Gh 528] He secretly incited the

Seljuqs, [F 695] and put heart into them, saying that they should fight on and that whatever number of troops they required of the Khāns, they would send, matching in number those of the Turkmens. The Amir became much distressed when he heard this latest news, since this was no small matter.

Then they arrested at the Oxus crossing a shoemaker who was acting somewhat suspiciously[104] and interrogated him severely. It was ascertained that he was a spy of Bughrā Khān's, that he was making his way to the Turkmens and that he bore letters addressed to them that he had concealed in a secret place. They sent him on to the court, and my master Bu Naṣr interrogated him in private and he confessed. He brought out the tools of his trade from the bag. The inside of one of the wooden instruments had been hollowed out, secret messages in minute characters secreted there, and then covered up with wood shavings that were painted over to look like wood and so that they would not be noticed. He said that Bughrā Khān had seen to this personally. Bu Naṣr consigned the man to a secret location, and took the secret messages to the Amir. All of them were stamped with the *tamghā*[105] and were addressed to Ṭoghrïl, Dāvud, Yabghu[106] and the Yïnāliyān.[107] Bughrā Khān had urged them on wholeheartedly and had belittled our power in the Seljuqs' eyes and minds, and had said, "Be resolute and press on, and ask for as many troops as you need, so that we may send them." The Amir was furious[108] and said, "A letter must be written to Arslān Khān, and a swift messenger despatched and these secret letters forwarded. He should be told that it is not right to let such things happen and for the Khān to let them pass." Bu Naṣr replied, "May the lord's life be prolonged! The Turks have never harboured much affection for us, and I have heard Amir Maḥmud saying on many occasions, it being his wont, 'The Turks[109] are only making these friendly approaches to us out of necessity, [F 696] and if ever they get the upper hand, they will dispense with all these niceties and protestations of friendship.' The wise course is for this spy to be sent to India for him to set up shop in the town of Lahore, and these secret letters should be kept somewhere under seal. Then a messenger can go to Arslān Khān and Bughrā Khān to mollify them with soothing words. In this way, open hostilities will be averted through Arslān Khān's intervention and Bughrā Khān will not get up to any further mischief." The Amir said, "That's an excellent suggestion," and he placed a seal on the secret letters and they were stored away safely. He gave the spy a hundred dinars, and my master said to him, "We have decided to spare your life. Go to Lahore, and carry on with your profession there." The man was taken there.

The Amir, the Vizier and Bu Naṣr b. Moshkān sat down together in a private conclave, and the choice for this mission fell on the Imam Bu Ṣādeq Tabbāni by virtue of the fact that Bu Ṭāher, his kinsman, had been previously involved in the matter. The Amir summoned him, made much of him and said, "Just take charge of this one mission, and when you get back, we'll bestow on you the judgeship of Nishapur and you can go there." He got ready, [Gh 529] and set off from Ghaznin, with a splendid outfit and array worth more than 10,000 dinars, on Tuesday, 7 Dhu'l-Qaʿda [4]28 [/22 August 1037]. He spent a year and a half in these wearisome negotiations and was involved in disputations and discussions such that Bughrā Khān commented, "He has all the discursive powers and skills[110] of Bu Ḥanifa",[111] and everyone averred that they had never seen a man of such rectitude and probity.[112] After prolonged negotiations and many a discussion, he made firm the agreements and made them all pledge their adherence to the mutual ties of friendship. Secret envoys carried reports of all these back to Ghazna, and the Amir studied them closely, on several occasions saying to the Grand Vizier and to Bu Naṣr, "Our father was not mistaken in cherishing this man." This Imam came back, but the local potentate (*vāli*) of Jerm[113] seized him on the road and took everything he had, for the local overlords in the mountains had become refractory and rebellious. He managed, however, to escape from the clutches of those villains through some ruse, [F 697] for his very life had been in danger, and came to Ghaznin, reaching here in the year 430 [/1038–39], just ten days before the date set for our departure to Balkh. He received from the Sultan a welcome beyond description, and the Amir was heard to say, "Whatever losses you suffered from the brigands, all will be reimbursed to you, and more, together with the judgeship of Nishapur which we had already promised."[114]

On Friday, 11 Dhu'l-Qaʿda [/26 August], before the worship, the Amir went off hunting to the plain of R.khā-margh, and my master and all the court accompanied him.[115] Good hunting was had, and large numbers of all sorts of game were found. He came back to the New Palace on Sunday, the twenty-first of this month [/5 September 1037].[116]

On Sunday, 4 Dhu'l-Ḥejja [/18 September], the Amir presided over the Mehragān festival. Gifts prepared and collected from the far horizons of the empire were brought forward at that time as presents, and the retainers and courtiers likewise brought forward many things. The poets recited verses and received largesse, since this lord used to commission poetry and pay very handsomely for it.[117] I did not set down those odes. If some critic should carp and say, "Why has he inserted the odes addressed to Amir Maḥmud but not those addressed to Amir Mas'ud," my response would be that this era, Mas'ud's reign, is closer to us, and the inclusion of all those odes would have made this account inordinately long; and in any case, it is obvious what kind of poetry is composed for these festive occasions. After listening to the poetry, he went on to enjoy the wine and the drinking session, and a joyous day drew to its close.

On the Saturday (i.e. on 10 Dhu'l-Ḥejja/24 September), the Festival of the Sacrifice was celebrated. There was much pomp and ceremonial on that day, including a parade [F 698] of the army, both the infantry and the cavalry, at the court, [Gh 530] and an unsurpassable display of equipment and finery, since the envoys of Arslān Khān and Bughrā Khān had come, as well as the troops of the governor of S.k.mān (?),[118] and there was a lavish spread of victuals and they drank wine.

The next day (i.e. Sunday, 11 Dhu'l-Ḥejja [/25 September]), ceremonial gifts (*khel'at*) were bestowed on Amir Mowdud, on a scale that he had never before experienced, including large kettledrums, standards and ordinary-sized kettledrums (*dabdaba*).[119] The governorship of Balkh was conferred on him and he was presented with an investiture patent for it, and with these honours Mowdud returned home. On the Sultan's orders, all the great men, the retainers and courtiers went to him—he was staying in the residence of Arslān Jādheb—and conveyed their respects on a most impressive scale through monetary offerings[120] to a degree that they had never shown before.[121]

On the third day (i.e. on Monday. 12 Dhu'l-Ḥejja [/26 September]), when the public audience was over, the Amir held a private session, and he kept back the Vizier, the Commander-in-Chief, the Head of the Army Department, my master and the Commander of the Palace Gholāms Begtughdï and the General Bu'l-Nażr. There was talk on the topic of the Amir's next move—which destination would be the wisest to adopt? Those present said, "The lord should let us know on which lines he has been thinking, since the right course will be that which the exalted judgement sees fit, and then we can say what we know." The Amir said, "This year, at Bost, when I had that illness after the incident on the river, I made a vow that, if God, His mention is exalted, should vouchsafe for my recovery, I would proceed to India so that the fortress of Hānsi might be conquered. Ever since I returned from there unfulfilled in my aims and out of necessity—since an illness supervened and I had to return[122]—I have nursed this grievance and the desire to conquer this fortress has remained with me; and the distance is not great.[123] In order to embark on this journey, I have decided to send my son Mowdud to Balkh, and the Vizier and the Commander-in-Chief are to accompany him with fully-equipped armies. The General Sübashï is at Merv with a powerful army, with the result that the Turkmens are afraid of encroaching on settlements and cultivated lands. Also, Suri is at Nishapur with a contingent of troops. There are fully-armed garrisons at Ṭus, in Qohestān, [F 699] at Herat and in other towns. There should not be any disturbances or mischief in Khorasan. If there should be any, you are all near each other and can see to it very quickly. The sons of 'Alitegin are quiescent, in accordance with the contractual agreement between us, and 'Abd al-Salām is at their court and giving further strength to our agreements (*'ahd-hā*).[124] According to what Bu Sahl Ḥamdavi has written, the Son of Kāku has no great force to reckon with, and his own people are thoroughly hopeless and inept, and the Turkmens[125] are not placing any reliance on what he says. No crisis should occur there either. Once I have acquitted myself from the vow, and after the fortress of Hānsi has been conquered, we shall not undertake any other commitment and will return, so that we shall be back in Ghaznin before Nowruz. We have thought this over, [Gh 531] and without question, this intended plan should be put into force.[126] Now tell us frankly what you think!"

The Vizier looked at those present and said, "What is your opinion on what the lord has just said?" The Commander-in-Chief said, "I, and those like me, are men of the sword: we obey the Sultan's commands and go wherever he bids us go, ready to sacrifice our lives if needs be. The merits and demerits of such matters are for the Grand Vizier to delve into, for he is closely involved with the important affairs of state, and he reads, hears, observes and knows things beyond our range. This has to do with the Vizier's craft and not with our profession," and he turned towards the other army commanders and said, "Do you agree with my words?" They replied, "We do."[127] The Vizier said to the Head of the Army Department and to Bu Naṣr, "The Commander-in-Chief and the other commanders have placed this responsibility on my shoulders and have absolved themselves from it. What do you say?" The Head of the Army Department, a hard-headed individual, said, "The nature of my job is well-known, and it is not feasible for me to go beyond it. [F 700] The work of the Army Department is so onerous that it leaves no room for any other concerns." Bu Naṣr Moshkān said, "The task, so it seems, has fallen on the Grand Vizier's shoulders, and, since the lord has thus decreed, some straight talking is called for. For my part, I, as a servant of the lord, will also say what I think, and I pledge myself upon all the bounty that the Sultan has bestowed on me that I shall not mince my words."

The Vizier said, "On no account do I consider it acceptable for the lord to go to India, since the wise course is that he should go to Balkh, and there too he should not tarry long but proceed at once as far as Merv, so that Khorasan can be recovered and Ray and Jebāl kept firmly under our authority. The vow can be fulfilled; if the intention is to conquer Hānsi, the commander of the ghāzis [in India][128] and the army of Lahore, and a general appointed and sent out from the court, will be sufficient for that affair. In this way, both that intention can be fulfilled and Khorasan remain under our sway. If the lord does not go to Khorasan, and the Turkmens do conquer a district—or not even a district but a mere village—and indulge in their usual habits of mutilation, slaughtering and burning, ten raids against Hānsi will not be a match for it. It was the expedition to Āmol and our return journey from it that brought about this present calamity (i.e. of the Turkmens' depredations in Khorasan); this proposed expedition to India is even more misguided. I have set forth my views and have thereby fulfilled my duty; it is for the lord to make the final decision and decree accordingly."

My master Bu Naṣr said, "I say the same thing, and I make a further point. If the lord deems fit, let him secretly appoint agents who can enquire of troops and subjects, lowly and noble, posing the question, 'The situation in Khorasan, Khwarazm, Ray and Jebāl has become disturbed to the extent that it now is, and the Sultan is going to Hānsi—is this a wise course of action [Gh 532] or not?', [F 701] and see what they say. I know full well that all of them will say that it is an unwise course of action. We are speaking openly, since the lord has given us permission to do so; but the ultimate decision will be the lord's."

The Amir said, "I am fully convinced of your affection and sincere counsel. But this is a vow that I have taken upon myself and will accomplish in person. Even if many disasters should occur in Khorasan, I should still hold it right that I should observe what is due to the Exalted God, and the Lord Most High will make all this come right." The Vizier said, "Since this is the situation, whatever is humanly possible will be done. It is to be hoped that, during this period of absence, no disaster occurs," and the Vizier and Bu Naṣr went back. The rest of those present likewise offered up their service and went back. When they had all come out, they gathered together privately and said, "This lord's intransigence knows no bounds. It is not possible to speak any more frankly than this, and it would be wrong to harp on further on this since it would be deemed disrespectful. We shall have to see what the Exalted God has decreed," and they dispersed.[129]

On Thursday, 15 Dhu'l-Ḥejja [/29 September], the Commander-in-Chief 'Ali was garbed in a very splendid robe of honour. He came into the royal presence and offered up service, and the Amir praised him and showed him consideration, saying, "The trust of the royal son, the Vizier and the army is focussed entirely on you. The Vizier is coming with you, and he is our deputy. He is responsible for formulating sound policy and collecting together money for the troops' salaries, while you are responsible for deploying the troops and making war. His orders should always be obeyed, and you must all act in unison so that no disaster occurs in our absence." The Commander-in-Chief kissed the ground and said, "I have but one life, and I hold it for fulfilling the lord's commands," and he went back. [F 702]

On Saturday, the seventeenth of this month[130] [/ 1 October], the Vizier was given a very splendid robe of honour, in conformity with what was the accepted rule, and much more besides, for the Amir was eager to keep the Vizier contented in every way, since it was clear that, during the Sultan's absence, he would be the mainstay of the realm. When he came into the royal presence, the Amir said, "May the robe of honour be blessed! While we are away in India, we place our trust first in God Most High and His favour and then in the Khᵛāja. We have made a vow and we shall fulfil it.[131] First of all, our son Mowdud, then the Commander-in-Chief, and all the retainers and troops who are left behind there, we entrust to him, and all must act in accordance with his commands." He replied, "I am your servant, and as such, will perform all my duties to the best of my abilities as befits a servant," and he returned home, where he was met by well-wishers and rewarded with very substantial offerings. [Gh 533]

On Monday, 19 Dhu'l-Ḥejja [/3 October], the Amir rode out early in the morning and stood on the plain of the Piruzi Garden while the army went past detachment by detachment. After that, towards the time of the midday worship, these three eminent figures, the royal son Mowdud, the Vizier and the Commander-in-Chief, dismounted, performed the rites of service and set off. My master appointed Khᵛāja Bu Naṣr Nuki,[132] in accordance with the exalted command, and he left with the Vizier, charged with the duty of reporting back intelligence and news.[133]

On Thursday, 22 Dhu'l-Ḥejja[134] [/6 October], the Amir, may God be pleased with him, set out from Ghazni along the Kabul road to India for the Hānsi raid, and he stayed in Kabul for ten days.

The History of the Year 429 [/14 October 1037–2 October 1038]

[Gh 533, F 702] The first day of Moḥarram fell on Saturday.[1] On Thursday, the sixth of this month [/19 October 1037], the Amir left Kabul.[2] On Saturday, the eighth of this month [/21 October], letters arrived from Khorasan and Ray, all bearing significant news, but the Amir took no interest in them at all and said to my master, "Write a letter to the Vizier, enclosing these letters with it, so that he can peruse them and take appropriate measures regarding the different issues raised by them, for we cannot be troubled by them ourselves." [F 703]

On Tuesday, 25 Moḥarram [/7 November], the Amir reached the Jhelum/Jehlam, and encamped on the bank of the river near Dinārkuta.[3] Here he was struck down by an illness, and was laid up for a fortnight, during which he held no court session. It also made him repent of his wine-drinking and ordered that all the wine that they had brought in storage with them[4] should be poured into the river Jhelum, and the instruments of music and revelry should be smashed. No-one dared to drink wine in public, since he had appointed agents and market inspectors[5] to impose the law and was most strict about it. He sent Bu Saʿid the intelligence agent on an important mission to the Indian Janki at his fortress,[6] and this was kept secret from everyone. We were still at the Jhelum when news arrived about the Great Rajah[7] and the Rajah of Kashmir's current condition, and we were there when we heard that the Rajah of Kashmir had died.[8]

By Saturday, 14 Ṣafar [/26 November], the Amir had recovered from his illness and held a court session. On Tuesday, the seventeenth of this month [/29 November], he left the Jhelum, and on

Wednesday, 9 Rabiʿ I [20 December], reached the fortress of Hānsi.[9] The army encampment was set up below the fortress, and they surrounded it. Fierce fighting raged every day and those besieged within the fortress put up a stiff resistance and fought back relentlessly, while the victorious army, and most notably the palace gholāms, [Gh 534] did full justice to the struggle. The fortress remained inviolate like a virgin bride. In the end, the besiegers dug mines in five places and brought down the walls, and they took the fortress by the sword on Sunday, 20 Rabiʿ I [/31 December]. [F 704] They killed the Brahman priests, together with all the combatants, and enslaved their womenfolk and children, and all the wealth and valuables fell to the troops as plunder. This fortress was known in India as "the Virgin Fortress" (*qalʿat al-ʿadhrā'*), for no-one had ever been able to take it before.[10]

From there, the return was made on Saturday, 26 Rabiʿ I [/6 January 1038], and he reached Ghaznin on Sunday, 3 Jomādā I [/11 February]. He emerged from the pass of Sakāvand.[11] There was exceptionally deep snow on the open plain. A letter had been sent on ahead to Bu ʿAli the castellan instructing him to turn out a corvée of men to clear the road, and this had been done; if it had not been cleared, it would have been impossible for anyone to have got through. The road now resembled a narrow passage-way, running from the Rebāṭ of Moḥammad Solṭān to the town. During those three days while we were approaching the town, it snowed continuously. The Amir Saʿid, the castellan, the mayor and others came out to meet us and escort us for the remaining two stages. The Amir installed himself in the Old Maḥmudi Palace and spent a week there while carpets and furnishings were being spread out in the New [Masʿudi] Palace and decorative features put in place. Then he moved to the New Palace. The baggage and impedimenta, the Amir's household[12] and the princes who had been in temporary residence in the fortresses, returned to Ghaznin.[13] During the whole time I was in the service of this great dynasty, I never witnessed a winter at Ghaznin as hard as that of this year. At this present moment, I myself have grown old and worn out, since I have been here for twenty years, and under the auspicious power of the exalted Sultan Ebrāhim b. [F 705] Nāṣer Din Allāh, *may God make his sultanate last for ever*, it is to be hoped that, if God so wills, the sultanate will revert to its former glory.[14]

On Tuesday, 26 Jomādā I [/6 March], the Amir held court in celebration of the festival of Nowruz, and the subjects[15] did full justice to the occasion by bringing presents, while the Amir likewise gave out presents, in observance of the usual custom. Wine drinking went on in a most appropriate manner, for he had drunk no wine since the time of his act of repentance at the Jhelum until this day.

On Tuesday, 3 Jomādā II [/13 March], very important letters arrived from Khorasan and Ray. During this period of absence, the Turkmens had come at the beginning of winter, had plundered Ṭālaqān and Faryāb,[16] and other places had suffered disasters, since the victorious armies had not been able to move against them at such a season. Through the Sultan's going [Gh 535] to Hānsi, many calamities, limitless in extent, had befallen, and Ray itself had come under siege. The Amir now regretted that he had gone to India, but it was to no avail, and no-one can prevail over the Divine Decree. He ordered replies to be written enjoining them to remain stout-hearted, for when the weather grew better, the exalted banner would go forth.

On Sunday, half-way through this month, Amir Mowdud and the Commander-in-Chief ʿAli reached Ghaznin from Balkh, but on the Sultan's express orders, the Vizier remained at Balkh since he had many pressing matters requiring his attention.

On Wednesday, 3 Rajab [/11 April], the Amir ʿAbd al-Razzāq donned the appropriate robe of honour befitting for the ruler of Peshawar, and duly performed the rites of service. Two of his gholāms were given black robes for their status as chamberlains. The office of counsellor and administrator was given to Sahl, son of ʿAbd al-Malek, and he received a robe of honour. He was a highly capable man and the son of one of the servants[17] of Aḥmad b. Mikā'il. He had served for a long time as an assistant [F 706] under Bu Sahl Ḥamdavi. On Tuesday, the ninth of this month [/17 April], this Amir set off for Peshawar with much pomp and splendour, having with him 200 gholāms.

The next day, a letter arrived from Nishapur stating that Bu Sahl Ḥamdavi had reached there, having been unable to remain at Ray when Tāsh Farrāsh had been killed and several[18] of the notables captured. He himself had been shut up in the citadel for a lengthy period, and the Turkmens had secured the upper hand (I shall related these happenings in the special section which, as I have said, will be devoted to Ray and Jebāl, together with many remarkable occurrences and wonders), until he found an opportunity and escaped.[19]

At this time when Bu Sahl arrived in Nishapur, the Great Chamberlain Sübashï was there, and the Turkmens were at Merv.[20] Both parties were preoccupied with their own preparations for war and avoided confronting each other. The Amir was laying a heavy portion of the blame on the Chamberlain, and kept on saying that "He will never get this business done (i.e. of expelling the Turkmens from Khorasan), for he is having too good a time enjoying himself as ruler of Khorasan. He must be recalled and replaced by a commander willing to engage in full battle and face the enemy in the field." He was saying this because letters kept arriving from Saʿid Ṣarrāf, the counsellor and administrator and the postal and intelligence officer[21] for the army, reporting that "The Chamberlain used not to drink wine, but for the past year he has taken to it and has been drinking without a pause and dallying with moon-faced Turkish slavegirls, spending time shut away with them. Also, he keeps shifting the army around from place to place and, using the more than a thousand camels that he has at his disposal, he keeps on stocking up with grain and dragging the army to places where seven *man*s of grain can be got for a dirham, and then drags them off to a place where a single loaf of bread costs a dirham, and he says, [F 707] 'I am being careful and prudent,' and then he sells the wheat to the army and makes a great deal of money, [Gh 536], with the result that, on this pretext, he is pocketing the army's pay for himself."

The Amir was inevitably very upset at this news. But in reality, it was not as they were saying, for Sübashï was being careful and exercising foresight to such an extent that the Turkmens called him "Sübashï the magician." With the charges of procrastination and sloth hurled at him by the Amir surpassing all limits, the Chamberlain was thus forced into engaging in battle, as I shall relate. The Almighty God does not vouchsafe to anyone sight of the future. Since Fate had foreordained that Khorasan should slip from our hands and that this group[22] should flourish to such an extent, as they have, it was inevitable that all plans should prove failures; one cannot prevail against Fate.

Then on Wednesday, 12 Rajab [/20 April], Bu Sahl the doorkeeper, the trusted confidant of the Great Chamberlain Sübashï, arrived in Ghaznin after travelling by the Ghur road in fifteen days.[23] My master immediately took the letter from him and presented it to the Amir. It said, "They have prejudiced the Amir's mind against me with the amount of nonsense that they have written; but as reliable authorities will confirm, I have followed all advice and directions up to this present moment. Immediately an order arrived by hand of the *kheyltāsh* that I was to march out and engage the enemy in battle, I sought to travel from Nishapur to Sarakhs so that the campaign could be undertaken. But your other royal servants Bu Sahl Ḥamdavi and the head of the Divān, Suri, advised against it and suggested that, instead, we should be preserving and reinforcing our resources prudently, for once the battle itself starts, it will all be over in a day, and no-one can predict the outcome. The Judge Ṣāʿed and the elders of Nishapur were all of this same view. [F 708] I was afraid of criticism and blame, and I sought from them a legally-attested statement. They joined together in doing this, and they all put their signatures to it. I have sent it so that the exalted judgement may be informed. I await an unequivocal answer as to whether a full-scale battle should be embarked upon or not, so that I might act accordingly. I have sent this trusty confidant of mine, Bu Sahl, on this important matter, and he has been enjoined to reach Ghaznin by the Ghur road within fifteen days, to stay there three days and then to return to Nishapur in fifteen days. When he gets back, and if I am considered to be fit for the job, I will act according to the command, if God Most High so wills."

The Amir read this letter and studied the legally-attested statement. He sent for Bu Sahl and had a private session with him from the late morning till the midday worship. He summoned my master, and he questioned Bu Sahl about the situation, and the latter gave an account [Gh 537] of the Seljuq Turkmens, to the effect that "They divide themselves up into twenty or thirty sections,[24] and they derive succour from the steppelands just as we are sustained by our towns (lit. "the desert is father and mother to them just as the towns are for us"). Up to the present moment, your servant Sübashï says that he has confronted them, and advance guards have been sent out and there have been military clashes. Moreover, he has a thorough understanding of their strength and strategy, and has husbanded his resources so successfully that they were unable to establish themselves in any of the towns of Khorasan. The levying of taxes is in progress, and the lord's collectors and financial agents are at work. The episode of the killing and plundering at Fāryāb and Ṭālaqān, on one occasion in the summer and another in the winter, came as a complete surprise; your servant Sübashï was confronting their main body, but one group had split and gone off, and it had made a sudden attack, and the destruction had been wrought before your servant heard about it. It is not possible for this army to undertake a campaign unless it receives reinforcements, whereas the case of the rebels is different. What Bu Sahl Ḥamdavi, Suri and the rest who put their signatures to the legal attestation are saying is correct and honestly expressed: [F 709] it is not wise policy to campaign and seek battle in this way. But the correct judgement will be what the lord sees as such. I await an answer and am ready to proceed. If the requirement is to strike a single decisive blow and to seek a pitched battle, a letter should be written [to me] in the hand of Bu Naṣr Moshkān, and with the lord's signature and device affixed, and at the foot of the letter there should be some lines in the exalted handwriting giving a firm command that I must set out on this campaign. When this letter reaches me, I shall not remain in Nishapur for a single day but shall immediately set out for Sarakhs and Merv, and the military campaign will be launched, since there is no excuse now for holding back and there is an excellent army, completely armed and equipped, and with their salaries fully paid out in coin."[25]

The Amir said to Bu Naṣr, "What do you see in all this?" He replied, "This is not my department, and I always keep well clear of military matters. The Commander-in-Chief is here; it would be much more appropriate to consult him on this; and one could also write to the Vizier for his advice." The Amir said, "We can't keep Bu Sahl here while a letter goes to Balkh and a reply comes back; we will speak with the Commander-in-Chief tomorrow, and we will ponder over this matter today and tonight." Bu Naṣr expressed his agreement and came home in a very pensive mood. He told me, "A most crucial and delicate problem has arisen, and I don't know what the outcome will be. Arslān Jādheb was a crafty and wily figure, whose like no-one could recall. He had large quantities of weapons, matériel and troops, and an enemy who did not enjoy the strength and military power which these Turkmens have today. It is well recognized and crystal-clear how complex and difficult it was making warfare and combat with [Gh 538] them over a long period, and if Amir Maḥmud had not gone personally to Pushang and had not despatched the commander Ghāzi with such a well equipped army, that partial victory would never have been achieved.[26] The problem of this present group, the Seljuqs and their Turkmens, is different. People are giving the Sultan deceitful information, and this could lead to another shameful episode and loss of face similar to the matter of Begtughdï and that awful débâcle that occurred through a display of wilfulness and obstinacy. If, God forbid, some disaster should befall this Great Chamberlain Sübashï, there will be no course remaining but for the lord unavoidably to go in person, and all our honour will be lost at a blow. I know what should be done in this matter, but I don't dare to speak out. Let us see what is the will of God, the Exalted One. This is what happened in the case of Ray and Jebāl, [F 710] when such a well-arrayed army fell apart, and now we have Khorasan in this plight and troubles everywhere, with a pleasure-seeking and self-willed sovereign, and a fearful Vizier under a cloud of suspicion. The great commanders of the past have been all gratuitously overthrown,[27] and the deputy of this Head of the Army Department has destroyed the army through his economies, and the lord is being taken in by his trickery. I don't know how all this will end. At all events, I feel sick at heart. Would that I were no longer alive, for I cannot bear to see these calamities happening!"

[The end of the eighth volume (?)] [F 711]

[The beginning of the ninth volume (?)][28]

The Khʷāja Bu'l-Fażl, the secretary, the author of this History, relates thus: at that time when Sultan Masʿud b. Maḥmud returned to Ghaznin from India, and stayed there for several days, Bu Sahl, the (trusted) rider of the Commander (Sübashï), arrived at the court and he related, in a face-to-face interview with the Amir, what had happened. The Sultan studied the message exhaustively, and gave orders that the army should undertake a campaign and give battle.[29] [This account begins on] Sunday, 21 Rajab [/29 April] after Bu Sahl had arrived and had taken rest and refreshment.

The next day, when the court session broke up, the Amir talked privately until noon about this with the Commander-in-Chief and my master, and decided that the only way was for Sübashï to engage them in battle. The Commander-in-Chief went back. Bu Naṣr sent for the inkstand and paper and wrote the letter in the Amir's presence, and the Amir sent for his inkstand and pen, affixed his signature and device and wrote a section at the foot of the letter, as follows: "The Excellent Great Chamberlain is to place reliance on this which Bu Naṣr has written at our command and at our court. He is to march out and engage the enemy so that what God, the Exalted One, has fore-ordained may be accomplished. We are hopeful that God, the Exalted One, will grant victory. Farewell!"

The Amir summoned Bu Sahl into his presence [F 712] and he was given the letter, and the Amir said, "Tell the Chamberlain that he should take all the necessary precautions and exercise vigilance." He kissed the ground and went out. He received presents of 5,000 dirhams and five sets of clothing, together with a Ghuri horse, and set off back via the Ghur road. The Amir ordered a letter to be written to the Vizier on this topic, [Gh 539] and it was sent off by a courier of the postal and intelligence service. A reply came back two weeks later, "There must be[30] soundness and correct judgement in what the lord has deemed appropriate to do," and to my master he had written a private note in his own hand, stating in very outspoken terms, that "I did not see it as incumbent upon myself[31] to state categorically that this grave step should not be taken, for no-one can be certain how it will all end; one should have left it to Sübashï's on-the-spot assessment. But the deed is done, and God Most High willing, it will all end well." My master laid this letter before the Amir.

On Monday, 28 Rajab [/6 May],[32] the Amir went to the Maḥmudi Garden with the intention of staying there for some time, and the baggage and furnishings were taken there.

On Monday, 6 Shaʿbān [/14 May],[33] the secretary Bu'l-Ḥasan ʿErāqi died, God's mercy be upon him. They allege that his wives administered a poisonous drug to him because he had taken as wife a singer from Merv.[34] He was a most ill-tempered man and hard to please, but I do not know what really happened. However, during that week in which he died, I went to visit him, and I found him hanging on to life by a single thread but perfectly alert in mind. He spoke, and made his last testament, that his bier should be borne to the shrine of 'Ali b. Musā al-Reżā, *God's approval be upon him*,[F 713] at Ṭus and he should be buried there, since he had donated the money for this during his lifetime, and he had repaired the subterranean irrigation channel (*kāriz*) of the shrine, which had dried up, and made it to flow again and had built a caravanserai. He had also constituted, as a perpetual endowment for the upkeep of the caravanserai and the channel, the income from a grain-producing (i.e. productive and profitable) village with a low annual tax.[35] When I went to Ṭus in the year [4]31[/1039–40] with the victorious banner, before the time of the débâcle of Dandānqān, I went to Nowqān[36] and visited the mausoleum of Reżā, *may God be pleased with him*. I saw 'Erāqi's grave in the mosque at the shrine, in a vaulted archway (*ṭāq*) which was five *gaz*s high from the ground level to the top of the arch. I went to it and remained there full of wonder at the nature of this deceitful world, which within the space of eight or nine years raised up this man to such dizzy heights, and then he had to die so soon, and become as nothing.

At this time, the Amir was completely preoccupied with the matter of Sübashï and talked of nothing else, having put his trust in God's will in the matter.[37] He had given orders for riders to be stationed at regular intervals along the Ghur road in order to bring the most important items of news.

The golden throne, the furnishings and the audience hall that the Amir had commissioned and on which they had been working for more than three years, were now ready.[38] The Amir was informed, and he ordered that the throne should be placed on the great platform of the New Palace, and this was done. The palace was decked out, and for all those who had set eyes on that decorous sight that day, whatever they saw afterwards [Gh 540] would be bound to fail to impress by comparison. That, at least, has been my own experience; I cannot speak for others. The throne was made entirely from red gold, and representations and shapes like the stems and branches of plants were embossed on it. Large numbers of costly jewels had been set in it, and extensions for reclining[39] had been set up, all of them studded with various kinds of jewels. A small-sized covering[40] made of Rumi satin brocade had been used as a covering for the throne. There were four cushions sewn with gold thread and stuffed with silk—for use as prayer cushions and ordinary cushions—for supporting the back, and four other cushions, two for one side and two for the other. A gilded chain had been hung down from the ceiling of the hall which contained the platform to near the platform for the crown and throne, and the crown secured to it. There were four images made from brass in the shape of human beings, these placed on supports [F 714] secured to the throne in such a way that their hands were outstretched as if they were holding the crown. The crown did not weigh heavily upon the head because the chains and the supports were holding it firm, and it was suspended above the monarch's cap.[41] They had decorated this platform with *qāli* carpets[42] and brightly-coloured Rumi satin brocades and ones of variegated colours, all made with gold thread, and 380 trays[43] in the audience hall had been overlaid with gold, each tray a *gaz* long and less than a *gaz* wide, and on those there were pastilles of camphor, vesicles of musk and pieces of aloes wood and ambergris. On the front part of the throne there were fifteen settings of pomegranate-coloured and Badakhshāni rubies, emeralds, pearls and turquoises. A festal spread had been prepared in that Spring Pavilion, and in the middle of it a palace made from confectionery, stretching right up to the ceiling of the hall, and on it there were also large numbers of [roasted] lambs.

The Amir came back from the Maḥmudi Garden to this New Palace, and sat down on the golden throne on that platform on Tuesday, 21 Shaʿbān [/29 May].[44] The crown was held above his cap, and he wore a coat of ruby-coloured satin brocade decorated with gold, so much so that little of the actual material underneath could be seen. All along where the trays were placed were stood the palace gholāms, wearing robes of *saqlāṭuni* silk,[45] Baghdadi and Isfahani cloth, two-pointed caps, golden belts, straps hung down for securing weapons and with gold maces in their hands. On the platform itself, on both right and left of the throne, were ten gholāms with four-sectioned caps on their heads, with heavy belts, all of them set with jewels, and with swords whose belts were also bejewelled. In the main body of the hall there were two lines of gholāms. One line was standing against the wall, with four-sectioned caps, arrows and swords in their hands, quivers and bow-cases. The other line was positioned in the middle of the hall, with two-pointed caps, heavy belts mounted with silver and straps for securing weapons, and silver maces in their hands. Both these lines of gholāms wore coats of Shushtari brocade. As for the horses, [F 715] ten had accoutrements set [Gh 541] with jewels and twenty simply with golden ones. There were fifty Deylamites with gold shields, ten of these being set with jewels. The holders of court offices stood by, and outside the curtained entrance of the palace, numerous palace attendants and court troops stood in attendance, all with weapons.

A royal audience was given and the pillars of the state, the retainers and courtiers came forward, and limitless quantities of coins were distributed as largesse. The provincial governors and notables of the highest rank were given seats on that extensive platform, and the Amir sat there on his throne, holding court, till mid-morning, when the boon-companions came in, offered their service and distributed coins as largesse. Then he arose, mounted his steed and went off to the Garden, changed his robes, rode back on his horse and sat down to feast in the Spring Pavilion. The great men and the pillars of state were brought to the feast and given places. Other tablecloths were spread down outside the Pavilion, on this side of the palace, and the field officers, the *kheyltāsh*s and the various component groups of the army were given places at that spread. They began to eat, the musicians and singers struck up, wine flowed like water, so that they all went home from the feast in a drunken state. The Amir rose from the spread in a joyous mood, mounted and came to the Garden, where another similarly lavish reception had been laid on. The boon-companions came along, and the drinking went on until the time of the afternoon worship. Then they returned home.[46]

In the midst of all this, the Amir was extremely depressed and concerned about the fate of Sübashï and the army, since letters had come from Nishapur, saying "When Bu Sahl the door-keeper came back from Ghazna, the Great Chamberlain held a council, and Bu Sahl Ḥamdavi, Suri and a few others who were there sat down privately with him. He laid out the Sultan's letters before them and said, 'A royal command with these instructions has arrived, putting an end to any further debate; whatever happens, I shall go forth tomorrow in order to fulfill this task, in whatever way that God Most High has foreordained. All of you here must be vigilant, and stow away all the money and clothing that was brought from Ray in a safe place, for no-one can know how things will turn out, and there is no harm in being careful and acting with foresight.' They replied, 'This will be done. [F 716] We regard this expedition of yours with a great deal of misgiving, but since such an order has arrived and the decision firmly taken, one cannot ignore it.' The next day, the Chamberlain Sübashï set out along the road from Nishapur towards Sarakhs with a well-prepared army, amply equipped with matériel and weapons.[47] After his departure, Suri gathered together the money collected in taxation from Nishapur, together with his own money, [Gh 542] and he told Bu Sahl Ḥamdavi, 'Get ready what you have brought with you (i.e. from Ray) for sending to the fortress of the Mikālis in the rural district of Bosht,[48] so that if, God forbid, this affair takes a different turn, this wealth will not fall into the hands of anyone else.' He replied, 'You have appraised the situation very soundly, but this plan must be kept secret.' They fastened up everything that the two of them had, and chose agile and alert riders for that task secretly so that no-one should realize what was happening. They were sent off at midnight and reached the fortress in safety and entrusted the valuables to the custodian of the fortress of the Mikālis. Trusty retainers of these two masters, with a force of fifty infantrymen, were stationed there to guard the fortress. Suri gave instructions that the heavier and bulkier items at Nishapur, including clothing, carpets from Shādyākh, arms and other things that could not be transported to the fortress of the Mikālis, should all be placed in the treasury. These two masters then waited to see what would happen. Horsemen were placed at regular intervals along the road to Sarakhs so that any news there might be could be speedily conveyed."

I heard from my master Bu Naṣr, who said, "When these letters arrived, I showed them, that is, the ones which had arrived from Bu Sahl and Suri,[49] to the Amir. He told me, "We were too impetuous, and we can't tell what the outcome will be between the Chamberlain and the army and these enemies." I replied, " God willing, [F 717] it will all be for the best." The Amir drank no more wine during the latter days of Shaʿbān, for he was too pre-occupied and heavy-hearted. Confidential letters arrived from Sarakhs and Merv to the effect that "When the enemy heard that the Chamberlain had marched out from Nishapur to attack them, they were filled with apprehension and said, ' Now matters have come to a head,' and they sent their baggage and impedimenta deep into the desert of Merv together with their less capable riders.[50] They have assembled a fleet-footed army with little baggage to weigh them down so that they can proceed to Ṭalkhāb[51] of Sarakhs and give battle there, and if they should be defeated, they were speedily to withdraw, pick up their baggage and impedimenta, and head towards Ray, since if they should be thrown out of Khorasan, there would be no other place for them to go except for Ray and those regions which were only lightly held.

On Thursday (i.e. 1 Ramażān/7 June),[52] the Amir began his fast. He used to take his repast with the boon-companions and the courtiers during the month of Ramażān. He would hold court twice a day, and sit there for a great deal of time, as had been the custom of his father, the late Amir, [Gh 543] for he was extremely worried during this time—and justly so—but when the decree of Fate has come down, reflecting and pondering are to no avail!

On Wednesday, the fourth of this month [/10 June],[53] the Amir had held court on the great platform of the New Palace till almost the time of the midday worship, had executed all the business and then had arisen and gone up to the elevated pavilion. My master was about to leave the Divān for home when one of the riders who had been stationed along the Ghur road came in bearing a despatch bag, closed with a ring and with the seal securing it in the handwriting of Bu'l-Fatḥ Ḥātemi, the deputy postal and intelligence officer of Herat. My master took it and opened it. There was just a single pouch in it, likewise sealed. He read a couple of sections of the letter and was taken aback in dismay.[54] He refolded the letter and gave instructions for it to be put back in the pouch [F 718] and for the despatch bag's seal to be replaced. He summoned Bu Manṣur,[55] the Guard of the Divān, sent a verbal message by him, and Bu Manṣur went off. My master became extremely downcast and worried, so that it became evident to all the secretaries that some great disaster had befallen. Bu Manṣur the Guard came back without the letter and said, "You have been summoned." My master went off and remained with the Amir till the time of the afternoon worship. Then he came back to the Divān, gave me that confidential letter from Bu'l-Fatḥ Ḥātemi, the deputy postal and intelligence officer, and said, "Seal it up and deposit it in the store for important official documents,"[56] and then went home, and so did the secretaries.

I then read that confidential letter myself. It said, "Today Sübashï came to Herat, accompanied by twenty gholāms, and the tax collector and financial agent Bu Ṭalḥa Sheybāni provided him with a comfortable lodging and sent along ample quantities of food and sweetmeats. At the time of the afternoon worship he went to him, accompanied by myself and the notables of Herat. He was feeling extremely despondent, and everyone was trying to cheer him up, saying, 'Ever since the world began, things like this have happened. May the exalted Sultan endure for ever! There are large numbers of troops, equipment and weapons, and calamities such as these can be retrieved. Praise be to God that the Great Chamberlain has been preserved alive!' He wept and said, 'I don't know how I shall be able to look the lord in the face. The battle between me and the enemy went on from early morning till the time of the afternoon prayer, and no more fiercely-fought battle has ever been known. Just at the moment when victory was in sight, our own ignoble and cowardly supporters let me down, and I was wounded and compelled to leave the field in the condition in which you see me now.' [Gh 544] The people went away, but he kept back Bu Ṭalḥa and myself and had a private talk with us, saying, 'The agents charged with reporting events back to the Sultan deceived him: [first,] through their reports on the enemy, making the latter appear feeble and negligible to him, while I was endeavouring, by patient tactics, to bring them to the point when they would, from sheer necessity, be compelled to flee; and [second,] they used trickery and obfuscation to turn the lord's mind against me, with the result that he gave me a categorical order that I must march out and give battle. [F 719] When I made contact with the enemy, they were an unencumbered and highly agile force, having made the necessary arrangements and having been relieved of the need to look after their baggage and impedimenta. Battle was joined, in the fiercest manner imaginable, until the time of the midday worship. Our troops strove valiantly and were on the point of gaining the victory when they were overcome by lassitude, and each one started worrying about attending to an ass or a wife. I had made a hundred thousand appeals to them not to bring any womenfolk,[57] but they paid no heed. As soon as the enemy saw what was happening, they came on with a bolder impetus. I gave instructions for an awning to be put up in the midst of the battlefield, and I made this my base so that the troops could follow my example and fight on so that no disaster should occur; but they did not do this, and they abandoned me and followed their own fancies, leaving me isolated. The leading men and senior commanders can all bear witness that I did everything possible, and if asked, can give the full story, up to the time when the disaster occurred. I was struck by an arrow and was compelled to turn back. With the help of a couple of horses and a body of twenty gholāms, I reached here (i.e. Herat). Everything belonging to me and to those cowardly and ignoble ones fell into the enemy's hands, as I later heard from several horsemen who were arriving closely after us. I have been here for some days, waiting for any stragglers who may be on the way to catch up, and then I shall travel by the Ghur road to the court and give a verbal report of the events. What you have heard from me in this present letter will need to be more fully explained'."[58]

At the time of the afternoon worship on this day, the Amir did not hold a court session and did not emerge from his quarters to break his fast and eat. It was said that he only broke his fast by drinking something but ate nothing, since what had happened was no small matter. I saw that my master too ate nothing, for I was there with him at the spread. The next day the Amir held court, and after this had a private meeting with the Commander-in-Chief, the Head of the Army Department, Bu Naṣr, the Commander of the Palace Gholāms Begtughdï and the General Bu'l-Nażr. He explained these events, and my master read out to them the confidential letter from the deputy postal and intelligence officer [F 720] of Herat. All those assembled there exclaimed, "May the lord's life be prolonged! Such things are bound to happen in this world, and this situation can be retrieved. Perhaps it would be wise policy to send one of the trusty confidants to the Great Chamberlain in order to strengthen his resolution and that of his troops, for it will serve as a soothing balm placed on their hearts." He replied, "I will do it, there is time enough for that and I shall issue the necessary commands; but what about here and now, what do you suggest should be done?" They said, "Until the Great Chamberlain arrives back, nothing can be done about this. But if the exalted judgement [Gh 545] deems it appropriate, a letter could be written to the Grand Vizier letting him know that something like this has happened, even though this news will have already reached him, so that whatever occurs to him regarding this matter he can set forth in his reply." He answered, "That's a wise course of action," and he gave instructions to my master for a letter to be written. Those who were present there tried to console the Amir in different ways, expressing their devotion and willingness to sacrifice their wealth and lives for him, and then they left. A very full letter was written to the Vizier on this matter and his opinion sought. Hitherto, people had felt free at the royal court to pour scorn on the Turkmens and their feebleness and insignificance, but now, after this calamity, no-one dared to utter anything untoward,[59] and when one or two individuals did, he bellowed at them and chastised them. He was in a very dispirited mood.

In the remaining part of the month of Ramażān [/later June-early July], alarming pieces of news kept arriving daily and, indeed, hourly, until a letter came from the postal and intelligence officer of Nishapur, Bu'l-Moẓaffar Jomaḥi,[60] saying that [F 721] "I am on the run and presently hiding somewhere underground. When the news reached Nishapur that the Great Chamberlain and the divinely-aided army had suffered such a disaster, Suri immediately opened up the prison, and a few of the inmates were beheaded and the rest let loose. He and Bu Sahl Ḥamdavi hurriedly departed and went off to the rural district of Bosht; all the men of our army who happened to be in the town went with them, and it was not clear where they would finally head for (i.e. after leaving Bosht). It was not possible for me to go with them since Suri is thirsting after my blood. Fearing for my life, I have gone into hiding here in a safe and secure place, and have posted agents in different spots to gather news; one can but wait and see what happens and how things turn out. Whenever possible, I shall send messengers to report the news. I will send very important items of information in code to the Vizier so that he might lay these before the exalted judgement."

When the Amir read the letter, he became very downcast, and said to my master, "How do you think Bu Sahl and Suri will fare, and where will they go? What is going to happen to that wealth?" He answered, "The lord knows that Bu Sahl is a man of wisdom and judgement, and Suri is a bold and strong-minded person. They have devised a way out, or are in process of doing so, so that no enemy will get hold of them. If they see that they can make it, they will find their way to the court by the route through the desert of the Ṭabaseyn,[61] [Gh 546] travelling via the Bosht district, since they have gone in the direction of the rural district of Bosht. But if something unexpected happens, we would not know where they would go, but we can be sure that they will never surrender themselves to this bunch of rebels, since they know full well what would happen to them." The Amir said, "At all events, they will not be able to proceed to the region of Ray, since the Son of [F 722] Kāku is there with the Turkmens and plenty of troops. They will not go to Gorgān either, since Bā Kālijār has likewise slipped away from our control. I really cannot tell how their affair will turn out. But alas for these two men and such quantities of wealth and valuable possessions if they should fall into the enemy's hands!"

Bu Naṣr said, "No-one is going to be able to get his hands on that wealth since it is in the fortress of the Mikālis, which is impregnable, and that castellan there is a wise old man, and a loyal and ancient retainer of the lord's. He will guard the fortress and the wealth, since he has laid in ample supplies of food and fodder and water. Bu Sahl and Suri have posted riders at regular intervals along the road from Sarakhs to Nishapur. News of this disaster will have reached them within three days, and both of them will speedily have got away. When they secured the victory, the enemy will not have immediately gone towards Nishapur, for they would have needed a week's stay in order to settle their affairs, and then they will formulate their plans and spread out through the land. By the time they reach Nishapur, these two would be miles away."

The Amir said, "A letter must be sent to them by swift couriers, in such terms as you deem appropriate." Bu Naṣr replied, "There's no point in sending out a courier blindly until we know where they are. Once they have reached somewhere and feel secure, they will themselves despatch swift couriers in order to report on their situation and to seek royal guidance and command. But it is meanwhile imperative to send two or three couriers with confidential letters bearing the royal emblem and seal to the fortress of the Mikālis in order to reassure and strengthen the will of the castellan, and naturally, he too will respond and send a courier and a letter." The Amir said, "This must be written at once, for it is an urgent matter." My master came to the Divān and wrote out a confidential letter to which the royal emblem and seal was affixed, and two swift couriers went off with it. The castellan was told, "For the time being we have sent a letter, but we [ourself] shall lead an expedition into Khorasan after Mehragān, and we shall remain there for two years until all these defects have been eradicated. You must guard the fortress well, [F 723] take all precautions and be watchful."

On Friday (i.e. on 1 Shavvāl/7 July), the Festival of the Ending of the Fast was celebrated. The Amir did not listen to any poetry or call for a wine banquet because of the prevailing gloom, [Gh 547] for every hour yet another thunderbolt of calamitous news would descend upon us from Khorasan.

On Sunday (i.e. on 3 Shavvāl/9 July), the secretary Bu Sahl Hamadāni was appointed, on the Amir's orders, to go and officially receive the Great Chamberlain and the troops, to console them regarding the recent events and to convey hopes of future favour from the royal court, in order to allay their feelings of shame and grief. My master composed the text of an order on these lines, and the completed document was written out and validated by the affixing of the royal emblem and seal. At the time of the afternoon worship on the same day, Bu Sahl Hamadāni set off.

The next day (i.e. 4 Shavvāl/10 July), the Vizier's letter arrived. It expressed much sorrow and anguish at the great calamity which had occurred, but had then gone on to say, "Although the evil eye has befallen us in such a manner as this, given the evergreen and auspicious fortune of the lord, everything can be retrieved; but a new approach to the task is required." He also sent on the letter from Bu Esḥāq Ebrāhim,[62] son of the late Ilig, that the latter had written to the Vizier from Özkend,[63] with the comment, "The exalted judgement should peruse that closely, and look favourably at his friendly overtures, for although he comes from a lineage traditionally hostile to us, he is himself a man of valour and good judgement, and has managed to escape from the sons of ʿAlitegin,[64] with a contingent of well-equipped cavalrymen intact, and he enjoys a formidable reputation. Thus we will also save ourselves from a potential trouble on yet another front."

The Vizier had written a very long letter to my master pouring out his heart, saying, "The foreordained decree of God, the Exalted One, apart, these disasters have taken place as a result of the two expeditions, one to India and the other to Ṭabarestān. What is past is past and cannot be remedied. Today [F 724] our opponents have attained such a high position that no commander is a match for them, since they have already defeated two notable commanders[65] with massive armies and gained much plunder, and have become more audacious and daring. Only the lord's actual presence on the scene can rectify matters. Henceforth, the lord must conduct affairs in a different way.

He must curtail his love of pleasure, personally review the army and not delegate this task to anyone else, and give up this policy of cheese-paring and making false economies in the army. This letter should be presented to him, and what needs to be said should be said, until we can meet in person and matters can be expressed more openly."

My master showed this letter to the Amir and said what needed to be said. The Amir said, "The Vizier is right in what he says here. We shall listen to his good counsel and will act upon it. A reply must be sent to him in this vein, and you should also write to him personally and express whatever should be said on these lines. Regarding the matter of Böritegin[66], son of the late Ilig, he is of noble stock, [Gh 548] and we need men like him today. The Vizier is to write a letter to him and say that he has brought to our notice Böritegin's present situation, and that our response had been that "He should treat our abode as his own and feel thoroughly at home with us. He should send an envoy to our court so that we can see what he desires and issue the necessary orders." This letter was written and despatched by swift courier.[67]

On Sunday, 10 Shavvāl [/16 July], the Great Chamberlain Sübashï reached Ghaznin, and came straight from the journey to the court and rendered service. The Amir was most gracious towards him and consoled him, as also the several commanders who had arrived with him. They went back home [F 725] and people went to them at once to bring them comfort and cheer. One week after the Great Chamberlain's arrival, the Amir had a private session with him that went on for a very long time, and all aspects of the situation were ascertained. The Amir then summoned the newly-arrived commanders one-by-one and questioned them separately and thoroughly about the situation in Khorasan, the enemy, the Great Chamberlain and the battle which had taken place, until everything that had happened was crystal clear to him. Since this was not a time for carping and criticism, he spoke solely in kindly and soothing terms. Everything that had occurred was reported in writing to the Vizier.

On the last day of Shavvāl,[68] the letter from the Vizier regarding Böritegin arrived. He had said that a letter should go from the exalted court session to Böritegin, to the effect that "What he had written to Aḥmad [b. 'Abd al-Ṣamad, the Vizier,] has been relayed to us. Our house is at his disposal. After Mehragān we intend to set out for Balkh. At present, he should send an envoy, and explain in detail the circumstances of the move to Khorasan and his aims and intentions, so that we are well briefed and can ordain whatever is best for his welfare and benefit."[69] The Amir said to Bu Naṣr, "You should write in a way that would guard our interests, using a formal and established manner of address so that no harm is done should the letter fall into the hands of ʿAlitegin's sons." My master composed the text of the letter with his wonted skill, for he was an experienced hand at such things. He gave the form of address as "Excellent Amir" and referred to him as "Amir".[70] It was sent inserted within the folds of the letter to the Vizier.[71]

On Tuesday, 3 Dhu'l-Qaʿda [/7 August], confidential letters sent by Bu Sahl Ḥamdavi and Suri, the head of the Divān [of Khorasan], arrived from Gorgān by swift couriers. They had written that "When a catastrophe of that magnitude struck the Great Chamberlain and the divinely-aided army, and the news speedily reached us because riders had been stationed at regular intervals along the Sarakhs road [Gh 549] for bringing news, we immediately left Nishapur by the road to Bosht and came to the foot of the royal fortress[72] [F 726] intending to install ourselves there within the fortress; but then we decided against it. We summoned the castellan and his trusty retainers, who were stationed at the foot of the fortress guarding the wealth stored there, and gave the necessary instructions for them to take careful precautions in guarding the fortress. We gave money to cover a year's payment of salaries for the castellan and the infantrymen. When we had completed these crucial tasks, we cast around trying to choose which road to take in order to reach the court. All the routes were long, and the enemy was getting nearer and nearer, and there would have been further danger if we had revealed our presence in this region. We had good guides. We pressed on by night and came by means of roads and across trackless country via Esfarāyen to Gorgān. Bā Kālijār was at Setārābād , and he was informed of our approach. He immediately came and declared himself a servant of the Sultan's and assured us that we had done well to come to this region, since, so long as he had life in his body, he would protect us so that no enemy should lay his hands on us. He went on to say that 'Gorgān is strategically vulnerable,[73] and it is unwise to remain here. You should come to Astarābād[74] and remain there so that if—God forbid!—the enemy should launch an attack on this region, I would take it upon myself to oppose them and you can go to Astarābād, since they won't be able to penetrate into those narrow and restricted terrains, and no-one will be able to get his hands on you.' We went to Astarābād, and Bā Kālijār remained in Gorgān with his troops waiting to see what would happen. We are at present at Setārābād, with an army composed of all sorts of ethnic groups in addition to the court household troops. Bā Kālijār is providing them all with provisions and sustenance, and in terms of benevolence and hospitality he cannot be faulted. If the exalted judgement deems fit, he should be conciliated in all possible respects, even to the extent of foregoing the stipulated tribute imposed upon him,[75] since he is taking upon himself such manifold cares and pain, and especially now that the court retainers and servants have taken refuge with him and he is having to look after them. He should be told that, very soon, [F 727] the exalted stirrup will lead an expedition, for this is a credible possibility, since Khorasan cannot be abandoned to such a bunch of marauders (i.e. to the Turkmens). Thus the man's courage and resolve will be strengthened, for when Khorasan is cleared of the enemy, Ray, Jebāl and these regions will be recovered. Moreover, in regard to us servants and the band of troops with us, such reassurances will come as a blessing and comfort to us, since we have been left far away from the exalted court, and as a result of this, nothing untoward will occur."

The Amir became jubilant after reading these letters, for he had been worried about the safety of these two servants and the enormous amount of wealth that they had with them. Their messengers were brought into his presence, [Gh 550] and they gave answers to all the queries put to them, saying, "The Turkmens have seized control of the roads in order to keep a close watch, and we had to use much ingenuity and use abandoned tracks and traverse through the wilderness in order to get here." Meanwhile, the official charged with looking after the envoys had them lodged at a secret location, so that no-one might see them. The Amir ordered letters to be written in reply, to the effect that "Careful precautions must be taken, and if the Turkmens mount an attack on Astarābād, you are to go to Sāri, and if Sāri is attacked, you are to go to Ṭabarestān, for it is not possible for them to follow you in such difficult terrain. You are to keep in constant touch with us through letters and the regular despatching of swift couriers, and we will do the same from this end. Know that we intend to lead an expedition after Mehragān, bringing to Tokhārestān and Balkh an army whose like has never been deployed in any previous age, and we shall stay firm in Khorasan until the fire of this disturbance is extinguished. You must keep a stout heart, for there have been many such phases of adversity and weakness in the world, and we shall retrieve the situation and make amends. Whatever it was necessary to write to Bā Kālijār has been written and despatched, so that they will be fully informed of the contents and inform others."

A letter was written to Bā Kālijār on this topic, couched in extremely approbatory terms, stating that "All the money which he is expending is to be considered as expenditure by ourself, and what is being done for our trusty retainers will not go unacknowledged. [F 728] We are about to come, and when we have reached Khorasan and have redressed the present plight, we shall see to it that in recognition of his loyal acts of service he will be raised to such a prominent position which he could hardly imagine now." He affixed his official emblem and seal to this letter and swift couriers bore it away. Immediately after them several other couriers were despatched with other important letters likewise on these topics.[76]

On Saturday, 7 Dhu'l-Qaʿda [/11 August], a confidential letter arrived from Bu'l-Moẓaffar Jomaḥi, the postal and intelligence officer of Nishapur. He had written:

I write this from where I am hiding, and have had to deploy a great deal of subterfuge in order to send this courier.[77] I write to inform you that twelve days after news arrived of the disaster that happened to the Great Chamberlain Sübashï, Ebrāhim Yïnāl reached the outskirts of Nishapur with a force of 200 men. He sent a verbal message through an envoy, to the effect that "I am the advance guard for Ṭoghrïl, Dāvud and Yabghu. If you wish for war, I can go back and report your decision; but if you do not want war, let me enter the town and have the *khoṭba* changed (i.e. in favour of the Seljuq leaders), for there is a large army at my heels.

They brought the envoy into the town, and a great tumult arose there. All the notables came to the Judge Ṣāʿed's house and said, "You are our Imam and leader;[78] what do you say about this message which has arrived?" He replied, "What do you yourselves think about it, and what are your intentions?" They said, "You are perfectly aware of this town's situation; it is by no means impregnable and can at best act as a minor irritant to an invading army[79] [Gh 551], and its people are not used to wielding weapons. A mighty army like that of the

General Sübashï was defeated by them, so what chance do we have? This is our view."

The Judge Ṣāʿed said, "Your assessment is a fair one; ordinary folk cannot be expected to face up to an army. You have a powerful lord like Amir Masʿud; if this province is of any use to him, perforce he will come himself or send someone to secure it. But for now, a fierce fire is leaping up [F 729] and is spreading, and a horde ready to shed blood and bent on pillage has appeared on the scene; we have no choice but to comply."

The Imam Movaffaq, who was the *ṣāḥeb-ḥadithān*, and all the notables agreed that "This is the only sensible course of action, or else we would have allowed the town to be sacked for no good reason. The Sultan is far away from us. We can seek pardon for our present conduct later, and he will accept it."[80]

The Judge said, "When the troops of the Ilig, led by Sübashïtegin, came from Bokhara, the people of Balkh put up a fight, with the result that he set about killing and looting, whereas the people of Nishapur did then what they are about to do just now (i.e. they submitted). When Amir Maḥmud came back to Ghaznin from Multan, he spent some time there, made preparations and then set out for Khorasan. He reached Balkh and saw that the Lovers' Market, that had been constructed on his orders, had been burnt down.[81] He castigated the people of Balkh, saying, 'What have ordinary subjects to do with making war? It was inevitable that your town should be destroyed and that they should burn down a property of mine which used to bring in such a large revenue. You should have indemnified us for this, but we have let it go. Watch out that you do nothing like this in future. If any monarch shows himself the stronger at a given moment, and demands taxes from you and extends to you his protection, you must hand over the taxation and thereby save yourselves. Why did you not consider the example of the people of Nishapur and of other towns, who went out and offered their submission? They acted quite rightly in doing that, with the result than no plundering took place. And why did you not consider other towns, from which no further taxation was demanded, since that had already been paid?'[82] The people of Balkh repented and promised never to commit a similar mistake in future. The problem today is the same as it was then." They all agreed that it was indeed exactly the same.

Then they summoned Ebrāhim's envoy and gave the reply that "We are subjects, and have a lord, and as a rule, subjects do not fight. The Amirs (i.e. the three Seljuq leaders) should come, since the town is open to them. If the Sultan regards the province as of any value, he will come after it personally or send someone else. However, you must know that the people have become fearful of you because of what has happened up to now in other places: the plundering, mutilations, killings and beheadings. You must alter your conduct, [Gh 552] for beyond this present world lies another world. Nishapur has seen many like you in the past, and its people have always had the weapon of dawn prayer with which to defend themselves. If [F 730] our Sultan is far away, the Almighty God and His servant the Angel of Death, are always within reach."

The envoy went back. When Ebrāhim Yïnāl had studied the reply, he moved from his position at that time to one a parasang away from the town, and sent the envoy back again with the verbal message, "You have appraised the situation very sensibly and have spoken very wisely.[83] I have written this instant to Ṭoghrïl and explained the situation to him, since he is our chief,[84] so that he may station Dāvud and Yabghu at Sarakhs and Merv and the other numerous leading figures at other places, and Ṭoghrïl, who is a just monarch,[85] will come here with his personal retinue. You must maintain stout hearts, for the plundering and unlawful behaviour that was happening up till now unavoidably arose from the rank-and-file of our following[86] who were engaged in warfare. Today the situation is very different. The province is ours and no-one has the temerity to act unlawfully. I shall come to the town tomorrow and install myself in the Khorramak Garden. Then things will be made known."

When the notables of Nishapur heard these words, their peace of mind was restored. A herald went round the markets and explained the situation, and the general mass of the populace was reassured. They laid out furnishings and carpets in the Khorramak Garden and prepared food and sweetmeats, and got ready to go out and greet him. Bu'l-Qāsem, the Sālār of Buzgān, a most capable and gifted member of the notables, who had in the past been beaten and ill-treated by Suri, threw himself whole-heartedly into preparing the reception of the Turkmens.[87] The *ṣāḥeb-ḥadithān*, the Imam Movaffaq, and the other town notables assembled together and came out to meet Ebrāhim

Yïnāl, with the exception of the Judge Ṣāʿed and Sayyed Zeyd, the marshal of the ʿAlids,[88] who did not go.

At a distance of half-a-parasang from the town, Ebrāhim appeared with two or three hundred horsemen, a banner,[89] two beasts that were being led, and wearing a generally ragged and worn outfit. When the reception committee came up to him, he reined in his horse, and they found him a most handsome young man. He spoke pleasant words and made everyone feel reassured. He rode on. An extremely large crowd of people had turned out to watch. The older men were secretly weeping for they had only ever witnessed the troops of Maḥmud and [F 731] Masʿud parade, and derided the contrast in pomp and retinue.[90] Ebrāhim alighted at the Khorramak Garden, and they brought for him large quantities of food and sweetmeats which they had prepared. Each day, people came to present their greetings. On Friday, Ebrāhim went to the congregational mosque, appearing now in a more soigné and presentable state. The Sālār of Buzgān had brought three or four thousand armed men, since he was in league with Ebrāhim [Gh 553] and had been corresponding with him, and had become friendly with all their leaders[91]—all this on account of Suri's tyranny, for in truth Khorasan was lost because of him. They had pressed the official preacher Esmāʿil Ṣābuni[92] very hard though discreetly to pronounce the *khoṭba*.[93] When this was made in Ṭoghrïl's name, a fearful uproar arose amongst the people, and there was danger of an outbreak of unrest until they were calmed down. They performed the worship and went back.

A week after that, some riders arrived bearing letters from Ṭoghrïl to the Sālār of Buzgān and Movaffaq. Ṭoghrïl had written to Ebrāhim Yïnāl that, since the notables of the town had acted with befitting wisdom, Ebrāhim and his followers must in turn see what could be done for the welfare of the notables and the entire populace. He added, "We appointed our brother Dāvud and our paternal uncle Yabghu, together with all the army commanders,[94] to take charge of the troops. We have come with the advanced guard and with our personal retainers so that the people of those districts should not suffer any harm, seeing that they showed themselves submissive and careful of their own interests." The people were reassured by these letters. Furnishings and carpets were laid out in Ḥasanak's former garden at Shādyākh. [F 732]

Three days later, Ṭoghrïl arrived in the town. All the notables, with the exception of the Judge Ṣāʿed, had gone out to meet him. He was accompanied by 3,000 horsemen, most of them wearing mailed coats. He himself had a strung bow over his arm, with three wooden arrows fastened at his waist and was fully armed.[95] He wore a coat of *molḥam* cloth, a headdress of Tavvazi cloth and felt boots.[96] He installed himself in the Garden at Shādyākh, together with as many troops as could be accommodated there; and the rest encamped round the perimeter of the garden.[97] They had prepared large quantities of food and sweetmeats and brought them there, and provided food and fodder for all the troops. On the way there, he only talked to Movaffaq and the Sālār of Buzgān, and the Sālār was attending to everything.

The next day—and after a great deal of prompting the previous night—the Judge Ṣāʿed went to pay his respects to Ṭoghrïl, accompanied by his sons, grandsons, pupils and a large number of followers. The marshal of the ʿAlids also came along with all the Sayyeds. The audience hall appeared devoid of all splendour and glitter. A group of riffraff were milling around with no apparent order or sense of decorum, and anyone who wished could go boldly up to Ṭoghrïl and speak with him. He had seated himself on the lord Sultan's throne in the foremost part of the dais.[98] He rose to his feet for the Judge Ṣāʿed, and a cushion was put down at the foot of the throne and he sat down. The Judge said, "May the lord's life be long! Take note that this is Sultan Masʿud's throne that you are sitting on. Such unforeseeable events[99] do happen, and one cannot know what further happenings will emerge from the Unseen. Be circumspect, and fear God the Exalted One. Render justice, and listen to the words of those who have suffered oppression and are reduced to misery. Do not allow these troops free rein to act tyrannically, for injustice will bear ominous results. With this visit I have fulfilled my duty to you, and I shall not come again because I am occupied in study, and apart from that do not give my attention to anything; and if you think about it wisely, the advice that I gave you will be sufficient."

Ṭoghrïl replied, "I do not wish to trouble the Judge with more visits, for matters can be relayed through messages. I am willing to carry out your words; we are new to this land and as strangers, and [F 733] unacquainted with the manners and customs of the Persians.[100] The Judge should not refrain from sending me messages of advice." The Judge expressed his consent and left, and the notables who had come with them also departed.

The next day, he handed over the administration of the town to the Sālār of Buzgān, and the latter donned a robe of honour, comprising a gown (*jobba*) and a woollen robe slit open at the front (*dorrāʿa*)[101] which he himself had prepared, and also golden saddle accoutrements of Turkish type. He went back to his house and embarked upon his administrative duties. In his black woollen robe, he appeared to people as a most impressive and fearsome dignitary, for it was he (i.e. as a king-maker) who was making Ṭoghrïl into an Amir.

I myself, Bu'l-Moẓaffar, am at present staying with Sayyed Zeyd, the marshal of the ʿAlids, who has proved singularly loyal. After writing this, my couriers will be sent off, for thanks to the exertions of this ʿAlid I am able to complete this act of service.[102]

The Amir studied closely this confidential letter, and was totally dismayed. At the time, he said nothing. The next day he said to my master in a private talk, "Do you see to what extent these Turkmens have been successful?" He answered, "May the lord's life be prolonged! Ever since the world began, such things have been happening. The truth will always remain the truth, and the false, the false. With the expedition of the exalted stirrup, there is hope that all wishes and desires will be achieved." The Amir said, "A reply must be sent to Jomaḥi's confidential letter in extremely heart-warming terms and unstinted praise, and a confidential letter to the marshal of the ʿAlids so that he will take great care that Bu'l-Moẓaffar Jomaḥi remains safe and secure. Confidential letters should be sent to the Judge Ṣāʿed and the rest of the notables, with the exception of Movaffaq, and it should be clearly stated that 'We are at this moment in process of leading an expedition with 50,000 cavalry and infantrymen and 300 elephants, and on no account will we return to Ghaznin until that time when Khorasan is cleared of the enemy,' so that they will be in good heart and do not transfer their allegiance and affections to that group, the Turkmens." Bu Naṣr obeyed and came back to the Divan, sat down by himself and composed the texts of the letters, and I [Gh 555] wrote the slim, confidential letters and the Amir affixed his emblem and seal. The courier was given a handsome present, and he set out.

I am able to set down these events so extensively because I was, at the time, [F 734] a trusted confidant. None of the secretaries knew about such events except my master Bu Naṣr who used to compose the texts and I who used to write out the confidential letters. For as long as Bu Naṣr lived, letters to the rulers of adjacent kingdoms, the Caliph, the Khāns of Turkestan and everything of grave importance were dealt with in the Divān in this fashion. This is not an idle boast on my part nor a case of blowing my own trumpet. On the contrary, it is an apologia that I wish to make in regard to this History, since I have in my mind that readers should not be given the impression that I am writing purely out of my own head. The just witness to what I said is in the form of the dated records for each year[103] which I have in my personal possession, all of them eloquent witnesses to the correct remembrance of these events. Anyone who does not believe this should come and attend the judicial court where Wisdom sits in judgement, so that the dated records can come in front of the judge and present their testimonial, and resolve his doubts and misgivings. That's it!

On Sunday, 8 Dhu'l-Qaʿda [/12 August], the letter from the Vizier arrived, in which the decision of the exalted judgement was sought: whether he should remain at Balkh and in Tokhārestan or should come to the capital. He went on to say that he felt anxious and wished to be at the lord's side so that he could have his say regarding the important issues and concerns which had recently turned up. The Amir ordered a reply to be sent that "The time for our expedition is very close, and will take place after Mehragān. The Vizier should proceed to Valvālej and remain there,[104] and should give orders for a month's supply of food and fodder (*ʿalaf*) to be got together there, and supplies for twenty days at Rāvan, Baruqān and Baghlān,[105] so that under no circumstances should there be any lack of provisions. A trusty agent of his should remain at Balkh to make plans concerning the rest of the supplies of food and fodder (*ʿolufāt*) so that, when our banner arrives there, we shall not find any lack of provisions." This was written out and sent off with a courier of the postal and intelligence service.

On Wednesday, 9 Dhu'l-Ḥejja [/12 September], the Amir sat in state for the festival of Mehragān, and [F 735] people brought large numbers of presents. It was the day of ʿArafa.[106] The Amir fasted, and no-one dared to indulge in any feasting or drinking, whether clandestinely or openly. The next day they celebrated the Festival of the Sacrifice; and the Amir had made great efforts, both in laying out a spread as well as in regard to the troops, since two armies had come together,[107] and it had been some time since he himself had indulged in any drinking. After [Gh 556] the worship and the slaughtering of the sacrifices, the Amir sat down at the feast, and the pillars of state, courtiers and retainers were brought in and set down at the spread. The poets recited verses, since no poetry had been heard at the celebrating of the Festival of the Ending of the Fast,[108] and after them, the musicians and singers struck up and began to sing. Wine flowed, and they staggered home in an intoxicated state. He ordered the poets to be given presents, and the musicians and singers too. He rose from the table, having drunk seven bowls of wine, and went into his quarters in the inner palace. Those present were all sent homewards.

After this, he drank wine continuously for a week, mostly with the boon-companions.[109] He ordered the musicians and singers to be given 50,000 dirhams, and he said, "Keep on with your playing, since we are about to depart, and there will be no wine-drinking in Khorasan, so that we can deprive our enemies of their false hopes and illusions. Moḥammad Beshnudi[110] the lute player (*barbaṭi*), who was a very fine master of this instrument and on very familiar terms with the Amir, commented, (F 736] "Since the lord will have a continuous run of victories, and the boon-companions will sit there and recite lyrical quatrains, and the musicians will come along and play stringed instruments and lutes in the court session, what is the official verdict on wine-drinking on that day?" The Amir was highly pleased with these words, and ordered that he should receive a separate gift of 1,000 dinars.[111]

After this, he sat for a whole week, from early morning up to the time of the afternoon worship, until the whole of the army had been reviewed and inspected and the money for their salaries issued in one complete payment and not in instalments.[112]

On Tuesday, the Great Chamberlain Sübashï was given a very splendid robe of honour, as also were several of the commanders who had come back with him from Khorasan.

The next day the Amir rode forth and came to the plain of Shābahār. He sat on a dais there, and the troops passed before him in their battle formation, a huge army. It was said to number fifty odd thousand cavalry and infantrymen, all with equipment, fine horses and a complete array of weapons, or, according to better-informed sources, forty thousand. It took all the time between the midday and afternoon worships for the whole army to go past in review.

The History of the Year 430 (/3 October 1038–22 September 1039)

[Gh 556, F 736] The first day of Moḥarram fell on Wednesday. On Thursday, 2 Moḥarram [/4 October 1038], the great marquee (*sarāy-parda*) was brought out and erected on the wooden platform behind the Firuzi Garden. The Amir ordered that, on that day, Amir Saʿid was to be given a robe of honour so that he could remain behind at Ghaznin as its prince-governor. Precious robes of honour were likewise given to his chamberlains, secretaries and boon-companions [Gh 557] and also to the castellan Bu ʿAli, the head of the Divān (i.e. of Ghazna) Bu Saʿid b. Sahl, and the postal and intelligence officer Ḥasan b. ʿObeydallāh.[1] [F 737] The range of gifts bestowed [on Amir Saʿid] encompassed all the insignia of royalty.[2] The other princes, together with all the women of the royal household and their attendants, were transported at the time of the night worship to the fortresses of Nāy constructed by Masʿud and of Diri,[3] in accordance with the Amir's instructions. The Amir left Ghaznin on 4 Moḥarram [/6 October] and took up his quarters in the camp enclosure that had been erected in the Firuzi Garden, and he remained there for two days until the troops and other participants in their entirety embarked on the expedition, and then he too rode out with speed.

At Setāj[4] a letter arrived from the Vizier. He had written that "Following the royal command, I had plentiful provision of food and fodder got ready at Balkh, and when I left for Valvālej, Bu'l-Ḥasan, son of Hariva, remained behind as my deputy at Balkh in order to attend to any remaining business there. I exacted from the notables of the region a sworn pledge that they would put up a bold front, since the exalted banner would appear very soon.[5] When I reached Kholm,[6] a letter arrived from the postal and intelligence officer of Vakhsh[7] with the information that Böritegin was about to move to P.r.k.d[8] from his position amongst the Komijis with a group of these Komijis and Kanjina Turks[9] that had joined up with him in accordance with the alliance which he made with the chiefs of the Komijis,[10] and they are threatening Holbok;[11] and it is estimated that he has with him at least 3,000 cavalrymen. These troops have caused much havoc here, and in spite of Böritegin's continuing protestations that he is coming in order to serve the Sultan, the real situation is as I have described. Following the written instructions issued by the royal command, I stayed here for several days, while other letters kept arriving from the direction of Khottalān fulminating against him and [F 738] the pillaging and plundering that rages wherever those troops of his go. I considered it unwise to proceed to P.r.k.d, so I turned round and went towards Piruz-e Nakhchir[12] with the aim of going to Baghlān [Gh 558] and then to proceed from there by the Ḥashmgerd[13] road to Valvālej. If Böritegin sweeps into Khottalān and crosses the Panj river,[14] having presumptuous ideas in his head, I shall go to the S.n.k.v.y valley[15] and hasten to render service to the exalted stirrup, since there is no point in going to Tokhārestān; for ever since this disaster which befell the Great Chamberlain at Sarakhs, every scoundrel[16] has begun harbouring delusions of his own. Food and fodder have been collected together at Valvālej, and a letter despatched with instructions that both the tax-collectors and the military governor should be on the alert and watch closely over that region. In addition to all this, I wrote a letter to Böritegin and despatched an envoy and pointed out the deplorable happenings in Vakhsh and Khottalān, and I said bluntly that 'The Sultan has set out from Ghaznin. If your avowed intention in coming is to manifest your obedience, one can see no sign of it.' I have a feeling that, when this letter reaches him, he will stay put. I have set forth everything so that the Amir will be fully informed. I am eagerly awaiting a speedy reply so that I may act in accordance with the royal command, if God Most High wills."

The Amir was disconcerted by this letter, and ordered a reply to be sent in these terms: "We have now set out, and are coming by the road through the Ghuzak pass. The Vizier should come to Baghlān, and from there to Andarāb, where he is to join up with us at the stage of Chowgāni."[17] This letter had been despatched by swift *kheyltāsh*s.

The Amir travelled along very speedily, halted at Parvān for one day only and traversed the Ghuzak pass. When he reached Chowgāni, he halted there for a few days until the baggage and impedimenta, the armoury, the elephants and the troops came up. The Vizier arrived and saw the Amir, and they talked privately together for a very long time. The Amir said to him, "First of all, Böritegin should be tackled, for he is an enemy and the son of an enemy.[18] Since there was no room for him to stay with his brother 'Eyn al-Dowla,[19] and he is too scared of the sons of 'Alitegin, and likewise of the Amir of Chaghāniyān, to dare to cross the outskirts of their territories, [F 739], he has come to us. Our domain and power must be regarded as the most innocuous and feeble, since whoever is on the run and has nowhere else to go, has to come this way. The Vizier replied, "Once the lord goes to Valvālej, it will become clear there what needs to be done."

The next day, the Amir moved off, kept up a good pace and encamped at Valvālej on Monday, 20 Moḥarram [/22 October], made a short stop there, and came to Rāvan.[20] He made his plans to chase away Böritegin and declared that he would himself go to drive him out, and he made preparations to get to Böritegin. Böritegin had got news of the Sultan, [Gh 559] so he turned back from the Panj river and halted on its farther bank. He had written a reply to the Vizier's letter, stating that he was coming to render service, and that what had occurred in Vakhsh and the region of Holbok had taken place without his knowledge. The Vizier said to the Sultan, "Perhaps it would be wiser if the lord did not embark upon this attack but remained here at Rāvan[21] until Böritegin's envoy arrives and we can hear what he has to say. If he talks sense,[22] we can summon Böritegin, welcome him with favours and set up all the necessary binding agreements, for he is a sprightly and valiant individual, and has a powerful contingent of men. We can use him this way, with a strong army and commander, against the Turkmens, for he is better acquainted with their methods of warfare. The lord should stay at Balkh and control and mete out resources from there. The Commander-in-Chief should go to Merv with a fully-equipped army, and the Great Chamberlain should make his way with another army towards Herat and Nishapur; they should attack the enemy and do their utmost to destroy them so that they are all dislodged, killed, captured or put to flight and the banks of the Oxus secured. I myself will go to Khwarazm and recapture that region, for when the Sultan's troops who are there, and the former troops of Altuntāsh, know about the Amir's coming to Balkh and my own marching on Khwarazm from here, they will abandon Altuntāsh's sons and return to obedience, and the region will be purged of sedition." [F 740]

The Amir answered, "The Vizier's proposals are all unsound. I intend to deal with this myself, and that's why I have come in person; for the troops are not doing what I have told them to do, but in my personal presence they will sacrifice their lives, willingly or not. Böritegin is worse than the Turkmens, since he is an opportunist who seized the occasion to invade and plunder the greater part of Khottalān; if we had arrived any later, he would have devastated those regions. I shall start with him, and when I am finished with him I shall then tackle the rest (i.e. the Turkmens)." The Vizier said, "We servants must set forth and explain all the aspects and considerations which we deem and know to be the best policy; but the lord's judgement is superior." The Commander-in-Chief, the Great Chamberlain and the commanders who were present in that private session said, "Böritegin is a mere brigand on the run; why should one attach such importance to him for the lord to lead an attack in person? What then are we useful for?" The Vizier concurred with them. The Amir replied, "We'll send our son Mowdud." The Vizier said, "That, too, is not a wise course of action." In the end, they agreed that the Commander-in-Chief should go. In the course of this same session, the names of 10,000 cavalrymen were registered (i.e. for the expedition). They went back and got everything ready, and the army set off for Khottalān the next day, Thursday, [Gh 560] 24 Moḥarram [/26 October].

I heard from my master Bu Naṣr, who said: When we had finished this private session, the Vizier said to me, "You see these acts of wilfulness[23] and misguided measures which this lord has embarked upon? I fear that Khorasan will slip away from our possession, since nothing augurs well for us." I replied, "The Vizier has been away from us for a long time; [F 741] this lord is not that same person whom he knew in the past, and has no time for any advice. God the Exalted One has a preordained plan in these matters, which no human being can comprehend. We have no choice but silence and forbearance. Nevertheless, we owe it to the Amir to speak our mind, whether it be listened to or not."

When the Commander-in-Chief departed, the Amir set off for the borders of Guzgānān.[24]

An account of ʿAli Qohandezi and his arrest

There was a man in those regions called ʿAli Qohandezi who had been in those lands for a while and had carried out some robberies and pillaged a few places. A bunch of sharp and cunning criminals had joined up with him, and they would attack caravans and plunder villages. News of this had reached the Amir, but no matter whom he sent to enforce the law, the trouble could not be put down. At the time when the Amir came there, this ʿAli Qohandezi had secured control of a place which was called "the citadel" (*qohandez*) and which held a strong fortress in a network of tunnels at the top of a mountain.[25] In no way was it possible to storm it by direct attack. He shut himself up there and installed many thieves and desperadoes (*ʿayyār*)[26] there with their baggage and possessions. During this period of weak control over Khorasan, they perpetrated many atrocities, preying on travellers along the roads and killing people, and ʿAli had acquired great notoriety. When he heard the news that the exalted banner had reached Rāvan,[27] he crept into this cavernous hideout and prepared for war, since he had very extensive supplies of food and fodder, running water and pasture on that mountain, with only one means of access; and he felt sure of its impregnability.

The Amir encamped on the banks of a river on this road, at a distance of half-a-parasang from this subterranean stronghold. The army collected a great deal of food and fodder, and there were no shortages; all around them [F 742] was green with vegetation, for there is no limit to that in the region of Guzgānān, a land of excellent pastures and extensive grasslands.[28] By virtue of the fact that he was governor of Guzgānān, Nushtegin Nowbati[29] sought to lead that military campaign. Although his beard was still not yet grown,[30] and he was part of the palace household,[31] the Amir consented, and he and a force of fifty beardless gholāms [Gh 561] of his went to the foot of that cavernous fortress. A force of 500 palace gholāms also went off with him and some three or four thousand men from various groups of the army likewise accompanied him: some came to participate, while others looked on. Nushtegin led the attack and battle was joined. They made little impression on the defenders of the fortress, who showered them with stones.

Bāytegin, my master's gholām, had also come along with his shield to give a hand. (This Bāytegin is still alive, an adroit and capable fellow, a warrior and cavalryman, a master in wielding all kinds of weapons, so that he is peerless in the game of polo.[32] At this present moment, the year 451 [/1059], when I have brought the History thus far, he is in the service of the lord, the mighty Sultan Abu'l-Moẓaffar Ebrāhim, *may God illumine his proof*, and performs his duties within the immediate royal vicinity, overseeing the polo playing, the use of weapons, the javelin and archery, and other physical and military exercises (*riyāżat-hā*). Thus my master's charismatic powers and aura, and his satisfaction with Bāytegin's conduct, finally bore fruit and secured him such a lofty position.)

This Bāytegin threw himself before Nushtegin Nowbati. The latter said, "Where are you going, for ahead of us rocks are pelting down, and each can bring down a man? If any harm comes to you, no-one will escape the wrath of the Khᵛāja 'Amid Bu Naṣr." Bāytegin answered, "I'll go ahead a little way, and indulge in some reconnoitring." He went off. Stones were raining down, but he [F 743] managed to protect himself. Then he shouted out, "I've come as an envoy, stop hurling stones!" They stopped doing this, and he went on as far as the foot of the cave. They let down a rope and pulled him up. He found himself in an impregnable place of fearful aspect, and he said to himself, "Now I'm trapped!" They took him into the presence of 'Ali Qohandezi, passing through a large number of men on the way, all armed to the teeth. 'Ali questioned him, "What brings you here? If you had seen Bu Naṣr before coming, you would never have risked your neck like this, for Bu Naṣr would never have agreed to such a venture; and who is this boy whom you have come with?" He replied, "This youth who has sought to attack you is the Amir of Guzgānān, and is just one gholām out of a total of 6,000 gholāms that the Sultan possesses. He has given me a verbal message for you, to the effect that 'It would be a pity if, through a man like you, the populace and the province should be brought to ruin. Come in peace so that I can take you to the lord's presence and secure for you a robe of honour and a senior military command'."

'Ali said, "There should be a guarantee of safe conduct and some token of assurance." Bāytegin had a seal-ring set with jade which he drew out, and said, "This is the lord Sultan's ring. He gave it to Amir

Nushtegin, and instructed him to send it to you." [Gh 562] The end had come for that benighted fool, and he was taken in by these words. He arose with the intention of coming down, but his followers clung to him and tried to frighten him off by telling him that he had been duped, but he took no heed, until he approached the entrance to the fortress. Then, however, he had second thoughts and turned back. But his hour had come; Bāytegin brought his full arsenal of deception into play at a time when 'Ali's own powers of reasoning had been impaired by his brazen acts of violence and brutality, and he agreed to come down. Meanwhile, a very large force of royal gholāms had arrived at the foot of the cave and they forced open the door. 'Ali was grabbed by the sleeve by Bāytegin and brought down. His capture meant the end of the siege, since our troops came along and the fortress fell readily into their hands. [F 744] They plundered it and took all the fighting men as prisoners. The news reached the Amir. Nushtegin took all the credit for himself, and he rose in rank and repute, though it had all been Bāytegin's doing in reality. Bāytegin was at that time very young and yet could perform such deeds. Today, when a monarch of such greatness—*may God perpetuate his rule*—has raised him up and made him one of his intimates, if he now finds great fortune and favour, one can imagine what great achievements he will be capable of accomplishing. I have thus done justice to my master's protégé Bāytegin, who is just like a brother to me, and I have fulfilled my obligation to history by describing how this fortress was taken. The Amir ordered that the accursed villain, who had wrought such evil deeds and had unjustly shed so much blood, should be held prisoner in the guardhouse together with his fellow-malefactors. On the Wednesday, this 'Ali and 170 others were hanged (may we be kept away forever from such an evil fate!).[33] These gallows were in two lines and stretched from the door of that subterranean fortress as far as they could go. That network of underground passages was dug out and the fortress destroyed so that no evildoer should ever make it his refuge.[34]

The Amir moved off from there, and headed for Balkh. En route a letter arrived from the Commander-in-Chief 'Ali with the information that "Böritegin has fled and taken refuge amongst the Komijiis. What are my instructions? Should I go after him from Khottalān, should I remain there, or should I come back?" He was told that he was to come to Balkh so that he could be given his instructions. The

Amir reached Balkh on Thursday, 14 Ṣafar [/15 November 1038] and encamped in the Garden. The Commander-in-Chief ʿAli also arrived eleven days after us and saw the Amir, saying, "It would be advisable to go after this enemy, since he is harbouring all sorts of evil designs in his head," and he described how [F 745] the people of Khottalān had suffered under Böritegin and his troops, and how he and his followers had bragged and said that, if it was right and acceptable for the Seljuqs to conquer Khorasan, it was even more justifiable and proper for Böritegin to conquer Khorasan, since he was, after all, of princely lineage.[35]

Next day, the Amir had a private session with the Vizier and the notables, and he told them that the matter of Böritegin[Gh 563] should take precedence so that he could be done away with that winter, and then, when spring came round, the Turkmens could be attacked. The Vizier had meanwhile remained silent, and the Amir urged him to speak. The Vizier replied, "The business of waging war is a finely specialized matter for those who wield arms and lead the troops. I do my best to avoid speaking on such matters, for my words are not palatable to the lord." My master said, "The Grand Vizier has an obligation to express what is palatable and what is unpalatable alike, and even if the Sultan insists upon a course of action, when he has thought it over, he may accept the words of sincere and disinterested advisers." The Vizier said, "I consider it totally inadvisable for an army to be deployed in such a freezing time of the year. Armies should be deployed at two seasons only: either around the time of the New Year (Nowruz) when the grass has already sprouted, or at the time when the wheat is ripe.[36] We have a more urgent task at hand, and it would be most unwise to divert our troops to engage Böritegin. In my opinion, letters should be sent both to the governor of Chaghāniyān and also to the sons of ʿAlitegin, who are sworn allies of ours, enjoining them to pursue this man and drive away his followers. In this way, the task may be accomplished; moreover, if there is a débâcle, it will be a matter for one of our two allies (i.e. the governor of Chaghāniyān or ʿAlitegin's sons) and it would be their loss, not ours." All of those present said that this was a sound piece of advice. The Sultan said, "Let me have time to think about this thoroughly," and they went back.

Afterwards, the Amir said, "The best course of action is that an attack should be launched against this man," [F 746] and on the eighth of the month of Rabiʿ I [/8 December 1038] a letter went off to Begtegin Chowgān-dār,[37] the former retainer of Maḥmud, with the command that a bridge was to be thrown over the river Oxus, because the exalted stirrup was intending to undertake a campaign in the very near future. (The Amir had given the custodianship of the fortress of Termez to this Begtegin after Qotlogh, the former retainer of Sebüktegin; he was a redoubtable and stout warrior, and he held many army commands, as I have mentioned in several places in this work.[38]) The answer came back that "An extremely strong and firmly-built bridge has been constructed from both banks, with the island in the middle. Equipment and materials, and boats, were all on site, left over from that time when Amir Maḥmud had ordered a bridge to be constructed. Now that the bridge has been constructed on both this bank and the other one, I have placed some guards to be on watch night and day lest some enemy attempt to sabotage and destroy it."[39]

When this reply arrived, the Amir began to prepare to move off, with the intention of going there in person.[40] No-one dared to say anything on this topic, since the Amir was highly perturbed by the volume of sundry reports of fresh disasters arriving daily.

The previous nine years had witnessed a repeated series of unwise measures,[41] [Gh 564] and now their repercussions were at last beginning to be felt. The wonder was that the Amir did not abandon his wilfulness; and yet how could he, since the Most High Creator's foreordained decree had been lying hidden in wait? The Vizier said to my master on many occasions, "Do you see what he intends to do? He is planning to cross the river at such a time as this (i.e. in mid-winter) to repel Böritegin because he came into Khottalān and crossed the Panj river! God only knows what this will lead to, for it is beyond comprehension." Bu Naṣr replied, "The only way is to hold one's tongue, for there's no point in offering advice if it rebounds and begets mistrust. [F 747] The army leaders at court were all aware of this, and debated its various aspects once they were outside the court, and had even pressed the Chief Inspector (*moshref*) Bu Saʿid to write (i.e. to deter the Amir from his intention), but to no avail. Once in the Amir's presence, however, they would trim their words to accord with his views, or else they would have to face his wrath.

On Friday, the thirteenth of the month of Rabiʿ I [/13 December 1038],[42] the secretary Bu'l-Qāsem [b. Ḥātemak,] who held the post of postal and intelligence officer of Balkh, died. I have already given an account of this Bu'l-Qāsem elsewhere in this History, and there is no point in repeating this.[43] Next day, the Amir gave the office of the postal and intelligence service back to Amirak Beyhaqi.[44] My master had given him strong support in this matter, and had repaired the breach between him and the Vizier so that the way was clear for him to resume that office. He was given a fine robe of honour.

On Saturday, the sixteenth of this month,[45] a letter arrived from Ghaznin with news of the death of Amir Saʿid, God's mercy be upon him. The Amir was in the inner quarters of the palace, drinking wine. They left the letter in its place and did not dare to give him such news when he was in the midst of wine-drinking. The next day, when he assumed his place on the throne but before he declared the court session open, they had arranged that a servant should bring in this letter, present it and go back. When the Amir read the letter, he came down from his throne and let out a great sigh of lamentation, which resounded in the inner regions of the palace. He ordered the servants who had raised the curtain giving admittance to the portico to lower it, and an announcement came that there was to be no court session that day. The gholāms were sent back, and [Gh 565] the Vizier, the retainers and the courtiers came into the loggia and sat there in the open until the mid-morning in case the Amir should sit publicly for the mourning ceremony; but he sent a verbal message telling them that he would not do so and that they should go home, and they went back. [F 748]

The death of this young prince, before he could see anything of this world, is a tale that I must ineluctably narrate. The Amir held him the most dear of all his sons,[46] and wished to have him as the designated heir to his throne, but the Almighty God had decided on Amir Mowdud as his father's successor; what then could the father do? Before the news of his death arrived, letters came that he was stricken with smallpox. The Amir was deeply perplexed and fraught and was saying, "This son has already had smallpox once; a second attack is most odd." But it was not smallpox that had struck this unfledged youth. He was not able to function properly as a man, and lie with a woman and enjoy sexual intercourse. They had not consulted a physician who would have treated him in a proper professional manner, for he was not constitutionally impotent, and with young people temporary impotence is a common occurrence. Instead, in their usual wily and insidious way, the women had claimed that the prince had been rendered impotent through sorcery.[47] An old woman split open a goat's gall-bladder and drew out from it a liquid, threw some concoction into it and gave it to this dear youth to drink. No sooner had he drunk this than his entire body[48] went limp and he went into a coma for eleven days and then passed away.

The Amir had mourned the death of this son in the inner chambers of the palace and had openly displayed his desolation and grief. This unexpected death had also other unfortunate repercussions; henceforth no-one was able to tell the Amir that it would be unwise to cross the Oxus river, for he was not receiving anyone for an audience and had, unheralded, mounted his steed and set off for Termez.

Within these two days the Vizier received the verbal message that "I must of necessity set off. You, together with my son Mowdud, are to remain at Balkh with the army, comprising palace gholāms and other elements of the troops, which we designated here. [F 749]. The Great Chamberlain Sübashï is to go to the Vale of Gaz, where he has stationed palace gholāms and horses and weapons, and he is to take with him 2,000 Turkish and Indian cavalrymen as well as his own gholāms and cavalrymen. The Commander of the Palace Gholāms Begtughdï is to remain here[49] at the head of the force of gholāms. The Commander-in-Chief is to come with us,[50] together with troops of the army including the senior commanders, field officers and chamberlains[51] who have been registered for such duties. All this must be attended to." [Gh 566] The Vizier in turn relayed his obedience and remained at the court until around the time of the evening worship until everything was arranged.

The Amir set out from Balkh heading for Termez on Monday, the nineteenth of this month [/19 December 1038]. He crossed by the bridge and encamped on the plain facing the fortress of Termez. My master accompanied the Amir on this journey, and I went with him. It was bitterly cold, colder than anyone could remember in their lifetime. He left Termez on Thursday, the twenty-second of this month [/22 December] and reached [the town of] Chaghāniyān[52] on Sunday, 30 Rabiʿ I [/30 December]. From there he set off on Wednesday, 3 Rabiʿ II [/2 January 1039] and travelled along the road of the valley of Shumān[53] since there were reports that Böritegin was there. The cold there was of another degree of intensity, and snow fell continuously. The army suffered more hardships on this expedition than on any other.

On Tuesday, the ninth of this month [/8 January], a letter arrived from the Vizier, brought by the riders [F 750] who had been stationed at regular intervals along the road. He had mentioned that "Reports have arrived that from Sarakhs Dāvud had headed for Guzgānān with a strong force and with the intention of taking the Andkhud road and reaching the banks of the Oxus. It appears that his intention thereby is to destroy the bridge, seize the territories along the river and stir up a great amount of trouble. I have set forth this state of affairs so that measures may be taken to deal with it, since I myself am in a difficult position.[54] If, God forbid, they destroy the bridge, there will be a great loss of prestige for the Amir."

The Amir became extremely worried and downcast. Böritegin had left Shumān and had seized control of the valley, since he was familiar with that region and had competent guides. On Friday, the twelfth of this month [/11 January], having failed to achieve his aim, the Amir turned back from there and pushed on speedily till he reached Termez. Böritegin bided his time and seized part of the Amir's baggage and impedimenta, and some camels and several horses which were being led along in reserve were also carried off, resulting in a loss of face and much concern.[55] The Amir reached Termez on Friday, 26 Rabiʿ II [/25 January]. The castellan Begtegin Chowgān-dār had accompanied the Amir on this expedition and had done various laudable acts of service. In the same way, his deputies and the field officers of the fortress had kept careful guard here. The Amir heaped lavish praises on them and ordered robes of honour for them. The next day he was in Termez itself, and then he crossed by the bridge on Sunday, the twenty-seventh of this month, and then came to Balkh on Wednesday, 2 Jomādā I [/30 January].

Letters arrived from Nishapur on Monday, the seventh of this month [/4 February], with the information that [Chaghrï Beg] Dāvud [F 751] had gone to Nishapur to see [Gh 567] his brother and had stayed there for forty days at Shādyākh in that very palace of Masʿud's. Ṭoghrïl gave him a present of 500,000 dirhams. It was the Sālār of Buzgān who had gathered together this sum of money and other monies that were involved in the transaction. Then he went back from Nishapur to Sarakhs, intending to make for Guzgānān.

On Wednesday, 8 Jomādā II [/7 March], the Amir celebrated the festival of Nowruz.[56] On the Friday, the tenth of this month [/9 March], the news arrived that Dāvud had come to Ṭālaqān with a powerful and well-equipped army. On Thursday, the sixteenth of this month [/15 March], further news arrived that he had come to Pāryāb and would proceed in haste to Shoburqān; wherever they went, there was plundering and bloodshed. During the night of Saturday, the eighteenth of this month [/17 March], ten Turkmen riders came up to the vicinity of the Sultan's Garden, bent on thieving, and they killed four Indian infantrymen. From there they turned to the citadel, where the elephants were kept. They saw an elephant and spotted a lad asleep on its back. The Turkmens came along and started to drive the elephant away while the lad was still asleep. They went on for a parasang from the town and then woke the lad up, saying, "Drive on the elephant faster, for if you don't, we'll kill you!" He submitted to their demand and began to drive it along, with the Turkmen riders coming up behind, pressing and prodding it with spears. By daybreak they had put a great distance behind them, and they brought the elephant to Shoburqān. Dāvud rewarded the riders with presents of money and ordered the elephant to be taken towards Nishapur. This incident resulted in much adverse comment, and people wondered at the amount of negligence that would allow the adversary to carry off an elephant from their midst. The Amir heard about this the next day. He became very annoyed, [F 752] and heaped reproaches on the elephant keepers. He ordered that 100,000 dirhams should be taken from them as the price of the elephant, and several of the Indian elephant keepers were beaten.[57]

On Monday, the twentieth of this month [/19 March], Altï Sokmān,[58] Dāvud's chamberlain, with 2,000 cavalrymen, came to the gates of Balkh, halted at a place there called Band-e Kāferān[59] and plundered two villages. When the news reached the town, the Amir became very concerned, because the horses, and the Great Chamberlain at the head of an army, were at the Vale of Gaz. He called for his weapons, so that he might gird these on and ride out with the palace gholāms who possessed horses. A great commotion arose at the court. The Vizier and the Commander-in-Chief came in, and they said, "May the lord's life be prolonged! What's happened that the lord is repeatedly asking for his arms? They have sent a man of a somewhat senior rank (*moqaddam*), so we should send someone of equivalent rank. If a more powerful and impressive figure [Gh 568] is required,[60] the Commander-in-Chief can go." He replied, "What am I to do? These chicken-livered troops of ours will not exert themselves and are bringing shame upon us!" (This was the usual harsh rebuke from this monarch.) Finally, it was decided that a general, together with a cavalry force, partly made up from the body of the *kheyltāsh*s and the rest made up of troops from various ethnic groups, should go. The Commander-in-Chief went off in pursuit of the Turkmens in a stealthy and low-key manner, with no fanfares or flags. At the time of the afternoon worship, battle was joined and a fierce engagement took place. Several people on both sides were killed or wounded. At nightfall, Altï retreated and came to 'Ali-ābād.[61] It was said that he remained there during that night; he informed Dāvud about what had happened, and the latter came from Shoburqān to 'Ali-ābād.

On Thursday, the twenty-second of this month [/21 March], news arrived, and a great clamour and hubbub arose from 'Ali-ābād. The Amir ordered the army to be prepared; the horses were brought back from the Vale of Gaz and the Great Chamberlain Sübashï came back with the army. The Amir set out from Balkh on Thursday, 1 Rajab [/29 March] and encamped at Pol-e Kārvān,[62] and the army contingents [F 753] arrived there. He ordered the army to assume its battle formation (I was there myself), and he set out from there with an army fully-equipped and arrayed for battle, together with thirty elephants, the greater part of them in rut hence in a most belligerent state.

On Monday, the ninth of the month [/6 April], the enemy appeared on the plain around 'Ali-ābād from the direction of the desert. The Sultan took up his position on an eminence, mounted on a female elephant, and the army gave battle. Everyone was saying of Dāvud, "What boldness and insolence to confront such a mighty sovereign on his own without his brother or leading men and people at his side!" There was intense fighting on both sides, and I witnessed the clash of battle formations such as I had never hitherto seen in my life! I thought that before midday our army would have cleared off the enemy from the field, since there were in our army 6,000 palace gholāms as well as other groups (*aṣnāf*) of the troops. But I was proven wrong, for the battle intensified, and while on the actual field of battle less than 500 cavalrymen were engaged in actual fighting, the rest of the army stood by watching, and when one contingent of troops grew tired, another contingent who were fresh and rested would take up the struggle. Things went on in this manner till round the time of the midday worship. The Amir became perturbed and called for a horse and in his fully-armed state exchanged the elephant for a horse as his mount. He sent a man to Begtughdï with instructions that he was to send a thousand hand-picked, warlike gholāms, fully fitted with body armour and with fine horses, and several other groups of soldiers also gathered round as reinforcements. The Amir personally led a charge into the field of battle, and then he halted and the gholāms pressed on and the enemy fled headlong, with every man anxious to save his own skin. A number of the enemy were killed and a group of twenty of them captured. The remainder went off in scattered groups towards the direction of the desert. The royal troops [Gh 569] wanted to pursue them, but the Amir sent troop commanders to restrain them from pursuing the routed foe, saying that "It would be wrong to run risks in the desert. Our aim is to wipe them out altogether, and those Turkmens who had come to fight us here have had a foretaste of our might." But if only he had gone after them, not one of the enemy would have escaped, for a month late, the true picture emerged. We learnt through our spies and agents [F 754] that the enemy had said, "No-one can possibly stand up against the military might of this monarch in a full engagement, and we would have been in a sorry state if they had come after us when we had taken to flight." The captured Turkmens were brought in and interrogated about their situation. They stated that "Dāvud came to this region without Ṭoghrïl's assent and instructions, saying, 'I'll just reconnoitre and test the waters for a while'." The Amir ordered that they were to be provided for and set free. He then came and encamped at ʿAliābād for a day and then turned back, entering Balkh on Saturday, 17 Rajab [/14 April], and he stayed there till the reinforcements he had requisitioned from Ghaznin arrived.[63]

A letter arrived from Böritegin[64] with a messenger, filled with excuses for his previous conduct. The Amir ordered a conciliatory reply to be sent, for when the ruler of Chaghāniyān had died while still young, leaving behind no sons, this man Böritegin went along and, with the backing of the Komijis, seized Chaghāniyān. Open and violent hostilities flared up between him and the sons of ʿAlitegin; and the Amir, facing troubles of his own, thought it for the time being best that there should be enmity between the two groups and to let dog eat dog (lit. "*the dogs should be at the cows' throats*")[65] and ensure that each should be entangled with the other, so that, during his own absence, no harm should come to his realm from them. But in the end, things did not work out that way. I shall narrate what in fact did happen, for it was most strange and remarkable, and it shows what the decree of Fate had in store, and how far beyond our reckoning and conjectures it was.

On Saturday, 15 Shaʿbān [/12 May], the Amir left Balkh for Sarakhs, with a complete panoply of troops and equipment. Everyone agreed that it was an army capable of subduing the entire region of Turkestan. There were short stops on the way to allow the troops [F 755] who had been commanded to come from other places to join up. On Sunday, 1 Ramażān [/27 May], he reached Ṭālaqān.[66] He stayed there for two days and then set out with his troops deployed in military formation.

Swift couriers [Gh 570] and spies arrived with the information that "Ṭoghrïl has arrived in Sarakhs from Nishapur, where Dāvud already was, and Yabghu too has come there from Merv. It is said that they have around 20,000 cavalrymen and have decided to come forward and engage in battle and see what happens. They intend to stand for battle at Ṭalkhāb and Dih-e Bāzargān.[67] Ṭoghrïl and the Yïnāliyān were saying that 'Ray, Jebāl and Gorgān lie open to us and there is only a bunch of troops busy feeding off the people[68] and some Deylamites and Kurds there. We should go there and distance ourselves from here for a long while, for we shall face no opposition on the borders of Rum (i.e. Asia Minor), and we should let go of Khorasan and these regions with its mighty ruler and his numerous subjects and vast army.'

"Dāvud replied, 'You are suffering under a great delusion! If you move one step away from Khorasan, you will not be secure from this monarch's machinations and from the powerful opponents which he will stir up against us from every direction. I was present at the military engagement at ʿAli-ābād. They have more than a sufficiency of men and equipment, but they are overburdened with baggage and impedimenta and are unable to extricate themselves from them since they can't survive without them. They are therefore stuck with the dilemma whether to fend for themselves or for their baggage, while we are footloose and travel light. The disasters that overtook Begtughdï and Sübashï stemmed from the heavy burden of their baggage, whereas our baggage is thirty parasangs behind us, and we are ready and prepared for action. So let us face battle valiantly and see what the Exalted God has decreed for us!' They all approved of this plan and decided to act upon it.

"Böritegin appeared particularly forward and eager to fight, and so were those men who had fled [F 756] to the Turkmens' encampment, comprising the former followers of Amir Yusof, the Great Chamberlain ʿAli Qarib, Ghāzi, Eryāruq and others.[69] Ṭoghrïl and Yabghu said, 'These people should not be given the opportunity to default somewhere, lest they have been seduced by letters (i.e. from their former sovereign, Masʿud)!' Dāvud said, 'It is unwise to place them in the rear supporting the main body. They are men whose masters have been killed, and they have come here out of necessity, with other senior commanders, such as Soleymān, son of Arslān Jādheb and the General Qadïr.[70] All these and the rest, whoever they are, should be sent to the front line and we'll see what happens. Only this way shall we feel more secure, for if there is some treachery afoot, some of them will go over and join up again with their former lord (i.e. Masʿud), and if they fight on our side, so much the better.' They said, 'This too[71] sounds like the right policy,' and they told the fugitives from the Ghaznavid ranks that 'The Sultan has come, and we are hearing that you have been suborned (i.e. from your new allegiance to the Turkmens) and that, in the heat of the battlefield, you will turn tail. If such is the case, go now, for [Gh 571] if you go over to them in the midst of the mêlée, it may be that you will be prevented from doing so and some harm may come to you, and all bonds of consideration and amity[72] will be dissolved.' They all replied, 'They killed our masters, and we came to you out of fear for our lives and out of necessity, we will fight (i.e. for you against our former sovereign) to our last breath. This is why we want you to send us in advance as your vanguard, so that you will see what we can do and how we will show our mettle.' The Turkmen leaders said, 'No cause for doubt remains!' They nominated Böritegin, and he went forth in the vanguard with a thousand cavalrymen, most of them former troops of Sultan Masʿud who had deserted from the Sultan's army camp and sought refuge with the Turkmens; after him there came Soleymān, son of Arslān Jādheb, with a similar number of troops."

The battle with the Seljuqs in the desert of Sarakhs, and their flight

When the Amir learnt of this state of affairs, he adopted a different approach. [F 757] He had been under the impression that once his battle standard appeared on the scene, those gholāms who had defected to the Seljuqs would return en masse. They had put out this delusory impression, and we had bought it. On Wednesday, 18 Ramażān [/13 June], towards mid-morning, the scouting parties of the enemy came into view, some 300 cavalrymen, near Ṭalkhāb. We had arrived in the vicinity of our halting-place, and our baggage and impedimenta were coming along behind. The Amir halted, being mounted on an elephant, while the tent was being erected. The enemy's scouting party swept in to the attack, and from our side troops went out to confront them and a fierce fight broke out. Their troops kept on arriving, while more and more men from our side also joined in. They erected the tents and the Amir encamped with the army. The enemy turned back. They took stringent precautions within the military encampment during that night to avoid any lapses of security. At daybreak, the large kettle-drums were beaten, the army mounted with all its arms and went off in battle formation. When two parasangs had been traversed, a large military force of the enemy came into view, and the advance scouts of both sides came together in a fiercely-fought battle. Both sides fought strenuously until there came into view the vicinity of Dih-e Bāzargān, which had a river and copious springs, and the plain there was largely composed of sand and stones.

The Amir was mounted on a female elephant in the centre of the battle formation, and he rode on until he came to a sort of eminence, of only moderate height. He gave orders for the great tent to be erected there so that the army could encamp by the side of the river. The enemy began to rush in from all four quarters and a fierce encounter took place, with the Ghaznavid army suffering untold damage [Gh 572] before it was able to encamp and set up the tents. There was a genuine fear of an imminent calamity, but the leading figures and senior commanders of the army struggled hard and did their utmost until the camp was set up. Nevertheless, the enemy drove off large numbers of camels and killed or wounded some of our men. The ferocity of the onslaught came mainly from the defectors from our side, who wanted to show the Turkmens how unjustly they had been depicted [F 758] and how true to their word they had acted in battle, so that the Turkmens could be reassured, as indeed they were, since not one of the defectors crossed back to the other side. Our spies had in the past fabricated many lies on this topic and had been paid handsomely for it.[73] It now became apparent that this was all deception.

When the army encamped in its battle formation, the Sultan had stationed himself at the centre, with the Commander-in-Chief ʿAli commanding the right wing and the Great Chamberlain Sübashï in charge of the left wing, while Ertegin looked after the rearguard. The enemy drew back, established their army camp in our vicinity on the fringes of a stretch of grassland and encamped there, so that the drum roll in one camp could be heard in the other. We had with us a numerous force of infantrymen. They dug defensive ditches all around the perimeter of the army encampment, and in the course of this day, every possible sort of precaution was taken, for the Amir was a marvel at deploying armies and did everything that was humanly possible, but his star was not in the ascendant, and God Most High had other designs, and it turned out as He intended. Throughout the whole of our army, it was not possible to lead one camel a single step, and everyone held his beast secured in front of his tent.[74] At the time of the afternoon worship, a strong detachment of the enemy appeared on the scene and prevented our own troops from bringing back water from that river. The Amir sent the Generals Badr and Ertegin with a force of 500 gholāms to wipe out the foe and to let the enemy catch a glimpse of the awesome power confronting them. When night approached, a strong force of scouts went out in all four directions as a defensive precaution.

The next day, the enemy came on in greater numbers and joined the fray on three or even on all four directions. [F 759] Because it was the end of the month of Ramażān, the Amir did not ride out personally to the fighting but chose to engage in battle after the Festival of the Ending of the Fast was over, in order to avoid shedding blood during this month.[75] There was fierce fighting every day on several fronts. It was a veritable struggle to find fodder for the camels and to bring it in, given the fact that the enemy was deploying one to two thousand riders [Gh 573] on the left and right flanks, who were as bold and daring as they could be; and this shortage of fodder was making things more difficult. The Amir was very concerned and held several private consultations with the Vizier and the leading commanders, saying, "I was unaware of the gravity of the problem posed by these Turkmens, and was misled about the real state of affairs and not given the true facts needed for adopting appropriate measures at the outset. After the Festival, we must engage them in a pitched battle, and after that, we must adopt a different approach towards them." Thus the matter became protracted and sporadic warfare went on during the remaining days of the month of Ramażān.

When the month of Ramażān came to an end, the Amir celebrated the Festival. The enemy, amounting to around four or five thousand, approached us as we were engaged in performing the worship and showered us with a hail of arrows. After the worship, our troops gave them a severe trouncing, killing some 200 of them and taking much delight in exacting retribution,[76] and giving them a sharp foretaste of their might. The Amir praised those commanders who had carried out this skirmish along the river bank and ordered presents to be given to them.

All through the night operations went on, and in the morning, the large kettledrums were beaten. The Amir mounted a female elephant, surrounded by an escort of fifty led horses. The senior commanders had come, and took up their stations on the right flank, on the left flank, on the wings, in the place where the reserves and supplies were held,[77] in the vanguard and [F 760] in the rearguard.[78] The Amir called out to the Commander-in-Chief and said, "Go to your assigned position and keep on the alert, and don't join in the battle as long as you can help it, since today we want to accomplish this work ourself, with the help of God, the Exalted One."[79] He ordered the Great Chamberlain, "You go to the left flank, and be alert, and keep your eyes and ears open for our commands and movements.[80] When we launch our offensive, you should engage with the enemy's right flank in a measured way while the Commander-in-Chief engages with their left flank. I shall keep watch and will send you reinforcements from the wings, and we'll see how things turn out." He acknowledged and obeyed the command. The Commander-in-Chief went off, and Sübashï likewise. The Amir then ordered Ertegin to stay in the rearguard with 500 of the most redoubtable palace troops and 500 Indian cavalry, and said,

"Stay on the alert so that nothing happens to the baggage. Watch the road closely, and if you see anyone of our troops deserting from the battle line, he is to be hacked in two halves on the spot." He acknowledged the order and went off.

When the Amir had finished assigning all these tasks, he urged on his elephant and the army moved forward from its place. It was as if the whole earth was shaking, and the very firmament was bedazzled by the tumult of men and the din of large kettledrums, trumpets and drums! When one parasang had been covered, the enemy appeared with a very powerful army, and a complete array of equipment and weapons. They had deployed themselves for battle in an orderly formation in the manner of royal armies.[81] The battle intensified on all fronts, and I and other Persian civilian officials like me [Gh 574] lost all sense of where we were and what was happening around us.

A wind arose at the time of the afternoon worship, blowing around dust and dirt and making it impossible for people to see each other and breaking up the battle formations. I became separated from the centre and my position behind the elephants.[82] Those attendants who were with me, including gholāms and retainers, became separated from me,[83] [F 761] and I was terrified[84] when I looked round and found myself on another mound. I came across Bu'l-Fatḥ Bosti,[85] whom five or six of his gholāms had lifted down from his horse, and he was weeping. He was unable to remain on his horse on account of the pain from his gout. When he saw me he asked what was happening. I answered, "Don't worry, everything is fine, it's the wind that is causing some confusion!" As we were talking thus, the Sultan's ceremonial parasol came into view. He had abandoned the elephant for a horse, and seemed to be keeping a low profile,[86] and had with him 500 gholāms of the personal guard, all wearing mailed coats and carrying short spears; the black battle standard had been left behind in the centre.

I said to Bu'l-Fatḥ, "The Amir has come, and there's nothing amiss." His spirits revived and he said to the gholāms, "Set me on my mount." I prodded my horse and caught up with the Amir. He had halted, and Khalaf b. Maʿruf b. Rabiʿ, the confidant and counsellor and adjutant of the Great Chamberlain Sübashï,[87] and Amirak Khottali,[88] the trusted confidant of the Commander-in-Chief, had galloped there and were telling him, "The lord need not worry; the army formations remain intact, and the enemy are beaten and are frustrated in their wishes. However, all three of the Seljuq leaders, Ṭoghrïl, Dāvud and Yabghu, are pressing against our centre with the choicest of their warriors, and the Yïnāliyān and other commanders have hurled themselves against us. The lord should give his attention to the centre lest some disaster occurs." The Amir said to them, "It was because these three were heading towards the centre that I removed myself from there and embarked upon laying an ambush in order to bring about a decisive blow. Instruct everyone to be vigilant and to tread carefully, for in this very hour, with the help of the Almighty God, our task may well be accomplished!" They rode off at once. The Amir speedily despatched troop commanders [F 762] to the centre, with the instructions for the troops, "Be alert, for the bulk of the enemy's army is heading towards you while I am busy stalking them. Keep your ears pricked for my command; go up round the left side of the enemy until they get locked in fighting with you, and I shall then come up from behind." He ordered Begtughdï to send him a thousand warlike gholāms in mailed coats. The reply immediately came back that "The lord should rest assured, since all the world cannot move this centre; the enemy have come and have been reduced to confusion, [Gh 575] and our right and left flanks are in place."

The gholāms arrived, as well as two thousand cavalrymen, all fighting fit, and 2,000 infantrymen—men from Sistan, Ghaznin, Ghur and Balkh. The Amir took a spear and rode off with this large and well-equipped army and positioned himself on another hillock. I was with him, having become separated from my own group. In the distance, I spotted, on a sandy hillock, three black flags, and I came up facing the hillock and saw that the three were the Seljuq leaders, who had learnt that the Amir was heading towards them from the centre. A large tract of the desert separated these two hillocks. The Amir sent down infantrymen who had long spears and broad shields, and after them, 300 cavalrymen. The enemy sent into action a thousand cavalrymen from each of the two sides, but when they reached the desert tract, our infantry blocked their way with their spears, and our cavalry too were pressing on and charging from behind. The fighting was becoming extremely fierce when one of the black flags on the hillock detached itself along with 2,000 cavalrymen clad in mailed coats and made for the desert. We heard that it was Dāvud's flag. The

Amir galloped forward at great speed and shouted out, "Forward, my men!" The gholāms rushed forward and the Amir positioned himself below the hillock, and the gholāms and the remaining troops chosen for the ambush clashed with the enemy and dust flew up into the air. I stayed on the spot with a cavalryman not engaged in fighting, [F 763] and kept an eye on the Amir's ceremonial parasol, waiting to see what would happen. The main nucleus of the Amir's designated troops left their position and joined in. The world was filled with the din of the battle and the clash of steel, as if a million blacksmiths' hammers were pounding away, and I saw the flash of spears and swords amidst the dust of battle. God[89] vouchsafed us the victory, and the three Seljuq leaders took to flight, and the rest [of the Turkmens] followed them so that not a single foe remained behind.

The Amir appeared in the howdah of an elephant and pursued the fugitives for half-a-parasang or so. I too rode off with the cavalryman until we caught up with the Amir. The Great Chamberlain and the senior commanders began to arrive. They kissed the ground and offered congratulations for the victory. The Amir asked, "What should be done now?" They answered, "A tent has already been erected on the edge of so-and-so river, on its left bank. One should proceed there and encamp in an auspicious state, since the enemy has taken to flight and has suffered a crushing defeat, and a commander whom the lord should nominate can pursue the fugitives." Bu'l-Ḥasan b. ʿAbd al-Jalil[90] said, "The lord should seize this chance (i.e. strike while the iron is hot) and go after the fugitives for a couple of parasangs, and take upon himself further trouble and pain in order that he may be free of them once and for all, and encamp there." The Commander-in-Chief shouted out at him—there was bad blood between the two of them—and said, "Are you now waxing lyrical about warfare too? Why don't you trim your words to suit your own state!" The other commanders all said the same, and the Amir was not too displeased with their words. [Gh 576] Bu'l-Ḥasan was reduced to silence. Subsequently, it turned out that the poor fellow had given the correct advice, for if the Sultan had gone after them in hot pursuit, the Turkmens would have found it impossible to fend for themselves. But no created being can prevail over its Creator, and since it was foreordained that these fellows, the Seljuqs, should attain to such heights, what chance had a sound policy of being implemented?

Böri,[91] the Master of the Royal Stables and a few other commanders were sent in pursuit of the fleeing enemy. They went off, already in an exhausted condition, with a force of cavalrymen feeling very much the same way. They flaunted themselves for a while[92] [F 764] and then found a place to take a rest and returned to the army camp at the time of the evening prayer. They said that they had covered a considerable distance but had not come across anyone, and that it was clear that the enemy had withdrawn into the sandy desert and the wilderness; and since the troops did not have the necessary supplies and equipment for operating in such a terrain (*ālat-e biyābān*), they had returned to avoid any potential disasters. This excuse of theirs was accepted.[93] I shall recount what happened after this. If the Amir had not encamped where he did and had gone after the enemy, all of the troops *would have obediently followed him*.[94] But I have said that God Most High did not will this, and the decree of Fate was thus. *There is no escape from His decree!*[95]

Meanwhile, the Amir called out to me, "Where's Bu Naṣr Moshkān?" I replied, "May the lord's life be prolonged! He and Bu Sahl Zowzani were together in front of the elephants, and I was there too. When the dust storm blew up, I found myself separated from them and alone, and I made my way here; by now they should have settled in the camp." He said, "Go, and tell Bu Naṣr to prepare the draft of a proclamation of victory (*fatḥ-nāma*)." I obeyed the command and went back. The Amir gave instructions to two troop commanders, telling them, "Go with Bu'l-Fażl as far as the army encampment." The troop commanders came with me. I had to go a long way to get to the army encampment. I found my master and Bu Sahl Zowzani seated there, with their coats and boots on, and with horses saddled, having already heard the news of the victory. They called out to me,[96] I sat down and gave my master the verbal message. He said, "This augurs well!", and questioned me about what had happened. I gave him a full report. He said to Bu Sahl, [F 765] "The right decision was the one that Bu'l-Ḥasan b. ʿAbd al-Jalil thought of, but they won't let this lord follow the right course." [Gh 577] Both of them mounted their steeds and went to meet up with the Amir. They gave due greetings and offered up benedictions and congratulations for the victory, and having discussed various topics, rendered service and departed. When my master got back, he wrote out a draft of this victory proclamation in a most elegant style. I myself wrote out the fair copy and took it along at the time of the afternoon worship. The Amir read and approved it, and said, "You must keep it, since tomorrow we are going to Sarakhs, and when we encamp there, more victory proclamations will have to be composed, and envoys conveying the good news can go out with it."

The next day, 3 Shavvāl [/28 June], the Sultan mounted, and with the army in its battle formation, set off in a very happy frame of mind. He came to within two stages from Sarakhs, and on Thursday, 5 Shavvāl [/30 June], they encamped by a stream with plenty of water. A scouting party of the enemy appeared there, but did not offer battle; instead, they showed their presence and then turned back. The town of Sarakhs, hitherto so verdant and prosperous, now appeared before us as a desolate wasteland. The fact that the enemy's scouts had been sighted here troubled the Amir, and he said to the leading men, "Can there be any people more impudent than these? We would have thought that, after that mauling which they received, they would not have reined in their mounts until they reached the Oxus shores and the Balkhān mountains." They replied, "That style of warfare and a complete withdrawal after defeat belongs to royal and princely armies, for when the Qarakhanids suffered defeat at the hands of the late Sultan,[97] no-one saw anything more of a single one of them. But here we are dealing with a bunch of rebels and misfits, and if they plan to return they will get a worse hammering than they got before." At the time of the afternoon worship, news arrived that the enemy had come back to within two parasangs. They had brought with them a work force[98] and they were diverting the waters of this channel and intended to deliver battle again. The Amir became extremely worried.

During the night, spies and swift couriers arrived, bringing with them confidential letters from the secret agents. [F 766] They had written that "These people sat down together and consulted with each other, and they said, 'It's not a good plan to go out and confront this monarch in a pitched battle; rather, we should keep to our own ways. We are not tied down by our baggage and impedimenta, and now that we are faced with such a formidable force,[99] we must disperse our forces and harass and unnerve him so that he has to go back, whether willingly or not. The winter months have gone and summer has come along.[100] We are people of the desert and accustomed to enduring hardship. We can put up with both the heat and the cold, whereas he and his army are not able to do so. They will only be able to endure hardships for a certain length of time, and then they will turn back'."

My master then laid these letters before the Amir, and he became most despondent and anxious. Next day, after the court session, he had a private session with the Vizier and the leading men. He told them about these reports and the confidential letters were read out to them. [Gh 578] The Amir said, "What do you suggest?" They replied, "Whatever the lord commands, we will do. What does the lord think about this?" He said, "I have come to the conclusion that I should remain here, prepare for desert warfare and confront them with another pitched battle, and when they are put to flight, go after them as far as the banks of the Oxus." The Vizier replied, "We must think of a better idea than this. It's a bad time of year and it would be wrong to take risks." As they were talking, the water stopped flowing in the stream.[101] They reported this to the Amir. It was early in the morning and our scouting party rushed in with the news that the enemy had appeared on all four sides of the army encampment. (The tents were pitched in such a narrow space and so close together that there was little distance between the army's right and left flanks and the centre, in a way that I had never encountered before.) The Amir turned towards the commanders around him and said, "Up you get! Arise so that we can mount and face the enemy!" They answered, "The lord [F 767] should remain where he is, since the commanders of the Seljuqs, according to what they are saying, have not come. We ourselves will go off and do whatever is necessary; should we need help, we will ask for it." They went back and prepared themselves for fighting and went off towards the enemy. The Vizier and my master remained with the Amir for a while and managed to console him. The arrangements for the despatch of the victory proclamations and their messengers were shelved for the time being to see how things would develop. Then they went back.

We were deprived of running water and had to use water from wells—there were many wells in this area where we were, only a short distance from the town of Sarakhs—and what was left of the ice[102] they were unable to fetch because of the enemy's raiding and their tight grip on us. There was fierce fighting until the time of the afternoon worship, and many men were wounded or killed on both sides. Our own troops came back in a deeply depressed state. Our opponents had the upper hand, and our men appeared listless and exhausted as if drained of all vigour and stamina. Informers from within the army's ranks relayed this news to the Amir, and the leading figures of the army and the commanders likewise secretly sent verbal messages to the Vizier by means of their confidential aides, lamenting the weakness of the troops, who were not able to function properly and were protesting about the dearth of food and fodder and their indigent state and complaining that "The Head of the Army Department has brought us to the brink of destruction through the excessive economies[103] he has made." We, the leading figures and the commanders had concluded, "are most apprehensive that a great calamity might occur here, for with our troops engaged in wrangling and arguments, and our foes coming on top, we may be facing a very dire predicament indeed." At the time of the evening worship, the Vizier mounted his steed and came along for a private meeting with the Amir. He remained there till the time of the night worship, explained the situation to him and returned. He and my master were discussing all this with each other all along the road, and they went back to the tents. [Gh 579]

The next day, the enemy appeared, stronger, bolder, in greater numbers and more eager for action, and [F 768] they engaged in fighting from all directions. The battle became fierce, and a clamour and tumult arose from the army camp. The Amir mounted his steed secretly, and went out incognito to one of the fringes of the camp and saw for himself what the commanders had said. He returned at the time of the midday worship, and sent a verbal message to the Vizier to confirm that he had now seen for himself[104] what the Vizier had reported. At the time of the afternoon worship he summoned the leading figures and said, "The fighting is going on in a very half-hearted and slothful fashion; what's the reason for it?" They replied, "May the lord's life be prolonged! The weather is extremely hot, fodder can't be found and the beasts are wasting away. A more decisive approach is required for fighting this bunch." They went on to say, "We had sent a verbal message to the Grand Vizier and had set forth our justifications for the poor showing of the troops, and doubtless he will have told you. Moreover, the lord has secret agents amongst the troops, and they must have informed him of the situation." The Vizier said, "I have had a session about it with the lord Sultan, and last night I was thinking about it all through the night hours, and came up with an idea which I have not yet mentioned to the lord but will do in private."

The leading figures all went back, and the Amir remained there with the Vizier and my master. The Vizier said, "May the lord's life be prolonged and all things proceed as he wishes! It is not as if it is only our troops who are worn out and exhausted, the Turkmens are even more weary and drained; but they happen to be far more resilient, and finding themselves in a perilous plight, are fighting for their very survival. It seems to me that the wise course would be for me to send an envoy to the enemy, and given the fact that they are still reeling from the shock of that one drubbing they have received,[105] offer them advice on my own initiative and say to them, 'If at that time the lord had come after you, not one of you would have been able to get away and save his skin, and if he decides to wage a battle against you now, not a single one of you will be left alive. You would do well to ask for mercy and show some signs of contrition so that I can take your case to the lord Sultan and convince him to accept your submissive and peaceful overtures and explain to him that your resistance was fuelled solely by fear for your own safety. I shall do my best to induce the Sultan to depart for Herat and allow you to remain in these regions and exchange envoys with you so that hostilities can cease and be replaced by an atmosphere of peace and amity'."[106] [F 769]

The Amir said, "This seems reasonable, but both friends and foes alike will realize that it stems from our own innate incapacity." The Vizier said, "That's true, but it's the best and safest course of action, and means that, given the present conditions, we can go back in safety. The lord has witnessed how they fight and has seen the situation for himself; should he wish to do so, he can march out from Herat after Mehragān against this group, with a full panoply of arms and with carefully thought-out plans. If they behave properly, according to an agreed arrangement, as is to be hoped, the affair will be finished; if, God forbid, the opposite happens, all honour will be lost, for a disaster may occur which cannot be retrieved. The lord [Gh 580] should look into this carefully and mull it over, so that whatever the exalted judgement decides upon can be put into effect."

The Vizier and Bu Naṣr went back. When my master came back to his tent, he summoned me and said, "You see to what level we have descended! I wish we were dead and did not have to face such ignominy!" He went on and told me everything that had gone on, and the circumstances upon which the Vizier had based his argument, and that the Amir was right to describe the Vizier's proposals as a sign of our impotence but necessary all the same. My master said that the Amir had told him, "O Bu'l-Fażl, the Vizier has discerned the sound course; perhaps this will turn out to be the correct plan and we may be able go to Herat with our honour intact. It is vital that no disaster should occur and that we should not be deterred by other distractions so that we can tackle this source of weakness and incapacity. May the Almighty God deal kindly!" We were engaged in this talk when one of the Sultan's household servants came and said, "The Amir is summoning you." My master arose and went off. I myself went back to my tent [F 770] in a very troubled state.

It was late into the night when my master came back and summoned me, and I went to him. He drew me aside privately and said, "When I reached the Amir's presence, he was in the large tent. He made me sit down on my own and sent everyone else away. He said to me, "This business has become extremely convoluted and drawn out, as you can well see for yourself. Our recently-defeated enemy has now come back as bold as brass, and I now realize, and have seen for myself, that it was not a wise move to send Begtughdï and Sübashï to fight against them. But what is past is past. What is required is an unfettered force similar to the enemy himself, well prepared and equipped[107] and without baggage and impedimenta, so that they can be destroyed. We keep talking to a lot of people about this matter but never get a clearcut answer. Our two eminent commanders (i.e. Begtughdï and Sübashï) having themselves suffered a thrashing from these people, prefer that this matter remains unresolved so that they remain exonerated from any blame. But the Vizier is altogether a man of a different stamp, and I cannot fathom him out. He will defer judgement to the Commander-in-Chief, and the Commander-in-Chief[108] then passes the buck back to him. We have therefore become very confused about all this. You are someone who always speaks the truth and who seeks nothing but our welfare. What do you see in all this? Speak freely, for amongst all our retainers, we have our eyes on you to speak your mind and banish our doubts and show us the right way."

I, Bu Naṣr, said, "May the lord's life be prolonged! The lord should tell me clearly what he thinks about the matter and what the lord's underlying concerns are,[109] so that [Gh 581] I can offer my advice according to my knowledge and ability and can avoid furnishing answers without knowing what the lord's wishes are."

The Amir said, "What the Vizier said today at the time of the afternoon worship came as sound advice: that he should despatch an envoy to bring about a tactical truce[110] with this gang. We shall go to Herat [F 771] and spend this summer there so that the troops can enjoy a period of rest and recovery. We will summon fresh horses, camels and arms from Ghaznin, and we shall adopt a new approach now that we are better acquainted with the ways of this gang. When Mehragān has arrived (i.e. in the early autumn), we shall make for Pushang, Ṭus and Nishapur. If the enemy challenges us and stands its ground, it will not pose a great threat to us since we shall be agile and not burdened with heavy baggage. If they don't stand fast but make off, we shall pursue them as far as Bāvard and Nasā. We shall prepare for this course of action throughout this coming winter so that, with the beneficent help of God Most High, Khorasan will be cleared of them."

I said, "This is well thought-out, but no-one, neither the Vizier nor the army commanders, is going to suggest that, while the war is still raging and the enemy remains undefeated, we should pack up and return, for they will be afraid that, the next day, when the lord has reached Herat, he will chastise them and say that it was their ineptitude that forced him to return here. Likewise, I too will not suggest this since it is not my proposal. However, a difficult problem has arisen here which I cannot avoid having to raise." He asked me what I meant. I replied, "Wherever there is an inhospitable terrain covered with thornbushes or strewn with rocks, that's where our army encampment will be, whereas this rabble bunch can pick for themselves desirable spots where there are fresh fields and plenty of fodder. They enjoy the luxury of flowing streams and supplies of ice while we have to make do with water from wells and have no access to flowing water or ice. They can graze their camels on pasture land and bring in fodder from faraway places, and we have to keep our camels at the entrance of our tents, for they cannot graze on the fringes of the encampment."

He said, "That's because they have no heavy baggage with them, hence they can come and go as they please, whereas we are weighed down with heavy baggage, and the onerous task of looking after it prevents us from attending to anything else. That's why I keep on saying that we should extricate ourselves from these encumbrances, [F 772] for the Turkmens by themselves do not pose such a serious problem and we can deal with them successfully." I said, "There's another matter too. No satisfactory decisions can be made without the presence of the Vizier, the Commander-in-Chief, the Great Chamberlain and the leading army commanders. If the exalted judgement thinks fit, a session should be held tomorrow so that they can discuss all this, adopt a fully-fledged scheme and bring it to fruition." He agreed that this was a good idea.

I continued, "May the lord's life be prolonged! There's another thing that, [Gh 582] out of diffidence, I hesitate to say." He replied, "You must have your say, and it will receive a sympathetic hearing." I said. "May the lord's life be prolonged! The atrocities being inflicted today by these people in Khorasan—wreaking evil, killing and mutilating people, and the abduction of decent Muslim womenfolk as if it was their lawful right—are on a scale beyond anything witnessed in the past or recorded in chronicles of the time. Yet despite all this, they are victorious in battles. What a wicked lot we must be that God the Exalted One has chosen to give such people power over us and has been vouchsafing them victory! The affairs of this present world and their good order are contingent upon kingship and the sacred law. The sovereign's rule and religion go together like two inseparable brothers.[111] When the Almighty God removes His care and favour from a monarch so that a group of people like these can get the upper hand over him, it must be a sign that God Most High has been displeased and vexed with him. The lord should meditate and ponder on how he has conducted himself *vis-à-vis* that Majestic Heavenly Court."

The Sultan replied, "I cannot think of having done any wrong to any person or any other deed that might have been displeasing to God Most High." I said, "Praise be to God! I have been behaving in a discourteous manner and am still persisting in it, but I speak purely out of affectionate concern. The lord is better able to look at his relationship with the Almighty God, and if there are any reasons for seeking His forgiveness for an offence, he should seek it. He should do it this very night and go before the Creator, place his face in the dust with supplications and lamentations, and make appropriate vows. If anything has arisen in the past between him and the Almighty God, he should show remorse and penitence, and he will see the very next day onwards the beneficial results, since there are no barriers placed before the supplications of kings when made from a sincere heart [F 773] and correct belief. If the lord sees me talking in such blunt terms, he should not take offence since he himself gave me licence to speak freely."

When I said this, he replied, "I shall do as you said, and you were entitled to say what you said and fulfilled the obligations due to myself and to my father. Go back, and whenever you wish, do speak in the same vein and offer advice, for there is no breath of suspicion upon you." I took my formal leave and went away. I hope that the Almighty God will reward me for the things I said. I do not know whether what I said was palatable to him or not; at all events, I performed my duty." I, Bu'l-Fażl, answered, "May the lord's life be prolonged! You did what was incumbent upon you, and you discharged the obligation of past favours and service to the ruling dynasty," and I went away.

There was a court session the next day, and all sorts of topics were aired and views exchanged. Those words which [Gh 583] the enemy had uttered and the deeds they had perpetrated were gone over. The decision was accordingly reached that the Vizier should send an envoy and offer them soothing advice so that they would disperse. Envoys from both sides would then come together, and they would go back to the original understanding. In that way, affairs would once more revert to a peaceable state, and warfare and hostility would be ended. When they left the Amir's presence, the Vizier summoned Master (*ḥākem*) Bu Naṣr Moṭṭavveʿi Zowzani. This last was a highly-skilled and eloquent person who had served for a long time such a distinguished military commander as Moḥammad Aʿrābi[112] and had become well-versed in affairs of state and how to handle them. After Moḥammad Aʿrābi's death, this monarch recognized his capability and his administrative skills, and made him responsible for the Arab troops and the overall management of their affairs. The Vizier rehearsed to him the terms of these discussions [F 774] and gave him instructions, saying, "On no account must it be revealed that the Sultan is cognisant of this. But since I am Vizier, and have to take thought for the welfare of the Muslims, of friend and foe, I must ineluctably speak regarding matters like these, in order that swords return to their scabbards, with no further bloodshed, and so that the subjects enjoy security again. You yourselves (i.e. the Turkmens) are experiencing much suffering, and are being attacked, hammered and killed. Here we have a most powerful monarch, and you have managed to antagonize him. On the morrow, he will not desist from hunting you down until you are totally destroyed. Although you have had some sporadic successes in this desert, it will not lead you anywhere. If you agree to toe the line and observe the royal commands, I will plead on your behalf at the royal court and will explain that 'The Turkmens are engaging in this warfare and contention, causing affliction and sowing confusion, simply out of fear for their lives and those of their women and children, since they have no place in the world where they can settle down and live. If through the royal bestowal of compassion and consideration they are rescued from their present plight and offered some pasture grounds and territory, they will display their obedience and allegiance to your lordship, and your own subjects will be relieved of these raids and military attacks. I will make sure that they are allotted a well-defined territory so that they can settle down there and live a life of comfort and security.'" He gave him these instructions and others in a similar vein, showing him how to pitch his talk to them and how to use the stick and the carrot, alternating between conciliatory words and stern warnings,[113] and then sent him off.

Master Moṭṭavveʿi proceeded to the encampment of those upstarts and delivered the Grand Vizier's message in a most comprehensive manner. He spelt out the matters which would redound to their own welfare and best interests, and he solemnly swore that "The most mighty Sultan Nāṣer al-Din knows nothing whatever about this mission; but the Vizier, because of [F 775] his concern for your welfare and that of the other Muslims, has sent me."

They received him with honour and esteem, took him to his designated quarters and sent him substantial offerings.[114] [Gh 584] Afterwards, all their leaders gathered together to discuss this matter and to decide how to respond to the Vizier's proposal. All kinds of ideas and opinions were debated and mulled over. At last they decided that, given the fact that they faced a mighty monarch with limitless troops, wealth and territories, it would be wise to follow the Vizier's advice; and they further argued that "Although we have met with several successes and have managed to defeat military expeditions and have seized some territories, in one single campaign when the Amir personally took charge he inflicted a mighty blow on us, and if he had at once followed it up by coming after us in hot pursuit, not a single one of us or our womenfolk and children would have escaped. It was thanks to our good fortune that they decided to stay where they were and did not come after us. The best course is the one that the Vizier has suggested."

When they had come to this decision, they summoned Master Moṭṭavveʿi on the next day, expressed their submissiveness to the Sultan, exhibited due decorum and said, "The position is just as the Grand Vizier has envisaged. He must now display his nobility and eminence and favour us with his intercession for us so that the exalted Sultan's feelings of animosity may be removed, and territory, steppe lands and pasture grounds may be ordained for us so that we may reside on and live within the realm of this Sultan and show ourselves his humble servants. As a result, the people of Khorasan will also be freed from further ravages of war." They appointed trusty agents of theirs to go with Master Moṭṭavveʿi and gave them a lengthy verbal message in these terms. They gave Moṭṭavveʿi an appropriate stay and send-off, and despatched him back homewards in the company of their own envoy. [F 776]

When they reached the Sultan's army encampment, Master Moṭṭavveʿi came on ahead and closeted himself with the Grand Vizier.[115] He gave a full exposition of the circumstances, saying, "Although these people have for the moment sent such conciliatory messages and are eager to win our approval, they can never be regarded as sincere in their approach, and the airs and graces of kingship and the delusions of grandeur which have been lodged in their heads will not be dispelled quickly. However, for the moment there will be peace and they intend to lie low.[116] I have described my experiences and impressions so that the Grand Vizier may decide and decree the best course of action."

When the Vizier became apprised of this state of affairs, he gave orders for the envoy of this upstart bunch to be summoned and brought into his presence. He offered laudatory greetings, and the envoy responded with due decorum, expressing his humble respects, and delivered his message.[117] He was then dismissed, led to his lodging in the guest-quarters for diplomatic envoys (*rasul-khāna*) and given ample hospitality. The Vizier went off in attendance on the Sultan. They had a private session, together with Khᵛāja Bu Naṣr, and the Vizier recounted what he had heard from Moṭṭavveʿi and communicated the verbal message that [Gh 585] the envoy had brought, and the exalted judgement was thus fully briefed. He gave orders to the effect that, "Although this course of action bespeaks of our weakness, since the Grand Vizier considers it as advisable and the right course in the present situation, let him put it into effect, as is required."

The Vizier went away. The next day the Vizier summoned the envoy—Khᵛāja Bu Naṣr Moshkān was also there in attendance—and they covered all aspects and settled all practicalities, [F 777] and the terms were enunciated by the Vizier as follows, "I interceded on your behalf, and I persuaded the monarch that you should remain where you are, while we go back and head for Herat.[118] He has commanded that Nasā, Bāvard, Farāva, and these deserts and borderlands should be put at your disposal, provided that you do not inflict any harm on the Muslims and that you leave the subjects well alone, nor should you make any confiscations and requisitions[119] in these three places where you are at the moment. You should go at once to your assigned territories while we turn back and make for Herat. Once there in your allotted territories, you are to send envoys to the Sultan's army camp[120] and make the stipulated offerings of service so that we may proceed in a judicious manner[121] and come to firm and irrevocable agreements. Thus the subjects and our territories can enjoy peace and tranquillity, and you too be saved from further escapades and strife and skirmishes."

The Vizier passed on the verbal message in the same vein, and fitting gifts and appropriate presents were bestowed upon the envoy of these parvenu people, and he was sent back well contented. Master Moṭṭavveʿi was once more designated for this important diplomatic task. He set out in the company of the envoy and reached the upstarts. Their envoy uttered profuse expressions of thanks and invocations to God, and the Turkmen chiefs had a private conclave with him. Master Moṭṭavveʿi likewise communicated the Vizier's message. They for their part made expressions of service and spoke fine words to him, and an atmosphere of appeasement and pacification seemed to prevail—even though they were never content and quiescent, for pretensions to royal power, to authority for making all crucial decisions and to seizing territories, had become implanted in their heads. They used honeyed words in their dealings and showed deference to Master Moṭṭavveʿi, with endless avowals of excuses for their past conduct, and said, "We [F 778] will give obedience to the Vizier's commands, but it is all the time necessary that the Sultan and his servants should be forthright with us and that we should not encounter any treachery or deceit from any quarter. Thus we will be able to live peacefully and there should be no need for renewed hostilities. It is further necessary that they should not go back on what they have decreed and that they should act in such a manner that the subjects and the troops on both sides remain at peace and that there is no unlawful bloodshed." Hence in accordance with this arrangement, they set out on the first stage of their journey, towards the territories assigned to them.

When the Turkmens had set out on the first stage of their journey and had departed, Master Moṭṭavve'i returned and came to the victorious army encampment. [Gh 586] He had a privy audience with the Vizier and recounted what he had seen and heard of the upstarts' affairs, their conduct and the mocking words they had been wont to utter. He said, "On no account can they be trusted. We should make it our priority to prepare our forces to topple them or to drive them out of our territories, and we should not be taken in by those deceitful declarations of theirs, for they will never behave in an upright manner, and these pretensions to royal power, giving commands and executing ordinances, will never be driven out of their heads except by the sharp blade of a sword. Now, because of that heavy blow inflicted upon them in that single attack which the king himself led, they have made a half-hearted tactical peace agreement[122] and have returned to their designated lands. But they will do their utmost to tempt and lure the gholāms to their side,[123] to encroach on our lands, to amass more forces and to recruit further manpower from Transoxania so that they can join forces[124] and swell their numbers. They will leave no stone unturned and will trample on their own words. There is much blatantly puffed-up talk amongst them, and it has become clear to me that they are of the opinion that 'This monarch feels helpless and despondent, and his vizier, acting on his own initiative, patched up the differences with us and put an end to the strife. Once their armies have rested sufficiently and have prepared for war, they will come after us [F 779] and will not rest until they have either driven us back or expelled us out from this land. They introduced this idea of a peace agreement and cajolement for this very reason, but it is also convenient for us to be at rest and free from these attacks for a little while, to get our affairs in order, gather together troops and be ready for war. We shall not relax our vigilance, but will be ready and prepared to face the enemy, so that when they suddenly launch an attack on us, we shall go out and confront them, give our riposte and fight to the death; we shall either come out on top or go down in defeat, since we have chosen a most mighty monarch to wrestle with.' They said a great many words of this kind, and went back in a confident and happy frame of mind, and set off. When we ourselves reach Herat, they will send high-level envoys and parade their might,[125] while at the same time coming forward and giving an appearance of rendering service and submissiveness, and asking for further territories, alleging that 'Our numbers have increased and what you handed over to us is no longer sufficient for us. When we find ourselves deprived of revenues and income,[126] there will be no choice but to resort to requisitions and raids for plunder, and giving out and acquiring further territories. They should not fault us for this since it is done out of sheer necessity.'" He also gave a full report of other matters that he had observed and had become apparent to him in this audience with the Grand Vizier.

The Vizier said, "I am aware of these facts, and I know what should be done. If the monarch heeds my words and acts according to my counsel, [Gh 587] I can, over a period of time, arrange matters in such a way that I can bar the Turkmens from any further encroachments until the entire lot of them are uprooted or thrown out of the land of Khorasan and have to cross the river for good,[127] and we can see an end to their turmoil through our own wise management and steadfast measures. [F 780] However, I know that others at court won't let this monarch alone and will raise objections to my counsels. Nor will they be content with that, but will despatch armies here and will throw into chaos these carefully-prepared plans and will provoke and alarm the Turkmens. Each day the situation is becoming more unruly, while these Turkmens become stronger and their horde more swollen in size. The whole of Khorasan and Western Persia will be lost, and there will be other reverses and disappointments in store for us, until the final decree of the Eternal and Almighty One is known. Let us hope that, God willing, everything will turn out well. Don't pass on to anyone else what you have told me and what I have told you till we see what happens."

The Vizier sent Moṭṭavveʿi away and went off to attend the exalted royal presence. Khᵛāja Bu Naṣr Moshkān came along, and they had a private session that went on late into the night. The Vizier gave a very complete and extensive exposition for the exalted judgement of what he had heard from Master Moṭṭavve'i and the questions he had put to him, and he reviewed the problems inherent in the situation and their possible solution in a manner that induced some reassurance for the time being. In this same session they also agreed to set out the next day for Herat (Hariv) and stay there so that the troops might find relief from their state of privation and shortage of food and might enjoy some rest and repose and fatten up the horses. Also, they were to seek from the capital Ghaznin and the outlying provinces all that they required in terms of equipment, supplies, treasuries, weapons and fresh troops, and become fully prepared for action. When this had been accomplished and they were ready for battle, with the army well rested and when more troops had joined in, they should see what these unruly outcasts[128] were up to. If they appeared calm and quiescent, and kept to their good behaviour, the royal army should stay put for a while and not stir them up. When the preparations had been made, and the army and detachments of court troops had come together, then action could be taken in the light of the prevailing circumstances.

His exalted majesty spoke many a complimentary and reassuring word to the Vizier, [F 781] and said, "Thanks to your statesmanship, this crisis has abated for the time being. From now on keep a constant eye on what pertains to the affairs of the realm and the state, for we shall not question your decisions. Thus with full confidence you can remove these blemishes through your incisive action and your sound and seasoned judgement." The Vizier rendered marks of service and made his obeisance. Having resolved upon these measures, they dispersed.

The next day, the royal escorts (*mavākeb*) and the other troops departed, and they encamped on the borders of the region of Herat. They proceeded at a slow pace until they emerged from those deserts (*biyābān-hā*) and found themselves in the open plain (*ṣaḥrā'*)[129] and could rest and amble onwards at a relaxed gait[130] till they reached Herat and encamped there. *God is the Most Knowing about what is the right course, and to Him is the return and the reversion!*[131] [Gh 588]

An account of the arrival of Sultan Mas'ud[132] at Herat and his taking up residence there, and a description of the events that occurred until that time when he went forth to attack the Turkmens and the ensuing events

In Dhu'l-Qa'da of the year 430 [/July-August 1039], Sultan Shehāb al-Dowla va-Qoṭb al-Mella arrived amidst much splendour in Herat. He ordered camp to be made and spent a few days resting with the troops. Then he devised a scheme to send armies into the provinces of the empire and made arrangements for advance parties of scouts and troop detachments to be deployed so that both the frontiers could be filled with men and also the army would find food and the animals get hay and barley and be rested. First, the Amir sent the Great Chamberlain to [F 782] Pushang with a powerful army, and he gave instructions for advance scouting parties to be held ready for proceeding from there to Khᵛāf,[133] a rural district of Nishapur; he sent the Commander Badr with a strong army to Bādghis and took the same measures with other districts, despatching strong detachments everywhere. They went off and took control of all the provinces of the empire. The financial agents and tax collectors got busy levying taxation. The Amir began indulging in merry-making and wine-drinking and took little rest from these prolonged activities. He was also giving audiences and seeing to the preparations. A letter went out to Bu 'Ali the castellan at Ghaznin, and various items were asked for, including equipment for waging war in the desert (*ālat-e jang-e biyābān*), horses, camels, gold and clothing, these to be despatched with haste. For collection from Herat and its adjacent districts, Bādghis, Ganj Rustā(q) and wherever else their grasp extended, assignments of money[134] for the army were written out, amounting to a million dirhams, and these were collected with some severity and violence, on the pretext that the people there had colluded with the Turkmens.[135] Things were different now, for this monarch was approaching his end, and no-one dared to initiate a debate with him and serve him with sound advice.

The notables of Herat, such as Bu'l-Ḥasan 'Alavi and others, had fled, and they had advised Bu Ṭalḥa Shebli, the financial agent and tax collector, to go into hiding but he had not done so. The Amir suddenly gave orders for Bu Ṭalḥa to be seized and imprisoned, and everything he possessed was confiscated. Then they flayed him alive. When the razor of the barber-surgeon touched him, he gave up the ghost, God's mercy be upon him! I saw his corpse thrown on top of a dunghill in the vicinity of the ʿAdnāni Palace, at the spot known as [Gh 589] S.k.y.n (?), with the chamberlain (*parda-dār*) Tegin Saqlābi[136] mounting guard over it. When the Turkmens defeated the Great Chamberlain Sübashï [F 783] and entered Herat, this Bu Ṭalḥa had gone out to greet them and had offered hospitality and gifts, and this had sealed his fate. Bu'l-Fatḥ Ḥātemi, the deputy official in charge of the postal and intelligence service at Herat, acting as the representative of my master Bu Naṣr, was likewise seized. He also had gone out to the Turkmens. My master did not intercede as it was not a time for any pleading. He was taken into custody along with Bu ʿAli b. Shādān of Ṭus, the counsellor and adjutant of the military governor of Khorasan, and then taken to the fortress of B.r.g.z[137] in the region of Peshawar and held prisoner there.[138]

Letters arrived with the news that Ṭoghrïl had returned to Nishapur, that Dāvud had taken up residence at Sarakhs and that the Yïnāliyān had gone to Nasā and Bāvard. The Vizier said to my master, "What do you think of the situation? The lord has forgotten what has happened and has occupied himself with merry-making, and there is no mention of the envoy, the enemy and the concluding of a contractual agreement with the Turkmens. To me this is most disturbing, for we still face the same problem but in a more intractable form." My master replied, "This situation has got beyond that point when it can possibly be salvaged, and it is better to keep unpalatable counsel to oneself. At present the words of old men like us sound odious to the lord; this is the situation favoured by these untested youths,[139] and it explains why they depict old men in such an unfavourable light. We have no choice except to remain silent." The Vizier said, "Just so. And if he does broach the subject and asks us about it, we shall remain silent."

On Saturday, the first day of Dhu'l-Ḥejja [/24 August 1039],[140] the Amir detailed five *kheyltāsh*s to go to Gorgān. He ordered a letter to be written to Bu Sahl Ḥamdavi, Suri and Bā Kālijār,[141] as follows: "We came to Herat in the assurance of victory and good fortune, and we have been here for some time [F 784] awaiting the arrival from Ghaznin of additional camels, money, horses, armouries and equipment for desert warfare, for which we asked. Then, when we are prepared and ready, we shall head for Ṭus and Nishapur. For we have now got the measure of the enemy and their ways and tricks and strategies in battle. We shall set against them troops just like them, unencumbered with baggage, while we remain with our equipment and supplies, so that the world may be made free of their presence. Bā Kālijār rendered highly meritorious service and acted in an impressive manner, and the rewards for that to be given out from our royal presence will be on a scale [Gh 590] that none of the servants of this empire have ever seen up to this time. We ordered these letters to be written to boost his morale. When our trains of troops and impedimenta (*mavākeb*) reach Nishapur, you are to come to the court with stout hearts. Keep the *kheyltāsh*s there so that they can come back with you." The Amir affixed his signature and emblem to these letters, and instructed the *kheyltāsh*s to take guides with them so that they could lead them to the borders of Gorgān by unmarked tracks; and so they went.

The Festival of the Sacrifice approached. The Amir ordered a magnificent display of unsurpassed extent and splendour. Herat is a town with a larger arsenal of weapons and armaments than any other town. On the day of the Festival (i.e. 10 Dhu'l-Ḥejja/2 September 1039), so many cavalrymen and infantry, with complete panoplies of weapons, came into the central square that trustworthy old men admitted that they had never witnessed anything on this scale before. The Festival was celebrated, trays of food were set down and wine handed out. Then after the celebration of the Festival, the Amir reviewed the army on the plain of Khodābān,[142] and all those witnessing the spectacle on the day averred that [F 785] they could not recall such an army from times past.

My master's allotted span of life was drawing to its close, and at these last days he was voicing unpalatable sentiments that the wise found hard to accept. For example, on the day of the army review, he passed by a cemetery (I was there with him), and he stopped and thought for a long while before moving on. Near the town, Bu Sahl Zowzani caught up with him, and the two of them rode on together. Bu Sahl's residence was on our way. He invited him to share his hospitality, and my master replied, "I'm in no mood for drinking wine, for I feel very low in spirits." But his protests were in vain, for the host was most insistent and he finally had to halt there, and I too went in. Bu Sahl ordered food to be prepared and arranged for boon-companions and musicians and singers to be present, until everything was ready, but my master was still buried in his thoughts. Bu Sahl said, "You look very despondent yet no mishap has occurred." He replied, "I am thinking about our present plight, and I fail to see any way out of this predicament and cannot stop myself thinking about it. I feel apprehensive, and it is as if I can see before my very eyes that we have been put to flight in the desert and are all dispersed and trying each to save his own skin, and I am left without any companion or a gholām, and have to surrender my life for naught and face the unknown in the Other World. When I came back today from the army parade, I passed by a burial ground and saw two graves, neatly made up and rendered with flesh plaster. For a while I wished, if only I were like them, with my dignity preserved, and would not have to face degradation and abasement: for that I have no stomach!" Bu Sahl laughed and said, "This is a case of acute melancholia: *drink and be merry, leave the cares of the world behind!*[143] Begin to eat!" Exquisite food and fine wines [Gh 591] were brought in, [F 786] musicians and singers and boon-companions entered. We ate bread and tucked into the spread. A most enjoyable day came to its end, since there was much bandying to and fro in refined talk and there was music and poetical improvisation, and we went homewards in an intoxicated state. Forty days later my master, may God be pleased with him, passed away, as I shall subsequently relate, and we set off from Herat. Seven months later, that great defeat and calamity occurred at Dandānqān near Merv, and we suffered many blows. Afterwards, while on the road, Bu Sahl said to me on different occasions, "Glory to the Almighty God! What a perspicacious man was Bu Naṣr Moshkān! It is as if he had seen with his own eyes this day in which we are now caught up!"

Bu Naṣr's utterances in this convivial session were reported back until they were brought to the Amir's notice, and it was said, "Given the fact that the head of the Chancery is one of the wisest of the pillars of state, there will be a great deal of trouble if his words reach the enemy, and they will be much emboldened by them." The Amir was much incensed as a result, but he kept back his wrath until Bu Naṣr passed away.[144]

I have said when recounting this story that, in that convivial session, there was much lighthearted flyting and reciting of literary vignettes. Even though, thanks to the length that it is acquiring, this History is becoming like the compendium of traditions (*jāmeʿ*) by Sofyān,[145] I am recording some verses from the poetic exchanges (*modhākarāt*) that took place in that session to round off the episode and make it complete. I did not have these verses myself, and will tell you how they came into my hands: There was in Herat a man called the Judge Manṣur. He had a complete mastery of all the branches of learning, poetry and penmanship, and many other talents. He was fond of wine-drinking and feasting, and had learnt that *"one should seize the day and shun all wavering and qualms"*[146] and should claim one's rightful portion in this deceitful world. He therefore adopted a different attitude to life (i.e. from the staid and earnest mode of life expected of a pious and ascetic judge), lived well, and ate and drank in style. He was such a great favourite[147] [F 787] amongst men of discernment that a gathering without him would be accounted a failure. He enjoyed a close and special friendship[148] with Bu Sahl Zowzani because of their mutual love of witty and cultured discourse, and they were always together and drank wine together. On this particular day, the Judge Manṣur had set out at dawn, and had plunged into a whirl of merry-making and had been deeply affected by the wine. Bu Sahl sent him some lines of occasional verse (*qeṭʿa*), and he at once responded using the same letter of the alphabet at the end of each line. Bu Sahl wrote another piece, and he once again wrote back a further rejoinder, but did not come in person and the day passed.

I yearned to have those pieces of verse until [Gh 592] I got hold of them, and it happened in this way. A learned scholar called Masʿud, who was related to Manṣur, had appeared. He had been frequently in the company of this Judge and had noted down all such incidents and occasions. When Herat fell into turmoil,[149] this noble-minded religious lawyer left his native land and went off on his travels until he arrived at the court of Arslān Khān b. Qadïr Khān, who was the ruler of Turkestan, and he remained there for several years in the most honoured and comfortable circumstances possible, since he was the outstanding figure of his age in religious and legal knowledge and in delivering homilies. When he perceived that that kingdom was going to fall into a state of instability and chaos because of the violent factionalism which had occurred and the divisions amongst the Khān's brothers and other family members—*and a wise person can smell trouble from afar*[150]—he sought and received permission to return.[151] He came back in the year 438[/1046–7] and through his eloquence won the hearts of everyone in the town, the noble as well as the lowly.[152] He was also welcomed and received much favour at the ruler's court, and this further enhanced his fame and stature amongst the public. At this present moment, in the year 451 [/1059–60], he has become even more highly famed since the Exalted Sultan Abu'l-Moẓaffar Ebrāhim—*may God prolong his royal power!*—thinks well of him. He is bound to rise further, for he is still young and has a noble disposition and is generous and courageous. Since he is a friend of mine, tested and trustworthy, and since we have enjoyed each other's company and conversation, I have mentioned his name in this History and have thereby observed the requirements of friendship. [F 788]

The verses written by the Sheykh Abu Sahl al-Zowzani[153]

1. *O outstanding scholar* (ṣadr), *to whose exalted status necks became lowered,*
2. *Respond to this call, and you will delight the boon companions, who are sorrowing*[154] *because of inexorable Fate,*
3. *And make it easy for the drinkers to swallow their grief, which wine does not assuage,*
4. *And attend, of your grace, in a gathering which is burning with yearning* (showq, i.e. for a meeting),
5. *And leave off excuses and pay us a visit, O one of pure stock and unspotted nobility!*
6. *Bitter separation from you is painful* ('adhāb), *and your noble qualities are sweet* ('edhāb).
7. *You are nothing but melodious song,*[155] *wine and youthfulness.*
8. *Your well-established bountifulness is an ocean and your all-sufficing liberality a rain-bearing cloud.*
9. *The present world is nothing but darkness, but your lofty qualities are a shining star.* [Gh 593]

The Judge answered him immediately:

1. *O outstanding scholar, one blessed with good fortune, a noble one, a stallion of noble breed,*
2. *Your face is the essential aspect of a matter, which illuminates, and your look is correct judgement.*[156]
3. *You encapsulate [the qualities of] the whole world, and I make them my resort.*
4. *Intoxication has pinned me down, and making a response has wearied me.*
5. *[He is] the summits of achievement, the one who has gathered within himself everything which is considered pleasing.*
6. *If only I were able, I would divide my body into two parts* (i.e. so that one could be with you), *and that would be pleasing,*
7. *But I am unable to do this, and my heart is full of burning passion* (i.e. for union with you).
8. *Hence I have set forth my excuse at length in lines*[157] *written down in a document.* [F 789]

Abu Sahl responded to him:

1. *O outstanding scholar, linger for a while, for I do not intend to go away from you!*
2. *All the qualities embodied in you are a source of pride and glorying, while everything which does not measure up to you is full of defects.*
3. *Your face is the full moon, but after the clouds have cleared away from it.*
4. *Your much-desired presence is a fertile garden, and your much-deplored absence is a tangled thicket.*
5. *Your return is eagerly awaited by me and is perpetually accounted a welcome event.*
6. *If you come back to us, it is as if youthfulness is returning,*

7. *Or as if life-giving rain has been poured on a parched land.*

8. *Nay, as if a dead man is taken out* (i.e. revived) *when the earth of the grave had hidden him.*

Manṣur wrote, after being overcome with intoxication:

1. *My legs have been overcome by sleep since I crossed the bridge* (i.e. between sobriety and drunkenness), *so approach, if you desire an excuse from me.*

2. *Indeed, this cup of wine is something remarkable; everyone who drains it to the lees, it renders intoxicated.*[158]

Behold, what great men these were! All three of them have departed, and we ourselves will likewise have to depart; may the end of our endeavours be crowned with divine favour, if the Almighty God so wills![159] [Gh 593]

The Amir celebrated the festival of Mehragān on Tuesday, 27 Dhu'l-Ḥejja [/19 September 1039], and a large number of presents were brought forward to the court and coins scattered. But no poets were commanded to be present, and he showed his anger with Masʿud Rāzi and ordered him to be exiled to India, since it was said that he had composed an ode in which he had proffered the Sultan many a piece of advice. That ode contained these two verses: [790]

1. Your enemies were mere ants, and have now turned into serpents; hasten and root out those ants that have become serpents!

2. Do not give them any more time and do not tarry, for given time, these serpents will become dragons!

It was an excellent piece of advice that this poor fellow gave, although in his prying into royal affairs he overreached himself;[160] such words from poets to kings are inappropriate.[161] The Sultan ordained no presents for the musicians and singers either, for at this time, that habitually gold-dispensing cloud and fount of largesse showed little rain, with its bounty having turned into a trickle; and there was much pinching and scraping. The Sultan's life had approached its end. This is the fate of mankind and the fortune allotted to us in this present world. These days of Mehragān and its celebration also came to an end.

[The History of the Year 431/ 23 September 1039–10 September 1040]

[Gh 594, F 790] In the year 431, the first day of which was Tuesday, the Amir made it incumbent upon himself that every day, before the court session, he would have a privy meeting, lasting up to the mid-morning, with the Vizier, the pillars of the state and the army commanders, so that they could discuss the serious situation facing them. The leading men would then go back while the Amir himself would sit down and attend to this matter until nightfall. Never in the past had anyone seen him devoting himself so whole-heartedly to a task. Letters were arriving from all quarters with the news that the enemy too were busy with their plans and had sent reinforcements to Böritegin, so that he had been able to engage the sons of ʿAlitegin in several fierce battles and defeat them, and that he had almost wrested the entire province of Transoxania from them. Moreover, Altuntāsh's son [Esmāʿil] Khandān had also allied himself with the Turkmens. They had opened up the barrier of the Oxus from both sides, and people began to come across the river bent on plundering Khorasan.[1] Things had reached such a pass that we read in a letter from Āmuy[2] that an old woman was seen, one-armed, one-eyed and one-legged, clutching a pickaxe. [F 791] When asked what had brought her there, she had replied, "I heard that they were digging up the treasures of the land of Khorasan from beneath the earth, and I came to help myself to a bit of them too." The Amir used to laugh at these reports, but those who felt the full gravity of the situation found these words too grim to bear.

The items that we had sought from Ghaznin started to come, and troop reinforcements were arriving. Bu'l-Ḥasan b. ʿAbd al-Jalil[3] had a private audience with the Amir, and said, "We Persian officials (*tāzikān*) possess large numbers of horses and camels, [Gh 595], and the Amir is in need of additional mounts for the newly-arrived troops; and we owe everything to his bountiful rule. A list should be drawn up, with a figure against each person's name."[4] He had not come up with this as an act of service, but he sought rather to write down something against the name of my master Bu Naṣr, knowing that, given Bu Naṣr's short temper and irascibility, he would object and speak out against it, and this would aggravate the situation and make the Amir feel more bitter about him. His pecuniary suggestions were not, however, displeasing to the Amir. Bu'l-Ḥasan drew up a list in his own hand and included in it all the leading figures amongst the Persian officials. It was shown to the Amir, and all the leading officials vowed to obey the command, though the Almighty God alone knew how they felt about this deep in their hearts. As for Bu Naṣr, he raised imprecations to the heavens, saying, "Even a single horse and a single camel cannot be spared, for they are all needed!" He was kicking up a commotion and saying, now that he has become reduced to such a position that they set down in a list his beasts at the bidding of a scoundrel like Bu'l-Ḥasan, he welcomes the prospects of prison, humiliation, impoverishment and death! He sent a verbal message through the agency of Bu'l-'Alā' the physician to the effect that "I am an old man now, and what little wealth and luxury I possess is intended as an offering to the exalted presence, and it is for the lord to command when it is needed and to indicate, too, the fortress where I should be sent and kept." Bu'l-'Alā' said, "I hope it is abundantly clear to the Khᵛāja that I am an old friend and devotee of his." He replied, "Yes, it is." He said, "It would be unwise to send this message, since the Sultan is not the man he was, and [F 792] he is picking quarrels with everyone. We must avoid instigating an incident. You should spare me from this, for I cannot bear to listen to unpleasant words said about you."

My master wrote out a sharply-worded document in which he gave a detailed list of everything he possessed, including land, goods and chattels, and this verbal message with which he was charging Bu'l-'Alā' was set down in the document in a more exhaustive form. He came to the chamber (*vothāq*) of Āghāji—and he had never abased himself like this before in his life—and he embarked on displaying much humility and submissiveness, and gave him the document.[5] Āghāji gave an undertaking to seek out an auspicious moment to present it. My master came back to the Divān, but was pressing Āghāji to hand in the document, so that he was forced to deliver it when distressing news had just arrived and the Amir was in an angry mood. Afterwards, Āghāji came out from the Sultan's presence, sent for me and said, "Inform the Khᵛāja ʿAmid [i.e. Bu Naṣr] that I delivered the message, and the Amir said, 'I have relieved him of the obligation to comply with this,' and tell him that the Amir uttered these words in a kindly and pleasant way in order to set his mind at rest. He gave the document back to me, and whispered to me confidentially, "Don't tell your master, for it will only upset him, but the Amir threw down the document and flew into a rage, saying, [Gh 596] 'Bu Naṣr is not to blame; it's our own fault that we abjured the 300,000 dirhams which had been laid on him.'"[6] I came to the Divān, set down the document before him and repeated the first message. He offered up expressions of service and became somewhat calmer. He went back, and then summoned me. When we had partaken of some food, he drew me aside and said, "I know full well that this is not what the Amir had said. You must have regard for our ties of friendship and loyalty and tell me if Āghāji has said something else, even if you have given him your word not to tell me, so that I can see what I should do." I repeated what Āghāji had said. He said, "I knew it, and this is what I expected; a curse upon any wretch who proffers his services to kings, for they lack any notion of loyalty, mutual respectful and compassion! I am ready to face any calamities, [F 793] and I don't give a fig for what a person like Bu'l-Ḥasan says." I went back. After this, he was habitually downcast and pensive.

Meanwhile, the Amir continued to treat Bu Naṣr with due respect. One day, he offered him wine and made much of him, and Bu Naṣr went back to his house reassured and in a happy frame of mind. He sent for Bu Naṣr b. Ṭeyfur[7] the physician—I was there at the time—and others, including musicians and singers, came along. Bu Saʿid Baghlāni, who was my master's deputy postal and intelligence officer at Herat, also joined us. In the course of the proceedings, Bu Saʿid said, "This little garden of mine is pleasantly situated at half-a-parasang from the city; let the lord bestir himself and come there tomorrow." He replied, "An excellent idea!" Bu Saʿid returned to make preparations, and we too went back.

Next day, it was my turn to act as duty secretary. I came to the Divān. My master went to the garden, and told Bu'l-Ḥasan b. Delshād, Bu Naṣr b. Ṭeyfur and a few others to come there. He came back at the time of the evening worship, since it was the eve of Friday. Next day, he came to the royal court and after the court session he went to the Divān. It was a bitterly cold day and very windy. He sat down on that dais in the ʿAdnāni Garden in the corner. Then he went into the Amir's presence, laid five or six letters before him, came back to the dais, ordered replies to be composed, and collapsed, and within the space of an hour was struck down by a paralytic stroke, hemiplegia and apoplexy. It was Friday. The Amir was informed, and said, "Could it be that Bu Naṣr is feigning illness to avoid accompanying us on the expedition?" Bu'l-Qāsem b. Kathir and Bu Sahl Zowzani replied, "Bu Naṣr is not of the kind to stoop to such devices." The Amir told Bu'l-ʿAlā' [the physician] to go there and find out. Bu'l-ʿAlā' came along. The man was lying in a collapsed state. He carried out an examination of the body, and went away dejected and told the Amir, "May the lord's life [Gh 597] be prolonged! This Bu Naṣr is beyond hope, and it is necessary to seek for another Bu Naṣr." The Amir let out a cry of distress and said, "What are you saying?" He answered, "It is just as I said. Within the space of one day, and indeed, one hour, [F 794] he was struck by three severe afflictions, each potentially fatal, and his life is now in the hands of God Most High. If he manages to survive, he will be paralysed on one side." The Amir said, "Alas for Bu Naṣr!" and arose. The senior Divān officials (*khᵛājagān*) came along to his bedside, shed many tears and mourned him bitterly. They placed his body in an elephant litter, and five or six porters took it up and carried him back to this house. He remained alive that day and the night, and died the next day, May God's mercy be upon him![8]

It was said that they had given him great amounts of *k.d.w*[9] wine, together with *nabidh*,[10] on that day when he was in that garden as the guest of the deputy postal and intelligence officer. The Amir mulcted that deputy official of 5,000 dinars. All sorts of stories were told about his death, but that is no business of mine. Only God the Exalted One is able to know, since all those concerned have passed on. To sum up my own views, I would not care for dominion over the earth, with all that it entails, including inflicting harm and shedding blood, for it is evident what a man takes with him when he dies, no matter how great a wealth or high a rank he may have had. As for this great master, was there ever anything that he lacked in fortune, wealth, status, wisdom, sound judgement and knowledge? And yet for three long decades he led a life of suffering and could not relish a single day of happiness. His achievements, and stories about him and his way of life, are those which are to be found in the *Maqāmāt*[11] and in this History. But [F 795] in truth, one must know that *"with him, capability, eloquence and intelligence reached their peak."* He is even more deserving of the words that were said of the secretary Bu'l-Qāsem Eskāfi, God's mercy be upon him: (Poetry)

1. *Did you not see that the chancery was brought to a complete stop with his loss, all its pens and its registers?*[12]

Since he held me dear, dearer than his own offspring, and I was at his side for nineteen years, receiving sundry favours and shown much kindness, thereby acquiring fame, wealth, status and exalted position, I feel it incumbent upon myself to repay one debt among the many that I owe him and to set down and expound some of his noble traits and virtues, even though I can cite but one-tenth of them.[13] Since my eulogy of him *(khoṭba)*[14] will round off the life and times of this noble figure and his name will no longer grace the subsequent pages of this History, I shall let my pen shed a tear or two for a while [Gh 598] and recite from the verse and prose of those great men of the past who have also faced such losses and misfortunes in order to bring consolation[15] to myself and my readers. I shall then return to the historical narrative, *if God Most High wills.*

Section

After his death, there never was a time when I did not think about those magisterial words of his, so full of meaning; one might say that it was as if I recalled to mind these verses[16] which Moẓaffar [F 796] Qāyeni the secretary[17] uttered elegizing Motanabbi, God's mercy be upon him, and those are as follows: (Poetry)

1. *May God not lead to pasture the flocks of this age when it visits us with a calamity such as the one involving that [eloquent] tongue!*

2. *People have never seen a second Motanabbi; what second one can possibly be seen for the unique one (lit. first-born) of the age?*

3. *He was, in his lofty spirit, in a position of exaltedness and in the grandeur of one exercising power.*

4. *He was a prophet* (nabi) *in what he uttered, but his miracles* (moʿjezātuhu) *were manifest in his poetic meanings.*[18]

I never passed by the door of his residence without reciting these two verses which Bu'l-ʿAbbās Żabbi uttered one day when he passed by the door of the Ṣāḥeb [Ebn ʿAbbād]'s residence after the latter's death, God's mercy be upon him, and those verses are as follows: (Poetry)

1. *O portal, why does deep distress overwhelm you? Where is that entrance curtain, and where are those doorkeepers?*

2. *Where is the one at whom Fate used to be terrified, when he is at this moment dust within the earth?*[19]

Bu Nuwās, God's mercy be upon him, expressed it so well when he said: (Poetry)

1. *O many a noble and ancient face, now in the dust, and O many a delicate beauty, now in the dust!* [F 797]

2. *O determined and courageous one in the dust, and O tall and slender stature, now in the dust!*

3. *Ho there, every living person is mortal, and is the son of a mortal, with a deep-rooted lineage amongst mortal beings!*[20]

And in Rudaki's words:

1. You who are sad and distressed, and justly so, and in seclusion allow the tears to stream and flow,

2. I have my reason not to address your grief by name; by its recall, greater hardship may be invoked, through the hands of fate.[21]

3. He, destined to leave, has left; those destined to come, have come; what is done is done, why grieve in vain?

4. All unruffled you wish the life on earth? Alas, that's life! How could it bear such quiet mirth?

5. Do not rail and bewail, for its ears are closed to your plaints; do not weep and cry, for its eyes are shut to your tears.

6. Tend to your loss, and mourn till the Judgement Day! When has mourning brought back those departed?

7. The revolving wheel will tax you even more, if every mishap can cast you down into such despair.

8. It's as if Fate's cursèd calamity keeps a beady eye fixed on those to whom you have bestowed your heart.

9. Not a cloud in the sky, and no word of any eclipse, and yet the moon is in a shroud and the world gone dark for you. [F 798]

10. Take it or leave it, but it's best to bow to custom; go fetch the wine and hand it round,

11. Batter the armies of despair; banish them from your heart, deny them their victory!

12. In bleak adversity they show their mettle: magnanimity, manly virtue and true nobility.[22]

The calamity of losing this outstanding man was not considered commensurate with that (i.e. the loss of Bu Naṣr was much greater than that of the person mourned by Rudaki), indeed, it was just as has been said,

[Khoṭba]

It seared the hearts and minds and tore at them and it wounded spirits and livers and consumed them with fire; it choked breasts with the cares which struck them, cast motes into eyes from sources of fear which seized them; it filled breasts with dismay and crushed minds into fragments. It left cheeks lacerated, tears flowing in torrents, powers crushed and ways of proceeding blocked. What a great one has been lost, and what a noble one is being placed in the grave! Indeed, I mourn him with lamentation for his virtues, I elegise him together with the shining stars, I am deprived of him with his noble qualities and excellences and I eulogise him for his lofty endeavours and virtuous deeds.

If it were possible to buy off the onslaught of death with a ransom of wealth and helpers, or indeed, with the senses of hearing and sight, then noble and free-born persons would find the ransom for that prominent figure, and by it his life's blood would be saved. Nevertheless, there is no calamity when there is faith, and no misfortune when there is the Qor'ān. The Book of God is sufficient as a consoler and is a soothing balm for the universality of death. Indeed, God Most High lightens the burden of the onslaughts of fortune, and He gives renewed consolation in time of disaster through mention of God's decree in regard to the Lord of the Messengers and the Seal of the Prophets. May God grant prayers over him and over them all, and may He be pleased with this ʿAmid and prominent figure and perfect one, and may he grant him contentment and make [F 799] *the Garden of Paradise his abode and place of refuge! May He forgive his sins and lighten his burden* (i.e. of past misdeeds), *and may He awaken us from the sleep of the heedless! Amen, amen, O Lord of the Worlds!*[23]

The Amir ordered Bu'l-Qāsem b. Kathir and Bu Sahl Zowzani to see to the arrangements for the funeral rites. They came along, and sat there all day until all arrangements were completed. His coffin was borne to the open country and many people performed the funerary prayers over him.[24] The Commander-in-Chief and the Great Chamberlain had come on that day, together with a large number of prominent people. A strange and remarkable thing was that there was a hospice (*rebāṭ*), adjacent to which were two graves, and Bu Naṣr had said of them, "Would that I might become the third of them!" They made a grave for him in that hospice. He was laid there for twenty days and he was then brought back to Ghaznin and buried in the garden of the *rebāṭ* that had been constructed at the army review ground.[25]

Those gholāms of Bu Naṣr who were especially suited for service and who were still slaves (i.e. not manumitted) were brought to the Sultan's palace, and the horses, camels and mules were branded with the Sultan's mark. (And to think that, when they had asked for some of these before,[26] he had become greatly agitated, but now he left them behind so easily and departed from this world!) Bu Saʿid the inspector came at the royal command in order to draw up an inventory for the royal treasury of whatever the man possessed. He reported back to the Amir the correctness of the document that Bu Naṣr had himself prepared previously for the Amir. He was apprised of its contents, and it finally appeared from the list that there was not a single thread additional to what had been previously set down. The Amir was astonished at the integrity and honesty of this man *both in life and in death*, and he lavished praises on him. Every time that his name was mentioned, he would express his grief and commiseration, and would revile Bu'l-Ḥasan b. [F 800] ʿAbd al-Jalil for his ingratitude.[27]

A private session was held in which the Amir entrusted responsibility for his Chancery to Khᵛāja Bu Sahl Zowzani, with myself appointed as his deputy and second-in-command. The Amir had said in private that "If Bu'l-Fażl were not so young a man, [Gh 601] we would have given the post to him, since before Bu Naṣr passed away, in that last wine-drinking session, he said to us confidentially, 'I have become an old man and am approaching my end. If I should die, Bu'l-Fażl should be kept on and looked after,'" and the Vizier had also talked approvingly of me.[28] At the time of the afternoon worship I went to see the Vizier and found him at court, and I thanked him for his kind words. He said, "Don't thank me, thank your old master, who has uttered such kind things in your favour before he died, and the Amir in his privy session today recalled them all." I gave grateful thanks in my prayers for both the living and for my dead master.

Things settled down, and Bu Sahl was coming to the Divān. He stationed himself at a corner in the garden until the time when he donned his robe of honour, a most magnificent one. He went home with it, and was showered with gifts and presents, since he enjoyed immense prestige.

On Wednesday, 11 Ṣafar [/2 November 1039], he took his place in the Divān, wearing his robe of honour, and embarked upon running the administration. He was very much out of his depth in the task.[29] I was trying to show due deference to his high status and dignified rank, but when I had a taste of his malevolent behaviour and evil temper, and I realized that in all things he was the exact opposite of Bu Naṣr Moshkān, I wrote out a memorandum to the Amir, in the appropriate form for a request, to be relieved of office as a secretary. I said, "Bu Naṣr was a source of strength for me, but when he departed this life, everything changed; and I felt bereft of that power. I have a long record of service, and I fear that that my present master, Bu Sahl Zowzani, may prove awkward, for he has an evil temper. The lord has at his disposal other posts; if the exalted judgement sees fit, let me become occupied with some other office." I gave this document to Āghāji. He delivered it [F 801] and brought it back. The Amir had written in his own hand on the top, "Even if Bu Naṣr has passed away, we are still here, and we have in truth recognized your worth. What's the reason for this despair?" I was much heartened by this regal response. This monarch's concern for his servants was such that, in a private session with the Vizier, he told Bu Sahl, "Bu'l-Fażl isn't your underling, he has been my father's secretary and confidant; treat him well, for I shan't be at all pleased if he has any cause to complain." He replied, "I'll obey the command." Then the Amir said to the Vizier, "I entrust Bu'l-Fażl to you, look after him." The Vizier informed me of this confidentially and raised my spirits.

My position remained secure and stable, and this new master of mine held me in high esteem and fully recognized my status as long as that monarch remained on the throne. Afterwards, things took a different turn, and a change came over Bu Sahl, and I too was partially to blame. Difficult times set in and I, though still young, fell down into a snare. Many wrongs [Gh 602] were committed, at a time when I passed through a period of hardship and suffered many ups and downs, and had to take the rough with the smooth.[30] Twenty years have elapsed and I am still afflicted by it all, and all those involved have passed on.

He was a great man, this master of mine, and I am not being perverse or injudicious, but what choice do I have but to expatiate on these happenings in this History? For since I had to give an account of the life and times of my friends and superiors, I had to include something about my own life too. But I revert to the main narrative so that it could not be said of me that I approach my task in the manner of Ṣuli, heaping praises upon myself. For Ṣuli composed a work on the history of the ʿAbbasid caliphs, may God be pleased with them, and called it the [*Ketāb al-*] *Owrāq*.[31] He expended a great deal of effort on it, since he was a man of deep learning and peerless in his time in belles-lettres, grammar and philology; it would be no exaggeration to say that seldom has the world seen his like. But he launched upon [F 802] praising himself and his own verses, of which he produced a great many, so that people protested in exasperation and only made allowances for him out of respect for his learning and erudition. For example, at the end of each ode he wrote "When I recited that poem to the vizier Abu'l-Ḥasan 'Ali b. al-Forāt,[32] I said, 'If the Vizier desires an ode from the poet Boḥtori[33] of the same final letter (*rawi*), metre and rhyme, he won't be up to it.'" The Vizier laughed and said, "That's very true." People have laughed at this all through the ages, and today's readers will no doubt find it amusing. Since I, Bu'l-Fażl, am fully aware of this potential pitfall, I shall not follow in Ṣuli's footsteps and indulge in self-praise. I have written in such a manner that if it is perused by the old and seasoned figures from the era of Maḥmud and Mas'ud, they would not be able to cavil at it. *May God preserve us from error and mistakes through His graciousness and the breadth of His grace!*

Amir Mas'ud's journey from Herat to Pushang[34]

On Wednesday, 18 Ṣafar [/9 November], the Amir set out from Herat towards Pushang with a mighty army, fully prepared, with war elephants, numerous infantry and less cumbersome baggage.[35] At Pushang, he ordered the army to take up its battle formation: the Sultan in the centre, the Commander-in-Chief 'Ali on the right wing; the Great Chamberlain Sübashï on the left wing; the Master of the Royal Stables Böri [Gh 603] , together with the Keeper of the Royal Vessels Begtegin [in charge of the rearguard]; and Sonqor and the General Bu Bakr with the whole of the Kurdish and Arab troops, and 500 *kheyltāsh*s, [F 803] in the vanguard. He ordered a splendid robe of honour to be given to the Palace Chamberlain Ertegin, and he gave to the Master of the Royal Stables a two-pointed cap and a girdle and made him the deputy of the Commander of the Palace Gholāms Begtughdï so that he might be able to convey what orders Begtughdï might need to give to the palace gholāms. There were many Indian troops, comprising both cavalrymen with mounts marked with brands[36] and also infantrymen, all with illustrious commanders; these had been distributed and stationed in the centre, on the right and left wings and in the rearguard, as were likewise the palace infantry, the greater part of them mounted on swift riding camels. There were in the expedition fifty war elephants of the highest calibre, and everyone averred that they had never seen such an army as this. A great clamour arose to the heavens when this mighty army moved off.

Ṭoghrïl was meanwhile at Nishapur. When the Amir reached the caravanserai at Senjed, where the road divides for Nishapur and for Ṭus,[37] he decided to make for Ṭus, hoping to instil a sense of security in Ṭoghrïl and induce him to tarry a while and postpone his departure from Nishapur. The Amir could hasten by the Nowq road in the direction of Ostovā and seize control of the road so that Ṭoghrïl would not be able to enter Nasā.[38] Ṭoghrïl might then have to opt for the Herat and Sarakhs road and thus give the Amir the opportunity to seize him. In accordance with this decision, the Amir travelled to Ṭābarān of Ṭus.[39] He remained there for two days at Saʿdābād[40] until the whole of the army came up. Then he went to the spring of Shirkhān.[41] He took a purging medicine, and then recovered from its effects and enjoyed a light sleep. At the time of the afternoon worship he called for a female elephant and mounted it, and gave instructions to the Vizier that he was to move off at the time of the evening worship, to be followed by[42] the infantry, baggage, the drums and standard, the Commander of the Palace Gholāms Begtughdï and a palace gholām. The army itself was to follow after the Vizier. He gave these orders and hurried on the elephant so that he could ride at great speed. He was accompanied by 1,000 palace gholāms, 2,000 cavalrymen from every ethnic group and 2,000 infantrymen, [Gh 604] heavily armed and mounted on swift riding camels. Before his departure,[43] the army, without being instructed, started to move off, in such a manner that [F 804] the Vizier was unable to hold them back, however hard he tried, till finally he gave the command that they were to go. At the time of the night worship, they took up their arms and equipment and moved off.

Ṭoghrïl had posted riders with good mounts all along the road. When he had heard that the army had gone towards Ṭus, it became evident to him that the Amir was planning to seize the roads and block his movements. He speedily headed towards Ostovā.[44] Amongst the remarkable combination of events and circumstances so ordained that Ṭoghrïl should not be captured, was the fact that the Sultan had taken a small amount of theriac, without sufficient sleep afterwards to counter its soporific effects. After the time of the evening worship he fell asleep while being carried on the elephant. When the elephant drivers became aware of this, they did not dare to urge the elephant on rapidly but drove it along at a measured and leisurely pace, while the Sultan slept on till near the dawn, forfeiting the opportunity to strike at the enemy. If it had not been for that sleep, he would have come upon Ṭoghrïl at the time of first light.

I was myself with the Amir. Early at dawn we travelled on rapidly so that in the course of the morning we were at Nowq. There a halt was made. He performed the dawn worship, and the large, brazen kettledrums, which were mounted on swift riding camels, were beaten. The Amir urged on the elephant ever faster, and the Commander Badr, with a force of Kurd and Arab troops, and the Commander Ertegin with 500 palace gholāms, set off at a cracking pace. When they reached Khujān, the chef-lieu of Ostovā,[45] Ṭoghrïl had left there in the course of the morning, since the sound of the large kettledrums had reached his ears, and he had left the district by the road of the pass crossing the mountains, in such a way that the Turkmens had in their haste abandoned heavy impedimenta in several places. The Amir arrived on their heels, the day being Sunday, 5 Rabiʿ I [/25 November 1039], and made camp, furious at forfeiting this opportunity [of catching Ṭoghrïl]. He was vexed with himself and people at large, uttering terrible insults and imprecations, and showing his disappointment and anger to an extent that I had never witnessed before. He immediately despatched Tegin J.y.l.m.y,[46] who was an outstanding and courageous champion warrior amongst the cavalrymen and who used to hold the headship of the gholāms housed in the palace barracks,[47] together with 500 fresh and rested gholāms [F 805] and 500 *kheyltāsh*s to pursue the fugitives. Other people too went after them, avidly bent on finding something. They returned at the time of the evening worship, bringing back all sorts of goods and fabrics, and they reported that "Ṭoghrïl had left in a very great hurry and had made use of fresh horses which he had stationed along the road, and we did not catch sight of him. But we reached a group of people who said that Soleymān, son of [Gh 605] Arslān Jādheb, and the General Qadïr were their leaders,[48] and that the valley was extremely narrow but that their leaders knew of a particular path to cross the mountains and managed to cross over with all their equipment.[49] It was evident that these people were not Turkmens."

The Amir encamped here for two days to give the army some rest and refreshment. Bu Sahl Ḥamdavi and Suri caught up with us here, together with the Commander, Keeper of the Royal Wardrobe, the Treasurer Gowhar-āyin, other commanders and 500 cavalrymen. The Amir instructed them thus, "You must proceed to Nishapur and take control of the town, for a letter has come from Bu'l-Moẓaffar Jomaḥi, the postal and intelligence officer. He has come out of hiding, and the 'Alids are assisting him, but the town notables have risen up and are causing trouble. You must proceed there so that the town may be restored to order, and you must collect and store as much food and fodder as possible, for we intend to spend the remainder of the winter there." They set out.

The Amir decided on a quick move and rode swiftly towards Bāvard, and he instructed the Vizier that he was to follow after him with the cavalry who had not been detailed for this expedition. The Amir set off in haste with riders on good mounts unencumbered with heavy equipment, and they followed unmarked tracks.[50] When Ṭoghrïl [F 806] reached Bāvard, he found Dāvud and the Yïnāliyān and the whole of the Turkmen forces already there. Orders had been given to the effect that "The entire baggage train should speedily go into the desert so that we can all be in the desert and indulge in a foray or two to gauge the enemy's strength.[51] For there is a different scale and magnitude to the threat from this monarch now." They were involved in these deliberations when the watchmen who were stationed on the hilltops all came down together in a rush and reported that the Sultan had come. They communicated the information to Ṭoghrïl, Dāvud and the other leaders of the Turkmen host, and they sent off their baggage. By the time we had passed through that terrain of hillocks and mounds[52] and reached the open country of Bāvard, they had managed to establish a little distance between themselves and us, and we would have succeeded in catching up with them if the Amir had proceeded swiftly.

But as Fate would have it, and as another proof of the fact that no scheme will succeed if God Most High does not wish it, they captured a young man of servile birth[53] and the chamberlain brought him before the Amir, and he was questioned about what the Turkmens were doing. He said, "It is some days since they sent the baggage and Ḥoseyn b. 'Ali b. Mikā'il[54] into the sandy desert of Nasā and Farāva. The leading men and commanders, with a numerous and well-equipped army, are on the fringes of the desert, at a distance of ten parasangs away from the road. My horse became lame, and I was left behind." [Gh 606] The Amir desisted from carrying on with the chase. Several cavalrymen, commanders of our vanguard, came in and told the Amir, "This young man is lying. They sent off their baggage this mid-morning, and we saw the dust flying up." The Commander-in-Chief ʿAli and the others said, "That was the dust raised by our army, since these fellows are not so careless as to keep their baggage as close to themselves as that." Their words weakened the Amir's resolve. He had travelled a long distance, and the day was hot. He encamped on the outskirts of Bāvard. If only he had pressed on with the same haste, or else had despatched a force of troops, all this gang of the Turkmens would have fallen into his hands, [F 807] since during the night, our spies came in and reported that "The Turkmens are panic-stricken and have despaired of their lives, and their baggage is very near to them. If the Amir had come up with them, a much-desired victory would have been his, but since the Ghaznavid army did not arrive, they rapidly sent off their baggage so that they might move to Nasā. For they have been overwhelmed by great fear and terror. If the Sultan proceeds to Farāva, they will certainly not be able to stand firm, since they are in desperate need of food and fodder, and they were saying, 'No matter how long they pursue us, we will press on ahead (i.e. further into the deep desert) until winter comes and makes the conditions too unbearable for them and forces them to turn back. Then in spring, unencumbered by baggage, we shall return to face them in battle'."

When the Amir had been informed of these reports, he took up his position at Bāvard. He summoned the leading men of state and discussed the situation with them. Bu Sahl, the Head of the Chancery, sought there in his department succinct versions of the reports, [and on the basis of them][55] retailed the information that the spies had brought back. All sorts of opinions were expressed. The Vizier said, "The lord's judgement is the best and the loftiest! From here, the way is not very long. I think that the wisest course for us is to proceed to Nasā and spend several days there and replenish our troops with food and fodder. This will strike more fear amongst our foes and make them flee even further afar. Moreover, the news will reach Khwarazm and have a beneficial impact, for it will become evident to people, whether distant or near, that on this occasion the lord is here to stay in Khorasan and will not return until all the troubles and disturbances have been addressed and resolved." The Amir commented, "This is indeed the best plan."

He set forth the next day and went to Nasā. There was much consternation in those regions. The enemy withdrew from Farāva into the desert and they transported their baggage to the Balkhān Kuh region. If only we had pursued and attacked them then, we would have fulfilled many of our aims. [F 808] A long time afterwards it transpired that the enemy had been reduced to such a state that for several days Ṭoghrïl had not been able to take off his boots and his breastplate, and that when he went to sleep he would make his shield his pillow. With their leader in such a state, one can well imagine the plight of the rest! [Gh 607]

The Amir stayed at Nasā for a few days and indulged in wine-drinking, since it was a pleasant region. The royal army[56] sent a secret, confidential letter from Khwarazm and made conciliatory approaches.[57] We composed confidential letters under the royal emblem and seal in reply to it. The Vizier said to me, "This is all blandishment. They know that we cannot go after them; for one thing, there is famine in these regions (i.e. in northern Khorasan), and the army cannot stay here long enough to make a move against Khwarazm; second, the enemy in Khorasan is in such close proximity to us, and it is for them that we have come here in the first place. They have tried to fob us off with empty promises and pledges.[58] It is nevertheless necessary to give a favourable answer to the Khwarazmians so that, if they harbour any evildoing in their mind, they will be put to shame and will be reduced to silence."

When the enemy withdrew into the confines of the desert, and the matter of finding food and fodder there [F 809] became critical, and the troops began to complain vociferously, the Amir came back from Nasā, by the same Bāvard and Ostovā road, and headed towards Nishapur. The judges, the religious and legal scholars and the sons of the Judge Ṣāʿed—the Judge Ṣāʿed himself being too frail to attend—came out as far as the urban centre (*qaṣaba*) of Ostovā, which is called Khujān, to greet and to escort him back. The Amir reached Nishapur on Thursday, 15 Rabiʿ II [/4 January 1040] and on the twenty-seventh of the month [/16 January] encamped at the Garden of Shādyākh.[59] Suri had ordered that the throne of Masʿud on which Ṭoghrïl had sat, and the furnishings and coverings of the dais, should be pulled apart and given to the poor, and the whole re-made. He had ordered much repairing and reconstruction to be done, and the stables which the Turkmens had constructed to be pulled down. The Amir was very pleased with this and heaped praises on him. Strenuous efforts had been made to gather together twenty days' food and fodder.

Nishapur was not the city I knew from the past; it now lay in ruins, with only vestiges of habitation and urban life. A *man* of bread sold for three dirhams. Property owners (*kadkhodāyān*) had torn off the roofs of their houses and sold them. A great number of people, together with their families and children, had died from hunger. The price of landed property had plummeted, and the value of the dirham had sunk to a *dāng*.[60] The Imam Movaffaq, the *ṣāḥeb-ḥadithān*,[61] had fled with Ṭoghrïl. After a week, the Amir [F 810] sent the General Badr to the rural district of Bosht (text, Bost), the General Altuntāsh to the rural district of Beyhaq, the Great Chamberlain to Khᵛāf, Bākharz and Esfand,[62] and the Commander-in-Chief to Ṭus. He filled all the outlying districts [Gh 608] with troops, and devoted himself to wine-drinking and pleasure. Meanwhile, the weather was bitterly cold and life was becoming hard to bear. Such a famine in Nishapur could not be recalled, and large numbers of people died, soldiers and civilians alike.

I saw some remarkable things in these times which I feel obliged to recount for they help towards a better understanding of this deceitful present world. In Nishapur there was a village called Moḥammadābād, adjacent to Shādyākh.[63] It is a much sought-after location where one ploughland of ground there, which is called a *jarib* in Nishapur, Isfahan and Kerman,[64] was wont to be bought for 1,000 dirhams as virgin land, and if it had trees and cultivation would fetch 3,000 dirhams. My master Bu Naṣr had a finely-built residence there, with gardens on three sides. That year when we came back from Ṭabarestān, and found ourselves spending the summer at Nishapur, he sought to purchase the remaining piece of land so that the house would have a garden on all four sides.[65] He bought this for 10,000 dirhams from three landowners, and a deed of sale was written out and attested by witnesses. When they asked for the price to be handed over—and I myself was there—my master said, "One part of the price[66] must be accepted in silver (i.e. in dirhams) [F 811] and the rest in gold (i.e. in dinars)." The vendors insisted that it should all be paid in gold. He thought for a while, and then picked up the deed of sale and tore it up, saying, "I don't need the land." The owners of the land regretted their words and offered their apologies, but he said, "I definitely don't want it," and the owners went away. He said to me, "What got into my head to make me want to buy land! With the state of the world as I see it, those who live long enough will find out that matters will get to the stage when a ploughland of ground will go for ten dirhams." I went back, telling myself that all this stemmed from my master's fiery and bilious temper.[67]

During this year, we came to Nishapur, and Bu Sahl Zowzani took up his residence in this house of my master.[68] One day I went to him. I found some of the local landowners (*dehqānān*) with him. They were negotiating the sale of thirty ploughlands of ground adjacent to this residence to Bu Sahl, so that his builder[69] might lay out a garden and residence there. They were asking for 200 dirhams per ploughland, and he was haggling until finally he consented. In the end, he bought it and the price was handed over. A smile appeared on my face, and he noticed it; he had a very suspicious mind and a trivial incident could arouse his suspicions.[70] When the group of vendors went away, he said to me, "I put a lot of effort into this in order to bring it about." I was about to return home when he said, "You smiled when the price was handed over for the piece of ground; why was this?" I told him about the episode involving my master Bu Naṣr and the land he sought to buy. [Gh 609] He thought for a long while, and then said, "Alas that Bu Naṣr has gone! He was wise and far-sighted! If you had told me about this before, I would never have purchased this land, but now that it has been bought and paid for, it would be unseemly to renege on the transaction." [F 812]

Subsequently, when these events befell us at Dandānqān, I learnt that matters had reached such a state at this place, Moḥammadābād, that a ploughland of ground was being offered for a single *man* of wheat, but there were no takers; and if one goes back to the time just before the events of this year,[71] a ploughland of ground would be bought for 1,000 dirhams, and after these events it would be sold for 200 dirhams, and afterwards, as mentioned, it would be offered for sale for a single *man* of wheat and there would be no-one to buy it over the course of a twenty-four hours' span.[72] There is a lesson in all this. Furthermore, I saw smooth-surfaced and polished glass drinking vessels,[73] including those of Baghdadi manufacture, which had been bought for a dinar[74] and which were now sold for three dirhams.

After we went back, a *man* of bread had become thirteen dirhams at Nishapur, and the greater part of the population of the city and its outlying regions died.

The position regarding food and fodder reached such a point that I observed one day—it being my turn as duty secretary in the Divān—that the Amir had sat down with the Vizier and the Head of the Chancery, and it took them until the midday worship to scrape together five days' supply of food and fodder. There was no bread or meat for the gholāms, and no hay or barley for the horses. [F 813] After the midday worship, we completed the business of the food and fodder. The Amir was relating this affair in a laughing manner, mentioning the strange and wondrous aspects of it, when at this very moment a courier of the postal and intelligence service arrived from Ghaznin. I presented the letter.[75] It was from the castellan of Ghaznin, Bu ʿAli. He read it and turned towards the boon-companions, and said, "The castellan has written and has said that 20,000 odd *qafiz*s of corn have been stored up in containers in the granaries—should he sell this or should he keep it? We have such a huge amount of corn in Ghazni, and such dearth and want here!" The boon-companions too were amazed at this. From this moment till the time when this monarch passed away, many strange things happened which I will relate in their appropriate places so that readers will agree that this present world is not worth a trifle. The position regarding food and fodder got so serious that camels were led as far as Dāmghān, and food and fodder brought back from there. It goes without saying that the Turkmens[76] did not harass or hover around us, since they too were taken up with their own welfare, since this dearth and famine had spread everywhere. [Gh 610]

Bu Sahl Ḥamdavi had been out of favour for some time with the Amir, and was most worried and upset about it.[77] The Vizier was also further muddying the waters in an underhand manner.[78] Finally, Bu Sahl brought Masʿud b. Leyth into the affair as an intermediary, and verbal messages went to and fro for several days until it was decided that he, Bu Sahl, should make a voluntary offering of 50,000 dinars to the lord. He gave a written instruction for this, and he sent the money to the Treasury secretly. The Amir ordered that he should be given a splendid robe of honour, and he used to come to the Amir's court circle and sit down as a boon companion. A few days after this, the Amir ordered him to go off to Ghaznin [F 814] and to set the affairs of Nishapur in order.[79] The wealth stored up at the fortress of the Mikā'ilis was to be brought forth, and he was to travel via the road through the rural district of Bosht[80] towards Sistan, and thence via the Bosht road to Ghaznin. He made preparations for his journey, and a commander[81] was detailed, together with 200 fully-armed and equipped cavalrymen to accompany him. A letter went off to the General Badr instructing him to go out as an escort for them along the road and conduct them to the border region,[82] and this he did. They reached Ghaznin safely, together with what they bore (i.e. the wealth from the fortress of the Mikā'ilis), and they did not witness that calamity which we had to experience (i.e. the Dandānqān disaster).

The Amir appointed Bu'l-Ḥasan b. ʿAbd al-Jalil as mayor (*ra'is*) of Nishapur, with exactly the same investiture patent and richly-embroidered official robes[83] that Amir Maḥmud had given to Ḥasanak. He awarded him a splendid robe of honour, a *ṭeylasān* and a *dorrāʿa*.[84] He came into the royal presence, rendered service and went back. The horse for His Eminence (the Great Khᵛāja), the mayor of Nishapur, was sent for.[85] He went back to his house, and people came to pay their respects to him with substantial offerings. The notables and military leaders of Nishapur all came to him and he was bragging in a self-congratulatory manner, saying that[86] "I too have a status like Ḥasanak's," but they excoriated him,[87] pointing out that the conditions at this time bore little resemblance to that of Ḥasanak's era.

At this time, letters arrived from the Caliph, *may God grant him long life*,[88] containing very cordial expressions of friendship. [F 815] He had instructed the Sultan, "He should stand firm in Khorasan until he has extinguished the flames of sedition fanned by the Turkmens. When he has accomplished that task, he should lead an expedition to Ray and Jebāl so that those regions too may be cleansed of usurpers."[89] The Sultan responded in the following terms: "The exalted command was received and obeyed. I had already the same intentions, but now that the command has come, it will stiffen my resolve." The Amir of Baghdad had likewise written a letter and had made conciliatory gestures, since he was fearful of this monarch launching an attack on him.[90] A reply also went back to him in favourable terms. The Amir further sent a very splendid robe of honour to Bā Kālijār, the governor of Gorgān and Ṭabarestān, through an envoy, [Gh 611] and a letter full of cordiality and encouraging words, since he had performed praiseworthy services at that time when Bu Sahl Ḥamdavi and Suri were there. The Amir re-appointed Bu'l-Ḥasan Karaji, who had been the treasurer of Western Persia and had come back with this group, to be a boon-companion and gave him a robe of honour. He had aged, and was not the same Bu'l-Ḥasan I knew in the old days. Times had changed, and so had the people and everything else besides.

On Thursday, 18 Jomādā II [/6 March], the Amir celebrated the festival of Nowruz. A large number of presents had been brought, and there was much celebration. He listened to verses recited by the poets, since he was in a happy frame of mind during this winter season and nothing untoward had occurred. He gave orders for sums of money and presents to be distributed, including also for the musicians and singers.[91] There had been intercessions for the poet Masʿud.[92] He ordered him to be given a present of 300 dinars in coinage[93] and a salary of 1,000 dinars per month from the taxation levied on the Jhelum province, but he also commanded him to remain in India.

After Nowruz, he embarked on the forthcoming military expedition, and the remaining tasks were completed. He told the head of the Divān,[94] Suri, "Get ready to accompany us, so that you too can leave the town at once, and your brother can act as deputy here at Nishapur." He replied, "I'll obey the command, and I myself was resolved to do this so that I may not for one instant be far from the lord's stirrup [F 816] because of what I suffered during this time." He made his brother his deputy and got busy with preparations. The Amir had also said that "Suri must be brought with me, for if Khorasan is cleared of the enemy, he can be sent back again (i.e. to his former office as head of the Divān of Khorasan), but if things turn out differently, this man must not fall into enemy hands for he will then turn the whole world against me." It was said that Bu Sahl Ḥamdavi instilled this idea in the Amir's head. The Amir ordered Bu'l-Moẓaffar Jomaḥi to be given a robe of honour, and he was confirmed in the office of postal and intelligence officer. He gave robes of honour to the ʿAlids and to the marshal of the ʿAlids, to whom he also entrusted Bu'l-Moẓaffar.[95] During this period, the Judge Ṣāʿed had seen the Amir on one occasion only, but his two sons used to come regularly to the court. Now the Judge came to bid farewell, and he sent up prayers for the Amir and offered counsel. The Amir gave robes of honour to both his sons, and they were sent homewards with great decorum and respect.

On Saturday, 28 Jomādā II [/16 March], this being the tenth day of Nowruz, the Amir led the army from Nishapur to the neighbourhood of Ṭus. He travelled by the Deh-e Sorkh[96] road and encamped in the plain at the meeting place of the roads going to Sarakhs, Nasā, Bāvard, Ostovā and Nishapur. He despatched detachments in all four directions to act as scouts, with able and alert leaders [Gh 612] and commanders of great repute. Our opponents were likewise on the move and came to Sarakhs with a large and well-equipped army, and they sent out their scouting parties to confront our own army. Both sides were proceeding warily and were on the alert, and there were some clashes and confrontations. The Amir had pitched his tent on an eminence, and the army had encamped in battle formation, fully armed and equipped. He was drinking wine, and was not going out in person with the main body of the army to confront the enemy [F 817] but was waiting for the supplies of grain to arrive. Prices had spiralled to such an extent that a *man* of bread went up to thirteen dirhams, but was still scarce, and as for barley, it was nowhere to be found. They ransacked Ṭus and its environs, and whoever had even a *man* of corn was forced to part with it. Suri truly devastated these districts. Many people and livestock perished from lack of food and fodder, for it is obvious how long one can survive on a diet of rough weeds and brambles. Things got to such a pass that there was a fear lest the lack of food and fodder should induce the army to break out in revolt, thus undermining the whole undertaking. The Amir was informed about this, and it was frankly stated that the situation was getting out of hand[97] and that a move must be made, since, if this were not done, things would reach a point when it would be difficult to retrieve the situation.

The Amir departed from there, heading towards Sarakhs, on Saturday, 19 Shaʿbān [/5 May]. Before we could reach Sarakhs, countless horses dropped dead on the road, and the men were all plunged in deep despair from prolonged hunger and dearth of food. We reached there on 28 Shaʿbān [/14 May].[98] The town looked parched and in ruins, and there was not a single shoot of corn. The inhabitants had all fled, and the plains and mountains looked scorched, with not a speck of vegetation in sight. The troops were dumbfounded. They would go and fetch from afar bits of rotten vegetation that rainwater had washed up and deposited on the surrounding plains in former times, and they would sprinkle water on them and would throw them before their mounts. The beasts would try a mouthful or two, but would then lift up their heads and just stare until they died from hunger. The infantry were in no better shape.[99]

The Amir was profoundly shocked by this state of affairs, and called a meeting with the Vizier, Abu Sahl, the great men of state and the leading figures of the army. He said, "What's the solution? If things remain like this, [F 818] neither the troops nor their mounts will survive. However, I do know that although the enemy have assembled all their forces, they too are suffering from these shortages." They replied, "May the lord's life be prolonged! The situation at Merv is quite different regarding abundance of food and fodder, and more favourable than everything else for them is the fact that now the corn harvest has ripened and the enemy is there to enjoy this. Before we can get there, their beasts will have rested and will be fattened up and in good shape, while we will not find anything along this road.[100] The wisest course appears to be that the lord should go to Herat, [Gh 613] since there is food and fodder there in Bādghis and the surrounding districts. We can stay there for a few days and then, being well prepared and ready, we can launch an attack on the enemy." The Amir said, "You are wrong here. I am not going anywhere except to Merv, no matter what happens, for that's where the enemy will be,[101] and I cannot keep on coming back to deal with this matter every single day." They said, "It's the lord's place to command, and we will carry out his orders wherever he may go."

They left his presence in a despondent mood and gathered together for a private discussion. They sent a verbal message through Bu'l-Ḥasan b. [F 819] ʿAbd al-Jalil and Masʿud b. Leyth to the effect that "It is not a sound idea to head towards Merv, for we are in a year of drought and have been told that there is no water or food and fodder on the way. The troops will be under great strain, and we do not want, Heaven forbid, any disturbances to occur, since it will then be extremely hard to salvage things." The two went off and delivered this message. The Amir flew into a violent rage, treated the two of them disparagingly and reviled them, saying, "You're all a bunch of pimps who keep putting words into each other's mouths.[102] You don't want this venture to succeed, so that I can go on suffering from this calamity (i.e. the problem of the Turkmens) and you can continue with your pilfering and thieving (i.e. I will be preoccupied, and you will be doing well out of the war), but I shall lead you into a place where the whole lot of you will fall into a pit and perish, so that I shall be free of you and your treacheries and you will be free of me. Let no-one bring a message on this topic a second time, or I'll order his head cut off!"

The two of them went back discomfited to the group who had sent them and sat down, without saying a word. The notables said, "What answer did he give?" Bu l-Fatḥ [b. Masʿud] b. Leyth began delivering a smoothly polished speech, but Bu'l-Ḥasan said, "Don't listen to him, for the Amir did not speak in this way. It would be wrong to mislead you, the great men of state, at such a critical juncture.[103] In fact, the Amir said such-and-such." The Vizier looked at the Commander-in-Chief, and the Great Chamberlain said to the Commander-in-Chief, "There's no place for further words. It is for the lord to command; we are servants, and the best thing for us is what the lord wishes for us." They arose and went out, and conveyed this information to the Amir.

Several things happened in this wise to the Commander-in-Chief, ʿAli Dāya, [F 820] which caused great vexation in the Amir's mind. One of these was that when we were at Ṭus a letter arrived from the General Altuntāsh, stating that, "The enemy are putting pressure on my front, and more troops are needed." The reply went forth, "Keep a stout heart, for we have given the Commander-in-Chief orders to join up with you." [At the same time,] a letter went to the Commander-in-Chief instructing him to go to Altuntāsh's assistance. The Commander-in-Chief said, "What use is it to me to have all the trappings of rank and status, the large kettledrum, the barrel-shaped drum and the ordinary-sized kettledrum[104] if I have to act as the subordinate of Altuntāsh?" and he gave orders for all the drums and other insignia of command such as banners to be ripped up and broken and then burnt. This news was brought to the Amir, [Gh 614] and he thought it advisable to send Masʿud b. Leyth to the Commander-in-Chief in order to mollify him. He went off on this mission, but it did not work and the Amir had to summon ʿAli Dāya himself and personally comfort and reassure him. Such things went on, and cracks began to appear. The Amir was acquiring a jaundiced view of his leading men. They, for their part, were going along with a heavy heart and in a despondent mood when that overwhelming catastrophe[105] occurred.[106]

While the Amir was in the private quarters and sitting by himself in the large tent, he conveyed his concerns regarding the Vizier and the leading army commanders to the household eunuchs,[107] and said, "They have absolutely no desire that this undertaking should go forward so that I may be freed of this pain and distress. That's how things went today. But come what may, tomorrow I will certainly set out for Merv." They said, "The lord shouldn't ask them, but should always be acting according to his own judgement and plans." The Vizier heard about this, and said to Bu Sahl Zowzani, "Alas for the land where it is the household eunuchs who make the decisions![108] We shall have to see what we can do." (There was one of those eunuchs, Eqbāl of the Golden Hands, who aspired to much wisdom. I am not saying that he was not clever and well-versed in his own personal affairs, but how could he have the necessary vision and understanding needed for such momentous undertakings?) Bu Sahl said, "If this is the case, the Vizier should persevere on the right course [F 821] and not throw up his arms in despair after just one or two attempts.[109] You should speak again." He replied, "That's what I thought."

He went back to his tent and sent someone to summon Altuntāsh. He came, and the Vizier had a private meeting with him and said,[110] "I have sent for you, out of the whole body of army commanders, because you are frank and sincere, and capable of suggesting the right course of action in a forthright manner. Myself, the Commander-in-Chief and the Great Chamberlain are of no use as far as the lord Sultan is concerned, for no matter what we say, and regardless of the sound advice we offer, he refuses to listen and holds us in suspicion. Now a calamity of such seriousness is taking shape, in that he is going to head for Merv and gives out that we are wrong-headed. For we are seeing that the one-horse trooper cavalrymen are all in a desperate state from hunger and lack of mounts. The palace gholāms are forced to ride camels rather than horses,[111] and the Commander of the Palace Gholāms Begtughdï is complaining volubly that these gholāms will not fight, since they are protesting and asking why they should go hungry, for they have tried hard to find wheat and barley but to no avail. They have never followed orders under a monarch in such conditions, and it is clear how much their endurance has been tested. The Indians and the rest of the infantrymen[112] are likewise suffering from hunger. What would you say is the best way to proceed?"

He answered, "May the Grand Vizier's life [Gh 615] be prolonged! I am a straightforward Turk, and tell the truth without fear or favour. From what I have seen of this army I can tell that they will not fight and will deliver us into the hands of our enemies, for they are hungry and in a parlous state. [F 822] I am afraid that if the enemy appears there will be an irretrievable disaster." The Vizier said, "Will you be able to tell the lord all this?" He replied, "Why shouldn't I be able to say it? I was the troop commander of Amir Maḥmud's *kheyltāsh*s. He left me at Ray with this present lord. I was promoted there to the dignity of Great Chamberlain, and he bestowed on me much beneficence and favour. Now I hold the rank of general (*sālār*). Why should I withhold such advice?" The Vizier said, "After the worship, ask for a private audience and set forth these views. If he listens, you will have conferred a great benefit on this dynasty and on us servants, and if he doesn't listen, you will have acquitted yourself of your responsibilities and will have fulfilled and acknowledged acts of grace and favour owed to the lord." He replied, "I'll do so," and went back.

The Vizier summoned me, Bu'l-Fażl, and gave me a verbal message for Bu Sahl with the words "So-and-so happened, and this is the last stratagem remaining for us, and we'll see what will happen. If he weren't such a simple and straightforward Turk, he wouldn't have agreed to do this." I myself went back and gave Bu Sahl the message. He said, "This man has done all he could in dispensing his sincere advice, now let's see what happens." The Vizier sent his trusty confidants to the Commander-in Chief and the Great Chamberlain Begtughdï, and explained that such a recourse had been adopted. They all thanked him for this. Between the time of the two worships (i.e. the midday and the afternoon ones), they all came to court, for everyone was anxious about the outcome. The Amir was in his large tent. They prodded Altuntāsh until he approached the attendants and requested an audience, saying that he had something urgent and important to say. He received permission, and entered, and poured it all out openly in the Turkish fashion, without mincing his words.[113] The Amir said, "They've set you up to talk in such an open way, otherwise, how would you have dared to behave like this? Go back, for we have forgiven you as you are an honest simpleton, but make sure you do not exhibit such boldness and temerity again." Altuntāsh returned and told the notables confidentially what had happened. They said, "What you had to do, you did, but keep this [F 823] to yourself." The Vizier then went back.

Bu Sahl had set all his hopes on this important matter. He sent me to the Vizier to find out what had happened. I set off and told the Vizier that he was asking for some news. He replied, "Tell Bu Sahl that the answer given to Altuntāsh was such-and-such. There will be a calamity here, and the foreordained decree of fate cannot be reversed. It is like the case of ʿAmr b. Leyth. His Vizier said to him, 'Go from Nishapur to Balkh [Gh 616] and look after your troops from there. Send the army by itself, for even if the army should be defeated, as long as you stand firm and unaffected there in your place you can retrieve the situation.[114] But if you go out in person and are defeated, you will have no further foothold on earth.'[115] ʿAmr answered, 'O Khᵛāja, the sensible course is what you say and suggest, and one should follow that, but there is something else at work here; it is as if the decree of fate has firmly tied a rope round the neck and is pulling hard at it.' The outcome of that was as you have read.[116] The case of this lord is the same. There is nothing to be done. We have all prepared ourselves for the worst, and you should do the same. Let's hope that things will turn out better than we think." I returned and informed Bu Sahl. He became extremely despondent and listless, for by nature he was of a dark and gloomy temperament.

The Amir was fasting. There was no court session at the time of the afternoon worship, and verbal message arrived from him with the instructions "Go back [F 824] and get everything ready and prepared. We intend to leave for Merv tomorrow." The notables and commanders went back in a state of despair, and got everything ready and in order.

On the next day, Friday, 2 Ramażān [/17 May], the large kettle-drums were beaten, the Amir mounted and he set off along the road to Merv, but his troops were going along in an apprehensive and despondent fashion, as if they were being pulled back from behind. The heat was fierce, there was a dearth of provisions, food and fodder were nowhere to be found, the beasts were emaciated and the troops were having to fast. On the road, the Amir passed several of the troops who were in tears as they led their horses on the way. He was struck to the heart and said, "This army has become reduced to a terrible state," and he ordered them to be given a thousand dirhams each.[117] This raised people's hopes that he might possibly turn back; but the foreordained decree of fate had the upper hand, for at the time of the afternoon worship, the Sultan himself put down those rumours, saying then, "All this suffering and hardship is only till we reach Merv." The next day, he moved off from there. The strange thing was that there was no water to be found along our way, and no-one could recall such a lack of water on this scale, for we would come across large streams but would find them all dry. The situation became so desperate that on the third day after leaving Sarakhs, wells had to be dug in order to get water. They dug extensively, and both sweet and acrid-tasting water came up. The reed beds had been set on fire (i.e. by the Turkmens), the wind blew and carried away the smoke from those beds, and it settled on the troops' tents[118] and blackened them. Incidents like these were not infrequent in the course of this journey.

On Wednesday, 7 Ramażān [/22 May], when we moved off in mid-morning, a thousand Turkmen horsemen appeared, said to be Yïnāliyān,[119] together with 500 cavalryman defectors from our own side, whose commander was reported to be Böritegin.[120] [Gh 617] They came in from all four sides, and [F 825] the situation became critical,[121] and they drove off large numbers of our camels. It was a bold and well-executed attempt; our troops went out and fought them off until they retreated to a position further off, but still following our trail and indulging in little skirmishes until we reached the next resting place. The Amir became somewhat more aware of the situation on this day when he saw the enemy taking the initiative and coming out on top, and it became obvious to everyone that he was regretting his decision.[122] At the time of the afternoon worship he held court, attended by the Vizier, the Commander-in-Chief and the leading figures. He raised the topic of these incidents and said, "Can there be anything worse than this state of affairs? Less than 2,000 of their cavalrymen show themselves, drive off our camels and act in a thoroughly brazen manner, and an army of this great size and in full military formation finds itself incapable of giving them their deserts!" The Commander-in-Chief and the Great Chamberlain said, "May the lord's life be prolonged! The enemy swooped down today and caught us unawares; if they come tomorrow, they will experience an encounter of a different kind!" They said this and rose to go. The Amir called them back again and, together with the Vizier and Bu Sahl Zowzani, held a privy conclave. Much talk went on until it was almost evening and then they dispersed.

Bu Sahl summoned me and had a private talk with me, saying, "How fortunate was Bu Naṣr Moshkān that he passed away in a dignified manner and does not have to witness this day and hear this bandying to-and-fro of words! However much they spoke with this monarch, it was to no avail. Today he had a little foretaste of things to come and it made him wake up and regret his decision, but what's the use of repenting when one is already caught in the snare? The notables and the commanders had made things perfectly clear at their meeting in the afternoon [F 826] and had said, 'Our cavalrymen are not giving of their best because they have suffered much and are in a despondent state. The generals and senior commanders are of course willing to give their lives in the lord's service, but it is clear that their numbers do not add up to much, and without the main body of the cavalry, we would never succeed, and the true remedy has eluded us.' However much the Amir went on speaking about this matter, they stuck fast to what they said, to the point that the Amir became desperate and asked, 'What, then, is the way out of this?' They replied, 'The lord should know this better than us.' The Vizier said, 'In no circumstances can we go back now that we are at the battlefront, since this would be tantamount to admitting defeat and retreating in the face of the enemy. There has not yet been a battle with the enemy, and no drubbing has been inflicted on them in such a way that one can say what is appropriate for the time and the situation. The wisest course in those circumstances appears to me that we should suspend warfare for a while, since the distance from here to Merv is short, and when we have reached Merv, the city and its supplies of corn [Gh 618] will come into our hands and the enemy will retire into the fringes of the desert, and the whole affair will be successfully resolved. And we must take extreme care in these last two stages of the way.' They all approved of this opinion, and arose having agreed that they would see to it that all blemishes and defects afflicting the army were removed."

[Bu Sahl continued,] "The Grand Vizier has come up with a sound solution, but I still harbour a great fear lest—may God forfend!—some crisis might occur within the army itself (i.e. a revolt in its ranks). For the Commander of the Palace Gholāms Begtughdï has reported privately to the Amir that the (Turkish) gholāms were saying today, 'Clearly, we cannot put up with riding on camels forever. Tomorrow, if the battle commences, we shall help ourselves to horses from the other (non-Turkish) troops,[123] since we cannot fight on camels.' The Amir had made no response but had been clearly disconcerted by this."

We were engaged in this discussion when a messenger arrived, and confidential letters from spies were brought in, to the effect that "The arrival of the news that the Sultan had left Sarakhs caused a great deal of fear and trepidation amongst the people here, and Ṭoghrïl gathered his leading men together and there was much discussion ranging over all topics. Finally, they said to Ṭoghrïl, 'You are our elder; whatever you consider is the wisest course of action, [F 827] we will carry out.' Ṭoghrïl said, 'The wise course seems to us that we should send our baggage and impedimenta forward and go to Dehestān and take possession of Gorgān and those regions, since the local Persian population (*tāzikān*) are poorly equipped and lack the armaments of war. If we are unable to establish ourselves there, we can go to Ray, since Ray, Jebāl and Isfahan are ours, and in no circumstances is the monarch likely to come after us once we have left his territory. For this is a great ruler; he has numerous troops and great amounts of armaments, equipment and territory, and he has learnt the technique of making war against us and will pursue us implacably. We all know how much hardship we have suffered this winter. Let us opt for submissiveness and compliance; it is preferable to lording it in such dire conditions.' They all replied, 'This is the most acceptable solution, and we should act on these lines.'

Dāvud had remained silent, and they said to him, 'What do *you* say?' He answered, 'What you have said and have decided upon amounts to nothing. We ought not to have acted thus at the outset and we should not to have crossed swords with someone like Masʿud. Now that we have launched strikes against him and antagonized him, and there have been battles and we have devastated several parts of his territories, we must fight to the death. If we defeat him, we shall be able to conquer the whole world, and if he defeats us, we will not fail in making our escape, for it is obvious that they will come after us if we are defeated. However, it is vital to have the baggage and impedimenta a great distance away, wherever we may be, for a footloose and unencumbered rider [Gh 619] is free of all worries. Know that if we go off without striking a blow, this ruler will think that we had become scared and had fled, and will come after us and will incite all the local rulers against us, turning our present allies into enemies. This famine which has afflicted us, and still is, has afflicted them in the same manner and still is, as we have come to know from reliable reports. We, at all events, have today enjoyed for some time past supplies of food and fodder, and the animals and our troops have enjoyed rest and refreshment, whereas they are just emerging from the desert wastes. [F 828] To give up now would be a sign of impotence; we shouldn't be afraid of him.'

Yabghu, Ṭoghrïl, the Yïnāliyān and all the commanders said, 'This is a sounder view.' They sent away their baggage, together with 2,000 riders, the ones who were more youthful and had poorer-quality horses for mounts. They reviewed the remainder of the forces and they amounted to 16,000 horsemen. Out of this lot, they will send forward a vanguard with the Yïnāliyān and Böritegin. Stringent precautions need to be taken, since this is the true situation as has been set forth."[124]

Bu Sahl mounted at once and went to the court, and I went with him. The Amir read those secret letters and became more subdued. He said to Bu Sahl, "We are heading for turbulent times before us. Our wisest course was to have proceeded to Herat and to have made a peace agreement with that bunch. But that's behind us now. Let us see what God, the Exalted One, has decreed, for it will be a mighty affliction: 16,000 good-quality horsemen confronting the body of debilitated and dispirited troops that we have." Bu Sahl said, "Everything that happens will be for the best. A great effort must be made so that we reach Merv, for once there, these matters can be resolved either by war or by a peace agreement." He replied, "That's so."

Attendants went off and summoned the Vizier, the Commander-in Chief, the Great Chamberlain and the leading figures, and these confidential letters were read out to them. Their spirits rose, and they said, "The enemy have become very fearful." The Vizier said, "This appears to be the work of Dāvud. It is as we decided in the previous discussion.[125] We must strongly endeavour to get our forces to Merv and must ensure that no crisis occurs, for once there, some way out of this affair can be put in place, since the state of the enemy is as the spies have written." They all replied, "That's so," and went back. They were making preparations for the battle all through the night. The generals gave words of advice and exhortation to the mounted troops and reassured them. The Amir summoned the General Ertegin, [F 829] who was the deputy of Begtughdï, together with the field officers of the palaces[126] and the most daring and outstanding of the gholāms; he gave them the necessary instructions [Gh 620] so that they would be highly alert. This, too, was a mistake, and it was most unfortunate that he had not summoned Begtughdï and had thus offended him, since the gholāms looked up to Begtughdï as their ruler, as it were, and did whatever he said. Everything was going badly, for Fate was bent on working out its will. *When God wills a thing, He prepares the means for it!*

The next day, Thursday, 8 Ramażān [/23 May], the Amir mounted, with the army deployed in full battle formation, and he rode forward. We had only gone one parasang when the enemy appeared from the direction of the desert, and in great numbers, to right and left, and joined battle. The situation became critical, for when they advanced boldly from every side, the defence on our side turned out to be only a half-hearted and desperate affair.[127] Our enemies were gaining in strength and the skirmishes continued as we rode on. On several occasions I observed that the royal gholāms who had defected[128] were joining up with us and riding alongside the royal gholāms mounted on camels and talking to them. The Commander of the Palace Gholāms Begtughdï was in a howdah on an elephant and was riding forward with his personal gholāms, since he could only travel on an elephant, had impaired sight and was afflicted in the use of his hands and legs. Whenever he was asked on that day about the disposition of the gholāms, what plan should be adopted or whether so-and-so detachment of the gholāms should be sent to a certain place, he would answer, "Ertegin knows, and the Sultan has given his orders to him and to the field officers. I can't see anything, and am no longer active; [F 830] what do you expect of me?"

The gholāms were fighting on half-heartedly while the mounted troops were just looking on. The enemy was increasing its hold by the hour, and our troops appeared more and more languid and spent. The high-ranking officers and the commanders were fighting bravely alongside the Amir. The Amir was indulging in fierce forays, and it was clear as daylight that they would lose him to the enemy. The wonder was that this calamity did not happen on this day, for it looked so imminent. The enemy carried off many camels and goods. The fighting continued until the time of the [midday] worship, when we had covered the assigned distance, so that from the place we had come to the bank of the river was three parasangs. We encamped on the bank of the river in a disorderly fashion,[129] like men who had lost heart, and all were in despair. It was evident that a great catastrophe was about to befall, and people began secretly to prepare swift-running camels for flight and to get together beasts that had sufficient strength for leading as pack-animals, to make plans regarding their possessions and equipment and money, and to say farewell to each other as if the Day of Resurrection were about to happen. [Gh 621]

The Amir had been reduced to a state of deep despair, but since he had no alternative but to appear resolute and at the helm, he acted thus. At the time of the afternoon worship he held a court session, and summoned the leading figures for a private session. There was much discussion, and they said, "There are only two more stages to Merv. As long as the day lasts,[130] we must remain watchful and on guard, and then when we reach Merv all our aims and desires will be achieved. The one-horse troopers took no part in the action today, and the Indian troops are not fighting at all and are, moreover, having an adverse effect on the morale of the rest of the army, for they take to flight even when there are ten Turkmens assailing five hundred of them. We don't know what has made them so prone to turning back and fleeing, when they had previously borne the brunt of the fighting in Khwarazm.[131] [F 831] The palace gholāms must give their utmost, for they stand at the heart of the army and are its core and mainstay, yet today they did nothing." The Amir said to Begtughdï, "Why is it that the gholāms are not fighting properly?" He replied, "Most of them lack horses, and the ones they have are weak from lack of barley. Despite all this, they did not fall short in their duty today. I will admonish them so that they will do their best tomorrow." A lot of elaborate talk went on in the same vein, and then they went back.

The Amir had a private session with Bu Sahl Zowzani and the Vizier, and said, "This situation is getting beyond control; what can we do?" The Vizier answered, "We ought never to have come, and everyone was saying so and I myself was protesting volubly, as Bu Sahl can testify. Now we cannot possibly go back, and we are approaching Merv. Begtughdï must be summoned ... Second,[132] Bu'l-Ḥasan, son of ʿAbd al-Jalil, had a violent altercation with him at Herat concerning the matter of the horses,[133] to the point that Begtughdï was brought to tears; that was not redressed either. The third thing is the matter of Ertegin;[134]

his presence makes Begtughdï livid. He is a grand and much respected Turk of enormous prestige, even if he is frail and past his prime. If, for instance, he were to tell the gholāms that they must sacrifice their lives, they would do so. If he is appeased and bolstered up, the gholāms will fight well, and there would be little to fear from the enemy. The commander of the Indian troops also [F 832] needs admonishing."

An attendant went to summon Begtughdï on his own, and he came. The Amir lavished affection on him and said, "You are like an uncle to us, and what took place at Ghaznin involving your men could not be rectified by means of letters but will be put right by our personal presence. When we reach there, you will see what has been commanded. Regarding Bu'l-Ḥasan b. ʿAbd al-Jalil, he is not worth complaining about; he received his deserts [Gh 622] and is still suffering from the consequences. As for Ertegin, it was you yourself[135] who asked for him and wanted him as your deputy and agent. If he is unsuitable, he will be removed." Begtughdï kissed the ground and said, "I don't deserve to be spoken to so kindly by the Amir and to be honoured with such words. The castellan is the Amir of Ghaznin, and he can't contemplate any other person exercising authority there. The Amir gave orders for what was necessary regarding the transgression which the castellan had committed, and I am not myself too helpless not to be able, under the aegis of the Amir, to exact justice from him. As for that nonentity Bu'l-Ḥasan the secretary, it was only out of my respect for the sanctity of the royal court that I did not mete out to him directly his punishment, for I would regard it as beneath my dignity to complain about him to anyone. Ertegin has turned out to be the most sensible and capable, and better suited to his task than anyone else, and there should not be anyone else. Regarding the gholāms' failure to engage in the fighting, it is because they lack horses. If the lord should see fit, he should give 200 well-chosen and sturdy Arab horses to the leaders of the gholāms, so that they can perform their task successfully." The Amir said, "That's a very sound plan. They must be given out this very night." The Indians were also summoned and admonished, but their commanders said, "We are ashamed at having to tell the lord [F 833] that our men are suffering from hunger, and the horses are weak, since for four months, men have been coming to us for barley, but with none for us to give. In spite of this, we will fight to the death and not fall short in our duty in any way, and whatever it's necessary to say this night we shall say to all the troops," and they went back.

Early into the night, Bu Sahl summoned me. He was extremely perturbed and dispirited, and he related to me all these circumstances. He summoned the gholāms and said, "You must get ready this night, and load up on swift-running camels all ready money and sleeping clothes. Nothing has happened, but one can never be too careful." They all loaded up their personal belongings on swift-running camels. When this was completed, he said to me, "I am full of fear and foreboding." I replied, "If God wills, it will all turn out well!" I also went back to my tent and took precautions along these same lines. The Amir remained awake and alert for most of the night. He was getting things ready, giving out horses to the gholāms, and sending instructions for precautions to be taken regarding the treasury and other matters. The generals and the commanders were all doing the same.

They performed the dawn worship, the large kettledrums were beaten and they set off. I saw surrounding the Amir fifty or sixty swift-running camels being led along, together with 300 heavily-armed gholāms and twelve elephants with armour on their bodies; [Gh 623] it was a most powerful and impressive array. We had travelled half-a-parasang on this day when a tumultuous roar arose from the enemy, and from all four sides large numbers of troops launched an attack in strength and engaged in very fierce fighting. The banners of Ṭoghrïl, Yabghu and Dāvud were nowhere to be seen, since it was said that they were in the rearguard, having sent forward all the choice, battle-hardened troops while they themselves remained behind the front-line troops, ready to go back to the baggage if something untoward happened. The fighting was so intense on this day that our troops were unable to make much headway along the road, [F 834] although they were striving hard and fighting well.

We were still engaged in fighting at close quarters, when near midday we reached the fortress of Dandānqān.[136] The Amir took up his position there on an eminence and asked for water. The rest halted too. The enemy also appeared, fully equipped, and halted, looking anxious and dejected. Many of the inhabitants had come on to the walls of the fortress and were letting down from the walls pitchers of water. The troops were standing there and were drinking, since they were extremely thirsty and disheartened. The large watercourses were all dried up and there was not a single drop of water. The Amir said, "Find out about water holes[137] for the beasts." They replied, "There are five wells within the fortress, and these will provide enough water for the army. Moreover, there are four wells outside the fortress, into which the enemy have thrown rotten carcasses and have capped them. We can get them in commission again within an hour. From here to that pool of water which the Amir has been told about is five parasangs, and there is no water to be found anywhere else."

They, the Amir's commanders and advisers, said to him, "We should halt here, for we did well today, and had the upper hand." He replied, "What kind of talk is this? How can seven or eight wells yield enough water for a large army? We shall proceed at once to the place where the pool is." How could we have halted there when such a momentous calamity (i.e. the ensuing military defeat) had already been ordained and had to happen? As soon as we set out, chaos set in: when the Amir rode on from that place, order broke down within the camp. The palace gholāms dismounted from their camels and started commandeering horses from the Persian troops, from everyone who was weaker than them, on the pretext that they were going to engage in battle. They seized large numbers of horses, and when they were mounted on them, they banded together with those who had acquired Arab and Khottali horses[138] during the night, and in one go, 370 gholāms, with their banners bearing the lion device, turned round and joined up with the Turkmens. Those gholāms who had deserted from our camp in the time of Böritegin came along; they clasped each other and sent up a cry [F 835] of "Our comrades, our comrades!", and they made a violent concerted charge. No-one in the Ghaznavid army stood by the side of his comrade, [Gh 624], discipline dissolved on every side and all our troops took to flight.

The Amir remained with Khᵛāja 'Abd al-Razzāq b. Aḥmad b. Ḥasan, Bu Sahl, Bu'l-Nażr, Bu'l-Ḥasan and their personal gholāms. I and Bu'l-Ḥasan b. Delshād also happened to be there by chance and witnessed the confusion of the Day of Resurrection occurring in this present world and unrolling in front of our eyes. Begtughdï and the gholāms were riding off into the fringes of the desert on camelback, with the Indian troops going off in flight in another direction, and there was no sign of the Kurds and Arabs. The *kheyltāsh*s had gone off in another direction and the order of the right and left wings had disintegrated. It was every man for himself.[139] The enemy had broken into the baggage and impedimenta and were carrying it off. They were launching fierce attacks, but the Amir was standing his ground. Then they launched an attack on him personally. He made a strong counter-attack, grasping a poisoned spear and struck down all his assailants, so that neither horse nor man remained. On several occasions, the enemy's champion warriors got near the Amir, shouting all the time, but were beaten off one by one and were falling back. If, on that day, a thousand first-rate cavalrymen had banded together and had assisted this monarch, he would have won the day; but this did not happen. I saw the Amir Mowdud, may God be pleased with him, with his face pressed down on the pommel of his saddle and with drawn sword in hand, urging on his horse and shouting to the troops, "O cowardly wretches, some of you cavalrymen come and join me!" but of course, not a single horseman responded so that he had to go back to his father in despair.

The gholāms of the Persians[140] stood firm with the Amir, and fought hard [F 836] with extraordinary tenacity. There was a commander from the close entourage[141] of Khᵛāja ʿAbd al-Razzāq, a gholām of lofty stature and fine appearance. A Turkmen confronted him and pierced his throat with a spear and hurled him to the ground. Other Turkmens rushed in and seized his horse and his weapons, and the gholām expired. The rest lost heart, and the Turkmens and the renegade gholāms made a strong assault, and a great catastrophe almost happened.[142] ʿAbd al-Razzāq, Bu'l-Nażr and the others said, "May the lord's life be prolonged! There's no point in standing our ground, we must move on." The general who was the Keeper of the Royal Wardrobe[143] also said, in Turkish, "Any moment now the lord is bound to fall into the enemy's hands unless we get a move on!"[144] (This gholām died of grief[145] when shortly afterwards they reached[146] Marv al-Rud.) The Amir rode off, and then gave orders that the road to the pool should be taken. He took that road, until a dry watercourse appeared. Everyone who [F 837] managed to get across to the far bank of the river bed was safe.

One of the Sultan's personal eunuchs, together with two gholāms,[147] managed through various expedients to get me, Bu'l-Fażl, across the river bed. [Gh 625] They themselves rode away with great speed, leaving me behind to fend for myself.[148] I went off swiftly with some others till we reached the bank of the pool. I found that the Amir had already halted there, with the leading figures and commanders all heading in this way and the rest also joining up. I thought that he had perhaps decided to make a stand there and was re-grouping his troops, but matters had gone beyond this and they were preparing for departure, dismantling the insignia and tarrying for a while waiting for the notables who were still on their way here. This went on till the time for the midday worship, when detachments of Turkmens came into view. They had thought that perhaps the Sultan had stationed himself there in order to make a revanche. The Amir mounted, together with his brother,[149] his son Mowdud and the whole body of leading figures, notables and prominent personages, and he rode off at a cracking pace, in such a way that many got left behind en route, and he took the road to the fortress,[150] taking with him two men from Gharjestān to act as guides. The Turkmens kept on pursuing them. One detachment would make a diversionary appearance, while others were busy plundering baggage and impedimenta. [F 838]

As the sun was setting, the Amir reached flowing water, a very large pool,[151] and I myself arrived there at the time of the evening worship. Swift-running camels had been tethered for the Amir. He intended to go off on one of them, since he had ridden and tired out sixteen horses. A young Turkish chamberlain would follow him, and would try to revive and prod onwards the exhausted horses that had been left behind, if they were of sufficient value. When I arrived, I saw a group of people and went up to them. It was the Vizier, the Head of the Army Department Bu'l-Fatḥ Rāzi and Bu Sahl b. Esmāʿil, and they were getting their camels ready. When they saw me, they exclaimed, "How did you escape, then?" I explained my tribulations and how fatigued I was. They said, "Come on, let's set off." I said, "I'm too exhausted." Someone shouted, "Get going, the Amir has set off." They also departed, and I followed behind them.

I did not see the Amir again for a week. He remained in Gharjestān for two days, as I shall relate in its entirety and in detail. It must be said that one would need several lifetimes and many years to witness anything like this again. I was travelling onwards till, during the night, I saw two female elephants, without their litters, ambling on at leisure. The royal elephant driver (*pilbān-e khāṣṣ*) was an acquaintance of mine, and I asked, "Why have you lagged behind?" He replied,

"The Amir went off in a hurry. He provided us with a guide, and here we are going along." I enquired, [Gh 626] "Who of the leading figures and great men were with the Amir?" he answered, "His brother [F 839] ʿAbd al-Rashid, his son Amir Mowdud, ʿAbd al-Razzāq b. Aḥmad b. Ḥasan, the General Bu'l-Nażr, Suri, Bu Sahl Zowzani, Bu'l-Ḥasan b. ʿAbd al-Jalil and the Commander of the Lahore ghāzis ʿAbdallāh b. Qarategin. On his heels were the Great Chamberlain and a large number of palace gholāms dispersed all around, and following them were Begtughdï and his personal gholāms. I was going along with these elephants, and people kept arriving in scattered groups. All along the road we were passing coats of mail, cuirasses, shields and other impedimenta which had been discarded."

At dawn, the elephants were driven off at a sharper pace. I fell behind them, and halted for a rest. In the distance, I saw the fires of the army encampment. At midday I reached the fortress of K.r.d.[152] The Turkmens had come there in pursuit. I somehow managed to cross over the B.r.k.r.d river.[153] I found that the Amir had gone to Marv [al-Rud]. I remained with a group of people I knew, and many trials and tribulations came upon us. On foot, and accompanied by a few friends, I reached the main town of Gharjestān[154] on Friday, [F 840] 16 Ramażān [/31 May]. When the Amir arrived there, he halted for two days so that the fugitives who were still to come might catch up. I went to Bu Sahl Zowzani. I found him in the town busy making arrangements for the onward journey. He greeted me warmly. Several members of my own retinue had arrived, all on foot. They bought some supplies of food, and we ate together with him, and then we came to the army encampment. In the whole of the encampment I saw only three tents,[155] one for the Sultan, the second for Amir Mowdud and the third for [the Vizier] Aḥmad b. ʿAbd al-Ṣamad. The rest merely had awnings made from cotton sheeting. We ourselves were out in the open.[156]

At the time of the afternoon worship we moved off, some seventy of us, and took the road to Ghur. The Amir likewise moved off, following on our heels, in the middle of the night. By morning, we had travelled as far as a staging post. There we found Bu'l-Ḥasan b. Delshād mounted on a horse, and I too acquired a horse which I bought on credit, and we fell in with a group of friends. Masʿud b. Leyth said to me, "The Sultan enquired after you several times, asking where Bu'l-

Fażl could have got to, and was anxious about you." At the time of the afternoon worship I went into his presence, wearing boots which were too tight for me and a worn-out coat, and kissed the ground. He laughed, and he said: "What happened to you? You've got on a smart outfit!" I replied, "I escaped with my life through the lord's auspicious power, and thanks to the lord's bounty there will be other sets of clothes!"

We moved off from there and came to Ghur and halted at a staging post. Other groups of stragglers [Gh 627] kept arriving and were bringing fresh news. I spotted here an acquaintance, a stout-hearted man of Sistan, [F 841] and I was asking him about all sorts of things. He said, "That day when the Sultan left the field, and the enemy won such a victory and started plundering, I saw Bu'l-Ḥasan Karaji lying wounded and groaning beneath a tree. I went up to him. He recognized me, and wept. I asked what had happened to him. He replied, 'The Turkmens arrived and saw my horse and all the trappings. They shouted at me to dismount. I started to dismount, but I was slow in getting down from the horse because of my old age. They thought that I was being very refractory; they speared me in the back and pulled it out through my abdomen, and seized the horse. I managed with an effort to crawl beneath this tree, but I am near to death. This is what has happened to me; you can recount it to any of my friends and acquaintances who may ask about me.' He asked for water, and after considerable difficulty I brought him a little water in a pitcher. He drank some of it, and then lost consciousness. I left the rest of the water near him and went away, not knowing what would happen to him. But I do know that he must have died during the night. Between the time of the two worships (i.e. between the dawn and the midday worships of the next day), I saw banners approaching, which were reported to be those of Ṭoghrïl, Yabghu and Dāvud. I saw the Son of Kāku[157] in fetters on the back of a camel, then they brought him down from the camel, broke asunder his chains and set him on a mule, one of those mules seized from Khᵛāja Aḥmad b. 'Abd al-Ṣamad, and they brought him to Ṭoghrïl. I myself went away, and I don't know what else happened." I told the Amir what I had heard.

The Amir was travelling swiftly onwards from one staging post to another. Three messengers, from our secret agents who had been keeping watch on the enemy, arrived simultaneously with secret letters. Bu Sahl Zowzani took those letters to the Amir at the staging post where we had halted. The Amir read them and said, "These letters are to be kept secret so that no-one hears about them." He replied, "I'll ensure that's done." He brought them [F 842] and gave them to me. I read them through, affixed a seal and entrusted them to the keeper of the Divān. The contents were as follows: "During these days, many extraordinary things took place. This gang (i.e. the Turkmens) had lost their nerve and had transported their baggage and impedimenta sixteen stages back and had made arrangements for their flight. Each day, they would pit every rider they had against the Sultan's army, expecting that, at any moment, there would be a reversal of fortunes with the royal army managing to turn the tables on them and charging at them and putting them to flight. But as it turned out, the palace gholāms acted in such a disobedient manner that we landed in the present dire situation.

Even more strange than this is that there is a youth of servile birth (*mowlā-zāda*)[158] who is knowledgeable about astrology, having been apprentice to an astrologer. He fell in with this gang, and several of his predictions turned out to be correct. It was he who insisted that they should stand their ground at Merv and said that if [Gh 628] his predictions proved false and they did not acquire rulership over Khorasan, he was prepared to die on the scaffold.[159] On the Friday when this fiasco occurred, he was all the time urging 'Stand firm for a while, till the time of the midday worship.' At that very moment, the renegade cavalrymen arrived there and their wishes were fulfilled and the Sultan's army retreated. All three Seljuq leaders dismounted from their horses and performed prostrations, and they gave the youth several thousand dinars on the spot and pledged to see him go far in the future. They rode onwards to that place where this disaster had occurred, pitched a tent and set up a throne. Ṭoghrïl sat down upon it, and all the leading men came forward and hailed him as Amir of Khorasan.[160]

Farāmorz b. Kāku was brought into his presence, and Ṭoghrïl [F 843] welcomed him and made much of him, saying, 'You suffered many hardships. Be of stout heart, for Isfahan and Ray will be awarded to you.'[161] Up to the time of the evening worship, the captured plunder was brought forward and distributed amongst them all. The astrologer received a great deal in the form of both immoveable and moveable property. The writing materials and the requisites of the royal chancery that had survived[162] were gathered together, but the greater part of them had been lost. A few official drafts and finished documents were found, much to their delight. Letters were written to the Khāns of Turkestan, the sons of 'Alitegin, 'Eyn al-Dowla[163] and all the leading figures of Turkestan announcing the victory. The official stamps and seals from the chancery equipment, and the banners of the Ghaznavid army, were sent by the couriers conveying the news.[164] Those treacherous gholāms who had acted so disgracefully had rewards lavished upon them: they were given governorships, large tents of the *darband* variety[165] and all sorts of things. The renegade gholāms themselves have become rich, since they have acquired plunder of unlimited extent. No-one dares to boast of achieving anything greater than them, for they would say that this victory is entirely their own work.[166] Orders were given that the fugitive infantrymen, of all the component groups of the Ghaznavid army that there were, should be pursued towards the deserts along the Oxus river so that the people of Bokhara and those regions might see them and so that the reality of the defeat might be confirmed. Immense quantities of gold and silver, clothing and beasts fell into the hands of this gang. [F 844] They seem to have agreed that Ṭoghrïl should go to Nishapur with 1,000 cavalrymen, that Yabghu should take up a position at Merv, together with the Yïnāliyān, and that Dāvud should march against Balkh with the greater part of the army so that Balkh and Tokhārestān may be seized.[167]

Everything that has happened so far has been narrated. After this date, whatever fresh news there is will be reported. But a more steady stream of messengers is required [Gh 629] and affairs should be conducted in a different way, for there has been a basic change in the situation. All this is in order that this intelligence service does not become less efficient."

When the Amir reached the vicinity of the village of Bu'l-Ḥasan b. Khalaf,[168] the leaders and headmen of that place came to render service,[169] and they brought out and set up tents, large and small, and whatever else that was requisite. A stay of two days was made there till the troops likewise got their affairs in order as much as possible. The Ghuris were extremely welcoming and helpful, providing lavish hospitality, and the Amir appeared more calm and consoled. He celebrated the Festival there,[170] but in a very subdued and lacklustre fashion.

At the time of the afternoon worship, I had taken up my place at court. He said to me, "What should be written to the Khāns of Turkestan regarding this matter?" I replied, "What does the lord ordain here?" He said, "Bu'l-Ḥasan b. ʿAbd al-Jalil and Masʿud b. Leyth have drafted two documents on this matter; have you seen them? I answered, "I haven't seen them, but what either of them writes will be of high quality." He laughed and said to the Keeper of the Royal Inkstand, "Fetch those documents." He brought them. I perused them. Indeed, they had guarded the lord Sultan's interests in an admirable manner, had written much in his praise and had alluded to the events in a veiled and cryptic manner. But they were at fault when they had written "We headed for Ghaznin, having left behind at Dandānqān household furniture, beasts and war equipment." [F 845] These two noble-minded men were always sneering at Bu Sahl, for they much coveted the office of the Head of the Chancery and were on the lookout for slips and mistakes on his part.[171] Whenever something would come up involving the fine points and difficult aspects of secretarial practice, and the Amir would say something regarding these last, they would say, "Bu Sahl must be instructed to draw up the draft document," since they knew that he was a mere novice[172] in such things. So I was forced to fend for him, and this I did.[173]

I read the draft documents and pronounced them to be very well done. However, the Amir, may God be pleased with him, said—and he was peerless in the world in his grasp of the finer points of the epistolary art—"They must be done better than this, for these set forth excuses, and the Khāns of Turkestan are the sort of people from whom happenings like these can't be concealed." I replied, "May the lord's life be prolonged! If there should arise at some future time a need for seeking military assistance from the Khāns, the letter must be couched in different terms." He said, "This will certainly be the case, for when we reach Ghaznin,[174] an envoy will be sent with letters and verbal instructions. At this present moment, concerning the calamity which occurred, a letter must be written while we are still on the road, and sent by a swift courier."[175] I said, "It will therefore be crucial to speak the truth in order to avert criticism, since, before our own letter can go off, the enemy's messengers will have set off, bearing our official stamps and seals and banners, according to the Turkmens' usual practice." [Gh 630]

The Amir said, "You are right. Draw up the draft document and bring it so that it may be perused." I went back. During the course of this night, the draft document was prepared, and the next day, at the next stage along the road, before I came up with the royal servants, I brought it into the royal presence. The Keeper of the Royal Inkstand took it, and the Amir read it, saying, "It's just as I wanted it; [F 846] read it out!" I read it out to those assembled there. The Head of the Chancery was present, together with all the boon-companions and Bu'l-Ḥasan b. 'Abd al-Jalil. All of them were sitting, whereas Bu'l-Fatḥ [b. Mas'ud b. Moḥammad b.] Leyth and myself were standing. When the end was reached, the Amir said, "This is how I wanted it." Those present expressed their approval at its excellence, *echoing what the king had said*, though a couple of people there were none too pleased.

I had to set down the intended meaning of that draft document, just as several other things have been recorded in this composition.[176] Whatever readers may say I regard as admissible. I am concerned to fulfil the requirements of my profession, and I related the story of events before this so that it may be known.

A record of the text of the letter to Arslān Khān[177]

In the name of God, the Merciful, the Compassionate. May God prolong the life of the exalted Khān, our kinsman! This is a letter from me to him written at Rebāṭ-e Karvān,[178] *seven stages from Ghazna. God Most High is worthy of praise in all circumstances! Blessings be upon the Prophet, the Chosen One, Moḥammad, and his excellent house! As follows:*

The Khān is well aware that God Most High decrees what shall be, just like a sharp sword whose path of cutting and incisiveness cannot be predicted in advance, and whose future effects cannot be comprehended. That is why man's helplessness is apparent at all times, for he never knows what the day has in store for him. The wise person is the one who places himself firmly in God's keeping and who does not rely on his own power and strength and on the panoply of arms and equipment which he possesses but entrusts his affair to God Most High, and who recognizes that good and evil, success and victory, come from Him; for if for a moment he relinquishes his trust in God, and exhibits pride and insolence, he will witness untold calamities beyond belief and will be left wretched and helpless. We seek from God Most High, with a sincere desire to please Him, an upright intention and a pure faith, that He will in all circumstances vouchsafe us assistance and will be our protector *in happiness and in misfortune, and in adversity and prosperity*, [F 847] and that He will not abandon us for one hour, nay, not even for one breath. We also pray that He will bestow on us divine inspiration in times of ease which He gives, and those of hardship which come along, so that we may, as submissive devotees, proffer patient endurance and thankfulness, and may hold fast to Him so that ease of life may increase as a result of gratitude and also that a heavenly reward may result from patient endurance. *Indeed, He, praise be to Him, is the best of those who vouchsafe success and who give help!* [Gh 631]

In the two years or so when our banner resided in Khorasan, the Khān was informed of everything that went on, the successes and the disappointments, the rough with the smooth, and we made sure that we shared it all and involved you in all matters; for true friendship entails that nothing, no matter how great or small, should be kept hidden away from friends. Our last letter was from Ṭus, five stages' distance from Nishapur, which we sent by hand of a mounted trooper acting as envoy. In it we explained that we had taken up our position there, with our troops, since this was the frontier bastion for the regions of Sarakhs, Bāvard, Nasā, Merv and Herat, so that we might see what action the circumstances required and what the upstart intruders (i.e. the Turkmens), who had infiltrated into the desert fringes, would do.

After the cavalry trooper bearing the letter had departed, we stayed on for six days. The state of affairs required that we should head for Sarakhs. When we arrived there it was the beginning of Ramażān. We found those regions devastated, with no crops or beasts there and barren, uncultivated fields.[179] The situation there had reached the point that a tiny amount of hay, for instance, could not be had even for a dirham. Prices had risen so high that the old were saying that such high prices had not been known for over a hundred years. A *man* [of flour] [F 848] had gone up to ten dirhams, but none could be found. There was not a blade of straw or of barley to be seen anywhere, and as a result, the mounted troops and the entire army suffered greatly.

Bearing in mind that even our personal guards, despite their many mounts and supplies, were in grave trouble, one can imagine how the rest of the leading court figures and retainers and mass of troops fared. The situation reached such a pitch that there were continuous and ubiquitous arguments and public disputes amongst the various elements of the army, and the troops at large and the palace guards (*biruniyān va sarā'iyān*) bickered over food, fodder and beasts, so that finally this quarrelling passed from the level of verbal exchanges to that of the sword. Our confidants told us about this, and those we had selected ourselves to be our counsellors and advisers were telling us in both plain and in diplomatic language that "The correct course of action is for us to head for Herat, since food and fodder can be found there in abundance, and it is near to all the parts of the province and is the pivotal point of Khorasan." The right course was indeed as they said; but we were overcome by a sense of sullen belligerence and obstinacy. Also, it would have meant that the problem of those upstarts would still remain tangled and unresolved, and we were keen to go to Merv in order to get the whole affair straightened out. Moreover, Fate was driving us forward[180] and making us confront unsuccessfully that unforeseen disaster which was about to happen.

We went towards Merv, and we could feel it in our bones that we were committing a grave error. The road was not as it should have been; there was no food or fodder and no water, and we had to face heat and the sand dunes of the desert. When we had gone three or four stages, [Gh 632] violent arguments broke out amongst all sections of the army about the length of the stages, fodder, our mounts, food, etc. [F 849] The commanders of the troops who had been appointed over the centre, the right and left wings, and other places of the army's line of deployment tried to calm down the situation, but the dispute had flared up[181] to such an extent that it could not be damped down sufficiently and was becoming more intense by the hour. Then on a certain day,[182] when we moved from a certain stage at the time of the afternoon worship with the intention of seeking to encamp at a further place, a detachment of the enemy appeared on the fringes of the sandy wastes of the desert. They sprang a daring attack on us[183] and tried to carry off plunder. The troops gave them a severe beating, and they failed to achieve their aim. Sporadic fighting continued late into the day. Our troops maintained their battle formation as they travelled on, and there were some clashes and skirmishes, but no fierce battle occurred, and the enemy steered clear of close encounters and intense fighting. If our troops,[184] our best warriors, had reacted more robustly to these clashes, they would have been able to chase the enemy away in all directions. We encamped at nightfall in a certain place,[185] there had been no mishaps and no prominent commander had been lost.[186] We took all the usual precautions, including posting guards[187] and sending out scouts so that nothing unexpected and untoward should happen to us in the darkness of the night. The next day was spent in the same way until we reached near Merv. [F 850]

On the third day, we set out with the army well-equipped and in formation *in tune with the occasion*. The guides had told us that once we passed the fortress of Dandānqān and travelled one parasang further, we would get to flowing water. We set off. When we reached the fortress of Dandānqān before noon, the enemy had filled up and blocked[188] the wells at the gate of the fortress to make it impossible to encamp there. The inhabitants of Dandānqān shouted down that there were five wells within the fortress which would yield ample water for the army, and that if we were to encamp there they would open up once more the wells outside the fortress, there would then be sufficient water and no cause for a crisis. The day was extremely hot, and the only sensible course was to encamp there. But foreordained Fate had to fulfill its brief, and so we set off. [Gh 633] A parasang further on, dried-up and deeply hollowed-out[189] beds of streams came into view. The guides were perturbed, because they had thought that there would be water there since no-one could remember a time when those streams had run dry.

The lack of water there worried the troops, and they became dismayed and disorderly. The enemy launched a fierce attack from all four sides, and I myself had to ride out from the centre and confront the enemy. We made strenuous attacks, and we thought that the compact formations[190] of the right and left wings were still intact. We did not know that a detachment of the palace gholāms mounted on camels had dismounted and were stealing the horses from anyone in sight so that they themselves might ride them into battle. This tussle over [F 851] horses, and the forcing of one another to dismount, became so intense that they started fighting amongst themselves and leaving their own stations. The enemy exploited this opportunity, and the situation became intractable, so that neither we nor our leading men could see a way out. We had thus to abandon our equipment and baggage to our opponents and leave the scene, and they became busy with plundering the captured baggage.

We rode on a parasang or so until we reached a large pool of standing water, and all the retainers and troops stationed at court, comprising our brothers[191] and our sons, the leading men and the subordinate ranks, reached there in good shape, such that there were no casualties amongst the leading figures. It was suggested to us that we should go away, since the situation was irretrievable. This seemed to us a fair assessment, and we set off. On the eighth day we came to the main town of Gharjestān, and spent two days there until the palace gholāms and the rest of the army caught up, so that no person of note was left behind. The only people who were left behind were some members of the palace infantry and others of no note and significance. From Gharjestān, we travelled by the road by the Rebāṭ of B.z.y.[192] through the mountains of Herat[193] and the region of Ghur and reached the fortress of Bu'l-ʿAbbās b. Bu'l-Ḥasan b. Khalaf, who is a faithful supporter of our realm and one of the chieftains of Ghur. We rested there for three days and then came to this *rebāṭ*, which is about six or seven stages from Ghaznin.

We thought we should have this letter written to the Khān, although it may perturb him, for it is better that he should read our account of the events than hear it from other sources; for doubtless our enemies will boast and brag a great deal and will make much of their own role and achievements. In truth, the fault and the cause of this extraordinary event can be traced to our own troops. [Gh 634] If [F 852] God Most High grants us a further lease of life, and with His help and through His favour, this situation can be retrieved. The Khān will know, by virtue of his exceptional wisdom and unique experience of the vicissitudes of Fate, that as long as the world has been in existence, such things have happened to rulers and armies. Moḥammad, the Chosen One, suffered at the battle of Oḥod, that memorable setback at the hands of the infidel Qoreysh, and yet this in no way affected his mission as Prophet, and afterwards he achieved his aims to the full. Right will always prevail. The wind which, at the moment, is blowing in favour of our foes, will doubtless die down in a few days,[194] for we are, God be praised, the mainstay of our realm and firmly and most auspiciously at the helm, and our sons and all our retainers and court troops—*may God grant them victory*—are in fine fettle. We can presently repair these reverses, particularly as we possess such an abundance of arms and equipment that it would be impossible to estimate their extent. Moreover, in the person of the Khān we have a friend and partner who clearly will not withhold from us any number of troops; and furthermore, if we beseech him to intervene in person in our cause, he will not deny us and will act to remove this blemish from our lives and will disregard his own comfort to that end. May God the Exalted One furnish us with the Khān's friendship and concord, [F 853] *through His beneficence and grace!*

This letter has been sent by this swift courier, and when we reach Ghaznin safe and sound, we shall from there appoint an envoy, one of our trusty confidants of the court circle, and will speak more explicitly about these matters, and what proposals need to be made will be set forth and what needs to be said will be said. We shall await a speedy answer to this letter so that we may know the Khān's opinion and thoughts on these matters, so that our friendship may receive a fresh impetus and we can once again bask in joy and happiness. We shall account that one of the greatest of gifts, *with the permission of God, He is magnified and exalted*."[195]

At that time when we got back to Ghaznin with the Amir, everyone was downhearted because of the scale of this catastrophe, and this great monarch, God's mercy be upon him, had not long to live. I had wished that, in the same way as I had composed this letter, penning an apologia for what had happened and depicting this defeat and flight from a more favourable and positive perspective, a learned man of letters [Gh 635] would compose some poetry in the same vein,[196] so that there would be an account of the events both in verse and in prose. But out of all the poets who had lived in these domains during the past twenty years, I did not find one whom I could ask to compose this poem until now that I have brought the History up to this point, and I asked the jurist Bu Ḥanifa, may God uphold and strengthen him. He composed it and did wonderfully well, and sent it along. *Every benefit which we enjoy comes from Him!* This learned man will go far, and I am seldom wrong in my predictions! [F 854] Indeed, recently, thanks to the gracious patronage of the lord Sultan Abu'l-Moẓaffar Ebrāhim and his lofty solicitude, he has received several marks of favour and handsome financial rewards. The office of the overseer (*eshrāf*) of Tarnak was entrusted to him, and Tarnak should not be belittled,[197] since it was the first official charge given to the Khwarazm Shah Altuntāsh. This is the ode:

Ode

1. Once the monarch leaves aside feasting and the rose garden, he can bring the realm under his sway, with ease.
2. A kingdom is wild and unruly by nature; this I know from the way it never becomes attached to any man.[198]
3. Only justice can be its leash, and once tied to justice, it becomes tame[199] and transfigured.[200] [F 855]
4. Friends and allies should not delude each other with their talk of massive troops numbers and many horsemen; recite to yourself the admonition "On the Day of Ḥoneyn when you set great store [about your numerical superiority, but to no avail]."[201]
5. The world is full of friends and comrades, and yet I have never encountered friends behaving like the Sun; shining through with honesty and transparent on both sides (i.e. devoid of hypocrisy).
6. The enemies of Jesus regarded him with contempt, for he had asked the heavens not for a sword but for a table of food.[202]
7. Who is it that dares to forbid you wine![203] Drink up, and beat the merry-makers at their own festive game![204]
8. Drink your fill,[205] but not so that, in the end, you crave for it impatiently like a suckling babe tugging at the maternal breast.[206]
9. But all this talk of how to eat and sleep does not concern a king; every schoolboy knows this![207] [F 856]
10. If the king is vigilant, he can succeed with ease and alacrity, and have his foe tied up and shepherded from the comfort of his garden down to the royal jail.

11. The enemy is a serpent and yet, if you want to preserve your power and authority, do not feel too secure even if you have pulled out its fangs.[208]

12. Fear the enemy most when he becomes a friend, and beware of the Magian priest (*mogh*) when he embraces Islam. [Gh 636]

13. A letter acknowledging bounties will proclaim its gratitude in its very title; the heading tells one what the letter itself is about.

14. If the Shah dons the coat of overweening pride, the enemy will slash it asunder as far up as the collar-strings.

15. Those who have suffered the discomfort and indignity of riding on a camel and a pack saddle will know better than to become haughty when offered the exalted status of riding on an elephant and its litter.

16. A man skilled in arts will never sit still: It is for some grand design that the Revolving Sphere maintains its diurnal rounds.

17. Such a man holds on to the monarch's body when he recognizes what the condition is of that true nature. [209]

18. [The Caliph] Ma'mun, he of all the rulers of the Islamic empire—no Arab or [Persian] *dehqān* ever saw his like—[F 857]

19. Had an ermine robe which he wore, so worn and frayed and old,

20. That it shocked his boon-companions, and they asked him for an explanation.

21. He answered, "In the lands of the Arabs and the Persians, it is the accounts of their deeds that the kings leave behind, not their robes of Tavvazi cloth and their fine linen."

22. If a king is used to reclining on silk and sleeping in fine brocade, he will find cuirasses hard to wear in times of war.

23. A kingdom won by means of the sword[210] and spear should not be squandered away through idle hours gazing at a pool amidst sweet-smelling herbs.

24. If the king does not keep his troops happy, whether at the court (i.e. in time of peace) or on the battlefield,

25. And he suddenly finds himself embroiled in a battle, he will find himself brought low by the very troops he had humiliated at the court.

26. Although money is the key to the troops' morale, they need the king's festive table and a portion of his heart-warming words too.

27. Treat your physician well when you enjoy good health so that he treats you well with his medicines and remedies when you are down.

28. If you wish to be secure from the malevolence of your contemporaries (*aqrān*), leave aside and do not dabble in astrological conjunctions (*qerān*) and turn instead to the Qorʾān.[211] [F 858]

29. Asceticism and abstinence (*zohd*) should be harnessed by religion, and knowledge with obedience to God; nobility is tied to generosity, and poems bound in a *divān*;

30. The mass of people (*khalq*) find strength from outer appearances (*ṣurat*), but moral character (*kholq*) is fortified through a sound inner disposition (*sirat*); religion is strengthened by innate virtue and the kingdom grows strong through the Sultan.

31. The Shah of virtuous conduct, the prince of princes Masʿud; good fortune is perpetually bound up with him in a firm covenant.

32. O you, by whom the age is permanently adorned, just like a garden in the month of April (Neysān).

33. If one could claim to be a prophet on account of great liberality, there would be no clearer sign of it than your ever-generous hands.[212] [Gh 637]

34. [For your hands are] the strength of Islam and the upholding of right belief, the succour of prophethood[213] and the proof of faith.

35. You have both a strong arm and an eloquent tongue, whereas Moses, son of Imran, was blessed with but one of these.[214]

36. Thanks be to the Lord that I enjoyed once more the privilege of seeing you in this portal of delight!

37. Now that you have reached the capital safe and sound, we do not have to fear if we hear that there have been losses,

38. For as the proverb has it, while the head remains in its place, a man can afford to have feeble arms.

39. It is not just at the present time that Khorasan has suffered from this sort of calamity; such things have happened as long as Khorasan has been in existence. [F 859]

40. The kingdom of the Lord of the World (i.e. God) is much larger than your kingdom; behold, is not the greater part of the world now in ruins?

41. If your enemy has seized by force of arms your possessions, did not demons seize the throne of Solomon in former times?[215]

42. If you suffered injury from your enemies, did not the planet Jupiter suffer injury from Saturn?[216]

43. Rain, an act of mercy and a blessing from God for the earth, is brought about by thunderbolts.

44. Our deeds recoil on us, if you look closely, just as with the axe in the tree, and the iron and the file.[217]

45. Renew your martial task, prepare fresh horses and unsheathe the swords, specially now that you know what lies ahead.

46. Once you win over and give heart to your soldiers and subjects, every lowly subject will become like two Rostams in strength.[218]

47. Since you are the lord of the monarchs of the age, and since God chose you out of all mankind,

48. Within the waters and in the depths of the desert, the lion, the sea monster and the eagle became alarmed and distraught[219] at hearing this news (i.e. the recent defeat).[220] [F 860]

49. No-one of your troops will have confidence in his own aggressive might[221] until you furnish them with the enemy's blood.

50. If even peris and human beings are enraged by these circumstances, one should not marvel if all the beasts and creatures feel the same (referring back to line 48).[222]

51. The tulip will not spring into leaf, nor the rose[223] laugh, unless you give them both, after this, the command.

52. You are the emperor of Iran, you always were and you always will be, even though your minions have become imperious in their revolt.

53. It is similar to the story of the one, who, in his ignorance, went off to fight God; his arrow was smeared in blood, when God had forsaken him.[224]

54. Pharaoh was drowned on that day when the Nile lured him on and he went forth[225] several steps, following Hāmān.[226]

55. Know that the firm foundation of the Nāṣeri and Yamini monarchy[227] is the strongest one in the whole world, [Gh 638]

56. For in the end, because of this terror-striking blow of the Ẓahiri sword, all the enemies will flee with their bodies covered in wounds.[228]

57. If a horse is not strong enough to bear you as its rider, an elephant will nevertheless be able to bear you like Rostam, the offspring of Dastān.[229] [F 861]

58. If your servant has erred, it was not intentional; it was the world that made him a hostage to worldly needs.

59. It would be right if you accepted this excuse, brought by the times, for he has repented and regrets his deed.

60. You possess translucent pearls from the sea (i.e. the vast extent) of your kingdom, while others hazard their lives after the (far less precious) red coral.

61. Yours is the crown of gold and a vigilant and auspicious fortune, while your enemy can be likened to an indolent cur slumped on a bed of straw.

62. When the rose does not withhold its scent from you, what need is there for tales about the acacia tree's thorns?

63. It is better not to let your heart become preoccupied by such matters (i.e. the problems of state), for these tales will not long remain secret from the world anyway.[230]

64. ...[231]

65. I do not normally compose poetry when I speak, but when I do, I do it this way, inserting in it the wisdom of Loqmān.[232]

66. It will be obvious that I do not speak in my poetry about the down of the cheek, the mole, the tress and the coquettish glance of fair ones.[233]

67. I, who utter praises of the Amir without desiring a reward, what should I ever know of such provision in the two worlds?[234]

68. There is still some verve and ardour left in my bald and ball-like head, even though my back has become prematurely bent like a polo stick. [F 862]

69. O Shah, the Lord has added to your span of life, whatever you lost in these recent wars.

70. I shall not draw breath except to express your praise, all I need now is fame, since I have obtained my sustenance.[235]

71. So long as the sun shines above in the heavens, just like a golden cup shining in a pool.

72. Live in happiness, and scatter silver and gold, keep a firm grip on your kingdom, and exercise the power of commanding and forbidding!

73. You must remain cheerful in countenance and buoyant, for your enemy will in the end fall as a sacrifice by your sword!

These words are becoming protracted, but it was with such words and using much artistry and finesse that he made a bejewelled crown out of his writing. It is a calamity when learned and illustrious men pass away; may this noble-hearted man live long! Since I am done with this, I now take up again the thread of the History. *God is the One who makes things smooth and easy, through His power and strength!* [Gh 639]

Before the Amir left Rebāṭ-e Karvān, a trusty messenger arrived from the castellan Bu 'Ali. He brought two black ceremonial parasols, a black banner and short spears, all placed in a black satin brocade bag, an elephant litter and a mule litter, together with other pieces of equipment, since all these insignia of royalty had been lost (i.e. in the flight from the battlefield). He had personally sent a great number of uncut pieces of cloth, necessary items and all sorts of things, and this act of service on his part came at a most opportune moment. The Amir's mother, as well as Ḥorra Khottali and his other aunts and sisters had likewise despatched trusty messengers with many things. The retainers and court troops and all the groups of the army had also been sent supplies and material by their relatives, for they were in a very wretched state. [F 863] The townspeople of Ghaznin came out to greet the Amir—and what an embarrassment that proved to be—for never before had monarchs and their armies returned to Ghaznin in such a fashion. *God does what He wills and decrees what He wills!*[236]

The Amir entered Ghaznin on Saturday, 7 Shavvāl [/21 June 1040] and took up residence in his palace. He was being comforted and reassured that the affairs of this world had their ups and downs and that, so long as he, the head, remained intact, matters could be rectified. But it was not as if he did not realize the magnitude of the disaster. For one day, when they were coming along the road through Ghur, this monarch was riding onwards with a group of people, including Bu'l-Ḥasan b. 'Abd al-Jalil, the Commander of the Ghāzis 'Abdallāh b. Qarategin and others. Bu'l-Ḥasan and this Commander were indulging in sententiously soothing words and saying, "This happening took place, and it was an unusual occurrence, arising not from the enemy's courage and alacrity but rather from the onslaught of Fate and other circumstances which are well known. When the lord reaches the capital safe and sound, fresh initiatives can be undertaken, since lo, 'Abdallāh b. Qarategin says that, if the lord so commands, he will go to India and bring back 10,000 picked infantrymen, who will be sufficient for conquering a whole world, and numerous fully-equipped cavalrymen. From this base, an attack on the enemy can be mounted, since the mode of making war on them is now known, and this disaster can be wiped out." Both Bu'l-Ḥasan and 'Abdallāh went on talking in this vein. The Amir turned towards Khᵛāja 'Abd al-Razzāq and said, "What are these fancies that they're babbling on about? We won it at Merv and we lost it at Merv."[237] The words of a monarch are always worthy of note, [F 864], especially such a monarch who was peerless in his time. He meant by these words regarding Merv that "It was at Merv that our father, the late Amir, Maḥmud, secured control of the governance of Khorasan when he defeated the Samanids, and it was here at Merv that we lost Khorasan." This story[238] happened in a remarkable way; *how strange are the ways of this present world!*[239] The late Amir had come [Gh 640] so that the matter of the governorship of Khorasan might be settled and that he might retain his status as one of the commanders giving allegiance to the Amir of Khorasan (i.e. the Samanid Amir); but God Most High desired him so to become the ruler of Khorasan himself and made this task incumbent upon him.[240] I consider myself obliged to set down this story since not everybody knows how these events happened. In this way, readers will derive profit and the events of past history will become known to people who wish to know the true nature of events. [F 865] By compiling and collecting these stories I perform my duty; *God is most knowing about the right course!*

The story of Amir Manṣur b. Nuḥ the Samanid

I have read in the historical accounts of the Samanids that when Amir Nuḥ (II) b. Mansūr (I) died at Bokhara, his son Abu'l-Ḥāreth Manṣur (II), who was the covenanted heir, was placed on the royal throne, and the retainers and courtiers all agreed on the choice.[241] He was a youth of very fine appearance, courageous and eloquent, but he had a violent temper[242] that instilled fear into all. He acceded to the throne in Rajab 387[/July-August 997][243] and appeared to have a very good grip on affairs, and proved himself a strong and capable ruler.[244] Begtuzun[245] was the Commander-in-Chief at Nishapur, and was at odds with Amir Maḥmud (i.e. the later Sultan Maḥmud). Amir Maḥmud was at Balkh and did not think it right[246] that Nishapur should be left in Begtuzun's hands. The Amir of Khorasan, Manṣur, was trying to keep both commanders happy, but was more inclined towards Begtuzun. When Amir Maḥmud realized how matters stood, he began to prepare an attack on Begtuzun. Begtuzun was alarmed, and complained to the Amir of Khorasan. The latter set out from Bokhara for Merv with his troops, accompanied by Fāʾeq al-Khāṣṣa,[247] and they sought to settle this matter by some means or other so that open warfare and hostilities could be avoided.

They stayed at Merv for some days and then headed for Sarakhs. Begtuzun [F 866] came with a large army to greet and escort [Manṣur, the Amir of Khorasan]. But he did not find the Amir of Khorasan as favourable to him as he had hoped, for the balance seemed to have tilted towards Amir Maḥmud. He said to Fāʾeq in secret, "This king is still young and green and tends to favour Amir Maḥmud; and if the latter becomes any stronger, it will signal the end for us." Fāʾeq answered, "It's just as you've said. The Amir has little regard for people[248] [Gh 641] and has no sense of gratitude, and is totally committed to Maḥmud's side.[249] He may well deliver us into Amir Maḥmud's hands, just as his father handed over Bu ʿAli Simjur to the father of this Amir Maḥmud, Sebüktegin.[250] One day, he said to me, 'Why did you acquire the honorific of "Lofty, Exalted One" (*Jalil*) when there is nothing whatsoever lofty and exalted person about you!'" Begtuzun said, "The wise course would be for us to oust him from his throne and install there one of his brothers." Fāʾeq replied, "You've hit the nail on the head, and this is the right decision," and the two of them plotted to bring this about.

One day, the Amir Bu'l-Ḥāreth (Manṣur) rode forth from the residence of the headman of Sarakhs, where he had been staying, and went out hunting. Fāʾeq and Begtuzun had halted on the outskirts of Sarakhs and pitched a tent. When Amir Manṣur came back, accompanied by 200 gholāms, Begtuzun said, "Will the lord join us in a feast which has been laid out in my tent, and eat and drink something? There's also a plan being made regarding Maḥmud." He replied, "Yes, that would be pleasant." On account of his youth and lack of foresight, and because of the foreordained decree of Fate, he halted there. When he sat down, he felt a commotion round him, and he became suspicious and apprehensive; and all at once, fetters were brought and he was bound.[251] This day was Wednesday, 12 Ṣafar 389 [/2 February 999].[252] A week later he was blinded[253] and sent to Bokhara. His reign had lasted no more than nineteen months. [F 867]

When Begtuzun and Fāʾeq had perpetrated this horrid deed, they set out and came to Merv. Amir Abu'l-Favāres ʿAbd al-Malek b.

Nuḥ[254] came to them, and he was still a beardless youth. He ascended the throne, and Sadid b. Leyth,[255] was appointed Vizier,[256] and he took up his task, but the affairs of the realm were very confused and muddled.[257] Bu'l-Qāsem Simjur came there with a powerful army and was well received. When this news reached Amir Maḥmud, he was filled with rage at the fate of Amir Abu'l-Ḥāreth, and said, "By God, if I ever set eyes on Begtuzun, I'll blind him with my own hands." He departed from Herat like an enraged lion and came to Marv al-Rud with a powerful army, and encamped over against Begtuzun's followers and his allies. They approached each other more closely, with both sides treading cautiously. Much mediation went on through envoys made up of important dignitaries, judges, religious leaders and jurists, until it was agreed that Begtuzun should be Commander-in-Chief of Khorasan and be given the governorship of Nishapur and other places which customarily went with his command, and that Amir Maḥmud should have the governorship of Balkh and Herat. An agreement was drawn up on these lines and solemnly made fast. Amir Maḥmud agreed to this arrangement, and ordered that a large sum of money should be distributed in alms since such a peace agreement as this had been negotiated without any bloodshed.[258] On Saturday, [Gh 642] 26 Jomādā I 389 [/15 May 999], Amir Maḥmud ordered the large-size kettledrums to be beaten. He stationed his brother, Amir Naṣr, over the rearguard and himself departed.

Dārā b. Qābus[259] said to the Sadidiyān, the Ḥamidiyān[260] and other groups of the army, "This was a most disadvantageous agreement that Maḥmud managed to get out of you for free. Go out now on a raid, and carry off items from his baggage and impedimenta." Many of the troops, avid for gold and clothing, launched an attack without any orders from their commanders or their approval, and fell upon the baggage of Amir Maḥmud and his troops. When Amir [F 868] Naṣr saw what was happening, he faced the situation valiantly and engaged them in battle. He also sent out riders to inform his brother. Amir Maḥmud immediately turned round, advanced and charged at them, putting the marauders to flight, and he persevered in this,[261] so that for two days there was much commotion in the battlefield until they gave up the struggle and tried each to save his own skin, and everything which they had fell into the hands of Amir Maḥmud and his army. The Amir of Khorasan (i.e. the Samanid ruler) retired to

Bokhara, defeated and deprived of all his possessions. Amir Maḥmud exclaimed, "*Indeed, God does not change what is in a people until they change their own natures.*"[262] These people made peace with us and gave their solemn word, and then went back on it. God Most High was not pleased by this and gave us the victory over them; and since they had so maltreated their prince (i.e. by blinding Amir Manṣur b. Nuḥ), He withdrew His grace and protective power from them, took away the land and the bounty He had bestowed on them and gave it to us."

In Shaʿbān of this year [/July-August 999], Fāʾeq died. Begtuzun fled before Amir Maḥmud to Bokhara, and Bu'l-Qāsem Simjur accepted a promise of pardon and safe conduct from Maḥmud.[263] From another direction, the Ilig Bu'l-Ḥasan Naṣr b. ʿAli led an army from Özkend.[264] At the beginning of Dhu'l-Qaʿda of this year [/14 October 999], he came to Bokhara, giving out that he had come offering obedience and military assistance. But one day later, Begtuzun and many of his commanders were suddenly arrested and put in bonds. The Amir of Khorasan, ʿAbd al-Malek b. Nuḥ, tried to hide, but they seized him, with all his brothers and relatives, and conveyed them to Özkend in litters. The rule of the house of Sāmān came to its end, and Amir Maḥmud, without any scheming on his part, became Amir of Khorasan so soon.[265]

This story has reached its end; it was intended to explain the meaning of Sultan Masʿud's words and also that a moral example may be derived from it, for from stories like this much profit may be discerned.

When Amir Masʿud realized that there was nothing to be gained from grieving, [Gh 643] he went back to feasting and drinking, but there were obvious signs that this gaiety was forced. [F 869] He manumitted Nushtegin Nowbati,[266] and he left the palace and spent his time with[267] Arslān Jādheb's daughter. After that, he sent Nushtegin to Bost with a strong military force, comprising cavalrymen and infantrymen, to act as military governor there, and he made him responsible for attending to all the problems of the region. He set out for that region.[268] The Amir sent Masʿud b. Moḥammad b. Leyth on a mission to Arslān Khān conveying letters and verbal instructions asking for military aid, co-operation[269] and assistance. He set out from Ghaznin via the Panjhir road on Monday, 24 Shavvāl [8 July 1040].

Confidential letters in code arrived from the postal and intelligence officer of Balkh, Amirak Beyhaqi. I deciphered them. He had written that "Dāvud had appeared at the gates of Balkh, with a powerful army,[270] thinking that the defenders were going to abandon the city and that they would hand it over to him without any struggle. I had seen to all the necessary measures and had brought in bands of irregulars (*'ayyārān*) from the surrounding countryside. The governor of Khottalān abandoned his town and came here, since he was unable to maintain himself there,[271] and we have now joined forces. There is fighting every day. The enemy were not at first pressing hard, and they sent an envoy hoping that we would hand over the city to them and leave. When they got a rough answer from us and encountered our swords, they despaired of the idea. If the lord sees fit, he should send us here a military contingent from Ghaznin under an alert commander so that we can retain control of this city, since the fate of the whole of Khorasan is bound up with this city, and if our opponents manage to capture it, all will be lost at one fell swoop.

Next day, the Amir had a private meeting with the Vizier, the Head of the Army Department, Bu Sahl Zowzani, the Commander-in-Chief and the Great Chamberlain, and discussed the confidential letter with them. He said, "They have held that city very well, [F 870] and Amirak has managed to hold there in the midst of all these troubles and failures. We must send an army so that Balkh remains in our hands, for if our opponents manage to take it, Termez, Qobādhiyān and Tokhārestān will be lost."[272] The Vizier said, "Amirak has presented the case extremely well. However, the present turmoil in Khorasan can only be resolved through the lord's own personal presence. Just a handful of souls holding on to the four walls of the city is not the solution, for the enemy can rely on additional help, and there are plenty of trouble-makers and malevolent folk inside Balkh itself,[273] and Amirak has no reinforcements. This is what I think, but of course the lord [Gh 644] knows best."

Bu Sahl Zowzani said, "I agree with the Grand Vizier. Amirak is under the illusion that the citizens of Balkh are as obedient to him as they were in former times. Furthermore, if we do send an army there, it should have at least 10,000 cavalrymen,[274] for with anything less, we shall have a disaster and lose face. An envoy has already been sent to Arslān Khān, and I think it is therefore prudent to delay making any decisions until we hear of the Khān's intentions. In the meantime, we should start to organise the troops, and if they (i.e. the Qarakhanids) are sincere and true to their word [F 871] and make a move and come down with their army, the lord too can embark on a campaign and the two armies can come together and carry out a successful mission. On the other hand, if they don't come and don't heed our words, and try to fob us off with false promises, then we can review the situation and take appropriate measures. But this idea of sending troops now to hold on to Balkh is not very sound." The Commander-in-Chief, the Great Chamberlain and other military commanders said, "This is exactly the case, but there is nothing to be lost if we send a commander with a contingent of troops to Tokhārestān, which is in our hands. If it proves possible for them to hold on to Balkh, so much the better, but if they can't, it will not be disastrous. But if we do not send a military force at all, the people of Khorasan, soldiers and subjects alike, will completely despair of this empire." Subsequently, they agreed that the General Altuntāsh should be despatched in all haste with 1,000 cavalrymen from all ethnic groups.

They went back, and set about arranging Altuntāsh's expedition with great urgency. The Vizier, the Head of the Army Department, the Commander-in-Chief and the Great Chamberlain were sitting down together and writing down the names of choice troops.[275] They were paying out silver coinage as salaries, until a powerful army had been got ready. We had written a reply to Amirak, to be conveyed by a messenger of the postal and intelligence service and also by swift couriers, to the effect that "Behold, a powerful army is coming, headed by an illustrious commander. You and the people of the city and others must stand firm and be thoroughly vigilant in keeping the city secure, for an army is coming in the wake of this confidential letter."

On Tuesday the Amir came to that elevated structure[276] which faces the review ground on the plain of Shābahār, and sat down there. This army passed him in review, in its battle formation and with a fine array, including full arms and equipment and good horses. The General Altuntāsh and his commanders came on to that elevated structure. The Amir said, "Go off with stout hearts, for we are sending another army with commanders behind you, and then we ourself will come after. What those opponents managed to achieve had nothing to do with their own efforts but [F 872] was the result of the famine which afflicted us all. The Khān of Turkestan is going to come with a numerous army, and we likewise are going to lead an expedition to restore the situation. Be resolute, and when you have reached Baghlān, see for yourselves whether you can make a surprise entry into the city of Balkh. Tread most carefully and go off and secure the city. Your appearance will reassure the townspeople and the troops there, and they will pull together as one. If, however, it proves impossible to proceed there, go to Valvālej and assume control of Tokhārestān until appropriate orders are sent to you, and keep your ears pricked for messages from Amirak Beyhaqi." They expressed their obedience and set out. The Amir embarked on a session of wine-drinking.

The Vizier summoned me and said, "Convey my verbal message to Bu Sahl, and say that 'Don't you see what is going on? An enemy of the calibre of Dāvud has come with a numerous army and has invested Balkh, and, having been taken in by the words of three or four wretched individuals, the Amir is placing this army in front of that vulture to pick at and tear to bits.[277] You'll see for yourself what will happen!'" I came and conveyed the words of the message. He replied, "This matter has got completely out of control, and one cannot improve upon the Grand Vizier's succinct and trenchant assessment. You heard what I said in support of that view, but it wasn't listened to. We're not here in the desert of Sarakhs now! Bu'l-Ḥasan b. ʿAbd al-Jalil is conducting the business of the vizierate now, and we'll see what the outcome will be."

On Tuesday, 17 Dhu'l-Qaʿda [30 July], the Amir went to the citadel, where the castellan [F 873] acted as host. A very lavish display of hospitality had been made. All the people at court were set down in front of the food trays, and they drank wine. The Amir heaped favour on the Commander-in-Chief and the Great Chamberlain Sübashï and lavished praise on them. At the time of the midday worship, all the participants went back, in a happy frame of mind. The Amir withdrew into his private quarters and remained there till late. The next day, Wednesday, the Amir held court in the citadel and heard complaints and requests for the redress of grievances. After this last session, there was a private session which went on until mid-morning. The Amir said, "Don't disperse and go your own ways,[278] for today the castellan has prepared for us a further feast."[279] The Commander-in-Chief came out, and they led him off to a small residence in the same entrance lobby and corridor which leads to the government headquarters building and treasury. There he was held captive. The

Great Chamberlain Sübashï was led to another small building of the treasury, and Begtughdï to a chamber at the castellan's residence: the very same routine that they had used on the previous day.[280] As soon as they were held there, all at once, just as had been planned during the night, the infantry in the citadel, [Gh 646] with their commanders and generals, went off and took control of the residences of these three commanders, and all their retainers were also arrested, so that not a single person escaped their clutches. The Amir had arranged this during the night hours with the castellan, Suri and Bu'l-Ḥasan b. ʿAbd al-Jalil, without anyone else being aware of it.

The Vizier and Bu Sahl were sitting in the Amir's presence, and I and the other secretaries were in that oratory in the entrance portico which houses the Chancery when monarchs visit the citadel. An attendant came out and summoned me. I went into the royal presence, and found Suri standing there with Bu'l-Ḥasan b. ʿAbd al-Jalil [F 874] and Bu'l-ʿAlāʾ the physician. The Amir instructed me, "Go with Suri to Sübashï and ʿAli Dāya, for there is a verbal message for them. You must listen carefully when the message is delivered and pay close attention to the response, for we've chosen you as our agent and informer[281] in this case to recount the occasion and then report back to us afterwards." He said to Bu'l-Ḥasan, "You and Bu'l-ʿAlāʾ are to go to Begtughdï and repeat to him our verbal message, with Bu'l-ʿAlāʾ acting as *moshref*." We all came out together, they went off to Begtughdï, and we to these other two commanders.

First, we went to Sübashï. His adjutant[282] Ḥasan was with him. When he saw Suri, his ruddy face turned pale. He said nothing to Suri but greeted me cordially, and I sat down. He turned to me and said, "What's the lord's command?" I replied, "We have a message from the Sultan that he (i.e. Suri) will deliver. I am here as a royal agent to take back the reply." He looked startled and then thought for a while, and said, "What's the message?" Suri sent the adjutant away, and he went out and was seized. Suri drew out from the side of his cloak a scroll, written in Bu'l-Ḥasan's hand, in which were listed, one after the other, Sübashï's acts of treachery, from the time when he was sent to combat the Turkmens in Khorasan to more recent days when the battle at Dandānqān took place, ending up with the admonition, "You deliberately delivered us into the enemy's hands so that your own defeat and flight from the enemy might be justified in retrospect."[283] Sübashï listened to all of this and said, "All this has been done at this man's dictation"—he meant Suri—"Tell the lord Sultan that I replied to all these [F 875] trumped-up charges when I came back from Herat to Ghaznin. The lord listened sympathetically and ascertained the falsity of all the allegations, and his exalted words were, 'I overlooked it, since the accusation was a lie,' and it would not be fitting if the lord brought this up again.[284] As for the insinuation that I deliberately schemed to bring about what happened at Dandānqān, it must be apparent to the lord that I committed no act of treachery, since I had said that we should not go to Merv. [Gh 647] I have no wealth or worldly goods left which could be of use, but if my being imprisoned will help in defeating the enemy and solving the present problem, let the lives of a hundred men like me be a sacrifice at the lord's command! And since I am guiltless, I hope that my life is not in danger and that my son may be brought up at the court so that he does not lead an idle and wasted life." He began to weep—in a way that made me feel extremely sad and distressed, while Suri exchanged some harsh words with him. After this he was held prisoner in this chamber for a period of time, as will be related in its proper place.[285] We left there, and on the way Suri said to me, "Did I err in any way in conveying the message?" I replied, "No, you didn't." He said, "See that you report everything." I agreed and thanked him.

We went off to the Commander-in-Chief. He was propped up against a chest and was wearing a robe of *molḥam* silk.[286] When he saw me, he said, "What's the lord's command?" I answered, "The Sultan has given a message to be given verbally, written by the hand of Bu'l-Ḥasan b. ʿAbd al-Jalil, and I am acting as the official responsible for conveying your reply." He said, "Deliver the message." Suri began to read out to him from another scroll. When he reached the end, the Commander-in-Chief said to me, "I understand. This is a load of rubbish that Bu'l-Ḥasan [F 876] and others have concocted regarding the tearing and destroying of the large kettledrums when on the road, and other things,[287] and our part in the débâcle. They have coveted my status and possessions, and have plotted to take them away. The whole affair is of your making. Tell the Sultan that I have grown an old man, and have used up my allotted time; as for the years between the passing away of Amir Maḥmud to the present time, I think I have overstayed my welcome in this abode. You'll see tomorrow what further tricks Bu'l-Ḥasan is up to! This Suri has been responsible for the loss of Khorasan; at all events, don't allow him a free hand in Ghaznin!" I went back. On the way, Suri said to me, "Leave out what he said about me." I replied, "I can't betray my trust." He said, "At any rate, don't retail it in front of the Vizier, because he is on bad terms with me and will rejoice at my misfortunes.[288] You should talk to the Amir in private." I said that I would.

I went into the Amir's presence, and the replies of these two men were rehearsed to him, except for the said episode (i.e. the denunciation of Suri for the loss of Khorasan). Bu'l-Ḥasan and Bu'l-ʿAlāʾ also came, and they likewise reported Begtughdï's reply, which was couched in similar terms. He had entrusted both his children, the boy and the girl, to the Amir, and said that he had lost all taste for life since he suffered from poor eyesight and felt frail and weak in the limbs.[289] The Vizier, Bu Sahl and ourselves went back, and all the rest of the courtiers were sent home and the place emptied, so that no-one of any note remained in the citadel.

The next [Gh 648] day no court session was held. At the time of the afternoon worship, the Amir came back from the citadel to the New Palace and he held a court session on Friday. This went on till late, since they had to go through the business of the commanders and the property and money, and horses and mounts belonging to those held in custody. They found nothing of Sübashï's, since his possessions had twice been plundered, but they came across a great number of possessions belonging to ʿAli and Begtughdï. Around the time of the afternoon worship, the Amir arose. I went up to Āghāji and said, "I have some private information to convey to the Sultan." He invited me in, and I related to the Sultan that passage about Suri, saying, "That day, [F 877] I delayed conveying that information because of what Suri said." The Amir commented, "I know this, and it's the truth, but if Suri asks you about this conversation, tell him something else." I went back, and Suri asked me. I covered up and misled him by saying, "The Amir said that people who are in deep trouble tend to say a lot of untrue and impossible things."

On Wednesday, 25 Dhu'l-Qaʿda [/7 August], the Commanders Badr and Ertegin were honoured and elevated in rank with two precious robes: Badr's being appropriate for a Great Chamberlain and Ertegin's for the Commander of the Palace Gholāms. They went back to their houses, and people came to offer congratulations and gifts in a handsome fashion. Each day they would come to the court with a show of splendour and a complete panoply of arms.

During the course of this week, the Amir heaped reproaches on Bu Sahl Zowzani, both face-to-face and by verbal messages, regarding the matter of Bu'l-Fażl Koronki, and he said, "You have been the cause of his rebellion, for the postal and intelligence officer there was your deputy, and he plotted and connived with him, and did not report truthfully on his activities, and if someone else tried to divulge what was going on, he would be after that person's blood. It was only through stratagem and guile that Bu'l-Fażl fell into our hands, but you and Bu'l-Qāsem Ḥaṣiri stood up to protect him and the two of you got him out of our grasp. Till this present time, he has been in continuous communication with the Turkmens, and when Khorasan fell into confusion, he rebelled and is at present launching an attack on Bost. You must now proceed to Bost, since Nushtegin Nowbati is there with a fully-equipped army, in order to put paid to his activities and rectify the situation, whether by peaceful means or by war."[290] Bu Sahl became very perturbed. He sought help from the Vizier and asked people to intercede for him. But the more they spoke, the more contentious the Amir became, as is [Gh 649] the wont [F 878] of monarchs in an affair in which they become aroused and obdurate. The Vizier told Bu Sahl confidentially, "This Sultan is not the man he was, and I've no idea what will happen. Don't be obdurate, give in and go, lest something awful happens, to the sorrow of us all." Bu Sahl became scared and agreed to go. How can anyone know what lies behind the curtain of the Unseen? *"It may be that you dislike a thing, when it is what is best for you."*[291] If he had not gone to Bost, with Amir Moḥammad having seized this monarch, Masʿud, at Mārikala,[292] the first person to be cut in half would have been Bu Sahl, because of Moḥammad's hatred for him. When he accepted to go, he appointed me as his deputy over the Chancery. He took a fresh letter of appointment (i.e. as Head of the Chancery) from the Amir because he was apprehensive lest his enemies should wreak some mischief regarding the Divān in his absence. I myself wrote out the contractual agreement concerning the Divān and the secretaries, and he wrote out the Sultan's responses to the clauses of the contract and issued orders. The next morning he saw the Amir, and received words of kindness and encouragement. He set out from Ghaznin on Thursday, 3 Dhu'l-Ḥejja [/15 August] and encamped in a garden on the outskirts of the town. I went there, and set up our mutual secret code for correspondence, said farewell and came back.

The Festival of the Sacrifice approached. The Amir gave orders that no elaborate arrangements should be made regarding the gholāms, the infantrymen, the retainers and the food tables. He came to the elevated structure overlooking the review ground, and the worship for the Festival was performed and the customary sacrifices made. It was a very low-key and subdued occasion; food tables were not set up, and the participants were all sent back homewards. The people [F 879] did not regard this as a good omen. Things like these were happening, for the Sultan's life was approaching its end, though no-one knew.

On Sunday, 27 Dhu'l-Ḥejja [/8 September],[293] a courier of the postal and intelligence service arrived from the Pass of (?) Sh.k.v.r.d[294] with a despatch bag, closed with a ring and with seals in several places.[295] I opened it. It was around the time of the midday worship. The Amir cleared the private quarters of the palace in order to read the courier's report. The postal and intelligence officer at the Pass had written: "Some fearful news arrived at this hour. I did not wish to send it on until the time of the afternoon worship came round, in the hope that an aide would arrive, since I thought that it might be a false report. At the time of the afternoon worship, the aide arrived with a confidential letter in code from Amirak Beyhaqi. I have sent this on so that it might be studied."

I deciphered the encoded text. It said, "As soon as the news arrived that the General Altuntāsh had left Ghaznin, [Gh 650] I began sending out to him one or two couriers every day, providing him with fresh news of what our spies were reporting concerning the enemy and would tell him [F 880] how to proceed on the journey and what sort of precautions he should take. He would act in accordance with what he read, and he was coming along in a watchful manner with his troops deployed ready for action. As soon as he left Baghlān and came closer to the enemy, those precautions were abandoned and they began to indulge in plundering, so that the local populace became desperate and went in haste to Dāvud and informed him of the situation. Dāvud had already heard that a general was coming from Ghaznin, and who he was, and had taken precautions to deal with the matter. When he saw the reports confirmed by what the local subjects were saying, he immediately used it as the occasion for appointing a general[296] with 6,000 cavalrymen and several senior officers, and sent them against Altuntāsh. He gave orders that ambushes should be set in several places, and he showed himself with 2,000 cavalrymen and engaged in fierce fighting. He then feigned a flight so that he could lure Altuntāsh's troops, who were avid for plunder, to pursue him past where the ambushes had been set. The troops hiding in the ambush would emerge, and they would therefore be able to make a two-pronged attack and engage in battle. When the spy's secret letter arrived with this information, I immediately sent a messenger to Altuntāsh and instructed him to proceed with caution when he drew near to the enemy, telling him what the situation was. But they had failed to take the requisite precautions in the army encampment, until there resulted a great disaster. Near dawn, the enemy fell upon him and launched an attack. Fierce fighting took place, and then they turned in a feigned flight. Our own troops, avid to get their hands on plunder, went after them, while the troops of the general and the commanders held back. The enemy released their troops from the ambushes, and they slaughtered large numbers and took many captives. Altuntāsh managed to make his way into the city with 200 cavalrymen, having fought off the enemy in skirmishes all the way. We comforted him and his followers [F 881] until things settled down. We don't know what became of the rest of that army."

I placed the letter from the Pass, together with the confidential letter in code and its deciphered text, inside a note and took it to Āghāji. He bore it inside the palace and remained there for a long time. Then he reappeared and said, "You've been summoned." I went into the royal presence,[297] and the Amir said to me, "This matter becomes more entangled every day, and we didn't foresee this as a possibility. Curses be upon Amirak! It is as if they have severed his birth cord from Balkh at the outset,[298] and he squandered away a whole army of ours! [Gh 651] Take this secret letter to the Vizier there so that he might become apprised of this situation, and tell him that the view expressed by the Vizier was the correct one, but they wouldn't allow us to follow our own judgement. ʿAli Dāya, Sübashï and Begtughdï made us do this, and now these acts of treachery have been committed by them, so that the Vizier cannot say that they were guiltless." I went into the Vizier's presence. He read the confidential letters[299] and listened to the Sultan's verbal message. He said to me, "Something like this happens every day; it is obvious that the Sultan will never abandon his self-willed conduct and his misguided ways. Now that these disasters have occurred, a reply must be sent back to Amirak urging him to hold on to the city tenaciously, and he must give encouragement to Altuntāsh so that these troops are not just squandered away. A plan should be drawn up so that they (i.e. Amirak and Altuntāsh) can fall back on Termez and find refuge with the castellan Begtegin Chowgāni, for I fear that the city of Balkh, and many of its God-fearing Muslim citizens, will become victims of Amirak's ill-judged vanity and his botched attempts at generalship."[300] I went back and told the Amir what the Vizier had said. He answered, "Yes, a letter should be written in these terms." It was duly written, and copies went off to the castellan Begtegin both via the courier and also by the hand of swift messengers. [F 882]

After this period of disasters, the Amir abandoned all hope for Ghaznin. The Angel of Death was at his door and had instilled in him such fear and trepidation that he fell into deep despair.

The Year 432
[/11 September 1040–30 August 1041]

[Gh 651, F 882] Friday was the first day of this month (i.e. of Moḥarram) and of the new year. The Amir had a private meeting after the court session with the Vizier, the castellan Bu Sahl Ḥamdavi, the Head of the Army Department Bu'l-Fatḥ Rāzi, the Great Chamberlain Badr and the new Commander of the Palace Gholāms Ertegin. The chamberlain of the Sultan's private quarters went away and summoned the prince Amir Mowdud. The register of the Army Department[1] was asked for and fetched. An attendant came to me and asked me to be there as well and to bring with me paper and inkstand. I went, and was seated in the royal presence—ever since Bu Sahl Zowzani had left on his mission,[2] the Amir had commanded that I should be given a seat while attending royal sessions for investigating complaints and grievances[3] and altogether regarded me in a different light (i.e. an implicit acknowledgment of his new status and duties). The Amir then instructed the Head of the Army Department to go through the names of the senior officers and told me to enter them in two separate divisions, and the allocations were so arranged that, in the end, most of the troops stationed at the court were assigned to proceed to Hopyān.[4] When we had finished with this, he summoned the palace secretary, who came with the register of the gholāms.[5] He made his selections [Gh 652] and I wrote them down: the more capable gholāms were assigned to the Hopyān expedition, and the more presentable and handsome gholāms of the royal household were kept back for himself.[6]

When we had finished this too, he turned to the Vizier and said, "Altuntāsh encountered difficulties, as we know, and had to seek refuge in Balkh with some of his mounted troops. But though the troops that accompanied him suffered a defeat and lost all they had, they have to return to the capital to be seen to and fitted out again. We intend to nominate our son Mowdud to go to Hopyān and [F 883] take up a position there with these troops whose names have been listed. The Great Chamberlain Badr, Ertegin and the palace gholāms are to accompany him, while you, Aḥmad, are to oversee the enterprise and act as Mowdud's counsellor and adjutant[7] until those troops reach you from Balkh and present themselves for review and receive their salaries and allowances from the Head of the Army Department's deputy. We are preparing other troops and will be sending them after you. At that time you are to proceed, with the vanguard of our army, and we will follow you, fully prepared and equipped. We will act with great alacrity and purpose, so that what God Most High has decreed may come to pass. Go back, and attend to your affairs, and whatever needs to be ordained, we shall ordain for you during the next [ten][8] days while you are still here." They acknowledged the royal command and went homewards.

The Vizier went to the Divān and sat in private and summoned me and said, "What's he up to now?" I replied, "I can't tell what is brewing up in his mind, but this much I know, that ever since the lord received the letter from Amirak with news of the Altuntāsh débâcle, his mood has changed drastically and he has fallen into deep despair." He said, "In that case, there's no point in pondering whether I should see him in person or not. You'll have to give my message." I signalled my willingness to do that, and he said, "Tell him that Aḥmad says as follows: 'The lord gave me a command that I should accompany the prince to Hopyān with the leading figures and the commanders, and that more troops will join up with us. The right way to proceed with this is for me to know what I am required to do. If the exalted judgement sees fit, I will draw up a contractual agreement and include all our needs, since this journey is a very delicate operation by virtue of [F 884] the fact that the prince and these leading figures will be in the vanguard and it appears that [Gh 653] the lord, in an auspicious state, will follow on our tracks. It is for the lord to command,[9] and for us, his subjects, to obey and to carry out whatever he orders to our last breath. But the lord should not keep hidden from his servant, who is the lord's vizier, whatever he has in mind, for that would have a most discouraging impact. On the contrary, if the lord consents, he should disclose his intentions to me so that matters can be arranged in accordance with what I hear from him and so that I can then act on the basis of the contract, while the prince and the senior army commanders will act according to the royal command. In this way, no breaches of security will occur. For it may be that your servant receives a royal command or he may have to proceed in great haste to Balkh and Tokhārestān, and in such cases it would be impossible to arrange matters through correspondence. Also, the prince has been chosen for a great task, and will today acquire the functions of being the lord's deputy and supreme commander of the army: It is vital that the resources allotted to him, comprising gholāms and everything else, should be on a grander scale than those bestowed on others. He must also have a counsellor and adjutant to take care of his own special affairs. This is essential, so that I can give the counsellor and adjutant some guidance on how to look after the prince's welfare."

I went and delivered this message. The Amir remained deep in thought for a long while, and then he said, "Go, and summon the Vizier." I went away and summoned him. The Vizier arrived and Āghāji took him in. The Amir was already in the small upper chamber when the Vizier went in—it had three doors[10] [F 885]—and he remained with him till a very late hour. Then Āghāji appeared and called me, and I went into the royal presence with inkstand and paper. The Amir instructed me, "Go to the Vizier's house and sit down with him alone so that he may tell you what I have said and commanded and may write out the contract. Come back by yourself at the time of the afternoon worship so that the royal response may be written out. Your dealings and what you hear from him must remain secret." I acknowledged his instructions and went back.

I went with the Vizier to his house. We had something to eat and rested for a while. Then he cleared the room of people and summoned me, and I sat down. He said, "You must realize that the Amir is now terrified of these enemies, and all my attempts to reassure him and instil some confidence in him have been to no avail. It is as if he is in the clutches of an inexorable decree of Fate against which we are powerless. He has got the idea firmly fixed in his mind that, since Altuntāsh fared so miserably, Dāvud will inevitably move against Ghaznin. I told him repeatedly that it would be impossible for them to launch an attack on another place, particularly on Ghaznin, when they have not finished with Balkh, but of course my words had no effect on him and he said, [Gh 654] 'I happen to know things that you are not aware of. We must get ready and presently proceed to Parvān and Hopyān.' The way I see it, as soon as I get there, he will set out for India. He concealed this from me, and he keeps saying, 'We intend to stay in Ghaznin for a short while, and then we shall follow in your tracks,' but I know that he won't come. It would be wrong to pursue the matter any further. He has ordered the contract to be written out so that you can bring it before him and, when the answers have been written down and the royal signature and emblem affixed, to return it to me. It has been settled that the office of counsellor and adjutant for the prince should be given to my son-in-law [F 886] Abu'l-Fatḥ Masʿud, who is the most suitable person for it."[11]

I said, "He's made a most excellent choice and, God willing, he will bring this matter to a successful end." He commented, "I'm worried about the way things are going at the moment," and he began to write out the contract in his own hand, and took a long time over it. (This lord, the Vizier, was a wonder in such matters, and what he wrote on his own could not be bettered by several people working together, since he was the most capable and the most proficient in secretarial skills of all the people of the age.) The contract encompassed the following: defining what was to be the extent of the services to be rendered for the prince; how much respect the latter was in turn to show to the Vizier; a detailed section on the palace gholāms and their Commander; a section regarding the Great Chamberlain and other senior army commanders; a section concerning modes of the army's proceeding and encamping while on the march, and on getting wind of news from the enemy; a section on the army's pay allotments and on the power of appointment and dismissal of the deputy of the Head of the Army Department;[12] and a section concerning money held in the treasury and the store of clothing which was to accompany them, and on the financial and tax officials charged with raising extra money if there were insufficient tax revenues coming in and unavoidable expenses.[13]

I took the contract and bore it to the court, and I had the Amir informed by word of a household attendant that I had brought it. He summoned me into his presence and gave orders that we should not be disturbed. He took the contract and studied it closely. Then he said, "How do you propose to write out the answers to these clauses? There's no doubt that you are best informed about how Bu Naṣr Moshkān used to write out such provisions as these." I answered, "I do, in fact, know this. If the exalted judgement sees fit, I will write down the answers to the various clauses of the contract and the lord can affix his emblem and signature in his own hand." He said, "Sit down, and make out the document here on the spot." I took the contract and started writing and set down the answers to each clause [F 887] and read them out. The Amir was pleased with this, but ordered a few changes to be made. I inserted his verbal corrections, and he approved of the final result, [Gh 655] with the Amir's answers below each clause of the contract, and he affixed his emblem and signature. At the foot of the document, he added in his own handwriting, "The Excellent Vizier, *may God perpetuate his strength*, is to place his reliance on these answers which have been written out at our command and have been strengthened by the royal signature and emblem. He is to display his capability and sincere counsel in every single one of these clauses in such a way as to make him worthy of being given praise and being relied upon, if God so wills." He handed the contract over to me and told me to arrange a code with the Vizier so that both sides could convey matters of crucial importance to each other in that code. He went on to say, "Tell him to summon Masʿud Rokhudhi (i.e. Abu'l-Fatḥ Masʿud) this evening, to pass on to him from us words of encouragement and hopes of future advancement, and to bring him to the court tomorrow with himself so that he may see us and so that we may entrust to him the office of counsellor and adjutant for our son and send him away with a robe of honour." I replied, "I'll do that."

I went to the Vizier, gave him the contract and conveyed the message. He was very pleased and said, "You went to a lot of trouble today on my account." I replied, "I am your servant. I hope that I can be of some service at times." I made a move to leave, but he said, "Sit down. You forgot this matter of the code." I replied, "I hadn't forgotten, but I intended to leave it till tomorrow since I thought that the lord must be tired by now." He said, "Let me tell you something. Never put off till tomorrow what you can do today, for each day that comes along brings its own tasks, [F 888] and it has been said that 'He who banks on tomorrow will have no tomorrow.'"[14] I replied, "The lord's company is always most instructive and beneficial." He took up his pen and devised before me a remarkably ingenious code. He then picked up a book from the reading stand and wrote down that code on the back of it, and gave the copy in his own handwriting to me. He said some words in Turkish to a gholām, who fetched a purse filled with silver and gold and some pieces of cloth, and laid them before me. I kissed the ground before the Vizier and said, "The lord must excuse me from accepting this." He answered, "I have been a secretary myself. One should not order secretaries to undertake a task gratis." I said, "It's for the lord to command." I returned home, and the money and the material were handed to one of my servants: there were 5,000 dirhams and five rolls of cloth. The next day, he brought Khᵛāja Masʿud along with him. He was a youth of good pedigree, intelligent, handsome and attractive, but still inexperienced and unfamiliar with the vicissitudes of life, for the young must of necessity experience the buffetings and ravages of Fate and the calamities of this world. [Gh 656]

The story of Jaʿfar b. Yaḥyā b. Khāled the Barmakid

I have read in the historical accounts of the caliphs that Jaʿfar b. Yaḥyā b. Khāled the Barmakid was peerless in his time in all the arts of political practice, learning, polite literature and etiquette, wisdom, self-control and capability, to such a degree that in the time of his father's vizierate he was called "*The Second Vizier*"[15] and used to carry out the greater part of his tasks. One day he had taken his place in the session for hearing complaints and grievances and was reading petitions and writing out responses as was the usual custom then. There were nearly a thousand petitions, to all of which he affixed his emblem and signature, with the words that in such-and-such a case, so-and-so should be done [F 889] and in such-and-such, so-and-so, and the last petition was a scroll with more than a hundred cramped and closely-written lines.[16] One of the royal household servants had come so that he could leave and not have to do any further work.[17] Jaʿfar wrote on the back of that last petition, "*Let it be looked into and let there be done regarding it whatever is done in similar cases.*" When at the end of the session Jaʿfar arose, those petitions were taken to the offices of justice and the vizierate and to those departments concerned with legal ordinances and regulations, charitable endowments, things given in fulfilment of vows, and the land tax, and were closely examined. People used to be astonished at his diligence and congratulated his father Yaḥyā. The latter replied, *"Abu Aḥmad,"* he meant Jaʿfar, *"is the unique figure of his age in every aspect of polite learning and secretarial expertise* (ādāb), *except that he needs to experience hardship and tribulation to refine him."*[18]

The situation of Khᵛāja Masʿud, may God preserve him, was exactly the same in that he came straight from home and school into the presence of the royal throne. Inevitably, he later went through many a testing time and had to see and endure a great deal, as I shall set forth in this work in its proper place.[19] Today, in the year 451[/1059], in accordance with the command of the lord of the world, the exalted Sultan Abu'l-Moẓaffar Ebrāhim, *may God prolong his life and uphold his supporters and retainers*, he remains in his house until there should arrive a command for him to come before the throne once more. It has been said that in order to thrive in this world it is better if one's fortunes suffer ups and downs,[20] for when everything goes to plan and there are no upsets, the person in question will suddenly suffer a mighty fall. *We seek refuge in God from adversity and upheavals in affairs!*

The Amir held a court session, and the Vizier and leading figures came into the royal presence. When they had all settled down in their places, Khᵛāja Masʿud was brought in, and he paid his respects and stood there. The Amir said, "We chose you as counsellor and adjutant for our son Mowdud. Be alert, and act in accordance with the Vizier's orders." Masʿud replied, "I'll obey the commands." [F 890] He kissed the ground and went back, and people came to congratulate him with lavish presents. He returned to his house and after an hour went to Amir Mowdud, and all the gifts brought to him were taken there. Amir [Gh 657] Mowdud made much of him. From there he came to the house of the Vizier, his father-in-law;[21] the Vizier showed him great favour, and sent him back.

On Sunday, 10 Moḥarram [/20 September 1040], Amir Mowdud, the Vizier, the Great Chamberlain Badr, the Commander of the Palace Gholāms Ertegin and others were given robes of honour of the most sumptuous kind, the like of which had never been bestowed before. The recipients came forward, paid their respects and went back. Amir Mowdud was given two elephants, one male and one female, barrel-shaped drums and ordinary-sized kettle drums, and much more besides. Others, too, had gifts lavished upon them, and all preparations were completed.

On Tuesday, the twelfth of this month [/22 September], the Amir, may God be pleased with him, mounted and came to the Firuzi Garden. He sat down on the elevated dais at the lower review ground[22] (that construction and the review ground have today changed out of all recognition, but were then in their pristine condition). He had ordered a very elaborate feast to be prepared and for dishes of *harisa*[23] to be set out. Amir Mowdud and the Vizier came along also and sat down with him. The army began to go past in review. First was the retinue of Amir Mowdud: the ceremonial parasol and broad banners;[24] 200 men from the palace gholāms, all with mailed coats and short spears; a great number of camels, both for leading and for swift riding; infantrymen with broad banners; 170 gholāms with a full panoply of arms; and his cavalrymen adorned with splendid, complete outfits. After this, there came the Commander of the Palace Gholāms Ertegin and eighty odd of his gholāms; then after them, [F 891] a contingent of fifty palace gholāms and, at their head, twenty field officers, highly decked out, with numerous camels for leading and for swift riding; these were followed by another detachment of field officers, also well turned out, until the whole parade passed by. The time of the midday worship having come round, the Amir ordered his son, the Vizier, the Great Chamberlain, Ertegin and the senior commanders to be given seats at the spread, and he himself sat down. They ate together, and then all those going on the expedition took their formal leave and departed. *This was the last time they ever had an encounter with this king, God's mercy be upon him!*

After their departure, the Amir said to ʿAbd al-Razzāq,[25] "What do you say? How about drinking a few large bumpers[26] of wine?" He replied, "Such a day as this, with the lord in a joyful state and the prince having departed with the Vizier and other notables all according to plan, and having all [Gh 658] just consumed *harisa* together, what better day could there be for festive drinking?" The Amir said, "We'll set out without any pomp and ceremony and drink in the Firuzi Garden." Much wine was immediately brought. He left the review ground for the Garden, and fifty huge goblets and two-handled flagons were set down in the midst of the summer house and the goblets began to circulate. The Amir said, "Be fair and keep the bumpers evenly topped up so that no injustice is done." Then they were passed around, with each bumper holding half-a-*man*,[27] the merry-making got under way, and the singers and musicians struck up. Bu'l-Ḥasan drank five bumpers, at the sixth he could no longer take it, at the seventh bumper he lost his wits, at the eighth he vomited the lot and the attendants carried him away. Bu'l-ʿAlāʾ the physician fell forward in a stupor at the fifth bumper and was carried out. Khalil, son of Dāvud, drank ten and Siyābiruz nine, and both were carried away to the Street of the Deylamites.[28] Bu Noʿeym drank twelve [F 892] and beat a quick retreat. Dāvud Meymandi fell down drunk. The singers and musicians and the jesters all became drunk and took to their heels. There remained only the Sultan and Khᵛāja ʿAbd al-Razzāq. The Khᵛāja drank eighteen, and took his formal leave, saying to the Amir, "This is enough for me: a drop more and my manners and my wits will desert me!" The Amir laughed, and gave him permission to leave. He got up and left with a great display of politeness and composure. After this, the Amir kept on drinking happily, and twenty-seven bumpers each of half-a-*man* were finished off. He arose, called for water and a washing bowl and for a prayer mat, rinsed out his mouth, and performed the midday worship and the afternoon worship, and he looked and behaved as if he had not had a drop. I, Bu'l-Fażl, witnessed all this with my own eyes. The Amir mounted his elephant and went to the palace.

On Thursday, 19 Moḥarram [/29 September], the castellan Bu ʿAli left Ghaznin with a powerful army and headed for the region of the Khalaj, bent on imposing some order on them either peacefully or by dint of war, for they had caused much trouble during the Amir's absence.[29]

After the Vizier's departure, the Amir used to seek Bu Sahl Ḥamdavi's advice and guidance on every topic, but the latter, believing that this was inappropriate, would try to extricate himself, and always strove to take the Vizier's side. He asked me to bear witness that every private meeting and policy deliberation that he had to attend was most distasteful to him. I was also present at these important deliberations. The Sultan's disenchantment with the affairs of the kingdom, and the weakness of his judgement, reached such a pitch that he had a private session with Bu Sahl one day, [Gh 659] with me standing there, and he said, "The provinces of Balkh and Tokhārestān must be ceded to Böritegin so that he may come with the army and troops of Transoxania and wage war on the Turkmens."

Bu Sahl replied, "The Vizier must be consulted over this." The Amir exclaimed, "You want to defer [F 893] to a dotard like him?"[30] and he ordered me to write out on the spot a formal document of cession and investiture[31] and letters, and he affixed his emblem and signature, and said, "You are to give it to a swift courier for him to deliver." I acknowledged the order. At that point Bu Sahl said, "The best course might be for the courier to go to the Vizier, and for the order to be confirmed and then for him to send the courier back." [32] He replied, "That's a good plan." A letter was written[33] to the Grand Vizier to the effect that "The Sultan is giving orders for such-and-such unwise courses of action; the Vizier knows better what courses he himself would ordain." Bu Sahl Ḥamdavi told me, "What I meant was that you should write on your own behalf and explain that I am innocent of any charges regarding these private deliberations and unsound decisions." I wrote out the message to the Vizier in code and explained the circumstances, and a courier was despatched. He came to the Vizier. The Vizier kept back the courier, the cession document and the letter since he knew that this was a wrong-headed course of action, and then wrote a reply to me to be brought back by the postal and intelligence service courier.

On Monday, the first day of Ṣafar (/11 October),[34] Amir Izadyār[35] set out from Naghar[36] to Ghaznin, saw the Amir and went back. During the night, Amir Moḥammad had been brought back from the fortress of Naghar in the company of this prince and conveyed to the citadel of Ghaznin, into the custodianship of the Commander of the Palace Guards Sengüy.[37] His four sons Aḥmad, 'Abd al-Raḥmān, 'Omar and 'Othmān, had also been brought back and were installed during the night in that elevated structure in the Firuzi Garden.[38] Next day, the Amir held a wine-drinking session from the early morning onwards. Towards noon he sent for me and said, "Go secretly and discreetly to my brother Moḥammad's sons and make them swear solemn oaths that they will give sincere and loyal service and not be rebellious. When this has been done, give them hopes of favour from us and give orders for them [F 894] to don robes of honour. Then you are to come back to us until Sengüy's son has lodged them in the residence prepared for them in the inner city."

I went off to that elevated dais in the Firuzi Garden where they were. They all looked distraught and apprehensive, and were clad in worn-out cotton robes. [Gh 660] I gave them the message, and they fell to the ground and were filled with great joy. I wrote out the texts of the oaths, which were oaths of allegiance (*eymān al-bey'a*). Each one of them read it out aloud, and I got them to place their signatures at the foot of each document. Then the robes of honour were brought out, made up of coats of expensive, parti-coloured, gold-thread woven cloth,[39] fine linen turban cloths and red boots, and they went into the house and put them on. They came out and mounted horses of noble breed, with gold accoutrements, and rode off. I myself came into the Amir's presence and related to him what had taken place. He said, "Write a letter to our brother saying that 'You should know that we ordered such-and-such for our brother's sons, and will bring them into our service and keep them with us at court so that they become conversant with our manners and ways, and then we will betroth our own virgin daughters to them: let this be made known to them'." He gave orders that the style of address for Moḥammad was to be "The Exalted Amir, Brother" *(al-Amir al-Jalil al-Akh)*. This was written out, he affixed his emblem and signature, and gave it to Sengüy, saying, "Take this to your son." He acted in this way so that no-one should find out that Moḥammad was being held in the citadel of Ghaznin.

The next day, those sons of his brother, wearing turbans on their heads, came into his presence and rendered service. The Amir sent them along to the Royal Wardrobe so that they might be garbed in robes of honour, comprising gold-embroidered coats, four-sectioned hats, belts ornamented with gold, and they were provided with fine horses. He further gave each of them presents of 1,000 dinars and twenty pieces of fine cloth, and then they went back to that palace. A supervisor was appointed to look after them, and awarded them generous stipends. They were coming to the court twice each day, morning and evening, to render service. The lady Gowhar was given to Amir Aḥmad b. Moḥammad, straightaway, until the time when he could designate other daughters[40] and the formal marriage ceremony [F 895] was performed.[41]

After this, he sent trusty agents, under the highest conditions of secrecy, to carry away all the treasuries containing gold, silver dirhams, clothing, jewels and whatever other forms of wealth were to be found in Ghaznin, and they got busy organising the work. A verbal message was sent to his mother and other noble ladies of the royal house, comprising paternal aunts, his sisters and his daughters, saying, "Prepare yourselves to come to India with us, and go about it in a thorough way so that you don't leave behind in Ghaznin anything that you really care about." Whether they liked it or not, they all began to prepare for leaving, and they sounded out the Sultan's aunt Ḥorra Khottali and the Sultan's mother about this and were told, "Let all those who wish to fall into the enemy's hands stay behind in Ghaznin," and no-one dared to say a word after that. The Amir set about dividing out the camels.[42] He used to spend most of the day with the accounting officer [Bu] Manṣur on this matter. Large numbers of camels were needed and there was a shortage, given the great size of the treasury. [Gh 661]

The retainers and the troops stationed at the court kept saying to me *sotto voce*, "What's all this about?", but none dared to speak out loud. One day, Bu Sahl Ḥamdavi and Bu'l-Qāsem b. Kathir said that it was vital that the Vizier should express his views on the withdrawal to India, since he must have read about it in the agent's letter.[43] I replied, "It may well be that he does, but he can't initiate anything and write a letter until the Amir himself broaches the subject." By chance the next day, the Sultan ordered a letter to be written to the Vizier, saying, "We have taken the decision to go to India and to retire for the winter to Wayhind,[44] M.r.manāra (?),[45] Peshawar, Giri[46] and those regions. You yourself must remain there at Hopyān until we set off and arrive at Peshawar, and a letter reaches you. At that point, you are to proceed to Tokhārestān [F 896] and winter there, and if it proves possible, you are to go to Balkh and topple the enemy."

The letter was written and despatched. I explained clearly in the coded message that "In spite of the fact that nothing untoward has happened, the lord is panic-stricken, and won't stop until he reaches Lahore. Confidential letters have been sent to Lahore to prepare for his arrival, but it appears that he will not tarry there long. None of the royal womenfolk nor any item of the treasuries will remain at Ghaznin. The retainers and troops stationed at the court who are here feel utterly impotent and bewildered, and all their hopes are concentrated on the Grand Vizier, and people are desperate for him to relieve us from this sorry state as soon as possible; and since he is several stages away from us (i.e. a safe distance away), he should write openly and without mincing his words, and perhaps this misguided plan will be renounced." I told the leading dignitaries of the court confidentially that the Sultan ordered a letter to be sent to the Vizier in such-and-such terms, and I wrote this out, but I also wrote on my own account a letter in code containing such-and-such. They said, "This was a stroke of luck, and if God Most High so wills, this wise old man will write a clear and comprehensive letter and will bring this lord back to his senses."

The reply to this letter came back, and indeed, he had given dire warnings and spoken directly, as if to an equal, deployed every weapon at his disposal, and had said bluntly, "If the lord is on the move because our enemies are fighting at the gates of Balkh, he should know that they haven't dared to enter the town and our troops have the upper hand [Gh 662] since they keep venturing out of the city and fighting them outside. If the lord gives the command, I shall go and clear the enemy from the region. Why does the lord have to reside in India? Let him pass this winter in Ghazni (*sic*), for praise be to God, we have no worries there since I myself have incited Böritegin against this gang of Turkmens and he will come. The lord must know for sure that, if [F 897] he goes to India, and takes all the royal womenfolk and treasuries to there, and this news becomes generally known, reaching friend and foe alike, the prestige of this great empire will be dissipated and everyone will become increasingly avid to get a share of it. Also, we cannot have so much faith in the Indians as to take to their land such numbers of womenfolk and such loads of treasure, for we have not treated[47] them all that well in the past. Moreover, what reliance can one place on the gholāms when the lord's treasuries will have to be laid open to them while traversing the open country? The lord has indulged in many wilful acts up to now and suffered the consequences, but this particular wrongheaded obduracy surpasses them all. If he now departs, the subjects will be left in a state of hopeless misery and gloom. I have given this advice and have fulfilled the obligations for his beneficence, and I am absolving myself of responsibility. It is for the lord to decide."

When the Amir had read this letter, he straightaway said to me, "This man has become a dotard and doesn't know what he is talking about. Write the reply, 'The right course is the one we have discerned. The Vizier set forth his view on a basis of giving sincere advice. He is to await the command, until what the Sultan deems necessary is ordained', for I can see what you are unable to see." The reply was written out. Everyone got to know about this and became plunged in despair. Preparations for the departure were begun.

The castellan Bu 'Ali returned from the expedition against the Khalaj, having successfully dealt with the matter. On Monday, the first day of the month of Rabi' I [/9 November], he went into the Amir's presence and was well received, and then he went back home. The next day, the Amir had a private session with him lasting till the time of the midday worship. I heard that he entrusted to him the town of Ghaznin and the citadel and the surrounding regions, saying, "We intend to come back in the spring. Great care must be taken so that no trouble occurs within the town itself, since our son Mowdud and the Vizier are stationed outside it with a powerful army. [F 898] We'll see how the enemy will fare this winter, and then in the spring [Gh 663] we'll steer a new course. The auguries are not good for this winter, so the astrologers tell us."[48] The castellan said, "It might be wiser to place the womenfolk and treasuries inside firmly-protected fortresses rather than transport them through the open countryside of India." He replied, "The wise course is for them to accompany us." The castellan said, "May God Most High crown this journey with safety, good fortune and success," and he went back.

At the time of the afternoon worship, the army leaders[49] went to the castellan, sat down with him and had a protracted session. But it was all to no avail.[50] God Most High moves in mysterious ways. They said, "Tomorrow we'll make yet another attempt[51] and we'll see what will happen." He replied, "Although there's no hope of success and he will become even more irate, it's the right thing to do."[52]

Next day, after the court session, the Amir had a private meeting with the accounting officer [Bu] Manṣur because a considerable number of camels was required for them to be able to leave, but these could not be found, and he was becoming very vexed over this. The dignitaries came to the court with [Bu'l-Ḥasan b.] 'Abd al-Jalil, but [F 899] Khᵛāja 'Abd al-Razzāq did not sit down[53] with them, and he said to me, "I haven't the stomach for listening to unseemly words," and he went back. The rest sat down at the iron gate of that domed chamber,[54] and they asked me to go along and tell the Sultan that they wished to talk to him.

I went off, and found the Amir engaged in a private meeting with the accounting officer [Bu] Manṣur in the winter building.[55] I repeated the message. He said, "I know they've brought a load of fanciful inanities.[56] Listen to their message, and then come back and tell me."

I went back to them and said, "*The scout does not deceive his own folk*.[57] Before he had actually heard the message, he said, 'They'll have brought a load of inanities'." They answered, "That may be so, but we wish to acquit ourselves of our obligations," and they stood there and gave me a lengthy verbal message on the same lines that the Vizier had written, but even more explicit. I said, "I don't have the temerity to convey these detailed points expressed in this form. It is best if I write it all down, for he'll certainly read through the whole written message." They all approved of the idea. I took up my pen, and it was set down in a very detailed manner, with them helping me along. Then they wrote some lines at the end, in their own hands, [Gh 664] verifying that this indeed was their message.

I laid it before the Amir and he took it, and he read it through twice slowly and deliberately. Then he said, "If the enemy comes here, Bu'l-Qāsem b. Kathir has gold and he can give it to them and assume the office of Head of the Army Department. Bu Sahl Ḥamdavi also has gold, and can use it to secure himself the office of Vizier, and the accounting officer Ṭāher and Bu'l-Ḥasan [b. ʿAbd al-Jalil] likewise. The right course for me is the one I'm taking. They must come [with us], and put an end to this talk." I came and related what I had heard. They became thoroughly dejected and distressed. The castellan said, "What did he say about me?" I answered, "I swear he didn't mention you at all." They arose, saying, [F 900] "We did what we had to do, and there's nothing further for us to say here," and they went back. Four days after this message the Sultan departed.[58]

This is the end of the present volume, and I have set down the history of events up to this point. I have left aside the departure of this monarch for India so that I can make a start on the tenth volume and can set down the two sections on Khwarazm and Jebāl, bringing the story up to this present time, as is the requirement of history. When I have finished that, I shall revert to the regular pattern of the History and relate the story of this monarch's departure for India up to the close of his life, and continue forward, *if the Almighty God so wills*.[59]

[The end of the ninth volume]

[The beginning of the tenth volume]

At the end of the ninth volume I brought the account of the reign of Amir Masʿud up to that point when he made the firm decision to go to India, intending to leave within four days, and with that I brought the volume to a close. I also said that, in this tenth volume, I am first going to set down two sections on Khwarazm and on Ray and on the stay at Ray of Bu Sahl Ḥamdavi and those retainers and troops of his, their return from there and the loss of that province to us. I am also going to give the complete story of Khwarazm and Altuntāsh and how the province slipped from our grasp, all so that the sequence of historical events may be correctly set forth. Then, when that is finished, I shall go back to the history of this monarch and shall relate the events of these four days and up to the end of his life, for there was little left of it.

I have now started on these sections, both of which contain a very considerable number of strange and remarkable points. It will become apparent to perceptive readers who reflect on these at length that human endeavour on its own will not bear fruit and will not set things aright, no matter how well furnished they may be with arms, troops and materials of war, but when the favour of God, His splendour is exalted, is present, all goes well. Which of the prerequisites that a monarch ought to have—court troops, servants, great men of state, masters of the sword and pen, numberless armies, copious numbers of elephants and riding beasts, and well-filled treasury—did Amir Masʿud lack? Yet, when Fate so decreed that he should endure so much pain and sorrow during his reign, and should lose possession of Khorasan, Ray and Jebāl, and Khwarazm, what [F 902] could he do but show fortitude and submission? For the divine decree is such that no human being can dare to struggle and strive against it. This king was not at fault, and even though he was admittedly self-willed and confident of his own powers, he fought hard night and day. But his plans went awry because God Most High had foreordained back in the remotest moment of past eternity[60] that, as I have related, Khorasan should slip freely from his grasp, and likewise Khwarazm and Ray and Jebāl, as I shall now relate so that it may be firmly ascertained. *God is most knowing about what is best!*

[The History of Khwarazm]

[Gh 665, F 902]

A description of the province of Khwarazm

Khwarazm is a province resembling a whole kingdom,[1] eighty [parasangs] by eighty [parasangs]. It has numerous mosques[2] and has always had its own separate seat of government there with its own illustrious kings. In the book *Lives of the Persian kings*[3] it is stated that a kinsman of Bahrām Gur, who was thus, by virtue of his lineage worthy of kingly rule over the Persians lands,[4] came there and conquered it, [F 903] but this account is thought to be spurious.[5] When the rule of the Arabs—may it endure for ever!—swept away the customs and practices of the Persians and secured the upper hand through the lord of all peoples, past and present, Moḥammad the Chosen One,[6] Khwarazm preserved its separate identity as before. As one can see from historical accounts and chronicles, it has always had its own king, and unlike Khottalān and Chaghāniyān, has never been considered a part of Khorasan. When, in the time of the Moʿādhis and Tahirids,[7] the ʿAbbasid caliphate underwent a period of strife and weakness, Khwarazm remained just as it had been. The reign of the Maʾmunids, whose power came to an end in the auspicious reign of Amir Maḥmud, bears witness to that. Given these particulars regarding the province, I thought it necessary to begin with an exordium at the head of this chapter and to say a few words about the remarkable history of the province and stories related to it, in such a way that informed readers will find acceptable.[8] [Gh 666]

Exordium (Khoṭba)

It is generally accepted that it is the mind (lit. "heart")[9] that sets apart human beings as a species and that their minds become weak or strong through hearing and seeing, for so long as they do not see bad and good, nor hear of them, they cannot know anything of the joys and sorrows of this world. Hence one should know that eyes and ears are the lookouts and [F 904] spies of the mind, for they transmit to the latter what they see and hear, and it makes use of what they transmit to it. The mind (heart) then transmits what it has apprehended from them to the intellect (*kherad*), which is the arbiter of justice, so that the true may be separated from the false, and what is useful may be retained and what is not, discarded. This explains the public thirst for finding things they have not heard of, or do not know, be they in the past or in the future. The past can be recovered the hard way by travelling round the world, enduring all sorts of personal discomfort, and by seeking out happenings and historical accounts; or else by studying reliable books and informing oneself by gleaning accurate information from them. As for what is still to come, the way remains closed for it is wholly inscrutable; since if a man could foresee everything good or bad, nothing bad would come upon him. "*Only the Almighty God, knows the Unseen.*"[10] Although this is the case, even the wise strive hard to decipher the future and attempt to examine it from all sides and discuss it in serious terms, hoping that, if they really do look into it properly, they would find the best way to plan ahead.[11]

Historical information about the past is said to be of two kinds, with no third way about it: either one must hear them from someone or read about it in a book. The necessary condition for the former is that the informant should be trustworthy and veracious, that one's intellect should find it sound and authentic, [F 905] and that it should be confirmed by the Word of God "*Don't give credence to any reports that are not acceptable to your judgement*".[12] The same goes for a book: for whatever one reads in a book, so long as it is not rejected as implausible by one's intellect, is held as being true by the reader, and the wise will also listen to it and take it in.

The mass of common people, however, are so constituted that they prefer impossible absurdities, such as stories of demons and fairies and evil spirits inhabiting the deserts, mountains and seas, as when some fool kicks up a commotion and a throng of likeminded people gathers round him, and he regales them with such things as, "In a certain sea, I saw an island, and five hundred of us landed on that island; we baked bread and set up cooking pots, and when the fire got going and its heat reached down into the ground, it moved, we looked, and lo and behold, the island was a fish." Or, "On a certain mountain I saw such-and-such things, and an old sorceress turned a man into an ass, and then another old sorceress smeared his ear with some kind of unguent and changed him back into human form," and other such nonsensical tales [Gh 667] that bring sleep to the ignorant when read to them at night. The wise—and they are very few in number—are those who test a statement for its veracity before they give credence to it; they welcome the truth in all its beauty and discard unseemly falsehoods. Bu'l-Fatḥ Bosti[13] has said, speaking very appositely, [Poetry]

1. *Human intellects have their own scales* (mavāzin), *by means of which right conduct can be assessed, and they are called experience.*"[14]

So I, who have taken up this History, have made it incumbent upon myself to write either from my own direct observations or from sound information heard from a reliable source. A good while ago, [F 906] I saw a book written in the hand of Master Abu Reyḥān (i.e. Biruni), who was peerless in his age in *adab*, learning, geometry and philosophy.[15] He would never indulge in exaggerations, and I have given this lengthy passage from Biruni's book so that it may be firmly established how scrupulous I have been in writing this History. Even though most of these people about whom I am speaking have passed on, and very few of them are still alive, and truth is, as Bu Tammām put it, [Poetry]

1. *Then those years have passed by, and the people of the time likewise, as if both, they and their years, are naught but dreams.*[16]

I have no choice but to complete this book, so that the names of these great men may remain alive through it, and also that some memory of myself may survive. For people will read this History after we are dead and gone, and the greatness of this Ghaznavid house, may it endure for ever, will be established for ever.

In the following account of Khwarazm, I thought it right to begin with the history of the Ma'munids, just as I copied it[17] from Master Abu Reyḥān, who has explained the reasons for the fall of their ruling power, how that province became part of the empire of Maḥmud, at what time the late Amir Maḥmud went there, how that land passed under his control, how he set up there the Commander Altuntāsh and then himself went back, and how the course of events there evolved after that, up to the time when Altuntāsh's son Hārun rebelled and became a turncoat, and the house of Altuntāsh was overthrown in Khwarazm. For there are many profitable things and wonders to be found in these historical reports, such that those who read and hear them can derive much benefit and insight from them. I seek success from God Most High for the completion of this work I am putting together. *Indeed He, praise be to him, is the best of those who vouchsafe success and give help!* [Gh 668, F 907]

The story of the Khwarazm Shah Abu'l-ʿAbbās

Bu Reyḥān has written in his *Mosāmara-ye Khᵛārazm* as follows.[18]

The Khwarazm Shah Bu'l-ʿAbbās Ma'mun b. Ma'mun, was the last Amir, since after his decease his house was overthrown and the reign of the Ma'munids came to an end.[19] He was learned as well as enterprising, and capable and steadfast in whatever he did. But along with these admirable qualities went some less praiseworthy ones, and I say this to make it clear that I am not being in any way partial and accommodating, since it has been said that *"Pronouncing a verdict on these sorts of things should be based on what is more preponderant and profuse, for the most meritorious person is the one who, when his virtues are assessed, the defects escape notice amidst his many merits, and if his praiseworthy aspects were to be enumerated, his bad qualities pale into insignificance within the whole ensemble."* The greatest virtue of the Amir Abu'l-ʿAbbās was that his tongue never uttered insults or engaged in idle tales (*khorāfāt*). I, Bu Reyḥān, who spent seven years in his service, never heard any abusive language from him; the worst insult in his repertoire which he would use if he became truly enraged, was "You cur!"

A firm friendship developed between him and Amir Maḥmud, and they made an agreement, and Ḥorra Kālji,[20] Amir Sebüktegin's daughter, was brought to Khwarazm and assumed her place in Amir Abu'l-ʿAbbās's harem. A continuous flow of correspondence, friendly contacts and exchanges of presents between the two sides was established.[21] In all matters Abu'l-ʿAbbās tried to preserve Amir Maḥmud's affections, and in this he went far beyond the accepted norms of courtesy, to such an extent that on the days when he held a wine-drinking session, he would summon the most illustrious of the retainers and troops stationed at the court, the boon-companions, the sons of the former amirs of the Samanids who were resident at his court, and others, and he would give orders that the envoys from neighbouring lands should be summoned in a courteous manner and be given seats. When he took the third draught in his hand, he would rise to his feet as an act of respect for Amir [F 908] Maḥmud and then would sit down. Meanwhile, all the assembled company remained standing, and he would command them one by one, and they would kiss the ground and then rise to their feet, till they had all gone through these motions. Then the Amir would give a sign for them to sit down and a household attendant would come along, followed by the presentation of gifts for the singers, each one receiving a valuable horse, a set of clothing and a purse containing 10,000 dirhams.[22] Furthermore, [Gh 669] he showed how far he was prepared to go in maintaining Amir Maḥmud's amity on the occasion when the Commander of the Faithful al-Qāder be'llāh sent him a robe of honour, an investiture charter, a standard and the honorific titles of *ʿEyn al-Dowla* ("Eye of the Realm") and *Zeyn al-Mella* ("Ornament of the Religious Community") by the hand of Ḥoseyn, the Commander of the Pilgrims.[23] The Khwarazm Shah thought that he ought not to alienate Amir Maḥmud, who might well instigate an argument questioning the propriety of the Khwarazm Shah's receiving a robe of honour and lavish awards directly from the caliph and without any intercession or mediation on his part. At all events, because of the need to conciliate Maḥmud, he sent out me, Biruni, to meet the envoy with due decorum midway in the desert.[24] I accepted those awards from him in secret and brought them with me to Khwarazm. I handed them over to Ma'mun, and he ordered that they should be kept concealed. So long as the state of friendly relations continued, this was never revealed, but subsequently, when inevitably the house of the Ma'munids was about to fall, it was brought into the open and what had to happen happened, and what had to pass away passed away.

The extent of the Khwarazm Shah's forbearance and magnanimity can be measured from the following incident. One day he was drinking wine as he listened to the music of stringed instruments—he paid a great deal of attention to refined culture and manners since he was himself highly learned and cultured[25]—and I was there in his presence, along with another person named Ṣakhri.[26] He was most learned and cultivated, highly eloquent and skilled in the epistolary art, but he was also at the same time extremely rude in his manners[27] and lacking in savoir faire, and it has been said that *"Innate good manners are superior to those acquired through learning."*[28] Ṣakhri held a cup of wine[29] in his hand and was about to drink. The horses kept tethered at the palace for immediate use[30] [F 909] made a great clamour and one of them let forth wind with a loud noise. The Khwarazm Shah cried out, *"In the drinker's moustache!"*,[31] but Ṣakhri, boorishly and lacking in manners, threw down the cup. I was filled with apprehension and thought that the Shah would order his head to be cut off, but he did not; instead he laughed and overlooked it, and behaved with forbearance and nobility of character.

I, Bu'l-Fażl,[32] heard at Nishapur from Khᵛāja [Abu] Manṣur Thaʿālebi, the author of the book *The Unique Pearl Concerning the Praiseworthy Aspects of the People of the Age*[33] and many other works, who went to Khwarazm and was for a long time a boon-companion to this Khwarazm Shah, dedicating several works to him.[34] He related, "One day we were in a wine banquet and were discussing polite learning. The topic of taking delight in visual contemplation (*naẓar*) cropped up, and the Khwarazm Shah said, *'I have an aspiration for a book that I can look into* (onẓoro fihi), *a handsome face that I can gaze* at (onẓoro eleyhi) *and a noble-minded person whom I can cherish* (onẓoro laho)'."[35]

Bu Reyḥān said, "One day the Khwarazm Shah was imbibing wine as he was out riding. [Gh 670] He arrived in the vicinity of my chamber and gave orders for me to be summoned. I was late getting to him, and he rode up to the door of the chamber allotted to me during my period of residence,[36] and was about to dismount. I kissed the ground and begged him upon oath not to alight, but he said,

1. *Learning is one of the noblest embodiments of power; all men seek it, but it does not always answer their call.*

Then he said, "*Were it not for part of the decorum and customs of this present world,*[37] *I would not have summoned you, for knowledge enjoys the highest position and nothing is superior to it.*" It could well be that he had read the historical accounts of the life and times of the Commander of the Faithful Moʿtażed, for I have myself read in those accounts that one day, as Moʿtażed was strolling hand-in-hand with Thābet b. Qorra[38] in a garden, he suddenly removed his hand. Thābet asked, "O Commander of the Faithful, why did you take your hand away?" He replied, "*My hand was above yours, but 'Knowledge enjoys the highest position and nothing is superior to it'.*" *Truly God knows best!* [F 910]

An account of the causes of the fall of the house of the Ma'munids and the transference of their kingly power to the Commander Altuntāsh

On the surface, Amir Maḥmud and the Khwarazm Shah Abu'l-ʿAbbās appeared to enjoy a most amicable relationship, with the mutual bonds of friendship firmly established through alliances and agreements. After the campaign of Özkend,[39] Amir Maḥmud decided to forge an alliance with the Khāns (i.e. the Qarakhanids), and to that end, field officers were sent off charged with negotiations. He also thought that an envoy of the Khwarazm Shah should accompany his own envoys, so that when it came to setting up the treaty with the Khāns he would be there and bear witness to it all. But the Khwarazm Shah would not be party to this and having turned it down, wrote in response, "*God has not endowed a man with two minds* (lit. "hearts") *within his body,*[40] and ever since I joined the Amir's camp, I no longer have any connection with the Khāns and in no circumstances will I send someone to them."

Amir Maḥmud appeared to accept this answer from him, but on the other hand, and given his suspicious nature, a feeling of animosity entered his heart. He said to the Vizier Aḥmad b. Ḥasan [Meymandi], "It seems to me that this man is not being straight with us, given the substance of what he has said." The Vizier replied, "I will put a proposal to the Khwarazmians and from that we will be able to ascertain whether they are being honest with us or not," and he explained what he had in mind and the Amir was pleased with the scheme. The Vizier said secretly to the Khwarazm Shah's envoy, "What are those futile thoughts that are clouding your master's mind [Gh 671] and why is he conjuring up such fantasies which induce him to talk like this about sending an envoy to the Khāns? He is inviting doubts upon himself [F 911] and insinuating allegations that are far from our Sultan's mind. If he wants to put an end to all these talks and speculations and to frustrate the covetous designs on his kingdom of outside powers, why doesn't he make the *khoṭba* [of Khwarazm] in the Sultan's name (i.e. acknowledge the Sultan's overall authority by citing his name in the exordium) so that he might be free of all this? In truth, I am saying this entirely on my own initiative by way of offering sincere advice, with the aim of dispelling the suspicions now held of him; the Sultan is unaware of what I am saying and gave me no instructions about it."[41]

An account of what happened regarding the khoṭba, *and the strife and the calamities which arose because of it*

Bu Reyḥān related: When this envoy reached us from Kabul—for this year, Amir Maḥmud had gone to India[42]—and he communicated this matter to us, the Khwarazm Shah summoned me and had a private session with me, relating to me what the Vizier Aḥmad b. Ḥasan had said on this topic. I replied, "Forget this issue. *Turn away from shameful things and don't listen to them, for not every speech addressed to one requires a reply*.[43] Take advantage of the Vizier's own words when he said that he was offering gratuitous and unprompted advice without his master's knowledge, and keep this all secret and don't tell anyone, for that could have a damaging effect." He said, "What are you talking about? He wouldn't have said any of these words without the Amir's explicit command, and how could such a subterfuge succeed with a man like Maḥmud?[44] I am afraid that, if I don't submit and make the *khoṭba* for him, he will resort to force until he gets his way. It would be best if we send an envoy with all speed, and there should be discussions on this matter with the Vizier, with the covert aim of letting them make a request to us for making the *khoṭba,* so that it may appear as an act of favour on our part, since we don't want the matter to be imposed by force." I answered, "It's for the Amir to command!"

There was a man called Yaʿqub Jandi,[45] an evil and avaricious scoundrel. In the time of the Samanids he had once been sent on an embassy to Bokhara, and he had nearly [F 912] lost us Khwarazm on that occasion. Now once again the Shah appointed him, and however much Bu Sahl[46] and others spoke against his decision, it was to no avail since the decree of Fate had come down, and the extent of this man's chicanery remained concealed from the Amir. Yaʿqub was despatched. When he reached Ghaznin, he gave out that the matter of the *khoṭba* and other things would be settled by him, and he bragged a great deal and appeared most patronising about it all. [Gh 672] But the exalted presence Maḥmud and his Vizier did not take him and his words seriously. Feeling slighted and rebuffed, he persisted in his devious ways and wrote a long missive to the Khwarazm Shah in the Khwarazmian language,[47] reviling Amir Maḥmud and fanning the flames of strife between them. A strange and remarkable thing was that, three years later, when Amir Maḥmud conquered Khwarazm, and official papers and the archives of Khwarazm were examined, this document came into Amir Maḥmud's hands, and he had it translated. He became enraged by the contents and ordered Jandi to be gibbeted and stoned to death. *Where is the profit when the capital itself is lost?*[48] One should be careful in what one writes, for spoken words can be retracted but what is set down in writing cannot be denied and once sent, cannot be retrieved. The Vizier wrote letters to the Khwarazm Shah, overawing him with his sober advice, for when backed by the sword, the pen moves more freely, and he could rely for support on a monarch like Maḥmud.

When the Khwarazm Shah realized what had happened, he became extremely apprehensive and suffered sleepless nights, dreading Maḥmud's retribution and regretting the way he had turned the wrath of the mighty upon himself.[49] He therefore assembled together the top commanders of the army [F 913] and the leaders of the civilian population and explained to them his decision regarding the *khoṭba*, pointing out that if the *khoṭba* was not made, he feared for himself, for them and for that land. There were loud protests from everyone, saying that in no circumstances would they agree to it. They came out, unfurled their banners and unsheathed their weapons, and they showered him with abuse.[50] He worked hard to cajole them into calming down, and managed to appease them by saying, "We were only testing you in this matter so that we might ascertain the state of your intentions and true feelings towards us."

The Khwarazm Shah then saw me in private and said, "You saw what happened? Who are these people who have the temerity to abuse their lord in such a fashion!" I replied, "I had told the lord that this was the wrong way to approach the matter. Now, since the deed is done, we have to go through with it in order to save face. You have brought all this upon yourself, since the position with this *khoṭba* could have been exactly the same as the Buyids' making the *khoṭba* for al-Qāder be'llāh:[51] it caught people unawares, being suddenly presented in public as a fait accompli, and no-one dared to say a word against it. We cannot abandon this course now, for that would suggest impotence on our part and we would lose Amir Maḥmud as a friend." He said, "Go back and hobnob with this bunch of people and see what you can do." [F 914] I went back [Gh 673] and managed to soften up and win over their more influential leaders with promises of silver and gold until they consented. Then they came to the court, and rubbing their faces in the dust of the threshold and weeping, admitted that they had done wrong.

The Khwarazm Shah summoned me in private and told me that he thought that this matter would not go away by itself, and I agreed. He said, "What's to be done, then?" I answered, "At the moment, we have lost Amir Maḥmud's goodwill, and I fear that the matter will come to the sword." He said, "When that occurs, what's going to happen with an army such as ours?" I replied, "I can't tell, since we face a most formidable enemy with extensive armaments and equipment and troops from every race and region. Even if his troops receive a hundred drubbings from us, they will return to the fight stronger than before. If, God forbid, they once inflict a defeat on us, that will be another story." He became very troubled at these words, to the extent that I detected in him a certain degree of antipathy and disdain towards my words. *My mentioning it to him was something I was accustomed to do.*[52] I replied, "There's one other thing, far greater in importance; if the royal command is vouchsafed, I will tell it." He said, "Speak on!" I said, "The Khāns of Turkestan have been annoyed by the lord, and they are Amir Maḥmud's friends. It is tough enough to prevail over a single enemy; when two of them join forces, the matter becomes far more serious. We must win over the Khāns—who are presently engaged in warfare at the gates of Özkend[53]—and strenuous efforts must be made through the lord's conciliation in order to bring about a peace settlement between the Khān and the Ilig, with no subsequent contraventions, for they will be grateful to the lord for this [F 915] and he will derive much advantage thereby."[54] He answered, "Let's think about it for a while," for he wanted it to look as if he alone had thought up this plan. Then after this he got busy and exerted himself, and he sent off envoys with great quantities of presents and gave orders,[55] so that through his intermediacy there would be peace between them and they would become reconciled, and would hold it as a great favour on the Khwarazm Shah's part, since his words were more acceptable to them[56] than those of Amir Maḥmud. They sent envoys, who brought the message that, "This peace agreement came from the Shah's beneficent concern and compassion;" they made an agreement with him and friendly relations were established.

When this news reached Amir Maḥmud, it worried him and his mistrust and suspicions focused both on the Khwarazm Shah and the Khāns of Turkestan. He set out and came to Balkh, and despatched envoys, reproaching the Khān and the Ilig over what had happened. They replied, "We regarded the Khwarazm Shah as the friend and son-in-law of the Amir, and still do. Indeed, there was such palpable harmony and cordiality that when the Amir sent envoys to us in order to conclude a treaty and asked him to appoint a representative to witness the procedure, he did not agree to it and did not send one.[57] If today he has for some reason become annoyed with the Shah, there's no need to reproach us [F 916] for it. [Gh 674] The best course is for us to act as mediators between the two sides, so that friendship and harmony may be restored to their former level." Amir Maḥmud did not send any reply to these words, since they had reduced him to silence; he kept quiet and nursed his suspicion of the Khāns.

On the other hand, the Khāns secretly sent a messenger to the Khwarazm Shah and told him about this state of affairs. He sent back the reply, "The wisest course is that we should send several detachments of two-horse troopers into Khorasan. We will send three men, with senior commanders to quickly spread out[58] within Khorasan with undercover groups.[59] Although Maḥmud is a mighty warrior and can move with great alacrity, he would be at a loss deciding which detachment to attack, and will find himself stuck; for whenever he tries to attack one group and heads in one direction, another group will appear from a different direction to disorientate him and add to his confusion. But we must obtain assurances from the outgoing troops, both those despatched by us and by you, that they will not antagonise the populace but instead promise them peace and comfort once those forays are over. This is the correct way forward, for there would be no sense in attempting to challenge an army such as Maḥmud's in a set battle, and the whole enterprise will only succeed if it is handled carefully."

The Khān and the Ilig conferred together over this matter, but they did not consider it wise to follow the policy suggested, [F 917] and sent the reply, "The Khwarazm Shah's aim is to ensure his own security and that of his land, but there is an agreement and covenant between us and Amir Maḥmud, and in no way can we break them. If he wishes, we can step in as mediators and help to mend his fences with the Amir." The Shah said, "That would be for the best."

Amir Maḥmud was at Balkh for that winter,[60] and was kept informed about these goings-on, since he had spies everywhere who made it their business to pry into the most minute details of people's lives and to relay the information back to the Sultan.[61] At first he became extremely perturbed by the news, but when he heard that they had decided on mediation, he calmed down. The envoys from the Khān and Ilig arrived, bearing a letter on this subject and conveying a verbal message. He gave a suitable reply, to the effect that there had only been minor misunderstandings and slight irritations, and those had now all been removed by their mediation and by what they had said, and the envoys were sent back home.

After this, Amir Maḥmud sent an envoy to the Khwarazm Shah, and he reminded him about what he had undertaken, saying, "It is clearly established on what terms the agreement and covenant between us was concluded, and how much respect and consideration he owes us. In this matter of the *khoṭba*, he kept our wishes in mind, since he knew where his best interests[62] lay, but his people put a stop to that. I am not calling these people 'retainers and subordinates' since they cannot be described as retainers if they can tell their king what to do and what not to do, for this is [F 918] a sign of impotence and weakness in a realm. When we saw how he was being treated by them and matters became complicated,[63] we decided to settle down here in Balkh for a long stay [Gh 675] until 100,000 cavalrymen and infantrymen and 500 elephants were assembled for the task of punishing and correcting those people who are showing such disobedience and are opposing their lord's intentions. We shall also awaken the Amir, who is our brother and son-in-law, and teach him how to rule, for a weak ruler is useless. Now we need a clear excuse in order to return to Ghaznin, and one of these two or three tasks must be performed: he must make the *khoṭba*, with all the obedience and willingness that he had promised, or he must send a complete array of offerings of money and presents, of a quality worthy of us, which will be secretly returned to him, since we have no need of additional wealth, and the very foundations of our fortresses are groaning under the weight of the burden of gold and silver; or else he is to send us leading persons, prominent imams and religious lawyers from that land, charged with asking for pardon, so that we may go back with the many thousands of troops we have brought."

The Khwarazm Shah was terror-stricken at this letter, and since Maḥmud's arguments were powerfully persuasive, he saw no alternative but to comply and to revert to a more friendly and conciliatory approach. He decided that he would make the *khoṭba* for Amir Maḥmud at Nasā and Farāva, which belonged to the Khwarazmians at that time,[64] and in the other towns, with the exception of [Madinat] Khwarazm (i.e. Kāth) and Gorgānj,[65] and that 80,000 dinars [F 919] and 3,000 horses, together with sheykhs, judges and leading persons of the land, should be sent, with the aim of settling this matter formally, of establishing friendly relations between them and of avoiding strife. *God is most knowing!*

An account of the deterioration in the state of affairs[66] *and the ascendancy of rebellious villains*

There was a powerful army of the Khwarazm Shah's at Hazārasp,[67] having as its commander his Great Chamberlain Alptegin Bokhāri,[68] and they all harboured treachery and deceitful designs in their hearts. When they heard of the plan to make the *khoṭba* in Maḥmud's name, they perceived that they had an excellent pretext for mischiefmaking. They raised a great clamour, saying, "Maḥmud has no claim on our allegiance."[69] They set off back from Hazārasp, bent on spilling blood, and killed the Vizier and the elder statesmen serving the Amir, who had given him wise counsel and had averted a great calamity, en masse. The remainder of the Amir's advisers all fled and went into hiding, for they were well aware of that unruly gang's aims and intentions. This unmanly and ignoble lot then turned to the government headquarters and attacked them. They surrounded it, and the Khwarazm Shah fled to the upper part of the palace. But they set fire to it, and when they came upon him [Gh 676] they murdered him. This happened on Wednesday, mid-Shavvāl 407 [/17–18 March 1017]. [F 920] The object of this atrocity was thirty-two years old at the time. They immediately brought forth his seventeen-year old nephew Abu'l-Ḥāreth Moḥammad b. 'Ali b. Ma'mun and set him on the throne. Alptegin secured control of the kingdom, acting through the vizierate of Aḥmad, son of Ṭoghān.[70] They consigned this boy, who had little knowledge or experience of the world, to a corner and did whatever they wanted, including killing, confiscating wealth and possessions, and extirpating whole families, and settling old scores openly and brutally. For four months they had a clear field; they destroyed the whole fabric of the kingdom with their own hands, and deeds were committed that would not have been done to Muslims in the lands of unbelievers.

When Amir Maḥmud heard the news, he said to Khᵛāja Aḥmad, son of Ḥasan, "No other pretext is necessary, and Khwarazm has fallen into our hands. We must ineluctably seek vengeance for the blood of our son-in-law and put to death his murderers and take the kingdom as the rightful heir." The Vizier replied, "The lord is right. If we falter now, God Most High will not be pleased with the lord and will question him about it on the Day of Resurrection; for, God be thanked, we have a complete and fully prepared army which is all we need for this venture. The greatest point in our favour is that the army has enjoyed a period of rest and has not been in action for one whole winter,[71] hence we will speedily achieve what we want. However, initially it would be better to send an envoy to put the fear of God into them for their recent atrocities, and to tell them that if they don't wish to see us come and avenge the bloodshed, [F 921] and if they would like us to leave this house on the throne, they should send the murderers to our presence (i.e. to Balkh, where the Sultan was at that time) and make the *khoṭba* in our name; for they will jump at this opportunity to get themselves off the hook and will produce a few ruffians and claim that it was they who had murdered the Shah. Our envoy must consent to that and pretend to go along with them[72] in order to make them feel secure and then proceed to suggest to them, on his own initiative as it were, that they would do well to send back the lord's sister with proper respect and decorum so that she could intercede on their behalf. This they would do out of fear regarding the crime that they had perpetrated. Meanwhile, we would be making our own preparations in secret and once the letter arrives confirming that the lady has safely reached Āmol, we will turn the heat on them and say things that we could not say before on account of the lady being there in Khwarazm. What we shall tell them is this: 'It was the army commanders, such as Alptegin and others, who initiated this calamitous event, and if you want to avoid being attacked, [Gh 677] they must be driven out and handed over to us in order to avert hostilities.'" The Amir agreed on this course of action. An envoy was chosen and briefed on his orders and taught how to dissemble and dupe them, and he set out. The Vizier secretly sent agents to Khottalān, Qobādhiyān and Termez, and these made preparations and got together a fleet of boats, and assembled supplies of food and fodder at Āmol.

The envoy reached Khwarazm and conveyed the messages as instructed, and with great dexterity and artfulness managed to lure that bunch into his trap[73] so that, out of fear of Amir Maḥmud, they immediately [F 922] made the necessary preparations for the lady, and she arrived in a seemly and respectful manner with a full-scale escort. They also seized five or six people and declared that they were the ones responsible for shedding the Shah's blood, and they held them in prison and promised that, when their envoy returned and a contractual agreement concluded, those arrested would be sent to Maḥmud's court. They appointed an envoy to accompany the Amir's envoy and undertook that, if no attack on Khwarazm was mounted, and if the Amir were to expunge thoughts of revenge from his mind and agree to an accord, they would hand over as acknowledgement of due service 200,000 dinars and 4,000 horses.

When the Amir saw this letter, he set out for Ghaznin, taking the envoys with him, and once there they explained the concessions offered. The Amir's answer was that Alptegin and the other commanders were to be handed over for vengeance to be taken on them. The Khwarazmians realized how they had been led on, and began to prepare for war. They gathered together the troops, a good 50,000 cavalrymen, and they made mutual vows to fight to the finish, since the Ghaznavid army was coming to wreak vengeance on them all. They said, "We'll go into battle shoulder-to-shoulder and do whatever is humanly possible."

The Amir had ordered letters concerning the killing of the Khwarazm Shah to be written to the Ilig and the Khān in Turkestan and despatched by swift couriers, narrating in full the enormity of the horror that had occurred, and had said bluntly that he was going to seek vengeance for the death of his son-in-law [F 923] and rule over that land and put an end to what had been as much a headache for them as it had been for himself. Although this proposition was not to their taste and they realized that, once in possession of Khwarazm, Maḥmud would be a constant thorn in their flesh, they wrote back the reply, "It's a well thought-out plan, and the dictates of honourable behaviour, statesmanship and piety prescribe the very course that he has adopted, so that, after this, no minion or underling[74] would dare to shed the blood of his royal master."

When all preparations had been completed, and despite the fact that the weather had become hot, the Amir embarked on the invasion of Khwarazm [Gh 678] along the road leading from Āmol, proceeding cautiously.[75] Moḥammad Aʿrābi[76] led the advance guard, but suffered a serious reverse; the Amir himself came up and retrieved that situation.[77] On the next day, Maḥmud came face-to-face with the rebellious regicides and saw confronting him a mighty army, with which one could conquer a whole world and defeat a host of enemies. But the wrath of the Creator, His eminence is exalted, had already confounded them and the spilt blood of the slain monarch was exacting its toll; they launched a strong assault aimed at the heart of Amir Maḥmud's army, but were routed and finally all captured.[78] The story of that battle is lengthy and well known. I do not propose to tell it in detail, but will return to the thread of the History lest I stray far way from my intentions. This [F 924] much will be sufficient.[79] ʿOnṣori has a most eloquent ode on this subject, and a perusal of it would convey the full significance of the event. Here are the opening verses (*maṭlaʿ*) of this ode:

1. In such a way does the imperial sword leave its mark; and this is how the great proceed when there is work to be done.

2. Leave aside the old chronicles and observe the deeds of the kingly sword, for his sword says it all and is far truer than the tale.[80]

Amongst his poems this ode stands out for its mastery of diction and subtlety of thought, and rightly so, given the stature of the recipient of praise and the magnitude of his victory.

After the army's defeat, the crack warriors, with their fine horses, pursued them, under the leadership of the Commander-in-Chief Amir Naṣr,[81] and plunged into the midst of those God-forsaken ones, bringing back many prisoners. In the end, Alptegin Bokhāri, Khumārtāsh Sharābi and Sāvtegin Khāni,[82] who were the leaders and instigators of the revolt, were seized, together with some others implicated in the bloodshed,[83] and all of them were brought before the Amir, with their heads bared.[84] The Amir was most pleased by the seizure of the culprits, and ordered them to be taken to the guard house and held captive.

The Amir came to Khwarazm, [F 925] occupied the land and took possession of the treasuries.[85] The recently-installed Amir, Abu'l-Ḥāreth Moḥammad b. ʿAli, together with all the house and kindred of the Maʾmunids, were arrested. When all this had been completed, he ordered three gibbets to be erected. The three ringleaders were thrown down before the elephants and trampled to death and then impaled on the elephants' tusks. They were paraded round, along with the public proclamation that anyone who killed his lord would be thus rewarded. Then they were stretched out on those gibbets and lashed to them with stout ropes. The front surfaces of those gibbets had been firmly cemented together with a mixture of baked clay and gypsum, making them like [Gh 679] three bridges, and the names of the three malefactors inscribed on them.[86] A large number of those implicated in the Shah's murder were torn in half or had their hands and feet cut off, and it all had a most compelling and overawing impact on the populace. He entrusted that province to the Commander Altuntāsh shortly afterwards, and ordered that the horse which went with the office of Khwarazm Shah should be brought for Altuntāsh and that Arslān Jādheb should remain there with him for a while until the region was finally pacified, and then return. The Amir turned back, victorious and conquering, and headed for Ghaznin. The train of prisoners of war stretched from Balkh to Lahore and Multan, and the Maʾmunids were carried off to various fortresses and held there.[87]

After the Amir's return from that region, Bu Esḥāq, Bu'l-ʿAbbās's father-in-law, collected a considerable force and launched a surprise attack to regain Khwarazm.[88] There was a fierce battle, and Bu Esḥāq was routed and fled, and the greater part of his followers were left abandoned. Arslān Jādheb gave orders for a massacre on a Ḥajjājian scale,[89] and by those means that region was subdued and pacified so that afterwards there was no need for further repression. Arslān now returned, and Altuntāsh remained there. He was a capable servant, [F 926] shrewd and with good judgement, as has already been mentioned in this History, citing his name and deeds and accomplishments.

At this juncture, an instance of his courage has come to mind, which I have not previously mentioned and which should be included. I heard from the Vizier Aḥmad b. ʿAbd al-Ṣamad, who related:[90]

"When Amir Maḥmud returned from Khwarazm and affairs became settled, there were 1,500 royal cavalrymen, with army commanders like Qalpāq[91] and others, apart from the gholāms. Altuntāsh said to me, 'Law and order must be strictly imposed so that there should be one overall authority and no-one should have the temerity to appropriate an inch of land which has been brought under protection,[92] since a large amount of money will be needed each year to pay out allowances for this army and to provide splendid presents for the Sultan and the great men of state. These people are under the illusion that this land is theirs to prey upon[93] and that they are free to plunder it. If this proves to be the case, we will be in dire straits.' I agreed whole-heartedly, and that only with such a policy would things go aright. We, that is Altuntāsh and myself, imposed firm rule and our authority was increasingly accepted and obeyed, and even the more headstrong and recalcitrant, who were obdurate at first, gradually began to toe the line.

One day, as I was about to ride to the court, Tāsh, the major-domo of the palace, appeared and said, [Gh 680], 'The gholāms are mounting their steeds and are saddling up the swift riding camels, and Altuntāsh is girding on his arms; we don't know what is happening.' I was most worried and concerned, and could not fathom out what might have led to all this. [F 927] I went off in great haste. When I caught up with him, he was standing there putting on his belt. I said, 'What's going on?' He answered, 'I'm going off to fight.' I said, 'There's no news of the approach of an enemy.' He replied, 'You're unaware of what's happening here? Qalpāq's gholāms and grooms have gone off to plunder the royal store of fodder, and if we let this happen, we shall be courting disaster. Why should I wage war against external foes when I am already facing home-bred ones?' I had to do a great deal to assuage and mollify him, until he sat down. Qalpāq came along, kissed the ground and offered copious apologies, saying, 'I regret my action bitterly, and this sort of thing won't happen again.' Altuntāsh calmed down and passed over this incident. With this single firm assertion of authority, he was free of worries from all the rest of them for as long as he lived. A man worthy of the name must know his craft."[94]

When he died at the fortress of Dabusi after he had come back from Bokhara, as I have already described at length,[95] Hārun was sent back from Balkh and then, after that, Aḥmad b. ʿAbd al-Ṣamad was summoned to Nishapur and invested with the vizierate. His son ʿAbd al-Jabbār returned from the embassy to Gorgān and was awarded a robe of honour for the office of counsellor and adjutant in Khwarazm, and he set off. Trading on his father's position as Vizier, he assumed a high-handed attitude[96] and gave Hārun and his entourage little elbow-room in matters of state. Hārun grew incensed and lost his patience, and slanderers and mischief makers thronged round him and secured an ascendancy over affairs. On top of this came the news of the death at Ghaznin of Hārun's brother Satï,[97] and they made out to him that he had been deliberately thrown down from the roof and that Khorasan was already being defiled by the Turkmens, before the Seljuqs had actually appeared. [F 928] Moreover, an astrologer had informed Hārun of his prognostication that Hārun would become Amir of Khorasan. Hārun believed this, and began to treat ʿAbd al-Jabbār's orders with contempt, to raise objections to his actions and to take over the direction of proceedings from him in the sessions for receiving petitions and hearing complaints of injustice. Things went so far that one day in the court session for these, he shouted out at ʿAbd al-Jabbār and belittled him, so that the latter left in a rage. Relations between them were patched up, and an uneasy truce[98] came about. ʿAbd al-Jabbār kept complaining about the situation, but his father was unable to come to his help, since Amir Masʿud would not hear a word against Hārun and was on bad terms with the Vizier. Hārun had the roads under his surveillance so that no-one had the temerity to write anything to his detriment, and had suborned the postal and intelligence service officer so that he would report only what Hārun wished to convey. His activities remained hidden until he had assembled a force of 2,000-odd gholāms [Gh 681] and had assumed the ceremonial parasol, the black banner and the despotic ways of monarchs. ʿAbd al-Jabbār and his followers were pushed out of a job. Troops began to pour in from all sides, his envoys went continuously to ʿAlitegin and other Amirs, and he broke out into rebellion. The Turkmens and Seljuqs joined up with him, since the custom had been that every year they would come from Nur of Bokhara to Andaghāz (?)[99] and would stay there a while.

Finally it got to the point that he decided to arrest ʿAbd al-Jabbār, but the latter had his own informers around Hārun and made plans to go into hiding, for it was not possible to flee the land and escape altogether. During the night of Wednesday, 1 Rajab 425 [/22 May 1034], accompanied by one of his trusty servants, he left his house incognito in the middle of the night so that no-one noticed, and sought refuge at the house of Bu Saʿid Sahli,[100] with whom he had already made an arrangement. Bu Saʿid [F 929] hid him underground beneath the portico, having dug out this[101] specially for this purpose in the preceding month, without anyone knowing about it. Next day, it was reported to Hārun that ʿAbd al-Jabbār had fled during the night. He was very worried, and sent out horsemen along all the roads, but they came back without having acquired any news or found any trace of him. It was proclaimed in the city that, if he were discovered in anyone's house, the owner of that house would be chopped in two by a sword. They set about searching, but found no information about him anywhere. Bu Saʿid came to be suspected regarding the matter of concealing ʿAbd al-Jabbār in a subterranean chamber, and his house, lands and property were all confiscated. Anybody who was connected with him in any way was extirpated. News about this situation was reported to Amir Masʿud, and he became very upset. The remarkable thing was that he was chastising the Vizier, charging him that Khwarazm had been lost on account of his son. There was nothing for the Vizier to do but keep silent; his very own offspring and household were being destroyed, and he did not dare to say a word.

After a while, it became clear to this monarch that Hārun was turning into an outright rebel, since secret letters arrived by the hand of spies that Hārun had made over the vizierate of Khwarazm to Bu Naṣr Barghashi[102] on Thursday, 27 Shaʿbān 425 [17 July 1034]. On the heels of those, a further secret letter arrived on Friday, 23 Ramażān 425 [/11 August 1034] with the news that the *khoṭba* had been changed and that Hārun had given orders that Amir Masʿud's name should be removed and his own name substituted. Our secret agents there got busy, and likewise, those of the Vizier Aḥmad. Swift couriers were arriving continuously, and [F 930] reporting on all Hārun's activities. [Gh 682] Amir Masʿud was particularly distressed at this state of affairs, for with Khorasan in revolt, he was unable to subdue Khwarazm. He had many private discussions with the Vizier and Bu Naṣr Moshkān, and secret royal messages were despatched to the royal forces in Khwarazm urging them to overthrow Hārun, but all this of course came to nothing.

Ṭoghrïl, Dāvud, the Yïnāliyān and the Seljuqs, together with extensive forces and unlimited numbers of tents, camels, horses and sheep, came to the borders of Khwarazm in aid of Hārun. He assigned to them pasture grounds and select spots at Rebāṭ-e Māsha, Shorāh-khān and Gāvkhᵛāra,[103] and sent presents and great amounts of food as a gesture of welcome, saying, "You must rest and refresh yourselves, for I intend to attack Khorasan and am making preparations for it. When I start out, you can secure your baggage and impedimenta here and go with my vanguard." They settled there in security since, when ʿAlitegin had died, his sons had displayed much antagonism towards them and they were unable to remain at Nur-e Bokhārā and its vicinity.

Between these Seljuqs and Shāh Malek there was a deep and ancient feeling of hatred and a long-standing blood feud.[104] Shāh Malek had set up spies. When he heard that this group had settled on the eastern fringes of Khwarazm, he rode out from his domains at Jand across the desert, and, with a powerful force, made a sudden surprise attack on these Turkmens at dawn, in Dhu'l-Ḥejja 425, three days after the Festival of the Sacrifice (i.e. on 13 Dhu'l-Ḥejja/29 October) and inflicted a severe defeat on them, killing seven or eight thousand of them, capturing a great amount of gold and horses, and taking many prisoners.[105] The fugitives passed, at the crossing of Khᵛāra/Khovāra, over the frozen Oxus, since [F 931] it was winter, and came to Rebāṭ-e Namak, with only their bare-backed and saddle-less horses with them.[106] There was a large village facing Rebāṭ-e Namak, and there were plenty of people about and they heard news of those fugitives. The young men took up their arms and said, "Let's go and kill them so that the Muslims will be free of them." There was an aged man there, ninety years old, amongst those village folk, who was revered by all and whose words carried some weight amongst them, and he addressed the young men, saying, "Don't lay your hands on the defeated and vanquished who have come to you seeking refuge, for it is as though they themselves have already lost their lives, for they are bereft of womenfolk, children, men or beasts." They desisted and did not venture out. *How remarkable is this present world, with its mutations and changes of circumstances!*[107] How could they have killed them, when they were destined to achieve such powerful status and such grandeur and rule over vast domains? For *God does what He wills and decrees what He wishes.*[108]

When this news reached Hārun, he became extremely concerned, but he kept his feelings to himself and sent someone secretly to the Seljuqs with assurances, [Gh 683] saying, "Rally round and summon up reinforcements, for I am keeping to my word and agreement made with you." They were reassured by this message, and went back from Rebāṭ-e Namak to the place where their baggage and impedimenta had been left. They found that they had lost the greater part of their children, their arms and equipment, and their beasts, and only a few were left. They started making preparations, and other tribesmen came back to there.

On the other hand, Hārun sent a messenger to Shāh Malek and reproached him on several fronts, saying, "You came and destroyed a people who were allies of mine and part of my troops, and in any case, if you have suffered because of them in the past, you have now meted out to them their due punishment. You should now have a face-to-face meeting with me so that we can pull together and fend for each other, and we should do our utmost to remove the rancour and acrimony that prevails between you and the Seljuqs, for I have a momentous task ahead and intend to conquer Khorasan." [F 932] Shāh Malek replied, "This is an excellent idea. I'll be on this bank of the Oxus, you should also set out and encamp on the other side so that our envoys can come together with their proposals and arrange a deal. When an agreement is concluded, I'll come to the middle of the Oxus in a skiff[109], and you should do the same. We can then have a meeting, and I'll give you a strong contingent of my own troops to assist you in the task ahead, and then return to Jand. But I make it a condition that you should refrain from any talk of a peace between the Seljuqs and myself, since both sides are thirsting for each other's blood and at daggers drawn. I intend to give them a drubbing, and we'll see what the decree of God Most High will be."

Hārun was reassured by this reply, and made preparations for coming to the encounter with a large, fully-equipped army of around 30,000 cavalrymen and infantrymen, and numerous gholāms and a great retinue,[110] on 27 Dhu'l-Ḥejja 425 [/12 November 1034], and encamped on the banks of the river opposite Shāh Malek. When Shāh Malek saw all that array of troops and armaments, he was filled with apprehension, and said to his trusty companions, "We have fulfilled one of our aims and subdued our enemies;[111] it would be sensible for us now to agree to a tactical truce[112] and go back, so that nothing can go amiss. It is such a comfort having the Oxus river between us and them." They all agreed. So the envoys went to and fro from both sides [F 933] and an agreement was concluded. The two leaders came into the middle of the Oxus, had a meeting and went back soon afterwards. Suddenly, without Hārun having any knowledge of it, Shāh Malek departed in the middle of the night and in great haste took the road across the desert to Jand, his realm. When the news reached Hārun, [Gh 684] he observed, "This man is a formidable opponent; he came to Khwarazm, defeated the Seljuqs, had a meeting with us and there was a peace agreement, and he's only able to come here from Jand in winter when this desert is covered with snow.[113] I myself am going to Khorasan and have a great task before me. When I leave this place, at least my mind won't be left worrying over what's left behind." They all agreed that this was indeed the case.[114]

Hārun also returned homewards and came back to Khwarazm, and set about preparations for his expedition in all earnest. Troops began to join him from all sides, and a large army, comprising Küjet, Chaghrāq and Qïpchaq (Khifchākh) aligned themselves with him.[115] He gave aid to the Seljuqs in the form of mounts and weapons until they grew strong, and he ordered them to halt at Darghān,[116] which is on the border of Khwarazm, and wait until he had come five or six stages from Khwarazm (i.e. from the capital Kāth), and then 3,000 or 4,000 of their cavalry should go forward and act as the vanguard of Hārun's army and make for Merv, while he would follow after them.

Amir Masʿud was kept informed of all these happenings through his spies, and he, the Vizier and Bu Naṣr Moshkān were engaged in frequent private discussions and deliberations. The Vizier Aḥmad b. ʿAbd al-Ṣamad said, "May the Sultan's life be prolonged! It had never occurred to anyone that this ill-fated minion[117] would be capable of all this mayhem. All the sons of Altuntāsh [F 934] have turned out badly, but this God-forsaken wretch beats them all. On the other hand, no person who followed a crooked path and who rebelled against his lord ever came to any good. The lord will see what will happen to this ungrateful wretch. I have devised a stratagem, and a letter in code has been sent to Bu Saʿid Sahli, in whose house my son is hiding, instructing him to expend as much money as is required to induce a group of men to kill this wretch. They are working hard at this, and have written back that eight gholāms from those closest to Hārun, including his arms bearer, the bearer of the ceremonial parasol and the standard bearer, have been suborned. They have decided that it would be feasible to do away with him on the road on the day when he leaves the city, for within the city itself any attempt would be impossible, since the household servant Shakar has imposed very tight security. We pray to the Almighty God that this affair will be brought to its successful conclusion, for when this dog is killed, things will become totally different; the army that he put together will disperse and never come together again." The Amir said, "This is an excellent plan; this crafty old fox[118] [Gh 685] must be helped along and given promises of future favours from us so that his scheme can proceed according to plan, [F 935] within four or five months."[119]

When Hārun had made all his preparations and the time of his departure drew near, his ill-starred camp enclosure,[120] together with other equipment, was taken away and set up at three parasangs' distance from the city. He mounted and set off from the city on Sunday, 2 Jomādā II 426 [/14 April 1035],[121] an auspicious time according to the astrologers,[122] and rode along with a fully-equipped army, with the intention of conquering Khorasan. However, Fate was mocking him, and he was destined to die within a couple of days. Other palace gholāms had sworn an oath and had joined up with the original conspirators. When he drew near to the camp enclosure,[123] he halted on an eminence, while the household servant Shakar was busy with making camp, and the palace gholāms and a sizeable force of shield-bearing[124] infantrymen were also left behind. Those palace gholāms involved in the plot charged at him with their swords, battleaxes and maces and felled Hārun to the ground. But he was still alive when they fled, together with a following of gholāms. Then the household servant Shakar arrived on the scene, in a frenzied state, and they lifted up Hārun and declared publicly that he had survived. He was placed in an elephant litter and they headed back to the city. A great tumult arose amongst the troops and order broke down, with everyone fending for himself and bent on getting back to the city. Much looting and plundering took place, with the strong taking advantage of the weak, and there was [F 936] universal chaos. They brought Hārun to the city, and cavalrymen went out in pursuit of the murderers.[125]

Hārun lived for three days and died on Thursday. May God have mercy on him, for he was a good man; but he committed a grave fault, in that he assumed his lord's throne, and it is impossible for a sparrow to aspire to a falcon's nest. From the time of Adam, peace be upon him, to this present day, the ineluctable rule has been that whoever has launched an attack on his lord has forfeited his own precious life. For the same favourable winds that sweep one into power are bound to die down again and leave one stranded. One should peruse closely the history books where one would see many clear examples of this, in all ages and within all dynasties. Consider, for example, the case of the deluded, God-forsaken Ṭoghrïl, who made an assault upon this house and assumed the throne of the Amirs Maḥmud, Masʿud and Mowdud, and see how events fell out and what the field officers deputed to kill Ṭoghrïl did with him and his associates![126] May the Almighty God grant a favourable outcome!

When the news reached the city that Hārun had passed away, a great tumult arose. The household servant Shakar mounted his steed [Gh 686] and put forward Hārun's brother Esmāʿil, called Khandān ("the laughing one"), together with all the dead lord's gholāms, and they left the city on Friday, 20 Jomādā II [/2 May 1035], and the city dissolved into anarchy. ʿAbd al-Jabbār now proved to be extremely rash and acted prematurely, for his allotted time in this world was also nearing its end. When Khandān and Shakar and their gholāms went off, he came out of hiding and tried to seize the government headquarters. Sahli kept telling him [F 937] that it was far too early to come out and show himself in public, and that he should bide his time until Shakar, Khandān and the gholāms were one or two stages away and the former troops and retainers of the house of Altuntāsh (*Altuntāshiyān*) had gone along likewise, and the royal armies could reach him, since the situation in the city was very volatile, with people divided into two parties. He paid no heed, and mounted an elephant, and a concourse of people came up and gathered round him, *just as it is said in the proverbial saying, "When they rally round, they are victorious, but when they disperse and are scattered, nothing further is known of them."*[127] He reached the review ground and halted there. Trumpets were blown and large kettledrums beaten, and ʿAbd al-Jabbār's partisans were emerging from wherever they had been hiding and a great commotion arose.

Shakar galloped back from the outskirts of the city with 500 well-armed and fully-equipped gholāms, and came up to ʿAbd al-Jabbār. Had ʿAbd al-Jabbār then behaved in an accommodating and favourable manner towards him, things might have calmed down. But he did not do this and instead called out to him, "You so-and-so!" Shakar said to his gholāms, "Let him have it!" and showers of arrows were directed at the elephant from left and right until they riddled the man with arrows like a sieve. No-one dared to go to his aid. He fell down from the elephant and expired. The rabble tied a rope round his feet and dragged him through the city with a great deal of fanfare.

Esmāʿil Khandān and the former troops and retainers of Altuntāsh gained the upper hand, and ʿAbd al-Jabbār's partisans, beaten or killed, disappeared from view. Messengers were sent to Esmāʿil with the good news about the successful outcome to the affair and he was urged to return to the city. He was filled with joy, and gave the bearers of the good news lavish gifts, made vows and agreed to distribute alms. He came to the city towards noon on Saturday, 28 Jomādā II [426] [/10 May 1035]. Shakar, the gholāms and the people of the city came out to meet him, and he entered the city and took up residence in the palace. Authority was imposed over the city, officials charged with police duties and keeping order[128] were appointed, and they were busy that day with this till the middle of the night, arranging the terms on which Esmāʿil was to assume power; pledges of allegiance were made [F 938] and accession money was given out. The next day, Sunday [2]9 Jomādā II 426 [/11 May 1035], Esmāʿil ascended the royal throne and held court. [Gh 687] The leading members of the army all came in a body and established him formally in the position of Amir, offering their services and gifts before returning home, and things went back to normal.[129]

When the news reached Amir Masʿud, he offered his condolences to the Vizier for that great calamity which had befallen the Vizier's son and his followers.[130] The Vizier answered, "May the lord enjoy a long, joyous and well-contented life! It is only right for those brought up within this court that they should offer up their lives[131] in its service. But that's in the past. We must now address the new problem facing us." The Amir said, "What's to be done with this unfortunate, new wretch[132] whom they have put up?" He replied, "An envoy should be sent, one unbeknown to Altuntāsh's army, and the lord should order letters under the royal seal and device to be sent to the Commander Alptegin and other senior officers from Maḥmud's army saying that, if possible, they should give appropriate counsel to this youth. Also, I for my part will write what need to be said to Bu Saʿid Sahli and Bu'l-Qāsem Eskāfi and we will see what they can do." The Amir expressed his approval and the Vizier went back. An envoy was chosen, letters in the royal style were written in the course of that day, and he set off [F 939]. He returned later and it became clear that it was the household servant Shakar who was running the country and that the child ruler, Esmāʿil, was more interested in feasting and hunting, and no-one took him at all seriously. Alptegin and other commanders had sent back replies, with formal expressions of servitude and apology, saying that the province could only be salvaged by wielding the sword and imposing severe punishments, since law and order had collapsed and the very fabric of administration and its workings corroded by Hārun's misdeeds. The Amir gave up all hope regarding the situation in Khwarazm, for he had many important matters facing him in Khorasan, at Ray and in India, as I have previously explained in this work.

Following the events in Khwarazm and Hārun's plight, the Seljuqs became even more despondent about their own future: they could not go to Bokhara, since ʿAlitegin had died, and his sons, who were a hopeless lot, had assumed power there; nor could they stay in Khwarazm out of fear of Shāh Malek. So they thought of moving from Khwarazm into Khorasan and seeking refuge there. Their people were all ready and prepared, so they suddenly moved off and crossed the Oxus. On that day, there were 700 horsemen who crossed the river, and then afterwards, large numbers joined up with them. They plundered Āmuy,[133] passed on, came to the region of Merv and Nasā, and installed themselves there at the time when we had returned from Āmol and Ṭabarestān and had reached Gorgān, episodes which have already been narrated in great detail in the History.[134] [Gh 688] The value of this section on Khwarazm is that it establishes clearly the origin of these events, how the Seljuqs came to leave Khwarazm and arrive in Khorasan, and how they rose to power and prominence. [F 940]

Shāh Malek sent an envoy to Esmāʿil in Khwarazm, with the verbal message that "Hārun gave fresh impetus to the Seljuqs, who were my enemies and whom I then defeated in battle, leaving them helpless and without manpower, food or shelter. He proved to be an ungrateful subject, launched an attack on his lord and the latter's province, in that he made the Seljuqs the vanguard of his army. As a result, the Almighty God showed his disapproval and he got his deserts, and now the Seljuqs have moved to Khorasan. If there was any agreement between myself and Hārun, that is all in the past, and today there is the sword between myself and you, and I am coming! Prepare yourselves, for I shall take Khwarazm and overthrow you and the rest of your ungrateful lot. When I finish with you, I shall go to Khorasan and, in support and service of the Sultan, dislodge my enemy the Seljuqs and send them into the wilderness for good. I know that Amir Masʿud will not grudge me this province once I have performed such a service and have uprooted his enemies from his province." (It was Aḥmad b. ʿAbd al-Ṣamad who had put these self-aggrandising ideas[135] into Shāh Malek's head so that Esmāʿil and Shakar were overthrown and Aḥmad's son and his followers avenged, although Shāh Malek too lost his life over this, as will be related in the reign of Amir Mowdud.[136]) Esmāʿil and Shakar realized that the Vizier Aḥmad b. ʿAbd al-Ṣamad was behind all this and that it was he who was pulling the strings. They sent back Shāh Malek's envoy with a tough rejoinder, saying, "We're ready. You can come whenever you like. It's Hārun who should be blamed [F 941] for your present delusions: for when he saw you with such a puny force facing his own mighty army, he should have instructed his followers the Seljuqs to finish you off there and then."

After a while, Bu Naṣr Barghashi, who held the office of vizier in Khwarazm, was arrested, and Bu'l-Qāsem Eskāfi was appointed vizier on 1 Moḥarram 428 [/25 October 1036], the pretext for his dismissal being given out that Barghashi was acting in Masʿud's interests.[137] Aḥmad b. ʿAbd al-Ṣamad used to provide him and Shāh Malek with aid, both in the form of sound advice and also with an envoy bearing letters from the Sultan, until the time when, having defeated Begtughdï and the Great Chamberlain Sübashï, the Seljuqs rose in power within Khorasan. The Amir had a private meeting with the Vizier, saying, "The Seljuqs' transgressions are exceeding all bounds. The province of Khwarazm must be made over to Shāh Malek so that he takes the bait, overthrows these ungrateful ones and takes possession of Khwarazm. His arrival there will relieve us of further headaches from both the Khwarazmians and the Seljuqs." The Vizier replied, "The lord's solution is a very ingenious one," and an investiture patent was written out in Shāh Malek's name, and a splendid robe of honour added to that. Ḥasan Tabbāni, a shrewd and discerning old man from the lower echelons of the trusted confidants [F 942] at the court who had been on diplomatic missions,[138] was appointed to go with several cavalrymen. He set off with the robe of honour, the investiture patent and verbal messages couched in incisive terms.

A great deal of time was spent on parleying and on the exchange of envoys between Shāh Malek and the Khwarazmians, since Shāh Malek was asserting his claim and producing proof that "Amir Masʿud is the rightful Amir, thus ordained by the Commander of the Faithful, and he has entrusted the province to me; you must hand over this land to me." The Khwarazmians were, however, sending back the reply that "We don't recognize anybody. The land is ours by conquest; it will have to be taken back from us by conquest and you'll have to come, and we'll see what God the Exalted One has ordained, and who will get the upper hand."

Shāh Malek encamped with a mighty army on a plain called Asib[139] and confronted Shakar on Friday, 6 Jomādā II 432[/11 February 1041]. A fierce battle ensued between them lasting three days and three nights, with much bloodshed[140] and many men killed on both sides. Ḥasan Tabbāni was with Shāh Malek, and he later told me, "I was present with Amir Maḥmud at numerous battles such as at Merv, at Herat, and against the Simjurids and the victory at the gates of Merv, and against the Khāns on the plain of Katār[141] and others, but I don't recall any as fierce as the one that took place between these two sides." In the end, Shāh Malek had the upper hand. On the third day, at the time of the midday worship, he defeated the Khwarazmians. They turned tail and came back to the city in flight and shut themselves up in the citadel. If they had persevered in fighting from within the citadel, [F 943], they might have made things difficult for their foes and prolonged the war; but they did not, since God Most High's abandonment of them had come upon them. Shāh Malek stopped for fifteen days at a *rebāṭ* in the place where he had defeated them, until the dead were buried and the wounded had recovered. Meanwhile, there was a constant exchange of envoys. The Khwarazmians sought peace and handed over an indemnity. Shāh Malek said, "I am claiming the province itself, for in accordance with the command of the deputy of the Commander of the Faithful (i.e. Amir Mas'ud), it is rightfully mine."

By pure chance, a second, well-armed and equipped army [Gh 690] reached Shāh Malek, and this gave him fresh heart[142] at a time when the Khwarazmians were being encouraged[143] by the hope that the enemy might return home at any moment. Also, by a strange concatenation of circumstances, an event occurred[144] which made Esmā'il, Shakar and the supporters of the house of Altuntāsh extremely apprehensive of the royal army and created a rift between them. Esmā'il and Shakar were convinced that the other faction of the Khwarazmians were going to seize them and hand them over to Shāh Malek. They believed that Amir Masʿud and his Vizier Aḥmad b. ʿAbd al-Ṣamad had plotted this and that the royal troops[145] were in league with them over this. On Saturday, 22 Rajab 432 [/28 March 1041], Esmāʿil, with Shakar and his followers, and the supporters of the house of Altuntāsh, fled from Khwarazm with the aim of making their way to their allies the Seljuqs. On the day Esmāʿil left, Shāh Malek sent a military force in his pursuit, [F 944] and they went as far as the frontiers of Khwarazm but did not reach them.

Shāh Malek remained outside the city for twenty days until he had settled matters and the city had become tranquil, and those individuals entitled to be received[146] came to offer service and to seek protection. When he knew that the situation had become stable, he entered the city and sat down on the royal throne on Thursday, 15 Shaʿbān 432 [/20 April 1041].[147] Coins were scattered as alms, the city was decorated, and peace and calm restored. On the next day, Friday, he came to the Congregational Mosque with a large force of well-armed cavalry and infantry and with a great retinue, and the *khoṭba* was made in the name of the Commander of the Faithful and then of Amir Masʿud, followed by his own name. One must give ear to the remarkable aspects of this situation: a while before that day when the *khoṭba* was pronounced there in his name, Amir Masʿud had been killed at the fortress of Giri.[148] Amir Mowdud came to Donpur[149] in this month of Shaʿbān when Shāh Malek had made the change in the *khoṭba*. He engaged in a battle and captured his uncle Moḥammad and his sons and those who supported him, and killed them all,[150] just as will be related in detail exactly as it happened and in its entirety in the remainder of the martyred Amir Masʿud's reign, and in the new reign of Amir Mowdud, if God wills.

The Seljuqs did not keep faith with Esmāʿil, Shakar and the partisans and supporters of the house of Altuntāsh.[151] For a while they treated them well, but in the end had them all imprisoned; only the Almighty God knows why. All the house of Altuntāsh and their partisans were humiliated and brought low. We shall relate what the fate of Khwarazm and Shāh Malek was in the time of Amir Mowdud, up to that time [Gh 691] when Shāh Malek, because of his support for the Maḥmudi house, fell into the hands of the Seljuqs and perished, and his womenfolk and children all fell into the hands of the same rebellious force, since all of these are remarkable stories and wonders.[152] [F 945]

This chapter on Khwarazm has come to its end. It has much to commend it, and could almost be regarded as a self-contained historical account, capable of standing on its own and offering many moral examples to its perceptive readers. Now that I have finished it, I have embarked on another section, so that I may fulfill my promise and complete the task, if God so wills.[153]

[The end of the book]